The Moving Image

The Moving Image

An International History of Film, Television and Video

John Wyver

Basil Blackwell

BFI Publishing

First published 1989

Basil Blackwell Ltd
108 Cowley Road, Oxford OX4 1JF, UK

Basil Blackwell Inc
432 Park Avenue South, Suite 1503
New York, NY 10016, USA

In association with the
British Film Institute
21 Stephen Street
London W1P 1PL

British Library Cataloguing in Publication Data

Wyver John
   The moving image: an international history
of film, television and video,
   1. Cinema films, to 1985
   I. Title
   781.43′09

ISBN 0-631-16821-4
ISBN 0-631-15529-5

Library of Congress Cataloging-in-Publication Data

Wyver John
   The moving image

   Includes Index
   1. Motion picture - History. 2. Television broadcasting - History.
   3. Video recording - History. 4. British Film Institute.
   II. Title
   PN1993.5.A1W95   1988   791.4′09   88-7722

ISBN 0-631-16821-4
ISBN 0-631-15529-5

Typeset and designed by
BH Graphics Limited
Perivale, England

Printed in Great Britain by
Butler & Tanner Ltd, Frome and London

Contents

For my parents, Ron and Marie

Foreword

by HRH The Prince of Wales KG KT GCB

Moving images have delighted and fascinated people all over the world for many centuries, from the Chinese shadow plays of 5,000 years ago to the satellite images of today. In our own century, the extraordinary technological advances in cinema and television have seen the moving image develop from the first flickering pictures to the computer-generated images of the present. Moving images now affect all of us, sometimes in ways we may not even pause to think about. They entertain us. They influence us — sometimes not always for the better. They also instruct us. They offer a fresh perspective on the way we see ourselves and peoples very different from ourselves.

Until now there has been no place which tells the whole story of this major influence on our lives; a place where we can see how the cinema, television and the newer forms of the moving image have developed and continue to develop. I am delighted that this gap has now been filled by the new Museum of the Moving Image. Here we can see, in one place, the entire history of the moving image — its artefacts, its technology, and of course the images themselves.

As befits a museum dedicated to a form which, as both industry and art, is constantly evolving, the Museum of the Moving Image is not simply an exhibition of objects from the past. It is an active museum, inviting those who visit it — and I hope they will be many — to participate in a changing programme of exhibits and events. In my own view the Museum offers a fascinating prospect to visitors. And it seems especially appropriate that, although MOMI will present an international view of every form of the moving image, there will be a particular emphasis on British achievements in cinema and television.

As patron of the British Film Institute, I am delighted to welcome the Museum of the Moving Image and this accompanying book. There is nothing like MOMI anywhere else in the world, so I hope it will become a considerable British success story.

Introduction

There is a sense in which a book such as this is impossible. No single volume can adequately encompass an international history of cinema, television and video. Omissions will quickly become obvious to the reader, who may find tiresome the sections of the text which almost (but I trust not quite) collapse into lists. Certainly every reader will take issue with many inevitable compressions and with what may appear as eccentric emphases or generalisations. But perhaps such arguments will also be part of the pleasure that the book can offer.

The pleasure in its writing has been derived from having to see the history of the moving image as a whole. In the research this has meant not only a thorough review of familiar subjects but also an exploration of unfamiliar ones, and I was delighted to discover how fascinating these new areas quickly became. The writing of the book consequently offered me a thoroughly enjoyable education, and I hope that traces of this remain for the reader.

The Moving Image is intended as an accompaniment and complement to the British Film Institute's new Museum of the Moving Image (MOMI). Neither a catalogue nor a guidebook, it was written with an awareness of the plans for MOMI, but it reproduces neither the museum's lay-out nor its original framework. Instead the book offers an independent introduction to the history of the moving image, and one which can be read and engaged with irrespective of whether the reader has visited the museum.

As well as my own viewing of films and tapes, numerous books and articles, both primary and secondary sources, have informed the writing. Such originality as I can lay claim to resides, in the earlier chapters at least, in the selection and juxtaposition of the research, ideas and responses of others. The later chapters should, however, offer at least a few surprises to the informed reader.

The strength of the book, I believe, is that it does, perhaps for the first time, draw together an outline history of both the cinema and television. For far too long writers have treated these two forms of the moving image as separate and distinct, whereas the connections and parallels, comparisons and contrasts are fascinating and significant, from as early as the 1930s, through the 1950s (when historians of one medium do often nod at the importance of the other), and on until the intimate intertwinings of the two media today.

Anyone who embarks on such a parallel history quickly becomes aware of the relative richness of film studies and the paucity of serious writing about television. Over the past decade, film historians, especially in the United States, have begun a thorough rethinking and re-examination of the whole history of Hollywood, often drawing on sources such as production accounts, studio memos and exhibitors' records. In part because of the younger medium's relative inaccessibility and, at least until recently, its lower cultural status, almost no such serious historical work has been undertaken for television. Nor is there anything comparable in television criticism to widely available and sophisticated analyses of, for example, aspects of the British cinema like Ealing and Gainsborough. The Museum of the Moving Image and the British Film Institute as a whole, as well as many other institutions and organisations, have much to do to stimulate interest in the responsible writing of television history.

The structure of the book is broadly chronological, with the story of the film and television industries forming the central spine. Complementing this throughout are explorations of the international cinema and television in Britain and elsewhere, as well as separate chapters on subjects such as animation, the avant-garde and video. The United States and Europe are prominent throughout, and I am acutely aware that in this I have reproduced the gross bias in Western media studies against the industries and distinguished film and television traditions in Asia, Africa, Latin America and elsewhere.

Although informed by the theoretical debates of the past fifteen or more years, this is quite definitely not a book of film theory. No history can avoid or separate itself from theory, but most of my assumptions, both conscious and unconscious, remain unexamined here. My central framework is one of economic and industrial history, and I have endeavoured throughout to place the more familiar approaches of national studies and individual author analyses within and against an understanding of – in essence – capital.

Finally, it should be said that this is not a work of rigorous scholarship. I have tried to make it fair, responsible and accurate, but the directions for Further Reading are intended for the reader unfamiliar with the area in question and not for the expert.

Many people have contributed to my knowledge and understanding of the history of the moving image. Individual authors important to my thinking are noted in the lists at the end of each chapter. Among those whose personal help, advice and friendship I have valued are, in Britain, Ruth Baumgarten, Edward Buscombe, David Curtis, Taylor Downing, Geoff Dunlop, Dick Fiddy, John Fordham, Carl Gardner, W. Stephen Gilbert, Alex Graham, Felicity Grant, Stuart Hood, Marc Karlin, Michael Kustow, Colin

McArthur, Don Macpherson, Tony Mechele, Mike Poole, Tony Rayns, Chris Rodley, Jane Root, James Saynor, John Stewart, Paul Taylor, Christopher Wicking, Judith Williamson, Linda Zuck and the late Peter Tasker; in Europe, Stefaan Decostere, Chris Dercon, Anne-Marie Duguet, Kees Kasander, Stephen Natanson and Jeffrey Shaw; and in North America, William Boddy, Peter Broderick, Bruce Ferguson, Jackie Kain, Lynne Kirby, Barbara Osborn, Catharine Richards, Ron Simon, Melinda Ward and Professor Brian Winston.

The chapter on the avant-garde was enriched by the thoughts and ideas of A. L. Rees, and the chapter on animation benefited greatly from an extensive revision by Irene Kotlarz. The mistakes and misjudgments throughout are, of course, all my own.

Threefold thanks are owed to the British Film Institute: to the Head of BFI Publishing Geoffrey Nowell-Smith for commissioning the book, and for persevering with me and it beyond duty and deadlines; to the unfailing support of all the staff of the BFI Library, without whom and which the book could quite simply not have been written; and to David Wilson, both for his extensive picture research (carried out in conjunction with the researchers at MOMI, notably Liz Heasman and David Watson) and for his immensely careful and beneficial editing.

The illustrations in this book have been prepared by the National Film Archive, and thanks are due to the staff of the Stills Department (in particular Markku Salmi and Tise Vahimagi for their invaluable help and advice). Acknowledgment is made to the distributors of the films and television programmes illustrated.

Special, warm thanks for help with the book and for much else are due to Paul Kerr and Michael Jackson. And the final, most heartfelt acknowledgment is to Clare Paterson, whose contribution to the book and to my life was, as it remains, paramount.

1
Before the Cinema – and after

In the early 1880s, more than a decade before the arrival of the Cinémato-graphe, entertainments in the Dutch town of The Hague included two rival spectacles. Both were enormous circular paintings, packed with vivid detail, known as Panoramas. And both were housed in buildings newly constructed to accommodate them. Entering through subterranean passages, curious spectators emerged on to a central platform from which they could marvel at the sweep of the vast canvases around them. One of the Panoramas, which had been imported from Paris, depicted Napoleon trouncing the Turks in 1798. The other, created by the noted local artist Hendrik Mesdag, illus-trated the view from a sand-dune at the nearby fishing village of Scheven-ingen. And among the first visitors to Mesdag's masterwork was Vincent Van Gogh, who apparently quoted an earlier critic's response to a canvas by Rembrandt: 'The only fault of this painting resides in its being faultless.'

One hundred years later, only the Mesdag Panorama continues to enter-tain tourists and local schoolchildren, for its companion was forced out of business within a decade. Most visitors to The Hague in the 1980s, however, prefer the more contemporary excitements of the town's Omniversum. There, seated in a steeply raked auditorium, the audience experiences a film projected above and around them on the curved roof of the building. Cocooned by dense multi-track sound, and by the huge, high-definition image, the audience is swept up in a sensory environment of startling power. A flight in a space shuttle, a journey to the Galapagos Islands, a lightning tour of Holland, can all be experienced courtesy of the Omnimax film system.

The Panorama is one element in the moving image's complex pre-history, the Omniversum one of its most sophisticated contemporary developments. Yet both satisfy similar desires for spectacle and surprise, and for the scrupulously detailed artificial rendering of the world. As did, two centuries before the Mesdag Panorama and on a rather more modest scale, the work of Dutch painters like Jan Steen, Jan Vermeer and Aelbert Cuyp. Their lovingly detailed domestic interiors, urban scenes and local landscapes can now be seen in The Hague's Maurithuis.

For a few days in late 1986 the experience of viewing these paintings in The Hague could be contrasted by participation in a contemporary art work installed only a few hundred yards away. Mounted then in the Filmhuis, but flexible enough to be shown elsewhere, Jeffrey Shaw's 'Heaven's Gate' comprises a high-definition video screen fixed horizontally some fifteen feet above the ground. Around it black drapes hang down to roughly the height of the human participant, who stands beneath the screen staring upwards. Positioned on a central pillar is a joystick with which the participant can move the image on the screen in its own plane. When the joystick is lifted, details on the screen are progressively magnified, as if the viewer were moving 'up' towards it. Then, at one point in this movement, the image dissolves to be replaced by one which is, or would be in conventional space, 'above' it. This image, too, can be manipulated in its own plane. In all, the work contains nine levels, which can be penetrated at any point, and going 'through' the final one returns the viewer to the base.

Although the moving images of 'Heaven's Gate' incorporate references to ancient hieroglyphics and baroque painting, they are entirely generated by a computer programme. No mechanical reproduction is involved at any stage, and the changing images are simply the product of digital instructions from a computer. Film produced by similar processes could also be seen at the Omniversum, in a collection of computer graphic animations titled *The Magic Egg* (1984). Applications of processes developed over the past twenty years, these are images from a quite new form of representation, which opens up almost limitless possibilities for the moving images of the future. Not the least of these possibilities is the interactive control available in a system like 'Heaven's Gate'. For each viewer, experience of the work is different, and is controlled by manipulation of the joystick. Moving images can now move in quite new ways.

Such a grouping of painting, Panorama, Omniversum and 'Heaven's Gate' is, of course, almost arbitrary. Yet it indicates the range of possible references in any history of the moving image. For some commentators this history begins as far back as 30,000 BC, with the cave paintings at Altamira in Spain. Certain of these animal drawings, it is argued, can be associated in groups intended as sequential progressions. A similar sense of implied movement between individual images has been ascribed to friezes on Greek temples. And the Greeks are also noted in some histories of the cinema because of Plato's famous simile in the *Republic*. Imagine a long cave, Socrates suggests, in which prisoners are held so that they can look only at a wall facing the entrance. On this wall they see the shadows, thrown by a distant fire, of men passing back and forth before the entrance. Then if the prisoners were to talk to each other, he asks, would they not assume that the shadows they saw were real men? For Socrates, this illustrated the essential ignorance of the human condition; subsequently, it has been celebrated as a first description of the cinema.

Skipping across two millenia, we can also incorporate the achievements of

6

the Dutch artists like Steen and Cuyp in such a chronology. Until the 17th century, most images had been produced for the Church or the aristocracy, but these painters produced a secular art for the new mercantile class. Paintings, together with the popular prints derived from them, were now bought to decorate quite modest homes. Over the next two centuries, advances in printing brought about an ever wider circulation of images. After about 1840 photography was contributing massively to this process, and by 1842 *The Illustrated London News,* the first pictorial weekly newspaper, was being published in England. For many people the world was becoming increasingly defined by a visual culture.

Such a breathless progress can be extended up to the Lumière brothers and their historic public presentation of the Cinématographe on 28 December 1895. But in any sketch of the pre-history of the moving image we must also explore the parallel developments of distinct technologies and their many connections with the complexities and contradictions of 19th-century history and thinking.

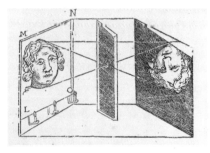

Engraving from Kircher's Ars Magna Lucis et Umbrae

Toy lantern made by Lapierre in France

Magic lanterns

One alternative beginning, to an account which should in any case resist simple linearity, can be found among the distinguished contemporaries of the 17th-century Dutch artists. Christiaan Huygens, a diplomat, poet and scholar, was also fascinated by optics, and he is credited by many historians as the first to construct, around 1659, a working 'magic lantern', which could focus and project light through a slide so as to produce an image on a screen. Just over a decade before, the principle of projection on which the magic lantern was based had been discussed by the Jesuit priest Father Athanasius Kircher in his book *Ars Magna Lucis et Umbrae.* The work of Kircher, Huygens and others stimulated enormous interest in these lanterns, and increasingly sophisticated models were soon being demonstrated across Europe. By 1700 Johannes Zahn had created a table model, illuminated by an oil lamp, which could create an impression of movement by the successive projection of glass slide images mounted on a circular disc.

Throughout the 18th century individual showmen popularised these entertainments across Europe, often walking from town to town carrying their lanterns on their backs. Animation was imparted to the images by the use of mechanical slides. One glass could be manipulated by a lever in front of another to show a ship moving up and down in the waves. Pulley slides could rotate images. And by superimposing two or more projections, primitive 'dissolves' could be achieved. Oil lamps were replaced by bright limelights, and in the later Victorian years sophisticated domestic lanterns, with two or three light sources, were used for both entertainment and education in many middle-class homes.

Public entertainment was also supplied, towards the end of the 18th century, by far more lavish lantern shows. One elaborate and extremely

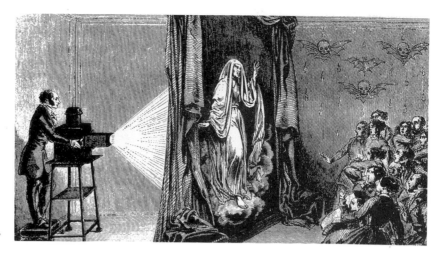

Robertson's Fantasmagorie

popular presentation was given during the 1790s in Paris by the Belgian showman Etienne Gaspard Robert, professionally known as Robertson. His Fantasmagorie, as he called it, was mounted in an abandoned chapel and included projections on to smoke and gauze of likenesses of Marat, Danton and Robespierre. As shows such as these became more complex, special theatres were built to house them. In 1823, for example, London's newly opened Egyptian Hall promised animated scenes like that of Mr Albert Smith's ascent of Mont Blanc. Also popular in the years after about 1780 were shadow theatres, developed from the shadow puppets of the Far East, which used lanterns to cast on a screen the outlines of detailed silhouettes. In the hands of a specialist showman like Georges Méliès, the technique could sustain lengthy dramas of considerable ambition. Lanterns were also used to incorporate slides into plays with live actors and a narrator. In the 1890s the American Alexander Black mounted melodramas lasting as long as two hours and using as many as four slides a minute.

A culture of the eye

The popularity of magic lantern shows and their variants during the 18th and 19th centuries is one indication of the change in the ways in which men and women perceived the world. In its fundamental shift from an understanding centred on the sacred to one with a secular focus, the Renaissance had introduced into European thinking the dogma that a work of art, while still created for the glory of God, should be a direct and faithful representation of an aspect of the external world. The rules and conventions of perspective had been formulated to serve this aim, and for three centuries artists had devoted themselves to its achievement.

The 19th-century forms of this impetus, which include the realist paintings of Courbet, Manet and many others, were a product of both the new scientific knowledge of the previous century and the changed social order which had emerged with the French Revolution. Recent advances in the science of optics now offered the possibility of achieving a fully mechanical

8

representation of the world. But prior to this, there was the demand of a new class for its own, original visual culture. The bourgeoisie of the early 19th century was concerned to consolidate and celebrate the achievements of its political and industrial revolutions.

Photography, of course, was the central contribution to this process, one element of which involved capturing, without the complex and possibly unwelcome mediation of an artist, the likenesses of the men who had made these revolutions possible. Another strand was the idealisation of an unsullied natural wilderness, the subject of so many early photographs, which could be projected as the appropriate complementary world to urban society. Rapid advances in printing, including the invention of ways to reproduce photographs, and the consequent spread of newspapers and illustrated magazines, were a parallel contribution to this visual culture. And although this process, and the forces acting on it, were more contradictory and complex than this account can suggest, further support for the argument is provided by the earliest films of the Lumière brothers. There can have been few more straightforward expressions of bourgeois pride than one of their very first films, *Workers Leaving the Lumière Factory* (1895).

A particularly revealing illustration of this fascination with the visual, with obvious parallels to both lantern entertainments and the cinema to come, is the enormous popularity of Panoramas and Dioramas. In the mid-18th century painters like Benjamin West were exhibiting huge painted canvases, often presenting them with the paraphernalia, and entrance fees, of a theatrical attraction. In the 1780s a portraitist in Edinburgh, Robert Barker, recognised the possibility of extending the large-scale canvas so that it encircled the spectators. Keenly aware of the commercial possibilities, he patented his idea in 1787, and soon afterwards created his first Panorama, a 'View of Edinburgh' which met with little success. A subsequent 'View of London', however, proved to be far more popular with both critics and public. The profits from its exhibition enabled Barker to build a rotunda in London's Leicester Square, where new Panoramas could be regularly unveiled.

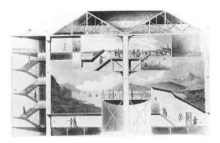

The Panorama: a section of the Rotunda, Leicester Square

Panoramas were soon popular across Europe. Battlefields and cityscapes, preferably from far-off lands, were particularly appreciated. Barker himself made an early modification when he revolved a view of the British Navy around an audience. And the influence of similar contemporary entertainments based on spectacle was to lead to further refinements. In 1781, for example, a painter and scene designer from Alsace, Philippe Jacques de Loutherbourg, had opened his Eidophusikon in London, which created a theatrical spectacle from painting, three-dimensional models and dramatic lighting effects.

Many of the possibilities suggested by both kinds of entertainment were brought together in a new form called the Diorama, first created in 1822 by Louis Jacques Mandé Daguerre and Claude-Marie Bouton. Vast transparent paintings, animated by changing patterns of light, were shown to an

9

audience, sometimes seated in a moving auditorium, who could view only a section of the spectacle at any one time. The excitement created by such shows meant that Dioramas were soon even more popular than Panoramas. Yet the images offered by Dioramas and the like were strictly framed by the understandings of the world which their audience wished to see given concrete form. They were celebrations of urban achievement, nationalist pride and Imperial fervour. But they were also sanitised views of battlefields and cityscapes, calculated to reassure and not disturb.

Panoramas and Dioramas continued to flourish, especially on Europe's mainland, although in Britain their popularity had significantly waned by 1860. The construction of Panoramas continued until the end of the century – and beyond. One showing the Battle of Stalingrad was recently inaugurated in the Soviet Union, and a new depiction of Bath went on show in London in 1987. Moreover, just as there were both public and personal versions of magic lanterns, so Panoramas were also eagerly appreciated in the form of portable peep shows, which would sometimes be elaborately concealed in decorative objects like peep eggs.

Optics

Parallel to this growing dominance of a visual culture, and making its own central contributions to it, the science of optics exercised an increasing fascination for European scientists in the early 19th century. Wave theory, the spectrum and the physiology of the eye itself were rigorously investigated, along with many related subjects, and the fruits of this research often emerged in the form of popular toys. The Thaumatrope, for example, first seen in 1825, was a demonstration of a phenomenon misleadingly described as 'persistence of vision'. A simple disc with a cord attached to two opposite edges, the Thaumatrope had different images painted on each surface. When it was spun on the cord, the images blended together, so that, for example, a bird (drawn on one surface) might be caught inside a cage (drawn on the other).

Thaumatrope discs and box: for 'seeing an object which is out of sight'

Ever since Newton, scientists had recognised the common effect registered by the eye which has been staring at a light and then looks away. The retina retains a bright after-image, which quickly fades. Usually known as 'persistence of vision', this effect has been used by numerous historians to explain how the eye and brain connect the string of static images projected as a film, and mentally create the impression of smooth movement. In fact, this process needs a more complex explanation. First, it has been recognised that observation is not instantaneous, and that the eye has to pass sensations to the brain which only then interprets them. Consequently there is a threshold below which repeated stimuli cannot be perceived as separate. And as stimuli come in, one which follows rapidly on another can mask the former, allowing the brain to compensate for likely changes. This information about changes is understood automatically, and in an area of the brain separate from the primary acts of perception. So as long as images are exposed at a speed below

10

the perceptual threshold (as with film's 24 frames per second) they will be read as continuous.

Nonetheless, although the idea of 'persistence of vision' has now been superseded by more recent research, as a theory it was of considerable importance in stimulating a number of key 19th-century experiments. In particular, at the same time as Joseph Nicéphore Niépce was making his first forerunner of the photographic plate, the phenomenon was being systematically researched by a Belgian, Joseph Antoine Plateau. In 1832 he popularised his work with a toy called a Phenakistiscope, a vertically mounted disc in which a number of radial slots had been cut towards the outer edge. On the back of the disc was drawn a sequence of images, which when viewed in a mirror through the slots as the disc was turned gave the impression of continuous movement.

Phenakistiscope disc

In the same year a similar mechanism was made in Austria by Simon Ritter von Stampfer, who called it a Stroboscope, and other refinements were soon to follow. Using the same principle, in 1834 William George Horner made a Zootrope, or Zoetrope. This had a cycle of images on the inside of a cylinder, which the spectator viewed through slots arranged opposite each separate image. Another Austrian, Baron Franz von Uchatius, was probably the first to combine the principle of these stroboscopic toys with magic lanterns. His crude but apparently effective technique was to arrange in a semi-circle a series of projectors, each of which held a different slide from a sequence. Holding a torch, he then ran around behind the projectors, so that the light passed through the slides in sequence, and created a moving image. The first Projecting Phenakistiscope is dated 1835, and this too gave the sense of movement on a screen when the Phenakistiscope disc was spun.

Zoetrope

Photography

The recognised inventor of photography is the Frenchman Joseph Nicéphore Niépce, who in 1826 first used a compound of silver to fix an image, after an eight-hour exposure, on a pewter plate. His process, which he subsequently developed and improved with Louis Daguerre, produced only a single, positive image, usually on glass. The next breakthrough was achieved independently by William Fox Talbot, who in 1835 employed a related process to create a negative image on paper. Five years later, as an eager public was first learning of Daguerre's work (Niépce had died in 1833), Fox Talbot discovered how numerous positive reproductions could be taken from each of his negatives.

The image which these and many other inventors had been striving to fix had in one way long predated their efforts. For almost three centuries the principles of a device called a *camera obscura* had been known and studied, and one motivation behind the experiments of Niépce and others was to capture the pictures produced only fleetingly with this device. The *camera obscura* had first been fully described by the Dutch mathematician Gemma-Frisius in 1544 and by the Neapolitan author Giovanni Battista della Porta in

Joseph Nicéphore Niépce, the inventor of photography

11

1558. But much earlier references were known. Aristotle in the fourth century BC had watched a partial eclipse of the sun using a pinhole; the ninth-century Arab mathematician Al Hazen had discussed the essential ideas in a treatise on optics, which was subsequently published in Europe in 1572; and Leonardo da Vinci had explored the principles of the device.

The observation common to all these writings was that if the sun's rays passed through a small hole into a darkened room (in Latin, *camera obscura*) they threw on to a wall or screen an inverted image of the scene outside. In 1589 Della Porta surprised an audience with moving images created in this way by actors outside the room. He also suggested how the principle might be used by artists, and by around 1650 portable devices were in use, presenting images on a screen which could be traced by hand to create a permanent representation. These sketching aids were gradually improved by, among other innovations, the use of lenses so that a sharper and brighter image was obtained. Nonetheless, they remained dependent on an artist's skill, and it was apparently Fox Talbot's dissatisfaction with such a device which acted as the spur for his experiments with the fixing of images.

In the early 1850s the new collodion process (which used a mixture of gun-cotton and ether) greatly facilitated the mechanical reproduction of images, and gave a further impetus to the rapidly growing popularity of photography. But a significant disadvantage, which was only gradually over-come, was the necessity of lengthy exposure times for the creation of a sharp picture. When a sequence of images was sought, perhaps for incorporation in an optical toy like Heyl's Phasmatrope, first shown in 1870, models had to be posed so as to achieve the needed result. Gradually technical improvements shortened exposures, and by the 1870s it was possible to create images from exposures of just 1/25th of a second, although at first only on glass plates.

Engraving of a large camera obscura, *with top and front cut away (Courtesy International Museum of Photography at George Eastman House)*

Among those exploring the potential of this new medium were scientists interested in the analysis of motion. Of these, the best remembered is Eadweard Muybridge, a British photographer who in the 1860s had successfully marketed his spectacular views of America. In 1873 he was commissioned by a former Governor of California, Leland Stanford, to settle a wager about whether all four feet of a running horse were ever off the ground at the same time. Although no photograph from his work at this time has survived, it appears that he did satisfy the Governor and his friends that this was in fact the case. Four years later, with Stanford's continued backing, he resumed work on the problem, and rigged up a battery of twelve cameras activated by trip-wires. When a horse ran past, a succession of sharp images were obtained, revealing for the first time all the details of a horse's movement. Soon he was applying the technique to human motion and to that of other animals. He also used the photographs in a device, called by him a Zoopraxiscope, which allowed him to project them in sequences so as to reconstitute the movement.

Muybridge's work was widely publicised, and in 1881 he was invited to Paris by the French painter Meissonier, who recognised how valuable it could be for artists seeking to understand anatomy. During his visit he met the physiologist Etienne-Jules Marey, who had already been corresponding with him. Marey was also interested in recording animal locomotion, and was particularly frustrated by his so far unsuccessful attempts to analyse the flight of a bird. After discussions with Muybridge, Marey began to work with the 'photographic revolver' which had been invented by the astronomer Janssen in 1874 as a way of recording the transit of Venus across the sun. Using a camera combined with what was essentially the mechanism of a Colt revolver, Janssen was able to take, at regular intervals, a series of rapid exposures on a single plate. Further adapting Janssen's designs, Marey

Frames from Muybridge's photographic demonstration of the movements of a horse

Janssen's photographic revolver

created a mechanism capable of fixing twelve successive frames in a second, and with this he was able to capture a photographic image of the motions of a bird in flight.

Initially Marey's camera recorded the twelve images around the edge of a revolving photographic disc, but about 1888 he recognised the potential of the paper strips of film, without perforations, which the Eastman Kodak company had begun to market. A new problem, however, was how to ensure a regular but intermittent movement of the film strip, for if the film was not static at the moment of exposure the result would simply be a blur. Marey's partial solution to this was a simple mechanism, similar to that long used in precision watches, based on a cog shaped like a Maltese cross. Perforated film was to produce significantly better results, but this was to come only after Eastman Kodak began to market, in 1889, an even more significant innovation—the first flexible film on celluloid.

Celluloid's importance derived from more than its being a transparent material which could carry photographic emulsion. Just as significant in its eventual adoption for moving pictures were its qualities of flexibility and strength, since during projection it needed to withstand extremes of tension, as the strip constantly moved, stopped, and moved again. But it had not been invented for the cinema. It had been developed from an earlier artificial substance called Parkesine by the Hyatt brothers of New Jersey who, in 1868, were seeking a tough, resistant material from which to manufacture printers' rollers. Other uses for it were soon recognised and in the late 1880s a photographic firm, Carbutt of Philadelphia, first used it as an alternative to glass as the base for individual photographic plates.

The photographic manufacturer George Eastman had introduced the first roll film on paper in 1884 or 1885. Utilising large-scale manufacturing techniques, he intended to create an extensive consumer market for still photography, an aim towards which he took another step in 1888 with his first Kodak camera. As the advertising said, 'You press the button, we do the rest', although initially this involved having the camera itself sent back to the factory for processing the film. In 1889 he recognised that if the roll film was made of celluloid these processing costs could be significantly reduced, and Eastman Kodak quickly introduced one of the last requisite elements for the attainment of motion pictures.

Thomas Alva Edison

Throughout the 1880s Muybridge continued his work, now supported by the University of Pennsylvania, and eventually published his eleven mammoth volumes of *Studies in Animal Locomotion*. In 1888 he encountered the inventor Thomas Alva Edison, already widely known as the creator of the electric light bulb and the phonograph. From the astute exploitation of these, Edison was building a major company, Edison General Electric (later just General Electric), and was able to fund a broad programme of new research. He was greatly impressed by Muybridge's Zoopraxiscope, and apparently

14

conceived a machine to record and reproduce images, much as his phonograph did with sound. Indeed his first idea was to extend the principle of the phonograph, and to find a way of etching tiny photographs on to a wax cylinder.

Another meeting, this time with Marey in Paris in 1889, may have suggested to Edison the possibilities of roll film, and also of adapting a principle from one of his own inventions, the automatic telegraph, so as to put perforations in film, an idea on which he took out an initial patent request in November 1889. Much of the actual work on this and subsequent innovations was undertaken by Edison's assistant W. K. L. Dickson, who also seems to have first seen the advantages of celluloid. In the autumn of 1890 Dickson finally succeeded in taking a sequence of photographs on film with a heavy, clumsy device which he called a Kinetograph. Fragments of these earliest films still survive, although the earliest complete film is acknowledged to be *Fred Ott's Sneeze,* probably shot in 1891, and featuring one of Edison's workers.

Edison protected his and Dickson's work with numerous patent applications, but uncharacteristically he failed to extend them to Europe, in part because he seems not to have realised how profitable this new invention might be. Concerned about the quality of reproduction, he resisted the idea of projecting the films, and encouraged Dick-

 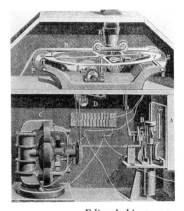

son to build a viewing cabinet, a Kinetoscope (patent applied for in July 1891), which patrons could use one at a time to see the films. He remained sceptical about this invention's potential for profit. In 1894 he wrote to Muybridge: 'I have constructed a little instrument which I call a Kinetoscope, with a nickel slot attachment and some twenty five have been made out. I am very doubtful if there is any commercial future in it and fear that they will not earn their cost.' Nonetheless, he seems to have thought that the poten-

Edison's kinetoscope

tial profits from Kinetoscope exhibition would be higher than from projecting films, which he feared would exhaust possible audiences too quickly. After several years' preparation, his first patents were granted in 1893, in time for an unveiling of the Kinetoscope at the Chicago World's Fair.

By February of that year, Dickson was working on a series of films in a curious studio adjacent to the Edison laboratory. Known as the Black Maria, it relied on the sun for illumination, and could be turned on a pivot to take the best advantage of this light. There Dickson shot simple, fixed-frame records of acts by many leading music hall and circus stars, including Annie Oakley and Colonel 'Buffalo Bill' Cody. Another of Dickson's early productions, *Fun in a Chinese Laundry* (1894), is a record of a vaudeville sketch, and

The Black Maria studio

Execution of Mary Queen of Scots (1895), made by Alfred Clark after Dickson had left the company, is a gruesome reconstruction of the Queen's death by the axe. In April 1894 the first Kinetoscope parlour was opened on Broadway, where these films, which lasted less than a minute, could be seen. This attraction's popularity, and profits, ensured that others were soon opening right across America, and abroad. And among those who marvelled at it in Paris were two brothers, Auguste and Louis Lumière.

Les Frères Lumière

In contrast to Edison's rejection of the potential for projecting films, a number of European inventors were directly addressing this problem. In 1876 Emile Reynaud had perfected a greatly improved version of the Zootrope, which he called a Praxinoscope. As in the Zootrope there was a cylinder, on the inside of which were drawn the sequence of images, but this

Emile Reynaud's Théâtre Optique, with the Praxinoscope. The images are drawings.

new toy had a polygonal drum of mirrors in the centre, which reflected each of the images in turn, and so produced a far brighter image for the spectator than had been possible by viewing through slots. In 1892 Reynaud presented to the public his Praxinoscope à Projections, which passed light through a succession of transparent images, reflected the beam off a spinning polygonal mirror, and threw the animated sequence on to a screen. Only the fact that his images were drawn, and not photographic, denies him the place in film history to be taken by the Lumière brothers.

In 1888 another Frenchman, Louis Augustin Le Prince, patented a machine to film and project images, using intermittent motion as in Etienne Marey's work. Marey, too, was discussing similar possibilities, as was the Englishman William Friese-Greene, who patented a system in 1893. But none of these figures appears to have actually built a projector, although Le Prince's achievements remain obscure since he mysteriously disappeared in 1890 on a train between Dijon and Paris. In America, a family of inventors with the name of Latham did build a combined camera and projector in

1895, using film 70mm wide. The Lathams gave a handful of showings in New York and elsewhere, but they were not able to make their work financially viable. Max Skladanowsky, in Germany, had also been developing a projection system, which used two parallel film strips and two lenses, and he gave some public showings in Berlin during 1895.

Among others tackling the problems were Auguste and Louis Lumière, two brothers who ran a profitable factory in Lyon which manufactured photographic plates. Intrigued by Edison's work, they considered the possibility of shooting their own films for the Kinetoscope, and early in 1895 Louis Lumière built an elegant machine which was a combined camera, processor and projector. Patented as a Cinématographe in March 1895, it was used to shoot one-minute actualities like *Workers Leaving the Lumière Factory*. Private showings of these films were given throughout 1895, and then on 28 December, in a basement room of the Grand Café in Paris, the Lumière brothers premièred a programme of work to a paying public. Immediately successful, their regular showings became the basis for a highly profitable international business. The cinema had finally arrived.

Interior of a single-lens camera-projector, ascribed to Le Prince

The next hundred years

The many fascinations of optical toys, of Panoramas and of the earliest cameras and projectors should not obscure the recognition that the invention of the cinema is not just a technological narrative. As the next chapter will explore further, the early cinema was closely linked with many of the 19th century's most common forms of representation, including theatrical *tableaux vivants*, documentary photography, magical illusions and comic strips. The influence of these representations was as significant to the invention of the cinema as the technical breakthroughs of Muybridge, Dickson, Lumière and the others.

Nor, of course, does the arrival of the cinema signal the end of more than one chapter in the history of the moving image. New technologies brought to the cinema have included sound, at the end of the 1920s; stereoscopic images, to give an impression of a third dimension, tried and quickly abandoned in the mid-1950s; and widescreen, first extensively adopted at the same time as 3-D, but ultimately proving to be rather longer-lived. Parallel to these developments was the growth of television. Foreseen as a domestic medium as early as 1882, in a series of remarkable drawings by the French artist Robida, television was developed with experimental broadcasts during the 1920s and introduced to audiences in the later 1930s. Closed down throughout the Second World War, it was established by the mid-1950s as both rival and interdependent partner to the cinema. At first relying on direct electronic transmission and on the use of film, it began around 1960 to adopt a new material for recording the moving image, videotape.

Workers Leaving the Lumière Factory (La sortie des usines Lumière, *1895*)

17

Video, too, has now become a domestic medium, with its own distinctive distribution and exhibition patterns, all of which are implicated in the structures established earlier by cinema and then television. In 1986 in Britain, six times as many movie viewings were from a videotape than from a cinema screen. Since the mid-1960s, video has also begun to explore its own aesthetics and production possibilities.

Genuinely three-dimensional moving images, created with the techniques of holography, were first achieved in April 1969. Two researchers in California produced a holographic motion picture of an aquarium, although the images were monochromatic, very grainy, and could only be viewed by one person at a time. Holographic movies have been foreseen ever since, but in the late 1980s they remain confined to science-fiction and patent applications. Another new medium, that of computer-generated images, also developed during the 1960s, is now far more established as part of our visual world. And far more than holography, or television, or even the cinema, it is a fundamental break in our systems of representation. Whereas holography still depends on making visual records of existing objects, computer-generated images are solely the products of digital information produced by programming. Freed from physical referents, computer imagery has the potential to show us moving images of which we cannot even dream.

Even in the more prosaic present both cinema and television are facing major changes. The impact of cable and satellite technology on distribution and exhibition remains uncertain. And there are, too, new technologies beginning significantly to affect production. In 1981 Francis Coppola shot his feature *One from the Heart* using a complex combination of film and video technologies, initiating what has been described as 'electronic cinema'. A widescreen television technology, with greatly enhanced picture quality, known as High Definition Television (HDTV), is now in use for the making of features, which can be shown by HDTV screens or transferred to 35mm without loss of quality. In 1986 the Italian television service RAI used HDTV for their drama *Julia and Julia*; *Crack in the Mirror* (1988) is the first American HDTV feature.

Alongside these new production technologies aimed at traditional exhibition sites, the 1970s and 80s have seen the growth of international circuits of purpose-built structures for screening Imax and Omnimax films. To date, these are the largest film gauges to be exploited commercially. Both use 70mm film but pass it horizontally through the camera, and subsequently through the projector. The result is extraordinary picture quality, which retains its brightness and detail when shown on a screen over 20 metres high, for Imax, or on the interior of a comparably vast dome, for Omnimax. In 1986 the first Imax film in 3-D was premiered at Vancouver's Expo.

All these technologies, actual and potential, suggest more than anything else the extraordinary range of possibilities which continue to open up for the moving image. Among those with their dreams of a bravura new world is Francis Coppola. In 1979 he described an idea for a film theatre specifically

The giant Imax screen at the National Museum of Photography, Film and Television in Bradford.

constructed to show his planned version of *Elective Affinities*, based on Goethe's 18th-century novel: 'We're going to build this incredible theatre there – 2,000 seats on the top of the Rockies. You go in there and it's just glass so you can see the view. Then, at a certain point, the glass gets dark and you're in a totally dark room and then – ultimately – you get a colour hologram.' 'It seems like a new film form,' his interviewer suggested. 'It is,' Coppola replied. 'It's a new kind of mental theme park.'

Further reading

C. W. Ceram, *Archaeology of the Cinema*, New York: Harcourt, Brace, 1965.

Thorold Dickinson, *A Discovery of Cinema*, London: Oxford University Press, 1971.

Gordon Hendricks, *Origin of the Motion Picture*, New York: Arno, 1972.

——— *Eadweard Muybridge: The Father of the Motion Picture*, London: Secker & Warburg, 1975.

Gerald Mast, *A Short History of the Movies*, New York: Macmillan, 4th ed., 1986.

Terry Ramsaye, *A Million and One Nights*, 1926; reprint, New York: Simon and Schuster, 1964.

David Robinson, *World Cinema: A Short History*, London: Eyre Methuen, 1973.

2
The Art and Commerce of the Early Cinema

By the early 1920s Hollywood was the overwhelmingly dominant force in world cinema. From the shadow of the famous sign, a small number of studios, linked with national and international distribution and exhibition companies, exercised effective control of a vast, hugely profitable industry then only a generation old. In many ways this structure, and Hollywood's dominance of it, remain essentially the same after more than sixty years and after the comfortable assimilation of television. But the structure was not born with the medium, and as it evolved in the early years it went through many changes.

A comparably complex development through the years up to the First World War can be seen in the evolution of film language. The first films were short, fixed-frame shots of vaudeville acts or everyday activities. Inside three decades, film-makers were to command elaborate narrative constructions which could sustain feature-length dramas and expertly move audiences through laughter, fear, pity and anger. But again, this language, for all that it continues to appear immediately accessible, is not 'natural' or in any way inherent to the medium. It too went through many changes, and was shaped by many influences.

European producers

As related in Chapter 1, much of the pioneering work in the cinema was achieved in Europe. And within a decade of the earliest screenings the French company Pathé was the first to demonstrate how the cinema as an industry could be organised to generate the most advantageous returns on investment. But there was to be a subsequent shift in power to the United States, effected during and just after the First World War. In retrospect, this can be seen as part of the broad shift in world economic dominance away from Europe, which had begun in the last years of the 19th century. As with other scientific endeavours, European breakthroughs were most effectively exploited by manufacturing concerns across the Atlantic.

Although their primary place in history is restricted to the first *regular* public projection of films, there is no dispute that the Lumières were also the first Europeans to establish the production and exhibition of moving pictures as a commercial operation. Like those who were to follow him, the dominant brother Louis demonstrated that a film producer needed to be part-inventor, part-artist and several parts showman. But of the qualities necessary for his success, acute business sense was, as it has remained, the most essential. Before his involvement with the cinema, Louis Lumière had designed, built and by 1895, with Auguste, successfully run a factory where 300 workers manufactured photographic plates to his own design. Once his Cinématographe was patented, he waited almost a year before giving the first full public demonstration, in part so that he could build more machines, train cameramen and be ready to exploit effectively the device's immediate success. The Lumières then refused to sell any copies of their invention, guarded each machine obsessively, and for two years, before they finally started to market their equipment, they organised their own highly profitable shoots and screenings around the world.

Poster for the Lumière Cinématographe (the film is L'Arroseur arrosé, *made in 1895)*

The fledgling industry, however, for all the protectiveness of the original inventors, could not prevent the rapid entry of many imitators. In Britain in 1895 the inventor Birt Acres and Robert William Paul, a scientific instrument maker, attempted to copy Edison's Kinematograph (which was not protected in Britain by the original patent) and to build a complementary camera. By May of that year they were shooting their own films. Just weeks after Lumière's representative unveiled the Cinématographe in London, Paul was mounting regular showings with his own projection system at the Alhambra music hall. In June 1896 he screened, within hours of the race itself, a film of the Derby which was seen by the Prince of Wales, owner of the winning horse.

Acres seems to have been interested in cinema largely as a scientific invention, but Paul quickly became one of the more notable early British producers. For the next fifteen years fifty or so films a year were made by his company, and in 1899 he built one of the first British studios, in Muswell Hill in London. Production at this stage was organised on an artisanal basis, usually by one man, who built the equipment, wrote and directed the films, often acted in them as well, and then marketed and even exhibited them himself. In Britain, as elsewhere, such producers were soon to be found throughout the country, and included Cecil Hepworth, the son of a well-known magic lantern lecturer; South Wales fairground showman Walter Haggar; and the Brighton portrait photographers G. A. Smith and Esme Collings. Another major figure, the American Charles Urban, came to Britain to act as the agent for Edison films. In 1898 he was Chairman of the Warwick Trading Company, which began to make its own films and also to distribute the work of the Lumières and others. Then in 1903 he set up the Charles Urban Trading Company, which earned a particular reputation for travel and war films. By 1910 he had developed a colour process, Kinemacolor, with G. A. Smith, which they successfully exploited, notably in a two-and-a-half hour film of the Delhi Durbar.

The magic of Georges Méliès

Across the Channel, the conjurer and illusionist Georges Méliès had established himself as one of the most significant, and most successful, of the earliest producers. Formerly a footwear manufacturer, he had purchased the Théâtre Robert-Houdin in 1888, and had become renowned as an inventive stage magician who worked imaginatively both with shadow puppets and magic lanterns. Witnessing one of the first Lumière presentations, he pleaded with the brothers to sell him a camera. Undaunted by their refusal, he purchased a projector from R. W. Paul in London and by April 1896 he was including films in his theatrical shows. He was captivated by the new medium, and he soon obtained a camera to shoot films himself.

His first productions were simple 'actualities', but one of the most popular legends in cinema history has it that while filming one day his camera jammed and, after a few moments, started again. The developed roll showed a 'magical' jump in the scene, and it was from this moment, so the story goes, that he began to create illusions with the camera. In fact, stopping and starting the film was a technique employed as early as 1895 by Edison's assistants, and Méliès may well have copied it from them. But this is not to belittle his remarkable achievements as the cinema's first magician.

Méliès magic: Voyage dans la lune *(1902)*

By 1897 his theatre was presenting just films, and he had set up a studio at Montreuil in which to create his elaborate fantasies. In *The Melomaniac* (1903) he presented a character, played by himself, who could remove his own head, have it replaced by another, and then throw the discarded head up on to a telegraph wire. *The Man with the Rubber Head* (1902) also used double-exposures, in this case to show Méliès inflating his own head to a massive size. And alongside these tricks he produced fairy-tales like his *Cinderella* (1899), which was composed of twenty scenes, as well as more sober reconstructions of contemporary events. For a decade or more the novelty of these films brought him continued success, but he suffered badly from plagiarism, and just before the First World War he was forced to sell his estate. Declared bankrupt in 1923, he also saw the Théâtre Robert-Houdin demolished in that year. Three years later, he met again one of his former stars, Jeanne d'Alcy. They married and together sold toys from a street kiosk. His role in the cinema's history was belatedly recognised by the French government before his death in 1938.

In common with other producers, Méliès had at first sold films outright to exhibitors and showmen. When these men found themselves with surplus stocks of old films, they started to hire out prints, and thus became the first distributors. Film exchanges, sometimes also run by producers like Méliès, began to circulate prints round a number of venues. Music hall programmes

22

featured many of the earliest screenings, but fairground showmen quickly adopted the new medium, and toured the rural districts with tents and caravans. Other exhibitors established rough-and-ready cinemas in empty shops or small halls. The first purpose-built cinema in Britain, the Central Hall at Colne in Lancashire, was completed in 1908.

In Britain as elsewhere, cinema almost immediately found an eager audience. Social changes in the 19th century had created a new urban working class. Poverty was still widespread, but union organisation was gradually improving the income of these workers, as well as gaining for them increased leisure time. Education was slowly improving, and the growth of public transport facilitated trips to a music hall or a film showing. This pattern of artisanal production and of exhibition to a largely urban, working-class audience was paralleled in the early years in other Western countries.

Gaumont and Pathé

Developments towards a more extensive industrial structure were first seen in France, which from 1906 to 1913 dominated the world's film markets. One company with a major role in this expansion was Gaumont, a still photography firm which diversified into the manufacture of projectors. Customers wanted films as well, and the company's head, Léon Gaumont, instructed his secretary Alice Guy to supervise their production. Between 1897 and 1906, she directed or oversaw the making of some 300 short films, as well as more than a hundred film and sound recordings of popular singers and entertainers. With her husband Herbert Blaché, who had formerly been Gaumont's chief cameraman, she later moved to America, where she established her own production company, for which she successfully produced and directed films until 1917.

Gaumont's activities, though profitable and significant, were overshadowed by Pathé Frères. Founded by Charles Pathé to develop his business of selling phonographs, the company soon began to reflect his fascination with the potential of cinema. In 1902 Pathé commissioned a camera which remained an industry standard for two decades, and with Ferdinand Zecca as head of production the company rapidly expanded its film-making activities. Production costs were kept low, so that they could be recouped by selling fifteen copies of a film. In fact an average of 350 copies were sold.

By the middle of the decade Pathé Frères were producing, distributing and exhibiting films, and were thus the first company to recognise how profitable such a vertically integrated monopoly could be. Pathé also began to export films, entering foreign markets earlier and more aggressively than companies from other countries. In 1910 French films accounted for 40 per cent of the British market (the United States took 35 per cent, and this would increase sharply in the next two years), with Pathé Frères making up more than half of this figure. By 1914 they had forty-one offices in cities around the world, as well as their base in Paris. No European company since has achieved a share of the world market which is in any way comparable.

The first films

Films in these years immediately prior to the First World War were increasingly ambitious and elaborate dramas, a handful of which now ran to the length we accept today as a 'feature'. But the earliest dramatic films had been *tableaux vivants*. Along with actualities, recordings of vaudeville artists and the visual jokes or tricks of a producer like Méliès, film programmes before 1900 included many single-frame restagings, lasting for around one minute, of recent or historical events. And although the technology was novel, audiences were familiar and comfortable with such entertainments. For each of these types of films was essentially an extension of one of the late 19th century's popular forms of representation.

The compositions, framings and angles of late 19th-century documentary photography were one clear influence on the earliest work of the Lumières and others. So too were drawings and engravings of historical events, either witnessed or imagined by the artist. A reconstruction of a trial like *L'Affaire Dreyfus,* made by Méliès in 1899, would consequently have felt quite familiar. Projected drawings and photographs were also well-known from magic lantern shows and educational toys like stereoscopes. Another key link was the recently introduced comic strips, with their elaborate tales unfolding across related frames on a newspaper page. It was in transformations of these representations, just as much as in the technological discoveries of Edison and others, that the cinema was invented.

Recognising the significance of all these pre-filmic representations, the historian Barry Salt has identified 'the first purely filmic device' in *The Kiss in the Tunnel* (1899), made by G. A. Smith. Here a studio shot, which is supposedly the interior of a railway carriage, is cut between two exterior shots filmed from the front of a train, the first as it enters a tunnel and the second as it emerges again. There is a clear intention of continuity. As such simple narratives developed, film essentially extended the serial progression of lantern slide shows, assembling first two scenes (which were often numbered like the acts in a stage play) and then a succession of scenes in a strict chronology.

Continuity had not posed a problem for lantern slides, because any gaps could be covered by a verbal narration. Narrators also accompanied many early film screenings. But only gradually did film develop *visual* continuity, to create a narrative which could be readily understood independent of

Tableaux films: William Haggar's The Life of Charles Peace *(1905)*

any descriptive text. James Williamson's *Fire!* (1902) is one of the earliest films to establish this continuity, but as late as 1905 Walter Haggar's immensely popular *The Life of Charles Peace,* about the notorious murderer executed in 1879, is still a series of static tableaux presented in long shot. Cecil Hepworth's *Rescued by Rover* (also 1905) shows a more sophisticated

24

sense of narrative, together with precise use of framings and a panning shot, in its Victorian morality tale of a middle-class baby kidnapped by a gypsy. As continuity evolved, so did other techniques, especially as the demand for films increased significantly after 1903. One important innovation was the division of a scene into several shots, probably pioneered by G. A. Smith in *Grandma's Reading Glass* (1900). Insert shots, dissolves, fades, camera movements, long-shot and close-ups were gradually added to the language, and by 1906 the fundamental formal features were established.

Narrative constructions, particularly as they evolved after the nickelodeon boom around 1905 spurred a great deal of new production, were similarly indebted to forms established in the late 19th century. Theatrical melodrama, which had reached the height of its popularity in the 1850s, was both a direct source for film narratives and a more diffuse general influence. Melodrama had served the same urban working-class patrons as early film, and this audience had looked to the theatre to see the problems and contradictions of its life dramatised in a simple, bold and engaging form. Immediate character recognition was demanded, and both psychological and moral subtlety was unwelcome. On another level, the early cinema also learned from the theatre's dexterity in scene changes and elaborate stage machinery.

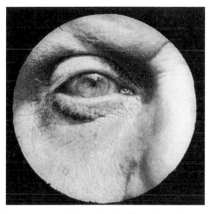

Innovations: Grandma's Reading Glass *(1900)*

Similar comparisons can be made between pulp literature around the turn of the century and early film narratives. Again, cheap novels and short stories were a source for the first dramas, and shared features include the often melodramatic stories and one-dimensional characterisations, and a stress on middle-class morality. In these first detective stories and Westerns lie the earliest elements of the movie genres which were to prove so fruitful for films in later years.

Les films d'art

Although it too is clearly indebted to the theatre, and specifically to the classical tradition, among the first genres fully developed by the cinema was the *film d'art*. In France, Pathé produced *L'Histoire d'un crime* (1901) based on waxwork tableaux from the Musée Grévin, and *La Vie d'un joueur* (1903), for which the source was tableaux at London's Madame Tussauds. Other such films followed, but a key development of this style came with the first production specifically identified as a *film d'art*, *L'Assassinat du Duc de Guise* (1908). Although it may be difficult today to appreciate the innovative qualities of this historical drama, its restrained performances and lavish settings were quickly recognised as the standard which respectable producers had to attain.

Le film d'art: L'Assassinat du Duc de Guise, *made by André Calmettes in 1908*

The works which endeavoured to emulate this success extended the length and ambition of film dramas, so that by 1912 Albert Capellani's adaptation of Victor Hugo's *Les Misérables* ran, in two parts, for three-and-a-half hours. The genre was much imitated elsewhere, and tempted the most famous theatrical actors, who previously had been mostly dismissive of the cinema, to appear before the cameras. Such productions, which included frequent adaptations of Shakespeare and comparable classics, imparted an intellectual respectability to the cinema which, in parallel with the building of more comfortable film theatres, helped it to attract larger sections of the middle-class audience.

The success of prestige adaptations was particularly important to the Italian cinema, which from 1908 produced numerous costume spectacles drawn from Dante, from classical history and from the 19th-century dramatic and operatic repertoire. Increasingly lavish, with ever larger sets and crowd scenes, these films are exemplified by two worldwide successes: Enrico Guazzoni's *Quo Vadis?* (1912), which made $150,000 in the United States alone, and Giovanni Pastrone's *Cabiria* (1914).

The lavish sets of Giovanni Pastrone's Cabiria *(1914)*

Melodrama and comedy emerged as the other staples of pre-war cinema. In Britain, after a period of undistinguished production and industry stagnation, there were successful domestic versions of the *films d'art*, notably W. G. Barker's *King Henry VIII* (1911) with Sir Herbert Tree and Cecil Hepworth's *Hamlet* (1913) with Sir Johnston Forbes-Robertson. But it was the release of Hepworth's melodrama *Rachel's Sin* (1911) which coincided

26

with the start of a period of greater vitality. *East Lynne* (1913), produced by W. G. Barker and directed by Bert Haldane, was the most polished of these pre-war successes.

British comedy, however, could not compare with the sophistication achieved in France and Italy. Comedians in both countries who had been trained on the vaudeville stage produced scores of short films, the most successful series of which attracted a loyal following. In France, Pathé dominated the market, partly because they had the services of the most popular comic of the day, Max Linder, who by 1910 had created his famous debonair persona. As the critic David Robinson has written, 'He broke entirely from the tradition of the Pathé clowns – naturals thrown into a world of frenetic and exaggerated activity. Max's comedy lay in the contrast between his own normality and elegance and the lunacy of the adventures that befell him.' In 1908 the Italian producer Giovanni Pastrone, noting the international appeal of French clowns, tempted one of them, André Deed, away from Pathé and into an Italian series of more than a hundred films where he starred as 'Cretinetti'. Success again spawned imitations.

British melodrama: East Lynne *(1913)*

Max Linder

One further significant genre of these years was the episodic crime series, initiated in France by Victorin Jasset at the Eclair company. In 1908 Jasset adapted *Le Guet-apens*, the first of a sequence of short films with the character Nick Carter, from American detective novels. Three years later Jasset began three episodic films centred on a brilliant criminal, Zigomar. But it is Louis Feuillade, at the rival Gaumont studio, whose achievements with the serial form – in *Fantômas* (1913-14) and *Judex* (1917) – are most feted. Set in contemporary Paris, and photographed with a keen sense of atmosphere and compositional beauty, these films constantly offer bizarre surprises conjured from everyday life.

Films d'art, comedy and crime ensured that French cinema, and particularly Pathé, remained buoyant, both in the domestic market and internationally, until the start of the First World War. Pathé had opened an office in New York in 1904, two years after Méliès' brother had set up an agency there. By this point Thomas Edison had been waging a legal battle for almost ten years to establish his monopoly in the cinema industry. Determined to stifle foreign as well as domestic competition, his company brought suits against both the French companies in November 1904. Under some self-imposed restraints, both firms continued to operate, and by 1908 Pathé was the largest single source of films in the United States. Their international success created new problems, however, for by 1912 only ten per cent of the company's profits came from France, whereas 70 per cent was being generated in the United States. This imbalance became increasingly difficult to negotiate, for many of Pathé's films were pitched at a sophisticated Parisian audience, which was not nearly large enough by itself to generate profits for high-budget productions. American films, too, were by this stage extremely popular with European audiences. In 1914, American imports to France for the first time earned more money than domestic productions.

Feuillade's Judex *(1917)*

Exhibition in America

Although Thomas Edison's peep-shows had been initially successful, there were soon indications that they were simply a novelty with which the public was becoming bored. In May 1895 Norman Raff, one of the Kinetoscope's marketing agents, wrote: 'The demand for Kinetoscopes has not been enough to even pay expenses of our company . . . Our candid opinion is that the Kinetoscope business – at least as far as the regular company is concerned – will be a "dead duck" after this season.' Raff and his colleague Frank Gammon were also aware of what the Lumière brothers were planning in France; and since Edison still refused to consider building a projector, they contracted for the rights to a projector with Thomas Armat and Francis Jenkins, two inventors from Washington, DC. The Edison company agreed to manufacture this and supply films, and Edison himself was announced as its inventor, since all parties involved accepted that this would generate the most publicity.

Early in 1896 Raff and Gammon recognised that they needed to premiere their projections before the Cinématographe arrived from France. So they hurriedly arranged for a debut at Koster & Bial's Music Hall in New York on 23 April 1896, just days before the Lumière company mounted its American premiere. Competition among vaudeville managers was intense during these years and, as elsewhere, projected films soon found their first home on the bills of theatres. But the Edison Vitascope operation, dependent on the vagaries of local electric power supplies, was dogged by problems, and the Cinématographe's simple, hand-cranked machinery quickly became the more solidly established system. This was not least because, unlike Edison's simple theatric images, the Lumière films exploited the scale and depth which could be achieved by filming in the open air, and Lumière operators were encouraged to film, process and project local attractions in the areas they visited. Vitascope finally ended its operations when Edison built a rival projector and undercut the prices of his former colleagues.

Vaudeville remained the primary exhibition site until after the turn of the century, not least because in 1900 a strike by artistes closed many theatres. Others stayed open by screening films, and the new entertainment became still more firmly established. Two years after this a Los Angeles entrepreneur, Thomas L. Tally, closed off a section of his peep-show arcade and set up an auditorium for projected films. Advertising 'A Vaudeville of Motion Pictures', he began to charge five cents for admission to matinee shows. Many arcade owners followed his lead, and from 1905 'nickelodeons' mushroomed across the country. In 1910 there were an estimated 10,000 such theatres in America, drawing perhaps 26 million people, or just under 20 per cent of the population, each week. As in Europe, the audiences were predominantly working-class, but with the important difference that many of them were newly arrived immigrants. The experience of cinemagoing drew them into the ways of American society, and as the cameraman Billy Bitzer recalled of a tour of nickelodeons on Manhattan's Lower East Side, 'We noticed that immigrants learned English by reading the titles aloud.'

Throughout this nickelodeon boom Edison's company harried with lawsuits its major manufacturing rivals, which by now included Vitagraph, set up by reporter and cartoonist J. Stuart Blackton, and American Mutoscope and Biograph. In particular, Edison claimed the exclusive right to the use of sprocket holes in film. His rivals, however, maintained that they were working with cameras and projectors which did not infringe Edison's patents. American Mutoscope and Biograph, for example, had in 1896 secured the services of W. K. L. Dickson, Edison's former employee, who first created an improved peep-show, the Mutoscope, which used photographic cards instead of film. With his new company he then built an original camera and projector, which utilised a larger frame-size than Edison and which punched perforations as it was operated. But in 1907 two important court decisions seemed to strengthen the veteran inventor's case. Edison's company now argued that it could control the manufacture and exhibition of all films, especially since it had an exclusive agreement with George Eastman, the sole American manufacturer of raw celluloid stock.

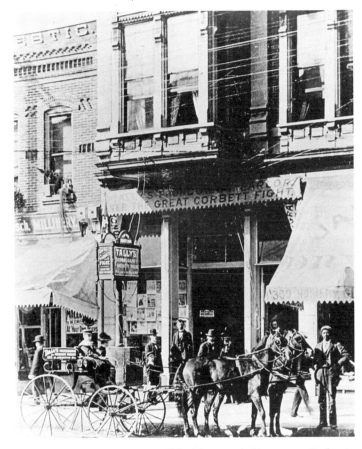

Tally's Phonograph Kinetoscope Parlor in Los Angeles

The Trust

Edison agreed to license a limited number of other companies, but Biograph, operating securely with a number of patents Edison did not control, established a rival licensing system. In 1908 these two groups agreed to form the Motion Picture Patents Company (known as 'the Trust', a derogatory term for illegal combinations of companies), which was intended to stabilise the industry, to keep control in the hands of a small number of producers, and to severely restrict foreign competition in the domestic market (only Pathé and the importer George Kleine were initially granted licences; Méliès received one later). Two years later the Trust extended its power with the General Film Company, which was soon almost the only domestic distributor.

Despite the Trust and its frequent resort to strong-arm tactics, which on occasion involved the employment of gunmen, independent companies were never completely forced out of the market. Often with the backing of the independents' organisation – the Motion Picture Distributing and Sales Company, set up in 1910 – many small operations continued to make and distribute films until one of the key patent holdings was disallowed in the courts in 1912. Three years later, further legal proceedings led to the MPPC

29

being declared a monopoly, and it was disbanded. But by then, protected at home and ever more efficient at production, American companies both within and outside the MPPC had been at work for five or more years on a systematic attempt to open up foreign markets. The war devastated European production, and the Americans were consequently able to achieve the dominant position which they have retained ever since.

This expansion abroad developed in parallel with the moves at home towards a smaller number of larger and stronger production companies. At first productions were mounted, photographed, directed and edited by a cameraman. Although the industry was still largely based in New York, W. K. L. Dickson produced actualities and staged scenes across America and abroad. Among many others, his early rivals included G. W. (Billy) Bitzer, who was to become D. W. Griffith's cameraman, and Edwin S. Porter. Porter is probably the most significant of the early American film-makers. In *The Life of an American Fireman* and *The Great Train Robbery* (both 1903), he demonstrated in crude form the principles of continuity and narrative development which were being explored at the same time in Europe. *The Great Train Robbery,* for example, contains a 'match' edit which preserves a continuity in space and time, as well as an early use of cross-cutting to create suspense.

Early continuity: Porter's The Great Train Robbery *(1903)*

With the huge increase in demand from the new nickelodeons after 1906, the industry began to allocate the staging of films to specialist directors, many of whom had experience in the theatre. Specialist writers, too, were brought in to increase efficiency, and, after new legislation in 1907, to protect companies against copyright claims. As demand continued to grow, and winter weather interrupted output, production companies dispatched director-led teams to better climates. A particularly favourable area was Southern California, which not only enjoyed good weather (the Los Angeles Chamber of Commerce boasted of sunshine 350 days a year), but offered many different kinds of scenery, a plentiful supply of cheap labour, including cowboys, and the proximity of several West Coast theatre companies. At such a distance from New York, there was also relatively little harassment by the Trust's representatives. One suburb of Los Angeles, called Hollywood, was particularly attractive, and despite the antipathy of residents by the early 1910s several companies were working there.

Location shooting remained unpredictable, and companies started to centralise production in 'factories', which were especially suited for shooting narrative dramas. Although audiences remained interested in seeing actualities, their production was more expensive and more unpredictable than the controlled possibilities of making short, studio-based story films. By the mid-1910s electrical lighting and interior sets were in general use. Detailed scripts were demanded prior to shooting so that the most effective use of resources could be made. Production tasks became more specialised, as the film industry adopted from other manufacturers many of the techniques of mass production.

David Wark Griffith

Even though his place and position are now much disputed by historians, the key figure in the decade after 1908 is D. W. Griffith. Despite the inaccurate attribution to him of the invention of almost all the significant additions to the language of film-making, his achievements were considerable, both in the numerous films which he made with Biograph between 1908 and 1913, and in his later, towering films *The Birth of a Nation* (1915) and *Intolerance* (1916).

An aspirant playwright, and an actor, Griffith began a reluctant career in front of the cameras with Edwin S. Porter directing him at the Edison studios in *Rescued from an Eagle's Nest* (1908). Soon he was at Biograph and behind the camera, which was invariably operated by his close collaborator Billy Bitzer. In more than 450 films for Biograph he applied to a medium about which he was at first completely ignorant what he knew of the popular theatre. Commercial success, and a relentless production schedule of a film or more each week, allowed him to experiment, and to work towards a more subtle and flexible film language than the tableaux-based style which he inherited. In particular he began to use the techniques, already explored by others, to break up a

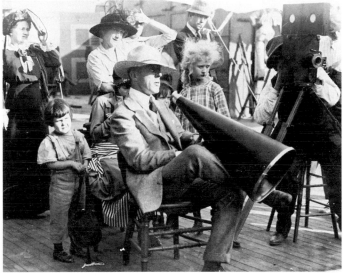

D. W. Griffith on location

scene into a succession of shots, taken from different angles and at different distances from the subject, and to combine these in ways which complemented the emotional content of the action. He subdued the extravagant, theatrical acting gestures previously thought appropriate, and worked closely with a company of carefully chosen actors, often rehearsing them before shooting.

Although the nickelodeons continued to produce healthy profits, exhibitors were always searching for new ways to attract audiences. As in vaudeville, a 'feature' attraction at the top of a bill was a significant draw, and one which could be strongly supported with advertising. Particularly distinctive films would bring in audiences, even with increased admission charges. Distributor George Kleine imported *Quo Vadis?* in 1913, and even though he was a member of the Trust (which only permitted the screening of one- or two-reel films), he chose to show it at its full length, with an admission price of one dollar. Kleine's returns were enormous, and other producers recognised a way of differentiating their output from that of the Trust companies.

With the spur of the imported Italian epics, Griffith wanted to move beyond one-reel films. But neither Biograph nor its distributor, the General Film Company, were interested, and both delayed the release of his first four-reel feature *Judith of Bethulia* (1913). Griffith broke with the company and moved to Reliance Majestic (Mutual), where he became Head of Production. After directing four films there, he put together with Mutual's founder Harry Aitken the biggest American production to date, an adaptation of Thomas Dixon's novel and play *The Clansman*, which on its release in 1915 was to be called *The Birth of a Nation*.

The Klan ride in Griffith's The Birth of a Nation

By this stage other American companies were beginning to produce large-scale films, but Griffith's family saga set in the Civil War was an unrivalled sensation. Its power to move, indeed to overwhelm audiences, was unprecedented. Yet it was a highly controversial film, and remains so today. Dixon's original novel glorified the Southern racist organisation, the Ku Klux Klan, and Griffith's film unproblematically reproduced this attitude (although Griffith always denied this). *The Birth of a Nation* was a key factor in the revival of the KKK, which had disbanded in 1869.

As the cinemas themselves became larger, more lavish, and more acceptable to the middle classes, such features were increasingly in demand. By 1916, when Thomas Ince made his epic *Civilization*, such films were widely accepted. But Griffith was eager to break boundaries once again. He first began work on a small-scale contemporary story called *The Mother and the Law*. Once this was shot, he started a second, with the same title but set in France. Then he made a third, with a biblical background. Finally, he began work on a fourth, to be staged in vast and spectacular Babylonian sets. Despite the huge profits of *The Birth of a Nation*, the scale of this enterprise meant that he had to invest much of his own fortune. And then he was faced with editing the four stories together in a coherent way. Eventually, he produced a film that ran for three-and-a-quarter hours, and in which the four stories ran in parallel. But for all that it was an aesthetic breakthrough, and a major influence on many later film-makers, the public were mystified by *Intolerance* and the enormous production costs were not returned at the box office. Although he was to continue making distinguished features through the silent period *(Broken Blossoms, Way Down East, Orphans of the Storm)*, the failure of *Intolerance* dogged Griffith throughout his life.

Stars and studios

Along with the new features, another popular lure for the pre-First World War audience was the star. Until 1910, producers refused to name actors and actresses, partly for fear that if they began to attract a personal following then, as was common practice in the theatre, they would demand higher fees. The action of independent producer Carl Laemmle to break this custom is another of the cherished legends of cinema history. Having recently signed Florence Lawrence, until then known only as 'the Biograph girl', he planted a false newspaper story about her death, and then angrily rebutted it with

32

advertisements. His initiative was rewarded at the box office, and other producers, particularly those outside the Trust, imitated his example and began to build distinctive images for their own stars.

Thus by the late 1910s the characteristic features of film production were in place, as was the central role of the star. Equally established was the film language which, with few adjustments, was to serve the American cinema for at least the next four decades. In addition, throughout the 1910s, the many small production companies were merging to form larger units, both for efficiency and for raising the finance necessary to make features. The same decade saw a crucial shift of power away from the individual producer towards a number of major corporations. By the mid-1920s a former nickelodeon owner, Adolph Zukor, would control an empire of production, distribution and exhibition, not only in America but around the globe. With such a vertically integrated monopoly, replicating the essential features of the Pathé model, Zukor's company was to dominate world cinema, with just four other similar enterprises, for the next three decades. The Hollywood system was firmly established.

Poster for Thomas Ince's Civilization. *Along with D. W. Griffith and Cecil B. DeMille, Ince is generally held to be one of the foremost directors of the silent cinema's middle period. A former actor, he began directing films in 1910 and became particularly known for his Westerns with William S. Hart. Ince operated a 'unit system', supervising the work of several directors to ensure that his passion for authentic detail was respected.*

Intolerance: *the Babylonian story*

Further reading

Roy Armes, *A Critical History of British Cinema*, London: Secker & Warburg, 1978.

John Barnes, *The Beginnings of the Cinema in England*, Newton Abbot: David & Charles, 1976.

Michael Chanan, *The Dream that Kicks: The Prehistory and Early Years of Cinema in Britain*, London: Routledge & Kegan Paul, 1980.

John L. Fell, *Film and the Narrative Tradition*, Berkeley: University of California Press, 1976.

John L. Fell and others, *Before Hollywood: Turn-of-the Century American Film*, New York: Hudson Hills Press, 1987.

Paul Hammond, *Marvellous Méliès*, London: St Martin's, 1975.

Robert M. Henderson, *D. W. Griffith: His Life and Work*, New York: Oxford University Press, 1972.

Rachael Low and Roger Manvell, *The History of the British Film 1896-1906*, London: Allen & Unwin, 1948; 2nd ed., 1973.

Rachael Low, *The History of the British Film 1906-1914*, London: Allen & Unwin, 1949; 2nd ed., 1973.

Lary Linden May, *Screening the Past: The Birth of Mass Culture and the Motion Picture Industry*, New York: Oxford University Press, 1980.

Barry Salt, *Film Style and Technology: History and Analysis*, London: Starword, 1983.

Richard Schickel, *D. W. Griffith*, London: Pavilion Books, 1984.

A. Nicholas Vardac, *Stage to Screen: Theatrical Method from Garrick to Griffith*, Cambridge, Mass.: Harvard University Press, 1949.

3
The Cinema before Sound

With only a touch of caricature, received wisdom about the years from the mid-1910s to the coming of sound in 1927 could be sketched as follows. In America factory-like studios, run by tyrannical moguls, became all-powerful by turning out indistinguishable 'product' for a mass audience. Creative directors who strove to express their individuality within this system, such as D. W. Griffith or Erich von Stroheim, were discouraged and ultimately destroyed by it. Across the Atlantic, however, artists like Feuillade and Gance in France, Lang and Murnau in Germany, and Eisenstein and Pudovkin in Russia were taking the poetry of film to new heights. But such a simplistic framework is of little help in reaching any real understanding of the silent cinema. The relationship between creativity and economics in the American industry was, as it has remained, both intimate and multi-faceted, just as it was, and is, in the European industries that fostered the 'timeless classics' like *Battleship Potemkin* and *Napoleon.* And it is the complexities of this relationship which must be investigated in any consideration of the culture of the moving image.

Adolph Zukor and Paramount

Of all the now legendary Hollywood moguls the most significant during the silent period was Adolph Zukor. Born in Hungary, the man who was to become the central figure in the rise of the studio system had opened a slot machine arcade in 1903 and a theatre in New York the following year. With the nickelodeon boom, he expanded the number of outlets which he controlled, and in 1912 became an independent producer outside the Trust. His success exhibiting Sarah Bernhardt's feature-length *Queen Elizabeth,* imported from France at the urging of Edwin S. Porter, persuaded him that there was a large audience for full-length prestige films. Together with Porter, he initiated the Famous Players partnership with the Broadway entrepreneur Daniel Frohman. After a number of successful productions with stars from the stage, several of which were directed by Porter in stolidly theatrical style, two further mergers greatly strengthened the company's position. One was with the independent producer Jesse Lasky, the other with

Adolph Zukor and Jesse Lasky with plans for Paramount studios, July 1923

35

'America's Sweetheart' Mary Pickford in A Girl of Yesterday

Gloria Swanson in Manhandled (1924)

the small but successful distribution company Paramount Pictures Corporation. The shrewd Zukor, however, retained overall control.

Signing stars like Mary Pickford and Douglas Fairbanks, Zukor and the new corporation were hugely successful in both production and distribution, and at the end of the war Paramount, as the company was now called, was making more than 200 films each year for nearly 5,000 cinemas. By now, after appearances in Paramount films like *A Girl of Yesterday* (1915) and *Romance of the Redwoods* (1917), Mary Pickford was Hollywood's most famous star, but Zukor was unwilling to match a million-dollar contract, together with artistic control, which was being offered to her by a rival company, First National. 'She taught me a great deal,' Zukor said long after they had parted company, 'I was only an apprentice when we started. She was an expert workman.'

The First National Exhibitors Circuit had been put together to counter Paramount's powerful distribution network, and by 1921 it was affiliated with 3,500 cinemas. In 1922 it set up its own production studio, and it also acquired exclusive distribution rights to Charlie Chaplin's films. Zukor was spurred to respond and, with Wall Street financing, Paramount began to buy up key first-run theatres across the country. By controlling such cinemas, particularly those in the large cities, Zukor was able to take larger cuts of the revenue from new releases. Healthy profits allowed him to extend and consolidate an ambitious production schedule. His new star was Gloria Swanson, a sophisticated and suggestively amoral contrast to Mary Pickford's innocent, and her pictures were usually slick comedies like *Why Change Your Wife?* (1920).

Paramount's taste for sensuality and exoticism was extended in 1921 when Rudolph Valentino was contracted to make first *The Sheik* and then *Blood and Sand* (1922). A rather different sex appeal was proffered by Clara Bow, whose image as a flirtatious 'flapper' was constructed in films like *Mantrap* (1926) and *It* (1927). Paramount was never to distinguish itself as a studio

Valentino in The Sheik

concerned with social problems, but it did produce a handful of major films which portrayed more than a round of parties and seductions. Directed by James Cruze and photographed by Karl Brown, *The Covered Wagon* (1923) is an epic picture of the westward migration of the 1840s; and William Wellman's *Wings* (1927) was a strong contribution to Hollywood's cycle of war films which had followed the 1924 success of *What Price Glory?* on Broadway. The studio also nurtured the young director Josef von Sternberg, who had startled Hollywood with his independently produced and location-shot *The Salvation Hunters* (1925). Sternberg's distinctive visual style, with its bold use of light and shade, was developed in *Underworld* (1927), scripted by Ben Hecht as the first serious study of gangsterism, and in the dark, violent *The Docks of New York* (1928).

Paramount's most trusted and consistent film-maker throughout the silent period was the director Cecil B. DeMille. One of the four original partners in the Jesse Lasky Company, he shot and cut with co-director Oscar Apfel the company's first production, *The Squaw Man* (1914), apparently with no more prior experience of film-making than a single visit to the Edison studio in New York. The film was hugely successful, as were many of the subsequent melodramas, Westerns and historical films which DeMille directed for Paramount through the 1910s. His 1915 drama *The Cheat* made distinctive use of the newly introduced artificial lighting, but it was less technical innovation and more his skills with delicate social comedy which made his films universally popular. His later fascination with epic spectacle was first evidenced in the ten-reel *Joan the Woman* (1917), and then given further rein in the making of his first version of *The Ten Commandments* (1923). He clashed with Zukor over the escalating budget, to a degree where he challenged the executive to sell the film to him for its production cost of a million dollars. Zukor backed down and the film proved to be a hit. But in 1925 DeMille left the studio to go independent, and he was not to return until 1932, when he made an early sound spectacular, *The Sign of the Cross.*

Light and shade: Sternberg's Underworld *(Clive Brook)*

37

Circuits and studios

In 1925 Zukor's cinema subsidiary, Publix Theaters, was put under successful theatre manager Sam Katz, who for the first time introduced to the film business modern retailing practices. Rapid expansion, centralised booking, advertising and accounting all rigorously controlled from New York, and a prominent corporate image partly created by lavish cinemas operating under the name Paramount, meant that by 1930 Publix was by far the dominant film circuit. Through this period Publix, and other chains following its model, competed fiercely to build increasingly more elaborate and fantastical 'picture palaces', which served as flagships for each company. Moorish, Gothic and oriental influences were plundered by architects in their creation of such wonders as Grauman's Chinese Theatre in Hollywood and Rothapfel's Roxy in New York, the world's largest cinema. By now the cinema was firmly established as a respectable activity for the middle class, and the prime locations of many of these new theatres reflected the importance of this clientele.

Grauman's Chinese Theatre in Hollywood

Paramount's success depended on the company's simultaneous control of production, distribution and exhibition, which became known as 'vertical integration'. Inevitably its operation was challenged throughout the 1920s not only by First National but by other large corporations created from mutually beneficial mergers. The producer who had first taken on the Trust, Carl Laemmle, had absorbed a number of small production companies and formed Universal. In 1915 he opened Universal City, a lavish ranch-size production facility in North Hollywood. From this base the studio made numerous low-budget action films and Westerns, which it distributed largely to rural audiences. But it failed to acquire key first-run exhibition sites, and although powerful as both a national and international distributor, the company was unable to consolidate itself at the level of Paramount.

Universal City: a Western street

Another immigrant showman, William Fox, had begun from an exhibition base of New York theatres, and had started to produce and distribute in the mid-1910s. But despite considerable success, and some notable work by directors John Ford and Raoul Walsh, like Universal and like the comparable Warner Bros studio, Fox Pictures was by the mid-20s still only a small-scale rival to what was emerging as the duopolistic control of Paramount and the new Metro-Goldwyn-Mayer corporation, established in 1924 as a subsidiary of Loew's Inc.

Metro-Goldwyn-Mayer

A former furrier, Marcus Loew entered the entertainment business in 1904, promoting mixed shows of vaudeville and moving pictures. Through the next two decades, working with his valued deputy Nicholas Schenck, Loew established an unrivalled and immensely profitable chain of theatres, retaining interest in both vaudeville and cinema. But by the early 1920s vaudeville was losing out to movies, and the vertically integrated corporations of Paramount and First National were pushing up the cost to Loew's of quality films. In 1920 Loew's Inc acquired the distribution and production company Metro Pictures, and in 1924 took over Goldwyn Pictures, which had interests in both production and exhibition. Establishing Nicholas Schenck as President, Loew also brought in the successful executive Louis B. Mayer, who was made vice-president in charge of production for the new combine Metro-Goldwyn-Mayer. Astute acquisition of further theatres in carefully targeted areas throughout the 1920s, combined with MGM's hugely successful production output, meant that as the industry faced the upheavals of introducing sound Loew's was the only serious rival to Paramount.

Prior to the merger Metro had produced a number of significant films, including *The Four Horsemen of the Apocalypse* (1921), directed by Rex Ingram. The new company continued with the policy of spectaculars, including *Ben-Hur* (1925), begun in Italy under director Charles Brabin and finished in the United States by Fred Niblo. Other major directors working for the studio were King Vidor – who made the immensely popular anti-war epic *The Big Parade* (1925) and a delightful version of *La Bohème* with Lillian Gish (1926) – and Erich von Stroheim.

Stroheim had arrived in the United States from Vienna around 1906, and had begun to work as an actor and writer for Triangle. During the war he was greatly in demand as a military adviser, for he falsely claimed to have been a cavalry officer in the Imperial army. He then persuaded Carl Laemmle to buy his screenplay for *Blind Husbands* (1919), which he both directed and starred in, as a seductive European aristocrat threatening an American marriage. The film proved to be a big hit for Laemmle's Universal, and was followed by *The Devil's Passkey* (1921, now lost) and *Foolish Wives* (1922). In the latter Stroheim is a Russian count and the backdrop is Monte Carlo, reconstructed in vast sets which ensured that the film was the most expensive since *Intolerance*. *Foolish Wives* was originally a sprawling canvas which may have stretched, in Stroheim's cut, to thirty-four reels. The one first screened in New York was fourteen reels long, and even this was subsequently further cut. The film was also widely attacked for its amorality and its celebration of casino society. But the controversy encouraged Universal to go ahead with an equally lavish project, *The Merry-Go-Round* (1923). After five weeks' shooting, Stroheim fell out with Laemmle's brilliant assistant, Irving Thalberg, and was replaced by the director Rupert Julian.

Stroheim was to cross swords again with Thalberg, at the newly founded MGM, when he delivered a forty-two reel cut of *Greed* (1924), a project begun for Goldwyn prior to the merger. A visionary melodrama based on Frank Norris' realist novel *McTeague*, the film now exists only in a mutilated version. Subsequently, the eleven-hour version of another mammoth project was rejected by Paramount, who were to distribute it, and cut into two films, *The Wedding March* (1928) and *The Honeymoon* (now lost). Stroheim's final extravagance was *Queen Kelly* (1928), begun with Gloria Swanson as both star and producer, who in the latter role fired him halfway through filming, and a much truncated version of the film was subsequently released. He was

Stroheim's Greed

39

to work as director on only one other film, *Walking Down Broadway* (1932), from which he was also removed, and he resumed his career as an actor. Memorable appearances included the German commandant in *La Grande Illusion* (1937), and Norma Desmond's butler in *Sunset Boulevard* (1950). An ageing, forgotten silent movie star, Miss Desmond is played by Gloria Swanson, and together they watch scenes from *Queen Kelly*.

The comics

Whereas in the years just prior to the First World War successful directors were quite likely to control their own production company, by the early 1920s most were working under contract for one of the major studios. Mack Sennett, for example, had begun as an actor working first at Edison and then for Griffith at Biograph. Styling himself as a protégé of the master, he started to write (his was the scenario for Griffith's 1909 film *The Lonely Villa*) and subsequently to direct. By 1912 he was able to find finance (from two former bookies) for the Keystone Studio, and as his distinctive comedies proved consistently successful he moved on from directing to become a supervising producer.

Mack Sennett

Crude farce, frantic improvisation and immaculate vaudeville timing were the hallmarks of Sennett's early comedy, which strung together visual gags with little regard for plot. But the Keystone Kops were complemented in the studio's output by more polished work, including a series of romantic comedies with Gloria Swanson. In 1915 Keystone was absorbed into the Triangle Film Corporation, but Sennett found no more satisfaction in this arrangement than his colleagues Thomas Ince and D. W. Griffith. After a further period as an independent, during which he worked frequently with Mabel Normand, in 1923 he began a long association with Pathé, where he was to launch the baby-faced comic Harry Langdon.

Another comedian who long pursued his career as an independent before acceding to the growing power of the majors was Buster Keaton. Given his nickname by the magician Harry Houdini, Buster was part of a family acrobatic act at the age of three, and was well-established in vaudeville when he entered the movies in 1917, in a series of films starring and directed by Roscoe 'Fatty' Arbuckle. Two years later Joseph Schenck set up a new company to make a series of comedy shorts with Keaton himself as the star. Among these elaborate two-reelers were *One Week* (1920), the bizarre, dreamlike *The Playhouse* (1921) and *Cops* (1922). Keaton's first feature, *The Saphead* (1920), was exceptionally well received by the critics, and with this success behind him he confidently developed his dignified, bemused character, whose deadpan expression never changes. Always determined to overcome whatever adversities life may offer, Keaton's character creates much of the humour from a constant, dogged resourcefulness.

In 1923 Keaton decided to concentrate solely on features, and his growing maturity as a director can be recognised in *Our Hospitality* (1923) and *Sherlock Jr* (1924), in which he plays a movie projectionist who inserts

40

himself into the action on screen. His biggest commercial hit was *The Navigator* (also 1924), for which he shared the star's role with an abandoned schooner, a strategy he repeated in *The General* (1927), where his constant companion through adventures in the Civil War is a train. But a new contract with MGM meant surrendering ultimate control of his films. He found it difficult to accommodate his perfectionism to the rigid production patterns of the studio, and his career rapidly declined. Like so many of his colleagues, he had found it hard to make a stand against the relentless economic pressures towards the consolidation of the larger companies.

Buster Keaton's former partner, Roscoe 'Fatty' Arbuckle, was at the centre of a notorious scandal in 1921 when a young actress called Virginia Rappe was taken ill at a party hosted by him. When she died four days later Arbuckle was charged with rape and murder, and became the target of vociferous attacks in the press, especially in those papers owned by William Randolph Hearst. After three contentious trials Arbuckle was found not guilty, but the decision neither saved his career nor helped to still the many reforming voices whose attention had been focused on the morals of Hollywood and its films.

Recognising the urgent need to deflect this criticism, fuelled subsequently by the death of morphine addict Wallace Reid and the murder of director William Desmond Taylor, the industry's moguls invited the then Postmaster-General, Will Hays, to establish a new body which would act as a voluntary watchdog. In 1922 he formed the Motion Picture Producers and Distributors of America (MPPDA), known as the Hays Office, and set about countering the adverse publicity. His most significant role was in offering informal, but almost always heeded, advice about the morality of planned features, and the consequent shift in tone was sufficient to prevent the government imposing its own censor.

Buster Keaton in Sherlock Jr

United Artists
The most famous attempt to resist the moves towards the consolidation of the large corporations was announced in January 1919, when Mary Pickford, Douglas Fairbanks, William S. Hart (who soon withdrew), Charlie Chaplin and D.W. Griffith set up their own distribution organisation, United Artists. 'This step is positively and absolutely necessary,' they proclaimed, 'to protect the great motion picture public from threatening combinations and trusts that would force upon them mediocre productions and machine-made entertainment.'

Much of the impetus for this unparalleled, and widely ridiculed, move came from rumours that the 'threatening combinations' were planning mergers designed to limit the power and the earnings of major stars. Production costs were rising rapidly, and Zukor was considering a merger with First National which would have tied up all the significant exhibitors. Pickford's and Fairbanks' contracts were coming to an end, and Chaplin had been shocked to have a proposed budget increase turned down by First

Fairbanks, Griffith, Pickford and Chaplin form United Artists. 'The lunatics have taken over the asylum,' said a rival studio boss.

41

National's board. Their own distribution company seemed an attractive option.

Like Pickford, her husband Douglas Fairbanks had moved from the stage to become, in less than five years, a major star. His first film, for Triangle, was *The Lamb* (1915), in which he exhibited the talent for acrobatic stunts which was to become such a part of his appeal. After thirteen pictures with the company, he was wooed by Zukor, who offered him greater, but ultimately not sufficient, autonomy.

Chaplin, too, had enjoyed a meteoric rise. In 1913 he was touring America with Fred Karno's theatrical troupe. Keystone hired him, and in his first year with them he made thirty-five films, often supporting more established comics. His tramp persona first appeared in the second of these, *Kid Auto Races at Venice*. Lured away by Essanay, who gave him the chance to develop as a director, he concentrated on making fewer and more sophisticated films, like *The Tramp* with its distinctive combination of comedy and pathos. After only two years in the business, he was recognised as the most popular star in the world. In 1916 he switched again, this time to Mutual, where he made a dozen inventive two-reelers, among them *The Floorwalker* and *Easy Street*. He then opted for full independence, with only a distribution contract with First National, and made his parody of life in the trenches, *Shoulder Arms* (1918), and his first feature, *The Kid* (1921), the returns for which had been bettered only by *The Birth of a Nation*.

The Gold Rush

During its first five years United Artists handled many of the best pictures of each of its members. Fairbanks honed to perfection a series of spectacular swashbucklers, which included *Robin Hood* (1922) and *The Thief of Bagdad* (1924), and Mary Pickford continued to satisfy her many fans with films like *Tess of the Storm Country* (1922). Chaplin contributed his features *A Woman of Paris* (1923) and *The Gold Rush* (1925). Griffith, too, made his best post-*Intolerance* pictures for release by United Artists, including *Broken Blossoms* (1919) and *Orphans of the Storm* (1922). Yet as more and more of the major theatres were taken over by Paramount, First National and others, United Artists pictures found it hard to gain access to the best sites. Nor could the founders deliver sufficient product for an efficient operation. Under a new chairman, Joseph M. Schenck, a financing and production affiliate was formed, which made, among others, *The Son of the Sheik* (1926) with Valentino and three of Buster Keaton's later films. In 1925 Gloria Swanson joined as a partner, as did, two years later, Samuel Goldwyn. In many respects Schenck's reorganisation was a success, and gave to United Artists a firm base from which to deal with the change to sound.

France and the European industry

Film production in Europe was decimated, along with much else, by the 1914-18 war. Deprived for the most part of their own country's productions, audiences continued to welcome American exports, and after the war New York distributors looked forward to consolidating their dominant position.

Cinemagoers were now accustomed to feature-length films with Hollywood stars, and it was clear that the greatly weakened European industries would have difficulty producing films as attractive. Moreover, the huge American domestic market continued to ensure that production costs were often covered before exploitation abroad, and consequently foreign exhibition charges could be kept comparatively low.

Lubitsch's Madame Dubarry

Only Germany had retained a significant level of production throughout the war years. The import of American films was prohibited from early 1916 to 1920, and government support had encouraged rapid growth in the industry. Even after the import ban was lifted domestic production was further stimulated by currency exchange problems which ensured that American films, paid for by exhibitors in dollars, were almost prohibitively expensive. In contrast, lavish historical epics made in Germany, like Joe May's *Veritas Vincit* (1918), could be sold relatively cheaply abroad. A cycle of successful costume dramas followed this initial success, and it was here that the director Ernst Lubitsch first attracted attention with *Madame Dubarry* (1919) and *Anna Boleyn* (1920).

In Britain, France and Italy, however, the film industries were unable to capitalise on the temporary advantage of currency problems. For a decade after the war the British market was rigidly controlled by American distributors who often filled cinema schedules more than a year in advance by 'block-booking' and 'blind-booking' of films (guaranteeing a particular attraction only if the cinema agreed to show a string of unseen, unproven films). This practice was eventually outlawed by the Cinematograph Films Act in 1927. In Italy, many of the smaller companies were integrated in 1919 into the Unione Cinematografica Italiana, but the production policy of attempting to emulate the lavish pre-war historical epics found little support with an international audience. UCI finally collapsed in 1925, after the disastrous reception of its remake of *Quo Vadis?* Domestic production stopped almost completely, and several of the country's most prominent directors sought work in France and Germany.

Until recently, French film-making in the 1920s has not received the close critical attention given to the German and Russian cinemas of the same period. A number of important restorations and revivals, however, together with several significant scholarly studies, have begun to suggest that French cinema then was as rich and as innovatory as that of Germany or Russia. Popular historical and literary epics were complemented by the more radical work of directors like Abel Gance, Marcel L'Herbier and Jean Epstein. Moreover, alongside the industry there was a thriving avant-garde, which was distinguished by the close involvement of painters, photographers and poets with film-makers like René Clair and Luis Buñuel.

Although new directors were soon to emerge, a number of significant figures from the pre-war industry continued to work. In particular, Louis Feuillade at Gaumont produced more of his successful crime series, although none of the later ones matched his achievements in *Fantômas* and *Les Vampires* (1915-6). A group of émigrés with experience in the pre-revolutionary Russian cinema also made their mark in France in the post-war years. Establishing themselves as the Société des Films Albatros, they included the director Alexandre Volkoff and the actor Ivan Mosjoukine, whose later work together included *Kean* (1924) and *Casanova* (1927). The Société des Films Albatros was to become one of the central producing organisations of the 1920s, often collaborating with younger directors like Epstein and L'Herbier. Another important group was the Société des Ciné-romans, which produced literary adaptations like Henri Fescourt's mammoth *Les Misérables* (1925), as well as co-financing bold features by L'Herbier.

Many of the younger film-makers were excited by DeMille's film *The Cheat*, first shown in Paris in 1916. They saw in it, and in other American films which followed, the possibility of cinema as an autonomous art which owed nothing to the stage. This aim was best expressed by the theorist and later director Louis Delluc, whose writings argued both for films which were the expression of individual authors and for the establishment of a truly national cinema in France. Two film-makers closely allied with him in the early 1920s were Germaine Dulac, who directed Delluc's script *La Fête espagnole* (1919), and Jean Epstein, whose later work embraced both spectacular fantasy, as in *La Chute de la Maison Usher* (1928), and explorations of everyday life like *Finis Terrae* (1929). Much of Epstein's work revels in exploiting the formal possibilities of cinematic technique, an interest shared by Marcel L'Herbier. Establishing his own production company, Cinegraphic, in 1922, L'Herbier supported young film-makers as well as directing critically controversial films like *L'Inhumaine* (1924) and *L'Argent* (1929), both of which contain remarkable experimental sequences. But for all their formal boldness, because such work was encouraged by the large producers,

'Formal boldness': L'Herbier's *L'Inhu-maine*

including Pathé and Gaumont, directors like L'Herbier were not confined to the margins of the industry.

The best-known figure from the 1920s in France must now be Abel Gance, thanks to the recent revivals of his epic *Napoleon* (1927). Gance wrote his first film in 1909, and ten years later he was enjoying enormous popular acclaim for melodramas like *La Dixième Symphonie* and *J'Accuse* (both 1918).

One of the triptych sequences from Napoleon

In 1920 he shot for almost a year in the railyards of Nice to make *La Roue*, an extraordinary amalgamation of tragical heroics and dazzling experiments with form and technique. *Napoleon* is even more impressive in its determination to extend the possibilities of cinematic language, an ambition most clearly demonstrated by the triptych sequences which close Kevin Brownlow's restored version. Almost universally admired as a spectacle, the film is only rarely questioned for its unqualified exaltation of Napoleon as a reactionary dictator.

The self-consciously artistic experiments of Gance, Epstein and L'Herbier were paralleled by vigorous avant-garde activity (see Chapter 8), and both tendencies were seen as important elements in a resistance to the contemporary American cinema. A more significant attempt to curb the power of the aggressive majors, however, was the possibility in the later 1920s of coordinated European resistance, a policy which came to be known as 'Film Europe'. France, for example, had initially banned German film imports, but this ban was relaxed when *The Cabinet of Dr Caligari* was shown in 1922. Subsequent mutual distribution arrangements, coupled with quota restrictions modelled on German legislation, did mean that in the late 1920s the circulation of European films was increased, although the success of this policy was always constrained by the still massive American dominance. Moreover, the Hays Office, looking after not only morality at home but also American business interests abroad, successfully fought the introduction of effective quotas in both France and Hungary.

Quotas and comparable measures were not, of course, sought only to protect the infrastructure of domestic film industries. It was recognised early on that American films created a demand for American products, and such increasing 'Americanisation', the effects of which are so familiar today, was resisted on both financial and cultural grounds. But 'Film Europe' was eventually to be defeated by politics. By the beginning of the 1930s right-wing elements were gaining increasing influence over both the German and the Italian industries.

German Expressionism

Despite the legacy of the war, Germany was central to the 'Film Europe' impetus because of the country's effective resistance in the early 1920s to American imports. Government support in these years, together with a number of innovative talents, had produced one of the most creative national cinemas of the silent period. Prior to the war, in contrast, the German cinema had been largely derivative. There had been the Teutonic equivalents of the *films d'art* and comedies. The detective thriller serial was another popular genre, but the films had few of the qualities that graced Louis Feuillade's work in France.

The herald of the new German cinema, which was almost immediately recognised as such around the world, was *The Cabinet of Dr Caligari*, made in 1919. By this point much of the industry, including the recently built, superbly equipped studios in Neubabelsberg near Berlin, was controlled by the mammoth combine Ufa, at first part-funded by the state and subsequently by the Deutsche Bank and industrial finance. But it was one of the smaller independent companies, Decla-Bioscop, which took a chance with a strange screenplay submitted by Carl Mayer and Hans Janowitz. Decla's producer Erich Pommer assigned the work to three designers – Hermann Warm, Walter Reimann and Walter Röhrig – who recognised in the story of a somnambulist and the doctor who instructs him in his murderous work the potential of creating an Expressionist work for the cinema.

Painted set in The Cabinet of Dr Caligari

Expressionism was an avant-garde movement which had been influential in German painting, literature and architecture for a decade. A central concern for its practitioners was the presentation of the world in ways which gave form to subjective ideas and emotions. Pommer was intrigued by the novelty of applying this to film, to create what the Italian Futurists had foreseen as 'living paintings'. He may also have thought that such a self-consciously artistic film would prove distinctive enough to find an international market. There was also a more prosaic reason for his support: the bold, stark, stylised sets, drawn and painted on canvas, could be cheaply made from the limited materials available.

Caligari was an immediate success, although the anti-authoritarian impulses of the authors (who saw the somnambulist as representing the innocents ordered to kill during the war) were toned down by a prologue and epilogue which revealed the tale as one told by a madman. Even so, sufficient continuities persisted between the story and its framing to suggest unsettling ambiguities. But it was the film's visual distinctiveness which made the greatest impact, and although the details were not widely imitated, at a more general level the style was to prove enormously influential. Visual distortion and exaggeration, chiaroscuro lighting and fluid framings, often combined with stories of horror and the fantastic, marked many German films in the next decade, with graphic visuals powerfully expressing the often turbulent feelings of the characters.

The style was to be most successfully developed in the work of two major directors, Fritz Lang and F. W. Murnau. Trained as an architect, Lang had begun to write scripts during the war for Decla, where he passed up the opportunity to direct *Caligari*. Two years later, he made another of the key Expressionist films, *Der müde Tod* (*Destiny*, 1921), which offers three variations, set in different historical periods, on a story about a woman's attempts to save her lover from death. Written in collaboration with his wife, the author Thea von Harbou, the film is a romantic, mystical fantasy which fully exploits the pictorial possibilities of its imagined, exotic locations. It was also one of the last films to be made by Decla before the rapidly expanding Ufa took over the studio.

Prior to *Destiny*, Lang had begun his sequence of successful thrillers which includes *The Spiders* (1919), *Dr Mabuse the Gambler* (1922) and, after the coming of sound, *M* (1931) and *The Testament of Dr Mabuse* (1933). Each of these contains Expressionist elements, and each combines imaginative lighting with striking sets. Lang's particular concern with the screen's ability to reveal grandeur on an architectural scale is even more apparent in his two-part telling of the Siegfried legends, *Die Nibelungen* (1923-4), and in his visionary fantasy *Metropolis* (1926). Just as the slave workers in this film are subject to a repressive, authoritarian regime, so the story's human qualities are swamped by the overwhelming sets.

Slave workers in Lang's Metropolis

Neither of these *folies de grandeur* (*Metropolis* was budgeted at DM1. 9m and cost DM5m) was a commercial success, partly because in 1924 the German mark was stabilised and American companies were once again able to operate effectively in the country. By the end of the year American films had captured almost half the German market, and production companies scrambled to enter transatlantic co-production deals, which the Americans were happy to accept since the product made helped to offset new quota regulations. In 1927 Ufa signed with Paramount and MGM, but the American interest was soon bought out by the industrialist Alfred Hugenberg. His new regime initiated drastic cuts in production and, as smaller companies went into bankruptcy, the industry started to look to the coming of sound as a possible saviour. Perhaps the difficulties of translation would act as a more effective stay on imports.

Europeans in Hollywood

Hollywood, however, was not only interested in selling its films into Germany. Eager to replicate the success of domestic talents, the moguls had been tempting away the German industry's best artists and technicians. Among those seduced by the prospect of working in what was now the movie capital of the world were producer Erich Pommer, art director and director Paul Leni, the innovative cameraman Karl Freund and several leading German actors, including Conrad Veidt, Pola Negri and Emil Jannings.

47

Perhaps the most successful transition was made by Ernst Lubitsch, who was invited over by Mary Pickford. Together they made *Rosita* (1923), and Lubitsch was launched on a brilliantly successful career as a director of 'sophisticated' comedies.

Nor was it only the German industry which was pillaged in this way. Since the war the two Swedish directors Mauritz Stiller and Victor Sjöström had been attracting international attention. Sjöström was particularly known for a trilogy of films from the fantastical novels of Selma Lagerlöf, an author to whom Stiller also turned in 1919. A later adaptation by Stiller of a Lagerlöf novel, *Gösta Berlings Saga* (1924), brought Greta Garbo to the screen. Stiller and Garbo were then invited to America, and to MGM, but the director, unlike his star, found Hollywood uncongenial. After working on a handful of projects he returned to Sweden, and to an early death.

Sjöström's The Wind

Nosferatu

Sjöström was at first more successful. He changed his name to Seastrom, and made two glorious silent pictures, both with Lillian Gish, *The Scarlet Letter* (1926) and *The Wind* (1928). But after the coming of sound, he too returned to Sweden. Greta Garbo, of course, stayed on, to play anguished women in *Ibanez's Torrent* (1926) and *The Temptress* (1926), before being paired with another of MGM's numerous contract stars, John Gilbert, in *Flesh and the Devil* (1927). MGM worried that sound might destroy her emigmatic beauty, and as late as November 1929 she was still working on a silent movie, *The Kiss*. As subsequent events were to prove, they need not have worried.

Neither Lang nor his compatriot Murnau ultimately resisted the blandishments of the American dream industry. F. W. Murnau's first triumph in Germany had been *Nosferatu* (1922), a startling, visually remarkable adaptation of the Dracula legend. His subsequent *The Last Laugh* (1924) is a psychologically acute study of a hotel doorman, played by Jannings, who loses his job and his self-respect. With one exception at the end, the film's narrative and emotions are expressed without any intertitles, illustrating how subtle was the potential of silent film language, and how total was Murnau's control of it. After two further films, *Tartuffe* (1925) and *Faust* (1926), he and scriptwriter Carl Mayer were invited to Hollywood by

48

William Fox to make *Sunrise* (1927). For his biographer, Lotte Eisner, as for many other critics, the film was his crowning achievement: 'All the skills which Murnau had developed in Germany in the years from 1919 to 1926 are here made manifest in the most dazzling manner: his marvellous sense of camera, lighting and tone-values, his mastery of the composition and the rhythmic ordering of images. And his gift for creating atmosphere as well as revealing the complexities of character.' Two subsequent Hollywood films,

Sunrise

The Four Devils (1928) and *City Girl* (1929), were less happy experiences for Murnau, who then went to the South Pacific to work with the documentary film-maker Robert Flaherty on *Tabu* (1931), a strange, silent utopian fantasy which was released just a week after his death in a car accident.

Lang had stayed longer in Germany. But when his *Testament of Dr Mabuse* was banned for its anti-Nazi sentiments he resisted Goebbels' blandishments and left for France, where he made one film before accepting an invitation to Hollywood. Beginning with *Fury* (1936), he was to have a successful American career, and he was to see how Expressionism as a style exercised a significant influence, first on Universal's horror films of the early 1930s, and subsequently on the dark cityscapes of *film noir*.

After the Revolution

Post-revolutionary Russia was the one major market closed to Hollywood (at least until the mid-1920s), and the one source of a vital cinematic culture which it was unable, as well as unwilling, to pillage. Before the war, rather as

49

Poster for Barnet's House on Trubnaya Square

Strike

in Germany, the Russian film industry had produced its comedies, thrillers and melodramas. But with the Revolution, cinema was seen to have a new place in society, as a medium of education and enlightenment of the masses. Despite severe shortages of film stock, mobile units known as agit-trains began to screen newsreels and propaganda films throughout Russia, and especially on the various fronts of the Civil War. The film industry was nationalised by a decree of August 1919, and Lenin's wife, Krupskaya, was appointed to oversee a special film branch of the Commissariat of Education. In 1922 Lenin himself was to make his famous declaration: 'Of all the arts, for us the cinema is the most important.'

As in the visual arts, in the theatre and literature, the ferment of the Revolution stimulated a radical rethinking of what cinema was and what it could be. Even before the events of 1917, painters like Malevich and Tatlin had, under the influence of European Cubist and Futurist work, been challenging the conventions of visual representation. A movement known as Constructivism looked forward to a new unity of science and art, a new understanding of art as production, which would be at the service of every individual. The energy and impetus which accompanied the building of this future produced a cinema in the later 1920s which was at least as rich as that of Germany in the earlier part of the decade. It is the work of two directors, Eisenstein and Pudovkin, which is most commonly referred to, but the industry was far from homogeneous and there were many different approaches to the task of creating a revolutionary cinema.

Theory enjoyed a central place in this cinema, not least because in the early days it was all but impossible to locate equipment or stock. Only after Lenin's introduction of the New Economic Policy in 1922, which permitted some private business, did pre-Revolution equipment become available again. One important centre was the new Proletkult Theatre in Moscow, where Vsevolod Meyerhold was creating an anti-naturalistic drama in opposition to the studied realism of Stanislavsky. Another major source of ideas was Lev Kuleshov's work at the State Film School in Moscow. Kuleshov was particularly influential for his exploration of 'montage'; that is, the manipulation of the spectator by the juxtaposition of images. In his most famous experiment, he demonstrated how an audience would interpret a shot of an expressionless face as either happy or sad depending on whether it was placed next to a shot of a small child or of a coffin. It was around this basic principle that many of the major Russian silent films were to be constructed. Montage was to be used as both the basis of narrative and as a technique with a powerful metaphorical force. As Pudovkin was later to write, 'The foundation of film art is editing'.

With others from the State Film School, Kuleshov directed the comic fantasy *The Extraordinary Adventures of Mr West in the Land of the Bolsheviks* (1924), which, like his second feature *The Death Ray* (1925), endeavours to marry the seductive power of American cinema with political satire. One of Kuleshov's pupils, Sergei Komarov, was to take this strategy a step further in

The Kiss of Mary Pickford (1927), which spices its satire on the movie industry with newsreel footage of Pickford and Douglas Fairbanks on tour in the Soviet Union. Another gifted follower of Kuleshov was Boris Barnet, whose comedies *The Girl with the Hatbox* (1927) and *House on Trubnaya Square* (1928) have received less attention in cinema history than they deserve.

The dominant figure in these years, however, was Sergei Eisenstein. After training as an engineer, he worked under Meyerhold in the theatre, where he staged anti-realist extravaganzas, using fantasy and folklore, among other weapons, to attack the bourgeoisie. In 1923 he mounted the play *Gas Masks* in the Moscow Gas Works, and the following year he directed his first film, *Strike.* Conceived as a generalised picture of pre-Revolutionary industrial conflict, *Strike* takes the proletariat as its hero and, in sequences influenced by Griffith, uses montage both to stress the contrast between rich and poor and to construct a dynamic presentation of the massacre of the workers.

Battleship Potemkin (1925), his next film, was commissioned as a panoramic celebration of the 1905 revolution. In the event, Eisenstein focused on two episodes from that year — the sailors' rebellion at Odessa, and the Tsarist reprisals — and the film was hastily edited. Its collision of images creates a powerful emotional impact. *October* (1927), which marked the anniversary of the 1917 Revolution, extends Eisenstein's exploration of montage, notably in the various techniques used to undercut the character of Kerensky, leader of the provisional government. Two years later, however, *The General Line* (also known as *The Old and the New*) failed to win Stalin's approval and was attacked for 'formalism'. Eisenstein was touring Western Europe, where he was much feted, with his collaborators Eduard Tissé and Grigori Alexandrov when he received an invitation from Paramount to work in America. But he was uncomfortable in Hollywood, and his film projects came to nothing. Finally he left for Mexico to work on the ill-fated *Que Viva Mexico!*, which he was to be prevented from completing. Back in Russia, he encountered comparable difficulties; and it was not until 1938 that he was able to complete the historical epic *Alexander Nevsky.* One more film was to follow, *Ivan the Terrible*, of which Eisenstein finished only two of the three planned sections before his death in 1948.

While Eisenstein was working with Meyerhold, Vsevolod Pudovkin, who had studied as a chemist, was working with Kuleshov's company in the State Film School. Pudovkin had been greatly impressed by Griffith's *Intolerance,* a copy of which had been smuggled into Russia in 1919, and like that of Eisenstein his later work was to be greatly indebted to the American film-maker's exploration of the potential of editing. He too was commissioned by the government to make commemorative films of the 1905 and the 1917 revolutions, and his *Mother* (1926), adapted from a Maxim Gorky story, reveals the impact of Eisenstein's *Strike.* But he was already disenchanted by Kuleshov's strictures about mechanical acting, and he worked with a cast steeped in the Stanislavskian method. As he wrote: 'I did not see how it was possible for me to limit myself with my organic need for inner emotions, to

Shots from the Odessa Steps sequence in Battleship Potemkin

the dry form which Kuleshov preached. . . I had a strong instinctive inclination for living people whom I wanted to photograph and whose soul I wanted to fathom.' Pudovkin's next feature, *The End of Saint Petersburg* (1927), covers much the same ground as *October*, but his editing technique creates effects with sequences of related images rather than utilising the clash of individual shots advocated by Eisenstein. In 1928 he made *Storm Over Asia*, an epic about Mongolian resistance to British imperialist forces, which combines lyricism with bravura action sequences.

'Living people': Pudovkin's Mother

Dovzhenko's Earth

Other aspects of the revolutionary cinema are to be found in the work of Alexander Dovzhenko and Dziga Vertov. The latter played a significant role in the early formulation of montage film-making, but he worked almost exclusively with newsreel material or specially shot documentary footage, and it is as a pioneer of the documentary that he is considered (in Chapter 11) in this book. Dovzhenko's work, in both its structure and emphasis, is closer to poetry. There is little narrative in either *Arsenal* (1929) or *Earth* (1930), elliptical works which draw together constellations of images to illustrate the revolutionary spirit in the Ukraine, and its closeness to nature and the land.

By the late 1920s, the government's cultural officers were beginning to express their misgivings about such film-making. Moving towards the imposition of 'socialist realism' in all the arts, they accused the practitioners of the radical cinema of 'formalism', and charged that their films meant nothing to the masses. The new official policy, formulated under Stalin's direction and intended to stimulate the production of art which was accessible to all, was finally imposed on the industry in 1934. Eisenstein, Pudovkin and Dovzhenko all continued to work, but with increasing difficulty and decreasing support, and the truly radical impulse of their work, and that of others, was crushed.

Their influence, however, had begun to make itself felt throughout the world. The late 1920s were a period of unprecedented exchange of ideas, and rapid assimilation of new possibilities. The stylisation in the settings, camerawork and performances of films by two other Russians, Grigori Kozintsev and Leonid Trauberg, is greatly indebted to the German cinema, which had begun to be imported into the Soviet Union after 1921. Kozintsev and Trauberg were associated with the touring theatre company F E K S (the Factory of the Eccentric Actor), and films of theirs like *The Devil's Wheel* and *The Overcoat* (both 1926) are clearly children of *Caligari* (though Kozintsev later denied this German influence).

An exchange in the opposite direction was stimulated by showings throughout Europe of *Battleship Potemkin*. The film was first shown in London, at a private screening in 1929, along with John Grierson's early documentary *Drifters*. Subsequently, Russian-style montage was to be a crucial element in the British documentaries of the coming decade. Another film which bears its imprint is Carl Dreyer's *La Passion de Jeanne d'Arc*, made in 1927. Indeed, the internationalism of the period is exemplified by this film. Dreyer was born in Denmark and had made eight previous films in Scandinavia, but he was now working in France. His designer, who opted for a rigorous simplicity and austere visuals, was Hermann Warm, who had collaborated on *Caligari*. The camera movements are reminiscent of pioneering French cinematography, whereas the film's editing style is clearly derived from the Russian cinema. Driven by the intensity of the actress Falconetti's performance, the film was to bring Dreyer international recognition. Yet for all the power generated by its skilled juxtaposition of images, it relies heavily on title cards, which tend to disrupt the viewer's involvement. Dreyer later said that he wished sound technology had been available to him during its making.

Falconetti in Dreyer's Le Passion de Jeanne d'Arc

For many critics and practitioners of the time, the silent cinema was by the end of the 1920s an international art form of considerable maturity. The coming of sound was seen by them as a catastrophe. Looking back almost fifty years, the director Basil Wright wrote: 'The anguish and breast-beating with which the intelligentsia, including myself, greeted the introduction of synchronisation now seems faintly silly. But many people at that time genuinely felt that the mimetic values of cinema were just beginning to reach their greatest heights. . . All this, it seemed, was to be destroyed.'

Throughout those fifty years the silent cinema, for all the esteem in which it had been held, began to slip away, to be lost both in memory and, as fragile prints decayed or were destroyed, in physical terms terms too. By the late 1960s the historian Kevin Brownlow could write: 'The silent cinema is regarded as prehistoric, even by those who work in motion pictures. Crude, fumbling, naive, the films exist only to be chuckled at – quaint reminders of a simple-minded past, like Victorian samplers.'

Since then, of course, Brownlow and many other scholars and archivists

53

have done much to bring about the re-evaluation of the silent cinema. New books and original academic research have been supported by important restoration work by archives such as Britain's National Film Archive, the Munich Film Museum and the UCLA Film and Television Archives in Los Angeles. Screenings, like those in the 'Thames Silents' series in Britain, have been enhanced by orchestral accompaniments, and these in turn have brought silent films to television in integral and often pristine prints. Brownlow's television series, *Hollywood* (1979, Thames TV), made with producer David Gill, illustrated the extraordinary power and range of the American industry prior to 1927.

Yet fundamental problems of awareness and understanding remain. Serious historical research is only beginning to document and analyse this period. The primary sources, in the form of production documentation, distributors' records and exhibitors' returns, are now being turned to as vital traces. Traces, moreover, which can be used to explore the complexities of a medium intimately related to the politics and social changes of its time. We need to continue to celebrate achievements like *Napoleon*, but we also need to understand their place in history.

Further reading

Richard Abel, *French Cinema: The First Wave, 1915-1929*, Princeton, N.J.: Princeton University Press, 1984.

Tino Balio, *United Artists: The Company Built by the Stars*, Madison: University of Wisconsin Press, 1976.

——(ed.), *The American Film Industry*, Madison: University of Wisconsin Press, 1984.

David Bordwell and Kristin Thompson, *Film Art: An Introduction*, New York: Random House, 1979.

Kevin Brownlow, *The Parade's Gone By*, London: Secker & Warburg, 1968.

——*Hollywood: The Pioneers*, London: William Collins, 1979.

——*Napoleon: Abel Gance's Classic Film*, London: Jonathan Cape, 1983.

Lotte Eisner, *The Haunted Screen*, Paris, 1952; trans. London: Thames & Hudson, 1969.

Douglas Gomery, *The Hollywood Studio System*, London: Macmillan/BFI, 1986.

Benjamin B. Hampton, *History of the American Film Industry: From its Beginnings to 1931*, New York: Dover, 1970.

Lewis Jacobs, *The Rise of the American Film: A Critical History*, 1939; reprint, New York: Teachers College Press, 1968.

Gorham Kindem (ed.), *The American Movie Industry: The Business of Motion Pictures*, Carbondale: Southern Illinois University Press, 1982.

Paul Kerr (ed.), *The Hollywood Film Industry*, London: Routledge & Kegan Paul/BFI, 1986.

Jay Leyda, *Kino: A History of the Russian and Soviet Film*, London: Allen & Unwin, 1960, 3rd ed. 1983.

Kristin Thompson, *Exporting Entertainment: America in the World Film Market 1907-34*, London: BFI, 1985.

4
The Emergence of Television

The many histories of the cinema, and the far fewer histories of television, mostly ignore the other medium until the early 1950s. Only then, it is suggested, did Hollywood finally wake up to television as a threat and respond to it with gimmicks like 3-D and CinemaScope. The reality was more complex. Television's development was closely tied to the already existing structures, corporations and marketing arrangements of radio. But there were also intriguing links between the introduction of the new medium and the progress of the film industry after 1930.

One early public television broadcast in the United States, and the first demonstration of a large-screen system, was to a movie theatre, in Schenectady, New York, in May 1930. Two years later the British pioneer John Logie Baird achieved one of his most notable publicity coups when he transmitted the 1932 Derby live to the Metropole Cinema at Victoria, where an audience watched the race on a screen 8ft high by 10ft across. In both countries, and in Germany, 'theatre television' was expected to have a profitable future. And the younger medium's respect for the older can be seen in the fact that one of the earliest Schenectady broadcasts transmitted the face and voice of D. W. Griffith across the country to Los Angeles.

By 1938 the film business in Hollywood was interested enough in television to set up a high-powered committee to consider the topic. As this group was recommending the installation of television in movie theatres, Paramount was buying into the DuMont Corporation, a television manufacturer and applicant for broadcasting licences. In 1940, in Chicago, Paramount set up the first television station owned by a film company. And at the end of the Second World War other film corporations followed Paramount's lead and sought new television licences. Yet within a decade television was established solely as a domestic medium and the cinema was battling with a formidable rival.

Radio and 'Visual Wireless'

As with the cinema, the history of television begins with a host of individual inventors, and then is quickly implicated in industrial, legal, economic and political structures. The first key figure was Guglielmo Marconi, the inventor in his early twenties of a radio receiver and transmitter which sent messages in Morse code. Despite the international effort in the late 19th century to perfect such wireless communication – other pioneers included James Clerk Maxwell, Heinrich Hertz, David Hughes and Alexander Popov – Marconi went unheeded in his native Italy, and so came to Britain with his family in 1896. The following year, encouraged by the Post Office, a powerful corporation was founded to exploit his discoveries. Within two years the Marconi Wireless Company of America was incorporated. Merchant and military shipping quickly recognised the potential of his device, as did a growing number of radio amateurs.

Two inventors working in the United States made the next important breakthroughs. Reginald Fessenden achieved the first voice transmissions, and Lee De Forest took them a stage further with his 'Audion' tube, a glass-bulb detector of radio waves, patented in 1907. At this point, and for at least the decade to come, radio was still seen as a means of point-to-point communication, and 'broadcasting' was of interest to only a few, including De Forest, who transmitted records, singers and speeches to anyone who might be listening in New York. The First World War, however, had a dramatic impact on radio activity. In Britain amateurs were banned immediately, and in America similar action was taken in 1917. But military needs greatly increased demand, which both stimulated technical advances and strengthened two American companies, General Electric, originally founded by Thomas Edison, and Westinghouse, both of which made light bulbs which could be modified as glass vacuum tubes for radio. Prior to the war, both companies, as well as the American Telephone and Telegraph Company (AT&T), were actively experimenting with radio and, to a lesser extent, with 'visual wireless', and all three groups held significant patents. Each was to emerge as a major force in post-war developments.

The search for visual wireless goes back to at least January 1884, when Paul Nipkow filed a patent in Berlin for an 'electric telescope', which was the earliest 'scanning' device: a disc with a spiral of small holes spun round between a lens and a selenium element. A decade before it had been discovered that, on exposure to light, selenium varied an electric current passed through it in response to the light. Nipkow's disc could now convert light reflected from successive tiny areas of an image and transform it into a modulated electric current. The image could then be reconstituted from this current, by reversing the process and passing the light generated through a second disc spinning at exactly the same speed as the first.

Mechanical scanning, as this system was known, was the basis of many of the early television systems, including that developed by Baird, but it was not to be the method finally adopted around the world. The alternative and eventually greatly superior system depended on the electron beam or cathode ray tube, invented in 1897 by Karl Braun. In 1907 the Russian scientist Boris Rozing filed a patent for using such a tube as a scanner. He directed the tube's beam of electrons to scan a thin plate, on which a photosensitive substance was reproducing an image. Working independently in Britain, A. A. Campbell Swinton suggested in 1908 that such a beam could also be used at the receiving end to recreate the image on a fluorescent screen. Rozing meanwhile worked on a series of prototypes, but he and others were discouraged by difficulties with the quite crude cathode ray tubes of the time and by the problems of electronic amplification. Mechanical scanning appeared to be the more fruitful course to follow, especially since by the First World War problems with the sensitivity of selenium had been overcome by the use of other substances, including potassium. Nonetheless, the spinning discs still limited the clarity of the picture and the problem remained of maintaining exact synchronicity.

The Radio Corporation of America

As the world readjusted to relative peace after 1918, the structures were established within which subsequent television developments would take place. In the United States the navy suggested that it should be granted a monopoly on the use of radio. Proposed legislation for this was forcefully opposed by amateurs, and so the navy accepted instead a private monopoly, in the form of the Radio Corporation of America, incorporated in October 1919. This new body took over American Marconi, and the founding corporation General Electric was by 1921 joined by three other partners: Westinghouse, A T & T and United Fruit. An equivalent of the early American cinema's 'Trust' had been formed, but inevitably there were soon intimations of anti-monopoly feelings.

Westinghouse had not at first been invited to join R C A, but in November 1920 the company initiated radio broadcasting from the roof of its East Pittsburgh works. Inspired by the amateur operations of an employee, Frank Conrad, Westinghouse started a regular schedule on the night of the Presidential election. The venture was such a success that R C A quickly drew Westinghouse into the alliance, and with the mass production of receivers opened the way to a broadcasting explosion.

A T & T contributed the next key development when in 1922 they started 'toll broadcasting', offering the chance to put a message, a song or a sketch to the American public – for a fee. When the actress Marion Davies gave a talk about make-up which was paid for by a cosmetic company, the response indicated how wide an audience could be reached in this way. Advertising revenue grew quickly, and A T & T was further encouraged by government support for a service seen as more democratic than other broadcasting stations.

Patent disputes among the members of R C A, however, were becoming ever more acrimonious, and there was now the real threat of anti-monopoly legislation. Throughout 1925 the companies considered the position and decided to establish a new central broadcasting organisation, the National Broadcasting Company. 'National radio broadcasting' was what R C A promised in an advertisement in September 1926, and early in 1927 NBC was operating two networks to supply an estimated 5 million homes with programmes.

The rapid growth in house building through the 1920s contributed significantly to an expanding market. Radio manufacturers worked with the producers of other consumer goods to create an idealised image of the modern home, and marketing campaigns fixed radio in a domestic setting. Group listening (as was common in Russia), and later group television watching (initially the only possibility in Germany), were never considered as options.

One final element in the setting up of the structure for broadcasting radio, and subsequently television, was the 1927 Radio Act, which created the Federal Radio Commission to allocate licences. As Eric Barnouw commented: 'The industry had now arrived at a structure that would hold for years: a nationwide system based on advertising; a network linked by cables of the telephone system; stations on temporary licences; a regulatory commission that was to base its decisions on the public interest, convenience or necessity.' Over the next two decades this structure was secure enough to accommodate television without strain.

Radio in Britain

In Britain after the war the Post Office began once again to issue licences to amateurs, and in 1920 the Marconi company started to broadcast Morse messages from Chelmsford. By 1922 Marconi were broadcasting from London, from Marconi House in the Strand (call sign 2LO). Transmissions could apparently be heard in many parts of the country and the total audience numbered about 50,000 people. Later in the same year, two other broadcast licences were granted, one of them to Marconi's rival, Western Electric, in Birmingham (5IT).

That year, too, the Post Office sought the views of the radio industry as to how the now rapidly growing medium should be overseen. A committee of manufacturers finally agreed on a private monopoly, the British Broadcasting Company, to provide a single service financed both by a share of the receiving licence fee and by a royalty on the sale of all BBC-marked receiving sets produced by member companies. Daily broadcasting by the BBC, from Marconi House in London, began on 14 November 1922.

The new company appointed John Reith as its General Manager, and it was Reith who presided over the BBC's transformation into a public corporation. Reith believed passionately in the educative potential of broadcasting, and by late 1925 both he and the Post Office agreed that broadcasting should be run as a public service, with a large measure of independence from both commercial and government interests. The Postmaster-General established the Crawford Committee to consider the future of broadcasting, which reported on 5 March 1926. Reacting strongly against the largely unregulated system now entrenched in the United States, the Committee recommended

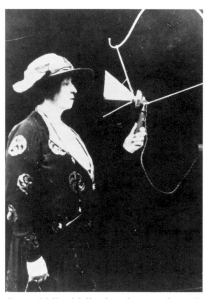

Dame Nellie Melba broadcasting from the experimental Marconi station at Chelmsford in 1920

that broadcasting should continue to be controlled by a single authority but that such a body should not be 'constituted on trade lines for the profit, direct or indirect, of those comprising it.'

In May 1926 Reith's BBC faced a dramatic trial, when during the General Strike it opted to retain only limited independence from the government position. Reith headed off threats of direct government takeover, and the BBC news bulletins were almost the only source of information throughout the country. In many ways the event marked the medium's coming of age. In July the government approved the BBC's metamorphosis into a public body, backed by a Royal Charter, and now to be known as the British Broadcasting Corporation.

Baird's first broadcasts

During the early 1920s, on both sides of the Atlantic, individuals and corporations had continued to tackle the problems of 'visual wireless'. Working for Westinghouse, Vladimir Zworykin, formerly a pupil in Russia of Boris Rozing, endeavoured to improve electronic transmission methods. But the efforts of most other experimenters were devoted to mechanical scanning. In Britain, Baird began his work with television in 1922, and after demonstrations of crude 30-line transmissions at his laboratory, a patent for his system was accepted in May 1924. An indefatigable entrepreneur and self-publicist, Baird arranged demonstrations in Selfridges in 1925, and the following year he was granted a licence (2 TV) for experimental broadcasts from his central London offices. The earliest of these were received in a house ten miles away.

Soon after his first laboratory transmissions, Baird attracted the attention of the Admiralty, which had apparently been considering for some time the military possibilities of a television system. Baird offered to withhold from the public details of new advances, but military experts recognised that

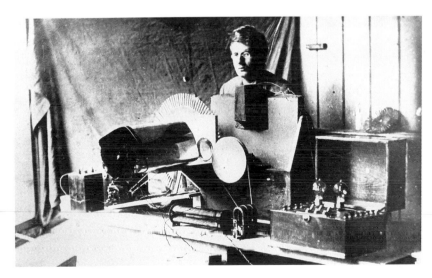

Baird in 1923 with some of his early television apparatus

59

commercial interest would best stimulate further work, and it is possible that Admiralty pressure contributed to the BBC's eventual accommodation with Baird.

Just months after Baird's showings in 1925 the American Charles Jenkins demonstrated a similar system. A team at General Electric were also working along the same lines, as were scientists at the Bell Laboratories owned by AT&T. In April 1927 this team gave a public demonstration of their system which included a speech by Herbert Hoover. Baird achieved a transatlantic transmission in February 1928, but by this point he was frustrated by the uncooperative attitude of the BBC, which was sceptical about the standards of his system and was refusing to consider broadcasts.

In May 1928, after experimental transmissions the previous year, General Electric began regular broadcasts from W2XAD, alongside the radio station WGY in Schenectady, and that summer transmitted Al Smith's speech accepting the Presidential nomination, and a drama, *The Queen's Messenger*. Charles Jenkins, too, had started a service in 1927, initially in vision only, and by the end of 1928 eighteen licences for experimental stations had been allocated. Baird finally began transmissions with the BBC on 30 September 1929, to what he estimated were twenty-nine sets, and the following March was first able to use two transmitters to broadcast synchronous sound and vision. In July 1930 a Pirandello drama, *The Man with the Flower in his Mouth*, was shown, and in June 1931 Baird televised the finish of the Derby. 'All that we ever expected or could see were the horses just flashing past the winning post,' Baird engineer Tony Bridgewater recalled. 'You wouldn't be able to tell one horse from another or one jockey from another, but you could at least tell they were horses.' So despite these and comparable achievements, including a 1932 broadcast to Copenhagen, the picture quality

In the studio for The Man with the Flower in his Mouth

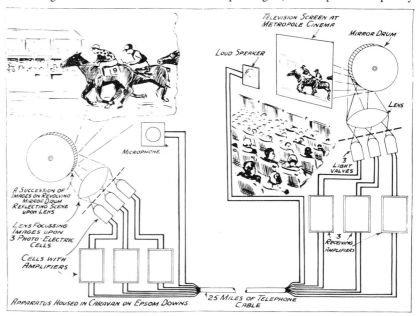

Diagram showing how the 1932 Derby was broadcast to the Metropole cinema in London

60

remained poor and in March 1934 the BBC terminated Baird's experimental licence.

Early electronic systems

By this stage the electronic systems were beginning to come into their own. Working alone in the American Mid-West, the nineteen-year-old amateur Philo T. Farnsworth took out a patent on a successful electronic camera in 1927. Zworykin, with his Iconoscope camera, was achieving similar results for RCA, and this research filtered into Britain after its subsidiary, the British Gramophone Company, became part of Electric and Musical Industries Ltd (EMI), a new electronics enterprise founded in 1931. Another of Rozing's students, Isadore Schoenburg, headed EMI's research team, which in 1934 opted to pursue an electronic system centred on a new camera, the Emitron. The extent of the connections with Zworykin's work remains controversial, but authoritative accounts suggest that the Emitron was essentially an Iconoscope – albeit a greatly improved one – by another name.

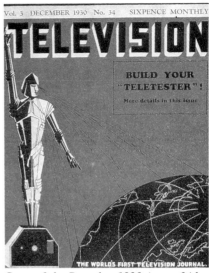

Cover of the December 1930 issue of 'the world's first television journal'

In Germany, regular television broadcasts began in March 1935 – the first regular service in the world. Initially transmissions were of 180-line pictures, produced with mechanical cameras, and were made only to public viewing rooms in Berlin. After a hiatus when fire destroyed the two transmitters, the service prepared to cover that summer's Olympic Games. The company Fernseh AG worked with mechanical cameras, which first shot images on film, developed them inside the camera within a minute, and then scanned these film frames (a technique known as the intermediate film system). Fernseh also used electronic cameras licensed from Farnsworth, but their rivals Telefunken, also covering the Games, used cameras based on RCA's Iconoscope. The two systems remained in use until the war, but it eventually became clear that Telefunken's was superior. Transmissions in fact continued until late 1943, when a bomb destroyed the Berlin transmitter.

It should not be assumed, however, that all the pioneering work on television's development took place in the United States and Western Europe. The Hungarian scientist Von Mihaly had demonstrated a mechanical system by 1928. In Japan, Kenjiro Tahayanagi had achieved laboratory transmissions the previous year. And in Russia, with Rozing and his colleagues building on their pre-war work, electronic systems seem to have been in operation as early as 1926. Semyon Katayev apparently built an electronic camera, similar to the Iconoscope, in 1931. Transmissions began in Leningrad, and then in Moscow, in 1938, but were closed down when the Soviet Union entered the war.

Television from the BBC

In Britain the government-appointed Selsdon Committee looking at the future of television recommended that television broadcasting should be entrusted to the BBC, which as soon as possible should begin a general

Adele Dixon in the first BBC television transmission from Alexandra Palace

television service, with a minimum standard of 240 lines. Baird and the new group Marconi-EMI would initially alternate broadcasts. After try-out transmissions from the new base at Alexandra Palace to the Radiolympia exhibition in August, a regular service began on 2 November 1936. A speech from the Postmaster-General, a newsreel, a song from Adele Dixon, jugglers and dancers, were all transmitted on Baird's system, and then an hour later, from a separate studio, by Marconi-EMI.

Influenced by a German 120-line film scanner, and straining to reach the minimum line standard, Baird was using an intermediate film technique. But his cameras had to be screwed to the floor (the Emitron was mobile), his pictures were less clear and his equipment less reliable, and it was soon apparent that Marconi-EMI's system would triumph, a choice officially endorsed in February 1937. Three months later came the first of television's celebrations of regal pomp, George VI's coronation, when three cameras broadcast the scenes at Hyde Park Corner.

Outside broadcasts: the first television Boat Race

Other early television events included Wimbledon, the Armistice ceremony at the Cenotaph, the Boat Race and, in August 1938, a Test Match against Australia at the Oval. Prime Minister Neville Chamberlain's dramatic return from Munich on 16 September was shown, with Richard Dimbleby commentating for both radio and television. There were regular plays and ballet, and numerous variety programmes. But the audience grew slowly, partly inhibited by the high price of receivers. When war came and transmissions ceased abruptly on 1 September 1939, there were still only some 20,000 sets, and most of these were within twenty-five miles of Alexandra Palace.

Throughout the years of experiment Baird had retained his contacts with the Admiralty. Recently released documents show that in parallel with the test transmissions from the BBC another trial was organised in secret by the British and French air forces at Farnborough and Hendon. Particular interest was shown in the possible applications of the intermediate film technique, but in the later 1930s this was overshadowed by the military's concern to prepare the new radar technology. Again there was an intimate connection with television, and it may well have been that television transmissions were begun at the direct request of the military establishment, which wanted to gear up British industry for the production of cathode-ray tubes. Engineers, too, needed to be prepared, and after the BBC television service shut down almost all its trained technicians were put to work at top-secret radar stations.

An early television receiver

Transmissions in America

In America, by September 1939, regular television transmissions had been in operation for just four months. Despite the fact that the technology had been available for five years, the industry and government had been engaged in lengthy discussions of technical standards. More significantly, the major corporations had been arguing among themselves, united only by a desire to prevent RCA gaining an unassailable monopoly.

By 1934 Zworykin's Iconoscope could produce pictures which almost matched the quality of 16mm film. This was the acknowledged goal of researchers, and it illustrates the conceptual grip of the older medium. (In the late 1980s the first productions are being made with 1200-line high-definition television, a standard fixed upon as equivalent in quality to 35mm film.) Farnsworth's Image Dissector was proving itself superior in the transmission of film, again a priority derived from the dominance of motion pictures.

From 1935 to 1941 there was interminable official consideration of which line standard to adopt, which delayed moves to set up regular transmissions. RCA finally broke ranks and began television broadcasts from the opening of the New York World's Fair on 30 April 1939. As in Britain, the schedule over the next months was a ragbag of vaudeville, drama, how-to demonstrations, opera and outside broadcasts. The first baseball game to be shown was covered with just a single camera. Almost all the movie companies refused to do business with this upstart, but a highspot of that summer's transmissions was a relay showing the stars and crowds at the premiere of *Gone With the Wind*. NBC did make the first transmission of a feature film in July, showing *The Heart of New York*, which was felt to have long exhausted its box-office potential. The following month an episode of the cinema serial *The Last Jungle* was shown. And in October the early days of a new medium echoed those of an older one when NBC screened Edwin S. Porter's 1903 film *The Great Train Robbery*.

The corporate structure of this new medium, however, was still fluid. Through the early 1930s there was conflict, eventually resolved, between AT&T and RCA (from which, in 1930, General Electric and Westinghouse had been forced to leave by Justice Department pressure). Just as AT&T had wanted its share of radio revenues, so it was concerned to find a place in the newest medium. It had already muscled in on Hollywood, owning the

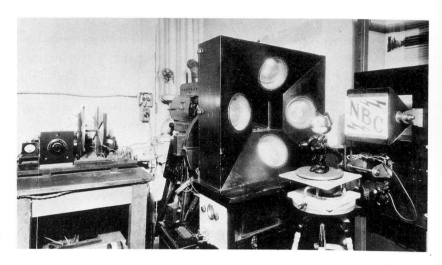

Television in America: NBC's first telecast, with Felix the Cat

Westrex sound system used, for a high price, by every major studio (except RCA's subsidiary RKO). And indeed the terms of a Westrex licence explicitly prevented any film made with that technology being sold to television. AT&T also had a deal with Farnsworth, but after 1936, when its Bell Laboratories had created a coaxial cable which could carry video signals, it saw that its main revenue could come from a source similar to that which it exploited in radio. A network of such cables was begun in 1937, with a link between New York and Philadelphia. AT&T and RCA could now develop in amicable partnership.

But there were other players in the game. In 1927 the Columbia Phonograph Broadcasting System, later the Columbia Broadcasting System (CBS), made its first appearance as a challenger to NBC. After a shaky start, it had grown throughout the 1930s under the leadership of William S. Paley. By 1938 its reputation for both news and drama was greater than NBC's, and inevitably it had been experimenting with television. Broadcasts in the New York area began soon after NBC's. Philco had continued its relationship with Farnsworth, and another young inventor, Allen B. Dumont, began experimental transmissions at the same time. By May 1940 twenty-three stations were reported to be telecasting in the United States.

That same month, however, the government agency responsible for interstate communications, the Federal Communications Commission (FCC), ruled that such transmissions were still only 'experimental'; and with the continuing argument about standards and the growing awareness of other priorities being forced on the country from Europe, the impetus behind television faded. Technical developments continued through the war, however, especially in work to perfect colour transmissions. And in 1941, as agreement on National Television System Committee standards was finally reached, RCA faced another anti-monopoly attack when the FCC forced it to sell off one of its two networks. NBC-Blue became the American Broadcasting Company (ABC); and the industry, which had been born in the

64

aftermath of one world war, awaited the end of another.

Hollywood had kept closely in touch with television throughout this decade. At first, because large investments in sound technology coincided with the Depression, the studios had found it difficult to fund their own research and development. But their interest grew throughout the 1930s. Among the major studios Paramount led the way, having flirted briefly with the new medium, from 1929 to 1931, by purchasing and then selling off a large share of CBS. The studio's interest culminated in the acquisition of wholly-owned stations in Chicago (1940) and Los Angeles (1943), and it also participated in two other stations. The historian Douglas Gomery, citing contemporary reports in the trade paper *Variety*, has even suggested that by the end of the war the studio's executives, lured by the potential of the small screen, were considering abandoning movies altogether. Other studios also sought licences, but anti-monopoly feelings, within the FCC and elsewhere, were to curb these ambitions.

Further reading

Erik Barnouw, *Tube of Plenty*, New York: Oxford University Press, 1975.
Asa Briggs, *The BBC: The First Fifty Years*, London: Oxford University Press, 1985.
Les Brown, *New York Times Encyclopaedia of Television*, New York: Times Books, 1977.
Eric Smoodin, 'Motion Pictures and Television, 1930-1945: A Pre-History of Relations Between the Two Media', *Journal of the University Film and Video Association*, Summer 1982.
Francis Wheen, *Television: A History*, London: Century Publishing, 1985.
Brian Winston, *Misunderstanding Media*, London: Routledge & Kegan Paul, 1986.

5
The Technology of Cinema

Since the days of Edison and the Lumière brothers, the mainstream cinema has three times adopted a transforming technology. But the technical means to achieve first sound, then colour and later a widescreen image were available long before the cinema adopted them. This suggests that the history of the cinema's relationship with technology has to take account of far more than technical innovations. To understand why and how the technologies were taken up by the industry at particular moments demands a consideration not only of their invention, but also of complex systems of economics, aesthetics and ideology.

For the French critic André Bazin each of these innovations was an inevitable step towards what he saw as the 'essence' of cinema, a means of representation which would eventually be capable of a totally realistic portrait of the world. Bazin's notion of realism, however, is far from obvious or unproblematic. Each innovation did, of course, introduce new representational conventions, and with these came new understandings of and responses to the world. But what the song in *Silk Stockings* calls 'glorious Technicolor, breathtaking CinemaScope and stereophonic sound' is no more 'real' than the projected picture available to Louis Lumière. Each development offers distinct possibilities and pleasures, but one is not superior to the other. They are, simply, different, from different historical moments, produced by different forces and answering different needs.

The sounds of silent cinema
Before the introduction of sound, the cinema was rarely either described or experienced as *silent*. Most screenings were accompanied by music in some form, created by full-scale orchestras in first-run houses or by pianos in the cheaper neighbourhood theatres. Commissioned scores became increasingly common in the 1910s, and were to attract the talents of major composers like Saint-Saëns, for *L'Assassinat du Duc du Guise* (1908), and at the end of the silent period Dmitri Shostakovich, for *New Babylon* (1929). Sound effects, such as explosions or thunder, were also frequently used, and were produced by a variety of ingenious devices. Singers and actors were

66

sometimes engaged to synchronise dialogue with the picture on screen. Moreover, particularly in the early days, certain presentations employed a master of ceremonies to comment on the projected images.

Edison Kinetophone

From the turn of the century there had also been numerous experimental attempts at the mechanical marrying of sound and image. Edison had developed a combination phonograph and Kinetoscope; and later, in 1913, the Edison company presented synchronised films to the New York public, again using a phonograph. Léon Gaumont had tried a similar system as early as 1901. In Britain around 1909 James Williamson and Cecil Hepworth devised what they called Vivaphone. Two essential problems, however, prevented the successful development of these prototypes. Amplification was crude, so that the volume necessary for large theatres seemed impossible to attain. And devices to synchronise the picture and sound were, at best, erratic.

The key invention in the development of amplification systems was the Audion, a triode valve which worked on a principle discovered by Edison in 1883, but which was first actually constructed in 1907 by Lee De Forest. The patents in De Forest's pioneering work, which facilitated faithful recording and reproduction at high volume levels, were soon purchased by the American Telegraph & Telephone company. AT&T's subsequent investment in the system, and in its exploitation, was symptomatic of an important shift. Two decades previously much of the key work on the development of the cinema was achieved by individuals, whereas film sound, like radio and television, was to be far more the product of corporate entities.

With limited resources individual inventors were unable to compete with the corporations. Nor did the film industry itself establish research divisions to work at the problem. The development of sound films in the early 1920s was consequently led by the large electrical manufacturers concerned to consolidate their rapid wartime expansion. With the Audion patents, AT&T's subsidiary Western Electric became one of the major producers of amplifiers and public address systems. Experimental work was conducted by their engineers and by those in AT&T's research division, Bell Laboratories, into both sound-on-film and sound-on-disc systems. Between 1922 and 1924 the latter technology, synchronising the sound on separate discs, showed the more rapid advance, even though the discs themselves were large and unwieldy. At the same time AT&T's rival General Electric was also developing a sound-on-film system, where the sound was converted into a photographic trace and printed alongside the images.

Initial contacts with the motion picture industry, however, were not encouraging. Adolph Zukor, among others, wanted nothing to do with such a potentially disruptive innovation. The industry structure which he had done

De Forest's phonofilm

so much to set in place was increasingly profitable and appeared increasingly stable. Paramount, like other corporations, had invested heavily in new theatres in the early 1920s, and was unwilling to take on the enormous costs which sound technology would entail, both in production and exhibition. Other problems foreseen at the time were the possible incompatibility of rival technologies and the likelihood of longer production schedules. There were also imponderables about whether the public would accept silent stars singing and talking. Above all, Hollywood feared that the introduction of talking pictures would destroy American domination of foreign markets. Silent films were easily exported, necessitating changes only in the title cards; films in English might find far more limited audiences overseas.

Warner Bros and sound

Hollywood's attitude began to change in May 1925 when Western Electric demonstrated their sound-on-disc system to the company's president, Harry Warner. In contrast to the other studio heads, Warner was immediately enthusiastic, envisaging the possibility of short films of vaudeville acts being shown in the small-town theatres with which Warners did much of their business. For as with many others newly introduced to the technology, his first thought was to use it to synchronise music. The idea of *talking* pictures came later.

At that moment Warner Bros was engaged in a major expansion programme. Run by four brothers, Harry, Albert, Jack and Samuel (who died in 1927), the company had had only limited success in production and distribution, although in the early 1920s director Ernst Lubitsch and then stars Rin-Tin-Tin and John Barrymore had increased corporate profitability. Concerned to develop the business, Harry had opened discussions in 1924 with the investment division of Wall Street's Goldman Sachs. Until the early 1920s New York financiers had largely cold-shouldered the movie business; now Goldman Sachs was sufficiently impressed by Warner Bros' business practices to begin to work with them. In 1925, with this new backing, Warner Bros acquired Vitagraph and its extensive distribution system; the company also bought and leased a number of first-run theatres, and set up a Los Angeles radio station.

In June 1925, in a complementary move, Warners signed an agreement with Western Electric for experimental work with sound, and the following April Western Electric licensed the Vitaphone Corporation, a Warner Bros subsidiary, for the production and distribution of sound films. Vitaphone's films first reached the screen on 6 August 1926, with a programme which included a filmed speech by Will Hays welcoming sound, and Warners' new feature, *Don Juan*, with John Barrymore and a synchronised score. Encouraged by excellent returns at the box office, Vitaphone released a second programme in October, and rapidly stepped up production.

The other studios' reaction to these developments, at least as they expressed it to each other, was caution. According to Alexander Walker,

'The "Big Five" of the film world (at this time MGM, Universal, Paramount, First National and Producers' Distributing Corporation) . . . met in secret session in December 1926 and agreed on a defensive strategy – none of them would adopt sound pictures until they all did and, if and when they did adopt it, they would all use the same device. They resolved, piously, it would not be the one Warners were using.' Yet behind this facade of solidarity Zukor had already approached Warners about the possibility of a deal, and another mogul had recognised that sound could transform his own company's prospects.

Movietone

Two weeks before the Vitaphone premiere William Fox had bought the rights to a sound-on-film system developed by inventors Theodore Case and E. I. Sponable. Similarities with a system pioneered by Lee De Forest, and Forest's brief professional association with Case Laboratories, have raised still unresolved questions about the originality of the Case-Sponable work. Nonetheless Fox and Case signed a deal establishing 'Movietone', and after showing a first programme of shorts in January 1927, unveiled a new sensation in April with the premiere of the first Movietone newsreels with synchronised sound. Warners' Vitaphone system involved the use of cumbersome apparatus, and while Movietone was still complex to operate, it was flexible enough to use for location recording, as at Charles Lindbergh's departure for Paris on the first solo transatlantic flight in May 1927.

Like Vitaphone, however, Movietone depended on Western Electric amplifiers and speakers, and this AT&T subsidiary now wished to establish itself in a monopoly position. After much contractual haggling, a new Western Electric subsidiary was set up to market sound equipment, Electrical Research Projects Inc (ERPI). Vitaphone was now assigned only a non-exclusive licence, leaving Western Electric free to deal with the other studios. In October 1927 Warners and Vitaphone released *The Jazz Singer* with four synchronised segments containing Al Jolson songs and the famous snatch of dialogue, 'You ain't heard nothin' yet'. All-dialogue shorts followed soon afterwards, but it was the huge success of *The Jazz Singer* which finally convinced Warner Bros and the industry as a whole that sound was here to stay. By early 1928 both Paramount and Loew's were negotiating with Western Electric.

It was not, however, the Vitaphone system which they were to adopt. After carefully considering the possibilities, the 'Big Five' agreed to opt for a Western Electric sound-on-film system which incorporated many of the advantages of Movietone. One key factor was that the Vitaphone discs were proving expensive and difficult to transport, and Warner Bros were to

Jolson speaks: The Jazz Singer

Hollywood
Wants
YOU
if you can use your voice

a hundred opportunities
today in the "Talkies"

discontinue the system in 1930. In addition, another rival, the technologically attractive Photophone system from RCA, would have entailed unacceptable contractual arrangements.

Radio-Keith-Orpheum

Along with Western Electric and AT&T, General Electric and its parent corporation RCA were the other major corporate concerns in radio in the 1920s. Building on experiments first carried out in the war, General Electric's laboratories had been developing their own sound-on-film system, called Photophone. Throughout the decade there had been an uneasy relationship in radio between AT&T and RCA. Part alliance, part bitter rivalry, it had recently settled into amicable co-existence. But RCA was now acutely aware that AT&T, through Western Electric, was capturing much of the sound market, particularly once Photophone was rejected by the 'Big Five'. In typically bullish fashion, RCA's David Sarnoff consequently set about creating his own market, first by an alliance with the low-budget studio Film Booking Office and then with the Keith-Albee-Orpheum theatre chain. In October 1928 they formed a new corporation, Radio-Keith-Orpheum, or RKO. Further deals, including with two major music publishers, consolidated the group and by the end of 1929 RKO was established close to the level of the four newly dominant groups in Hollywood: Paramount and Loew's as before, and now Warner Bros and Fox.

In production, Vitaphone had continued to make the running, with the first all-dialogue feature, a gangster film called *The Lights of New York*, which opened in July 1928. Soon afterwards the other studios began to catch up. In November, Paramount's first talkie, *Interference*, was shown. A year later, some three-quarters of Hollywood features included sound sequences, although until 1930 silent versions continued to be made, both for showing abroad and for the shrinking number of cinemas without new equipment. At the same time radio was beginning to make a major impact, and the two media complemented each other well. Promotional advantages meant that songs from musicals found extensive airplay, and stars whose voices had become familiar in homes throughout America soon crossed over to the screen.

Once the novelty was established, the disadvantages of the new technology became apparent. Cameras were noisy, and so now had to be enclosed in sound-proof booths which greatly restricted movement. Microphones had a limited range, which meant that actors had to bunch round mikes disguised as bowls of flowers and the like. Early dialogue was often stilted, and poorly delivered by actors new to speaking lines as though they believed them. Nonetheless, despite the despair of many serious critics at the re-emergence of filmed theatre, and the threatened eclipse of the mature filmic styles of the silent cinema, solutions were quickly found. At first, post-dubbed sound and music was used to enhance the sweeping camera movements in films like King Vidor's *Hallelujah!* (1929) and Lewis Milestone's *All Quiet on the*

Microphones hidden in the foliage: early talkies burlesqued in the 1951 Singin' in the Rain

70

Western Front (1930). The camera blimp, which stifled the sound of a camera's motor, was introduced, and the booths disappeared. Microphones were mounted on booms which could be held just out of frame. Striking new actors were culled from the stage, and many like James Cagney and Edward G. Robinson quickly made their mark. Soon, major directors were beginning to make creative use of the new possibilities. One of the best-known examples is Ernst Lubitsch's staging in *Monte Carlo* (1930) of the song 'Beyond the Blue Horizon' as a duet between Jeanette MacDonald and an express train. Another is Alfred Hitchcock's famous scene in *Blackmail* (1929), where the insistent pointing up of the word 'knife' signals a character's preoccupation with a killing.

Britain's first talking picture: Hitchcock checks the sound in Blackmail *(1929)*

Sound inevitably brought stylistic changes to the cinema. Narrative, motivation and shades of meaning were now explicitly expressed in words, rather than, as had often been the case, being implicit in the sets, lighting and composition. Acting styles, too, were significantly affected, for silent actors had had to use gesture and facial movement to express much of what was now being carried by the dialogue. Yet there was no radical break with the norms of silent film-making. After some uncertainties, the broad parameters of the established style easily adjusted to the new demands of sound.

The studios, too, had to evolve new working methods. In particular, location filming became a rarity because of the inevitable problems of controlling the recorded sound. To achieve exterior shots, the studios developed sophisticated background projection techniques. There were changes also in the types of film being made. Improvised shooting was almost impossible with the cumbersome new equipment, and so slapstick comedy became far more difficult to produce. Instead, verbal and character-based comedy began to thrive, as exemplified by the popular success of Laurel and Hardy. And, of course, sound nurtured the new genre of the musical.

Corporate shifts

The change to sound, and the resultant rapid rise in box-office takings, also initiated a number of fundamental changes in the industry's structure. Warner Bros graduated to 'major' status, acquiring first the Stanley chain of first-run theatres in 1928 and then control of the First National circuit. In common with the other studios, they also bought significant interests in music publishing. Fox, too, was able to expand, building a new studio and in 1928 briefly taking over the Loew family's share of Loew's Inc. Although this meant that the new combine was larger even than Paramount, pressure from incurred debts and from the Justice Department forced Fox to divest its Loew's holdings in 1931. Paramount, too, caught merger fever, and considered deals with Fox, Loew's and R K O. In June 1929 it had acquired half of the radio network C B S, and in September it finalised an arrangement with Warner Bros. The enterprise would have created a vast entertainment corporation, but again threats of a Senate investigation and anti-trust proceedings from the new Hoover administration killed the deal.

Both Western Electric and R C A were quick to export sound equipment and films to Europe, although the conversion of cinemas was rather slow. At the same time the studios faced up to the problems of exporting films to foreign-language markets. First M G M, in Hollywood, and then Paramount, in new studios outside Paris, began to make foreign versions of new films. Although this increased production costs by only one-third, it was soon realised that additional revenues were not covering even this extra outlay, and the studios settled for their films to be dubbed in Europe.

In Germany three scientists had developed a sound-on-film technology called the 'Tri-Ergon' system, but they had failed to interest their domestic industry. In response to the continuing pressure of American marketing, however, a German, Dutch and Swiss corporation, Tobis-Klangfilm, was established to exploit the patents. Arguing that it had sole rights on sound film technology in Germany, it successfully prevented a Warner Bros premiere in Berlin in May 1929. Hollywood responded with a boycott, but soon the studios were endeavouring to make a deal. By June 1930 representatives of Western Electric, R C A and Tobis-Klangfilm were sitting down in Paris and attempting to carve up potential world royalties.

The proposed cartel was too unstable and, with the confusion caused by further patent disputes, it was soon modified into many individual arrangements. But the coming of sound was one factor which contributed to the increased vertical integration of the European industries and to their growing dependence on financial institutions – processes which were directly paralleled in the United States. For perhaps the most fundamental shift in Hollywood brought about by sound was the now inevitable dependence on banks and other sources of external capital. Converting cinemas to sound involved major borrowing, and bankers became essential board members at all the major studios. In particular both the Morgan and Rockefeller banks were directly involved, the former through its connections with A T & T and Western Electric, the latter thanks to Chase National Bank's close links with R C A. The imminent Depression was to tighten this hold yet further.

Colour

Just as with the other new technological processes, early experiments with colour film photography were presented soon after the first cinema screenings, and by 1900 several systems were being demonstrated. Most early colour films, however, were painted by hand, frame by frame, as with much of Méliès' work. But as films became longer and more prints were demanded, this was clearly uneconomic and automatic stencilling processes were introduced. Even these proved too slow and costly, and the industry increasingly adopted 'tinting' and 'toning'.

In the tinting process, black-and-white film is passed through a coloured dye which imparts a uniform colour to each frame. Toning, in contrast, uses dyes which affect only the silver contained in the black portions of the frame, which are thus given a colour while the white sections are left untouched.

Both processes were widely used to create a mood for particular scenes – blue for night-time, green for a landscape, yellow for a lamplit interior. The effects were often startlingly intense and beautiful, and remain so even after more than fifty years. But although both processes were common throughout the silent period, with the coming of sound they were almost completely discontinued. At first the dyes interfered with the quality of sound reproduction; but even when a new range was introduced, their use remained extremely restricted. Tinted and toned pictures may have been felt to conflict with the new 'realism' of talking pictures. A new, more 'natural' colour process was needed.

Colour processes characterised as 'natural' are of two kinds: additive and subtractive. In additive processes two or three images each containing only one of the different primary colour elements of the master image are projected together on to a screen to reconstitute this master. Colour television works on a variant of this principle, but the additive processes designed for the cinema were too clumsy to be widely adopted. Nonetheless, the company which was to dominate colour film production until the 1950s started with an additive system. Founded as a corporation in 1915, Technicolor began by introducing a two-colour additive process. By 1922 the company had developed its first subtractive system. In filming with such processes, separate filters extract each of the primary colours from white light. Two or three negatives (which may be combined in a layered strip) record separate versions of the master image, each of which lacks one of the primary colour elements. From these negatives a positive print is made which reverses the colour values. When white projection light passes through this positive print, which is now effectively a three-colour filter, the colours of the original scene are reproduced.

Throughout the 1920s Technicolor's two-colour subtractive process was primarily used for distinctive sequences in black and white movies, although *The Black Pirate* (1926) and a few musicals were shot entirely in colour. Then in 1929, in line with their policy of constant innovation, Technicolor introduced a new two-colour process with a greatly improved printing method. Warners used this for *On with the Show!* (1929), and other studios followed. But print quality and cost remained major barriers. Another breakthrough, in 1932, produced a three-colour process, which used three parallel strips of film in a camera equipped with prisms to split the light three ways. It was bulky and cumbersome, but the colour quality was exceptional. Until that point, Technicolor had had only a precarious business existence, but the company was now to establish an exceptionally lucrative monopoly hold in Hollywood, and internationally, which lasted two decades.

With each new improvement Technicolor produced a prototype film which demonstrated the recent advances. For the three-colour process they worked first with Walt Disney, who made the animated *Flowers and Trees* (1932). Disney's subsequent *Three Little Pigs* was a comparable success, and both films won Oscars. Then independent producers Merian C. Cooper and

73

Tinting for mood: Hell in Dante's Inferno *(1924, directed by Henry Otto)*

John Hay Whitney formed Pioneer Films to make the first three-colour live-action short, *La Cucaracha* (1934). The following year Pioneer engaged director Rouben Mamoulian to shoot the feature *Becky Sharp*, but its disappointing performance at the box-office appeared to confirm the dominant view in the industry that colour contributed little to a film's commercial potential. And since the process could add $100,000 to the cost of a $200,000 movie, the major studios were slow to adopt Technicolor. Undaunted, Cooper and Whitney set up Selznick International with the producer David O. Selznick, and began to exploit their Technicolor contract in this new partnership. They concentrated on what were seen as 'quality' productions, and the brilliant successes of Selznick's *A Star is Born* (1937), *The Adventures of Tom Sawyer* (1938), and then, in 1939, *Gone With the Wind*, conclusively established the process.

As a company, Technicolor exercised a rigid control over their technology.

Three-colour Technicolor: Mamoulian's Becky Sharp

Around 1930, a number of untrained camera operators had tried out the Technicolor system of the time, and had produced shoddy results. To ensure that this unhappy experience was not repeated, Technicolor now insisted that cameras had to be hired from them (no Technicolor equipment could be purchased outright), that a Technicolor consultant was present during production at all times, that Technicolor make-up was used, and that Technicolor processed and printed the film in its own laboratories. Secrecy and rigorous security surrounded the whole process.

Although the major studios did slowly adopt Technicolor, its uses were confined to particular genres. Fantasy, the musical and historical adventure, in which stylisation and spectacle were paramount, became the favoured genres for colour. This attitude is clear in the decision to shoot in colour only the central fantasy sequences of MGM's *The Wizard of Oz* (1939). And during the war, as budgets were cut and film stock rationed, and as the external 'reality' imposed itself on much of the industry, the demand for Technicolor was reduced.

The first significant challenge to Technicolor's dominance came in 1947 when the Justice Department charged the company with restraint of trade. Three

Colour for fantasy: The Wizard of Oz

years later Eastman Kodak, itself subject to an anti-trust suit, introduced a single-strip colour process, and Technicolor's monopoly position was broken. Like Technicolor, Eastman Kodak had invested heavily in research and since the early 1920s it had been searching for a single-strip process. During the 1930s it had even jointly funded some research with Technicolor. Now it brought out a refined version of the German process Agfacolor. Within four years this had effectively replaced Technicolor, whose three-strip camera was last used on *Foxfire* in 1954.

Eastman Color could be used in any camera, and processing and printing were largely conventional. These advantages made it attractive to the studios, especially after the introduction of an improved version in 1953. At about the same time, Technicolor's printing was proving inadequate for the resolution demands of the new widescreen processes. Consequently Eastman Color was used to film *The Robe, How to Marry a Millionaire, Beneath the Twelve-Mile Reef* (all 1953), and many of the other early anamorphic films. Technicolor, of course, survived and adapted to the changes, concentrating on processing and printing, and on new research. Nor was the clarity, intensity and brilliance of its three-strip process surpassed until Eastman Color introduced the colour reversal internegative (CRI) printing process in the 1970s.

In the 1950s the impact of television had contradictory effects on colour film production. At first, colour was valued as one element in the newly stressed qualities of the cinema as spectacle. But as television came to be seen as a significant market for the studios, and as the new medium was still restricted to black-and-white, colour was regarded as unnecessary for the cheaper films. Only when television converted to colour in the mid-1960s did Hollywood adopt the process for all its output.

Widescreen, 3-D and Stereophonic Sound

A popular attraction at the Paris World Exposition in 1900 was a multiple-projector cinema spectacle which greatly extended the size of the screen image. Abel Gance experimented with a similar effect for his celebrated triptych sequences in *Napoleon* (1927). And in the late 1920s Hollywood showed serious interest in a number of different systems which projected a widescreen image from one strip of film. For certain road-show screenings of *Wings* in 1927 Paramount used the Magnascope process, which produced a screen area four times as large as the usual. In 1930 MGM explored the potential of a process dubbed Realife, which used a wider film stock reduced to 35mm for projection. In the same year Fox introduced Grandeur, a 70mm film projection system. Although these and comparable technologies suffered from focus problems and from the difficulty of achieving sufficient light levels, it appears that they were not widely adopted primarily because the industry, anticipating the effects of the Depression, did not expect the necessary investment to be covered by increased returns.

By the early 1950s, as cinema admissions fell rapidly, the figures looked very different, and the box-office potential of exhibition novelties stimulated the reintroduction of widescreen processes, together with stereo sound. Parallel thinking also led to the industry's brief flirtation with 3-D. As with other innovations, stereo sound had been technically possible for almost two decades, and 3-D worked with a principle applied in 19th-century stereoscopic photographs. Gance too had experimented with the idea for a sequence in *Napoleon*, and MGM made a number of 3-D shorts in the 1930s. 3-D films were also a significant attraction at the 1939 World's Fair. But it was only in late 1952 that both Cinerama, the first widescreen process, and 'Natural Vision' 3-D were first offered to the general public.

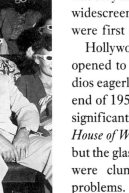

Watching 3-D

Hollywood's first 3-D feature, *Bwana Devil*, opened to sensational business. Most of the studios eagerly embraced the new process, but by the end of 1953 it was clear that its novelty value was significantly outweighed by the disadvantages. *House of Wax* (1953) grossed well over $5 million, but the glasses necessary to achieve the 3-D effect were clumsy and projection caused frequent problems. Moreover, few film-makers seemed genuinely interested in the unique dramatic potential of 3-D. Alfred Hitchcock intelligently exploited the process in *Dial M for Murder* (1954), but the exhibitors were no longer interested and the 3-D version was never released.

By 1954 the industry had recognised that it was widescreen and stereo which could far more effectively provide the sought-for differentiation from television. The first successful process was Cinerama, filmed by three interlocked cameras and shown with four projectors (one carried the sound track). At its premiere in 1952, its inventor Fred Waller screened the 1903 film *The Great Train Robbery* before unleashing *This is Cinerama*, a largely unimaginative travelogue which nonetheless thrilled audiences with a sequence of a rollercoaster ride and an impressive stereo soundtrack. In 122 weeks at a Broadway cinema, it grossed over $4.7 million.

The complex projection arrangements meant that Cinerama was restricted to special roadshow presentations, although in the early 1960s several features were shot using the process, including *The Wonderful World of the Brothers Grimm* (1962), *How the West Was Won* (1962) and *It's a Mad, Mad, Mad, Mad World* (1963). CinemaScope, however, which made its debut with *The Robe* (released in September 1953), was a single-film system and consequently far more flexible. The numerous other widescreen processes which were to follow were almost all single-film systems.

CinemaScope employed a conventional camera, and squeezed the image through an anamorphic lens so that it could be recorded on a film strip of normal width. A similar lens in the projector then reconstituted the image on the screen. The principle of anamorphism had been used by artists for centuries, and the lens itself was developed by Henri Chrétien during the First World War for use in tank sights. The French director Claude Autant-Lara had employed the process in his film *Construire un feu* (1929), but extensive commercial application only came after 20th Century-Fox purchased the rights from Chrétien.

The Robe, *the first film in CinemaScope*

Spyros Skouras, President of 20th Century-Fox, invested heavily in new CinemaScope productions, believing that the process would greatly benefit the financially troubled studio. An important initial stage was marketing the idea to exhibitors, not least because new screens were necessary. Derived from Eidophor, Fox's attempt to introduce theatre television, these were expensive and fragile and effectively restricted CinemaScope to the large first-run theatres. The accompanying stereo sound system was also expensive to install, so small independent theatres stood little chance of participating.

77

Nor was the process to be made available for the production of anything but lavish spectacles. Yet to ensure its success, Fox recognised that more CinemaScope films than the studio could produce would have to be released, and other studios had to be persuaded to take it on. M G M obtained a licence in March 1953; and after the spectacular opening of *The Robe*, Warners also adopted CinemaScope, even though they had been developing a rival system. Other widescreen systems were soon introduced. In 1954 producer Michael Todd, together with the American Optical Company, developed Todd-A O, a non-anamorphic process shot in 65mm and released on 70mm prints so that two-track stereo sound could also be incorporated. In the same year Paramount brought out VistaVision, which recorded a non-anamorphic image sideways on 35mm film, thus greatly increasing the area of the image.

The new aesthetics of the wide screen prompted much debate. George Stevens complained that the CinemaScope frame was more appropriate for filming a python than a person. But André Bazin welcomed widescreen as an important, and for him progressive, step away from montage-based cinema. The industry, inevitably, was more interested in the figures, and they quickly proved impressive. James Belton has recorded: 'In 1953, prior to Cinema-Scope, Fox pictures lost a total of over $6 million. But the first 25 Cinema-Scope features earned Fox a profit of over $47 million, *The Robe* alone grossing more than $30 million (at a negative cost of $4.5 million). The $10 million that Fox spent in developing CinemaScope and the increased average cost in making CinemaScope features, whereby the average negative cost rose from $1.3 million to $2 million, paid off.'

In 1957 the Panavision company introduced a 35mm alternative to CinemaScope which gave an improved picture quality and eliminated the distortion of close-ups. M G M immediately adopted the new system, and two years later used a further refinement, Ultra-Panavision, to make *Ben Hur*. Over the next decade Panavision established the industry standards. Further developments followed, like the introduction of anamorphic zoom lenses, and today Panavision manufacture the majority of cameras and lenses used in both standard format and widescreen production. *In Like Flint* (1967) was Fox's last film to employ CinemaScope.

Widescreen is now accepted, and indeed expected, by film audiences watching mainstream commercial films. The irony is that during the 1970s many of the large cinemas which could accommodate widescreen projection were either closed or converted into a number of small-screen theatres, where the impact of widescreen is greatly reduced. Equally, with showings on both television and videocassettes, widescreen compositions are destroyed, and the technique of panning-and-scanning across a widescreen frame invariably proves irritating. A handful of films, like *Revolution* (1986), are still made in 70mm, but true spectacle is now largely confined to specialist projection systems like Imax and Omnimax, which need purpose-built auditoria.

After the introduction of each of the transforming technologies of sound, colour and widescreen, Hollywood cinema comfortably absorbed the new aesthetic possibilities. Standards, conventions and expectations shifted a little, and certain genres proved more amenable than others, but the fundamentals of Hollywood's classical style have remained largely unchanged. Outside Hollywood, however, and beyond the international mainstream cinema, the potential of these technological innovations has been realised in stimulating and exciting ways.

Jean-Luc Godard, for example, has spent the past fifteen years developing a practice for both film and video in which, among much else, sound is used to counterpoint, challenge and overturn images, rather than simply to reinforce them. Godard's explorations with colour and widescreen have been equally remarkable, like the bold blocks of primary reds and blues which dominate the extended frames of *Le Mépris* (1963) and *Pierrot le Fou* (1965). Michelangelo Antonioni has made a similarly non-naturalistic use of colour in *The Red Desert* (1964), for which objects and sets were painted in uniform hues to suggest the state of mind of the central character. Comparably non-naturalistic widescreen compositions are fundamental to many films, including *L'Année dernière à Marienbad* (1961), directed by Alain Resnais, Akira Kurosawa's historical spectacles like *Ran* (1985), and Miklós Jancsó's elaborately choreographed allegories, such as *The Red and the White* (1967) and *The Confrontation* (1969). In Hollywood, too, directors like Nicholas Ray and Douglas Sirk and, more recently, Francis Coppola and Martin Scorsese, have endeavoured to exploit the aesthetics of colour and widescreen in bold and uncompromising ways.

Composing for the wide screen: Kurosawa's Kagemusha *(1980)*

79

Further reading

Charles Barr, 'Cinemascope: Before and After', *Film Quarterly*, vol. 16, no 4, Autumn 1963.

Fred E. Barsten, *Glorious Technicolor*, London: A.S. Barnes, 1980.

Edward Branigan, 'Colour and Cinema: Problems in the Writing of History', *Film Reader*, no. 4, 1979.

Raymond Fielding (ed.), *A Technological History of Motion Pictures and Television*, Berkeley: University of California Press, 1967.

Douglas Gomery, 'The Coming of the Talkies: Invention, Innovation, Diffusion' in Tino Balio (ed), *The American Film Industry*.

———'Writing the History of the American Film Industry: Warner Bros and Sound', *Screen*, vol. 17, no. 1, Spring 1976.

———'Economic Struggle and Hollywood Imperialism: Europe Converts to Sound', *Yale French Studies: Cinema/Sound*, no. 60, 1980.

Gorham Kindem, 'Hollywood's Conversion to Color: The Technological, Economic and Aesthetic Factors', *Journal of the University Film and Video Association*, Spring 1979.

Steve Neale, *Cinema and Technology: Image, Sound, Colour*, London: Macmillian/BFI Publishing, 1985.

Patrick Ogle, 'Development of Sound Systems: The Commercial Era', *Film Reader*, no. 2, January 1977.

R. T. Ryan, *A History of Motion Picture Colour Technology*, London: Focal Press, 1977.

The Velvet Light Trap, , no. 21, Summer 1985. (This edition devoted to American widescreen cinema contains a number of important articles.)

Alexander Walker, *The Shattered Silents*, London: Elm Tree Books, 1978.

6
'Those Miraculous Images'

'It is not generally recognised by the public,' the director Michael Powell wrote in his autobiography, 'that the most genuinely creative member of a film unit, if the author of the original story and screenplay is excluded, is the art director. . . It is not sufficiently acknowledged that the art director is the creator of those miraculous images up there on the big screen, and that besides being a painter and architect, this miracle man has to be an engineer as well.'

Powell's hyperbole, in praise of the art director Alfred Junge, is a valuable corrective to the too frequent invisibility of these craftsmen (and more rarely women) in cinema history. But his argument risks perpetuating the comparable invisibility of those who work closely with the art director – the cinematographer and the special effects team. All three participate creatively in the film-making process, each making central contributions to 'those miraculous images'.

Art Direction – the early years
Most of those who first worked as designers in the cinema were scene painters from the theatre, and they provided no more than crude backdrops against which tableau-style scenes were shot. Georges Méliès, in contrast, made his own fantastical designs an integral element of his films. Concerned more with visual impact than with narrative, he created convincingly realistic settings for his newsreel-style reconstructions, as well as often bizarrely baroque fantasies. *A Trip to the Moon* (1902), for example, includes the lunar face being struck in the eye by a spaceship; *The Conquest of the Pole* (1912) features the vast visage of a Giant of the Eternal Ice.

Elaborate scenic design was further extended by artists working for Pathé and Gaumont, where Robert Jules Garnier designed the strange worlds of Louis Feuillade's serials. Another important figure at Gaumont was the young scenic artist Ben Carré who, in Hollywood after 1912, worked on a remarkable cycle of films with director Maurice Tourneur. Their collaboration *The Blue Bird* (1918) is an elaborate visual delight, which won particular note for its imaginative use of silhouette. In Europe, a more

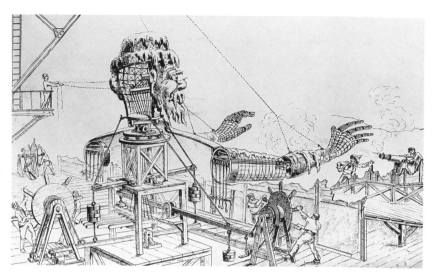

grandiloquent style emerged with the pre-war cycle of classical epics produced in Italy. The most spectacular sets of the time are in *Cabiria*, directed by Giovanni Pastrone in 1914, where ancient Carthage is a world of opulence and extravagance, which is both elaborately decorated and solidly constructed so that action could be staged in sharp perspectives and on several levels.

Cabiria was undoubtedly a major influence on the Babylonian set for Griffith's *Intolerance* (1916). This huge construction, designed by Walter L. Hall, with towers 165 feet high and ramparts which could carry chariots, was easily the largest set built until then in America. By this date theatrical backdrops had been supplemented both by extensive location work and by increasingly ingenious sets, often constructed so as to contribute to a comedian's carefully timed gag. *Intolerance,* however, introduced a quite new sense of scale, which was to be further developed by art director Wilfred Buckland in his mammoth settings for Douglas Fairbanks' *Robin Hood* (1922), for which he built a castle which cost a quarter of the film's budget.

During the 1920s German Expressionism, first brought to the screen in *The Cabinet of Dr Caligari* (1919), made its singular mark in Europe. The tormented vision of *Caligari* inspired few direct imitations, but its stylisation, chiaroscuro and external embodiment of internal emotions influenced many film-makers. Murnau's *The Last Laugh* (1924) was comparably significant. Designed by Robert Herlth and Walter Röhrig, many of the interiors are bare indications of a room with just one or two essential props, whereas the exteriors (all shot on a stage) are complex perspective constructions through which the camera moves with great mobility. In France directors Abel Gance and Jean Epstein encouraged bold art direction, and Marcel L'Herbier in *L'Inhumaine* (1924) choreographed a remarkable visual spectacle, employing as designers Claude Autant-Lara, Alberto Cavalcanti, the painter Fernand Léger and the progressive architect Robert Mallet-Stevens.

Perspective in an exterior set for Murnau's The Last Laugh

82

Hollywood: the studio years

From the early 1920s to the 1950s art directors were key members of each Hollywood studio. Visual style was recognised as an essential element in the production-line creation of films, and talented architects, illustrators and stage designers were persuaded to move from New York and Europe. They toiled in the art departments of the studios, only to see the credit for their visions being taken by the department's head, who while ultimately responsible for the overall style of the studio's output usually had little to do with the details of designing and building sets.

The man who designed the Oscar statuette, Cedric Gibbons, was head of the Art Department at MGM from 1924 to 1956. For his work there he collected eleven of the coveted awards, and he received a credit on every film made by the studio during those years. Yet he personally designed only a handful of films, including contributions to *Ben Hur* (1925) and *The Big Parade* (1925). Nonetheless, MGM's films from the three decades which he dominated have the most consistent style of any of the studios. Distinguished by opulence and glamour, MGM settings often bore the influence of international Art Deco.

MGM glamour: The Great Ziegfeld *(1936), designed by Cedric Gibbons*

Paramount German: Sternberg's The Scarlet Empress *(1934), designed by Hans Dreier*

No other designer or art department head challenged the almost legendary status of Gibbons at MGM. But each studio enjoyed the creative services of some remarkable artists. At Paramount from 1923 to 1950 Hans Dreier forged a distinctive studio style indebted to his experience in the early 1920s at the Ufa studios in Berlin. German Expressionism was also important to the work of Anton Grot at Warners. Between 1927 and 1948 his use of light and shadow defined one essence of that studio's style, which was always achieved on tight budgets. At RKO, Van Nest Polglase oversaw the cool, elegant visuals, with their *moderne* lines and Art Deco styling, in that studio's series of films with Fred Astaire and Ginger Rogers. Universal meanwhile profited from the talents of Charles D. Hall, who worked closely with Chaplin between 1925 and 1936, and who created the worlds of *Dracula* (1931), *Frankenstein* (1931) and *The Old Dark House* (1932). Another noted figure was Richard Day, who designed Stroheim's films from *Foolish Wives* (1922) onwards, and who worked for Goldwyn/United Artists during the 1930s and was Supervising Art Director for 20th Century-Fox after 1941. Of all the major art directors, Day was the one most sympathetic to an idea of documentary realism, evident in his work on *A Streetcar Named Desire* (1951) and *On the Waterfront* (1954).

Art Deco at RKO: Rogers and Astaire in Top Hat *(1935), designed by Van Nest Polglase*

William Cameron Menzies, in contrast, chose to operate strictly as an independent. A former commercial illustrator, and assistant to Anton Grot, he worked with Douglas Fairbanks on the spectacular fairytale *The Thief of Bagdad* (1924) and with Valentino on *The Eagle* (1925) and *The Son of the Sheik* (1926). Among the first art directors to make scrupulous sketches of particular shots, he made many demands on his directors, often specifying the lighting, camera-angle and disposition of actors. After a collaboration with Alexander Korda on the futuristic epic *Things to Come*, Menzies returned to Hollywood to work with producer David O. Selznick on a series of films culminating in *Gone with the Wind*. On this Menzies was a central creative force, and his detailed sketches established a unifying vision for the film's three directors (George Cukor, Victor Fleming and Sam Wood) and numerous cameramen. Menzies also directed many sequences himself, but Fleming apparently refused to allow Selznick to credit Menzies as associate director. Instead, the credit reads 'Production Designed by William Cameron Menzies', and the film was one of the first to recognise the co-ordinating role of a production designer, who took responsibility for every visual element.

Things to Come (1936), designed and directed by William Cameron Menzies

Under each of these supervisory figures, the studios set up teams of researchers, draughtsmen, carpenters, model-makers, painters and others. In the 1920s and 1930s employees might vary these roles, but in the early 1940s both management practices and the increasingly powerful craft unions brought about greater demarcation and specialisation. The studios also endeavoured to use their resources as efficiently as possible. Once a major set was built, either on a sound stage or on the backlot, it would often see repeated service. The staircase constructed for *The Magnificent Ambersons* (1942) appeared in a string of low-budget R K O dramas, and cowboys from many different films rode down the same Western street set.

European design

In the later 1930s and during the war the most distinctive French art director was Alexandre Trauner. In his work for Marcel Carné, especially *Hotel du Nord* (1938) and *Le Jour se lève* (1939), he did much to define the style subsequently known as 'poetic realism'. Stressing unusual details, he often drew sharply distorted perspectives, with a central corner or angle dominating the frame. During the war, Trauner was one of three designers on Carné's sparkling theatrical period piece *Les Enfants du Paradis* (1945), and since then he has worked with many of the leading American directors. In 1952 he was art director on Orson Welles' bold, graphic *Othello*, and almost three decades later

Poetic realism: Carné's Le Jour se lève, *designed by Alexandre Trauner*

he visualised Joseph Losey's glorious *Don Giovanni* (1979).

In Britain the most notable designs in the 1930s came from Vincent Korda. Initially a painter, he worked in the French film industry before coming to England to create the sets for his brother Alexander's hugely successful *The Private Life of Henry VIII* (1933). His subsequent films included *The Private Life of Don Juan* (1934), *Rembrandt* (1936), and collaborations with Menzies on *Things to Come* (1936) and *The Thief of Bagdad* (1940). Before Korda, and in many ways for long after him, British art direction relied on discrete naturalism, simply transferring to the screen tasteful interiors from the stage. Korda conceived grandiose, sweeping sets, built to display striking effects.

The most distinctive design achievements in the British cinema, however, must be the films made during and after the Second World War by the writing, directing and producing team of 'The Archers', Michael Powell and Emeric Pressburger. In their collaborations first with Alfred Junge and then

Design by Alfred Junge for Black Narcissus

with Hein Heckroth, they created mythical visions quite distinct from the traditions of the British cinema. Junge had trained at Ufa and his first film with the Archers was *Contraband* (1940). But it is for the Technicolor marvels of *The Life and Death of Colonel Blimp* (1943), *A Matter of Life and Death* (1946) and *Black Narcissus* (1947) that he is most noted. Much of *A Matter of Life and Death* takes place in a black-and-white Heaven, and its celestial spectacles include an escalator to the stars and a trial mounted in a vast amphitheatre. On earth, too, Junge's use of colour (and lack of it) is so striking that the film remains almost unparalleled as a design achievement. His former assistant, Hein Heckroth, created comparably dazzling images for *The Red Shoes* (1948) and *The Tales of Hoffmann* (1951).

The Red Shoes, *designed by Hein Heckroth*

Naturalism, however, continued to dominate British cinema design, as a studio style in the work of Ealing designers like Roy Oxley (*Passport to Pimlico*, 1949) and Jim Morahan (*The Man in the White Suit*, 1951, and *The Ladykillers*, 1955), and then as the basis for contemporary social dramas like *Saturday Night and Sunday Morning* (1960). Subsequent deviations from this norm have been rare, although noteworthy attempts include Ralph Brinton's exuberant sets for *Tom Jones* (1963), Assheton Gordon's work with bold colour for Antonioni's *Blow-Up* (1966), Derek Jarman's stylish designs for *The Devils* (1971), and Anton Furst's studio fairyland in *The Company of Wolves* (1984).

86

The Company of Wolves, *designed by Anton Furst*

Beyond the studios

In the decade after the Second World War the Hollywood studio system was transformed. The anti-trust decree of 1948 (see Chapter 12), together with the growth of television, substantially curtailed the economic power of the large corporations. Budgets were tighter, and elaborate studio re-creations became prohibitively expensive. The studio backlots became more valuable to their owners as real estate. New lightweight, portable cameras and sound equipment meant that location filming was a feasible alternative, as well as a financially attractive option. At the same time art direction was assimilating a range of influences, including the verisimilitude of wartime documentaries and the stark, street-based style of Italian neo-realism. Around 1960, these alternative appearances were supplemented by the vivid naturalism of *vérité* documentaries and the casual, everyday look of the French 'new wave'.

20th Century-Fox's cycle of urban thrillers filmed on location, beginning with *The House on 92nd Street* (1945), was the first and most obvious result of these new aesthetic and economic influences. But their impact can also be seen in *On the Town* (1949), an MGM musical with elaborately stylised dance numbers but featuring the streets of New York as one of its major attractions. Just over a decade later production designer Boris Leven achieved a comparable mix of authenticity and theatricality, location filming and studio work, for *West Side Story* (1961).

On the town in the studio: a New York rooftop in West Side Story, *designed by Boris Leven*

For all the attractions of fantasy, many directors and production designers today still aim for all-out authenticity. George Jenkins, who started as an art director on *The Best Years of Our Lives* (1946), built an exact re-creation of the *Washington Post* newsroom for *All the President's Men* (1976). For three months, *Post* journalists filled boxes with discarded letters and magazines, which were then used to dress the enormous set, built on two adjoining stages at the Warner Bros studio. Dean Tavoularis has a similar passion for detail. On *The Godfather* (1972), he insisted that the smells of garlic, oregano and paprika should permeate the kitchen sets.

Hollywood cinematography

One dominant tradition of Hollywood cinematography served its practitioners well for more than fifty years. Individual stylists like Lee Garmes and Leon Shamroy could distinguish themselves within its restrictions, and occasionally an innovator like Gregg Toland or James Wong Howe would capture on film images as startling as those in *Citizen Kane* (1941) or *Body and Soul* (1947). But the hallmarks of this studio style were restraint, subtlety, unobtrusiveness. One President of the American Society of Cinematographers, John Arnold, expressed this view when he said that the ideal 'is to so perfectly suit the cinematography to the story that the former is imperceptible, and the latter is subtly heightened.' In the 1960s these ideas, and the tradition which had been built upon them, were fundamentally challenged, partly by new styles from France and Italy, and partly by the influence of *vérité* documentaries.

In the cinema's earliest years, the cameraman invariably doubled as director, and developed and edited the finished scenes as well. Edison's former assistant W. K .L. Dickson worked in this way, as did Edwin S. Porter and 'Billy' Bitzer. Nor did they specialise in one type of work, each filming actualities, topicals and vaudeville acts as well as comedies and dramas. Interiors were at first shot in the open and lit by direct sunlight. From the early 1900s such scenes were produced in simple studios, and after 1904 artificial lighting, either similar to that already used in the theatre or new Cooper-Hewitt mercury vapour lamps, was introduced to supplement diffused sunlight.

The nickelodeon boom in 1905-6 greatly increased the demand for films, and to improve production efficiency specialist directors were introduced to film-making. As in the theatre, from which many of them came, they were made responsible for the staging of the action. The cameraman became one specialist in an ultimately complex hierarchy of labour, and the role itself subsequently divided further into Director of Photography (or cinematographer), who took overall responsibility for the images, and camera operator, focus puller, and so on. Only much later, with the availability of simple, lightweight film cameras, and then video, did directors again have the opportunity to undertake their own cinematography.

The increased availability of arc lamps after about 1908 encouraged cameramen to explore the creative use of 'effects' lighting, allowing attention to be directed to particular elements within the frame. Throughout the

1910s cameramen increasingly adopted a more selective style, rejecting blanket illumination of a scene. Theatrical spot lights were another important new tool for cameramen, as were powerful arcs, developed for wartime use but available to the film industry from 1918. By 1919, at least in America, it was completely standard to use combinations of these lamps to shoot all of a film's interiors in a blacked-out studio.

Soft and hard

Even with sophisticated uses of effects, the accepted norm in Hollywood during the 1910s was sharp, hard-edged lighting. But after Bitzer and Henrik Sartov's work on *Broken Blossoms* (1919), a softer style of cinematography, conjured up with gauzes, filters and smoke as well as shallow focus, became increasingly popular. In part this style was employed to separate central characters from peripheral backgrounds, but it was also seen, following accepted standards of portrait photography, as enhancing the beauty of the compositions. Among the masters of this style were John F. Seitz, whose work on Rex Ingram's *The Four Horsemen of the Apocalypse* (1921) was particularly influential, and Charles Rosher, who had been a noted still photographer before being taken on by Mary Pickford as her cameraman in 1917. The soft style became the norm after the introduction of sound, although the images of the early 1930s lack the dark blacks and sparkling highlights which still distinguish the best silent films shot in the soft style, like *Sunrise* (1927). In part, this was because sets were often lit for multiple-camera shooting, just as television studios were to be illuminated two decades later. Moreover, recently introduced automated developing processes contributed to a general fuzziness, as did the new incandescent, or tungsten, lights which had quickly become standard because they operated with minimal noise. They did not, however, help a cameraman achieve a crisp image.

Focus on the foreground: Broken Blossoms, *photographed by Billy Bitzer*

Rapid technical development in the 1930s by the manufacturers of film stock, lenses and lamps greatly increased the options open to cinematographers, but most chose to retain the soft style, which continued to be regarded as artistic. Some, like James Wong Howe and Hal Mohr, chose to experiment with rendering depth on the screen, but on the whole directors continued to stage the action in one plane, and it was not until after 1940 that films began to place a foreground close to the camera and in sharp focus. The visual quality known as 'deep focus', in which the different planes of a scene all appear in sharp outline, is usually associated with *Citizen Kane*, but this film was only one of several at the time, including *The Maltese Falcon*, which used the possibilities of recent advances in lenses and film stock. *Citizen Kane*, however, made a significant impact because the film's cinematographer, Gregg Toland, exploited deep focus in such a flamboyant manner. With director Orson Welles and designer Perry Ferguson, he

Deep focus in Citizen Kane, *photographed by Gregg Toland*

created enormous sets to highlight the impact of the deep focus shots. Toland claimed numerous innovatory aspects to his work on the film, including the introduction of oppressive ceilings.

European influences

Hollywood's dominance of distribution and exhibition ensured that throughout the 1920s and 1930s foreign cinemas were more influenced by American styles than vice versa. Nonetheless, the visual style of German Expressionism made its mark in Hollywood, and its most prominent and innovative cinematographer, Karl Freund, was invited to work in the United States in 1929. Among his later credits were *Dracula* (1931) and *Murders in the Rue Morgue* (1932), as well as the early episodes of the pioneering television series made on film, *I Love Lucy* (begun in 1955). Camera mobility really developed in France and Germany in the mid-1920s, and was only later used by a handful of American directors before sound technology significantly hampered its development. The Hungarian director Paul Fejos, however, oversaw the building of the first real camera crane at Universal Studios in 1929, and made extensive use of it for the non-dialogue sections of *Broadway*.

After the war, the unvarnished cinematography of Italian neo-realism had some influence on Hollywood style, as did wartime documentary camerawork. Photoflood bulbs and lighter cameras facilitated location work, and the associated visual qualities gained further adherents after the first films of the French 'new wave' began to be seen internationally. The work of Henri Decaë, who shot Claude Chabrol's first features and François Truffaut's debut *Les Quatre cents coups* (1959), and of former still photographer Raoul Cou-

The first camera crane, in the studio for Broadway *(1929)*

tard, exploited the natural light possibilities of documentary-style filming, and often used a handheld camera and rapid pans. Faster stock permitted Coutard, who worked frequently with director Jean-Luc Godard, to film interiors with natural light enhanced by photoflood bulbs fixed above windows and with light bounced off ceilings and walls. Television, too, has had a major impact on styles of cinematography. The improvised methods of many documentaries in the early 1960s encouraged the acceptance of a freer, rougher visual vocabulary.

Assimilating these various influences, and in many cases their practitioners, throughout the 1970s and 1980s, Hollywood cinematography is now distinguished by a far greater diversity of style. Gordon Willis' dark, ominous interiors have contributed greatly to Woody Allen's films, to both parts of *The Godfather* (1972 and 1974), and to the fluorescent world of *All the President's Men* (1976). Vilmos Zsigmond has adapted his soft impressionism to frequent collaborations with Robert Altman and with Michael Cimino, for whom he shot *The Deer Hunter* (1978) and *Heaven's Gate* (1980). For Spielberg, Zsigmond co-photographed *Close Encounters of the Third Kind* (1977); he also shot Spielberg's debut theatrical feature, *The Sugarland Express* (1974), which was the first film to make extensive use of the flowing movements facilitated by the Steadicam process. John Alonzo, another of the cinematographers who contributed to *Close Encounters*, first won attention with his glowing, heat-drenched images of 1930s Los Angeles in *Chinatown* (1974).

In Europe, cinematographers like Sven Nykvist (for Ingmar Bergman) and Carlo Di Palma (for Michelangelo Antonioni) had given their particular imprint to the films they shot. But perhaps the contemporary cinematogra-

Interior light: Godard's Breathless *(1959), photographed by Raoul Coutard*

pher with the most consistently distinctive style is Vittorio Storaro, who won international recognition for his collaborations with Bernardo Bertolucci, from *The Conformist* in 1970 to *Last Tango in Paris* (1972), *1900* (1976), *La Luna* (1980) and *The Last Emperor* (1987). With Francis Coppola, Storaro endured the intense physical demands of the shoot for *Apocalypse Now* (1979), for which he won an Oscar, as he did for his camerawork on Warren Beatty's *Reds* (1981). In all his work, Storaro has used diffused and reflected light, developing a programmatic sense of the dominant colours and their changes throughout a film. For him, cinematography has an almost mystical dimension: 'Photography, for me, really means writing with light . . . I am trying to describe the story of the film through the light. I try to have a parallel story to the actual story so that through light and colour you can feel and understand, consciously and unconsciously, what the story is about.'

Diffused light: Bertolucci's The Conformist, *photographed by Vittorio Storaro*

Special effects

As with so much in the moving image's past, any history of special effects begins with the fantasies of Georges Méliès. Using theatrical illusions, elaborate stage machinery and the 'magic' of a film camera, Méliès could transport his audience beneath the waves, to the polar regions, to the moon. Since then, journeys into space have often featured at the cutting edge of special effects technology: in Fritz Lang's *Frau im Mond* (1929), in *Things to Come* (1936), in *2001: A Space Odyssey* (1968), and in *Star Wars* (1977). The largely unremarkable sci-fi adventure *The Last Starfighter* (1984) might appear an incongruous addition to such a distinguished list, except that it was one of the first features to make significant use of computer graphics animation. Méliès achieved many of his effects with the same kinds of models, mirrors and masks which, in rather more sophisticated forms, were used by the teams working with Stanley Kubrick and George Lucas. In the future, computer-generated effects may eclipse this tradition, now nearly a century old.

Special effects are conventionally categorised as either mechanical or optical. The former derive from theatrical trickery, and include explosions, bullets and the like, while the latter extend many of the techniques initially developed by 19th-century photographers. Glass shots, mattes, rear and front projection involve the precise manipulation of the image, both outside and within the camera during filming, and also during the developing and printing. Méliès became as adept at this optical trickery as he was at mechanical effects, and there were many contemporaries who endeavoured to emulate his success.

Edwin S. Porter's famous 1903 Western *The Great Train Robbery* features an early application of in-the-camera mattes, which Méliès had adapted from the techniques of still photography. One scene has a telegraph clerk being overpowered as, through a window, a train can be seen drawing into the station. The image is a composite, created by first inserting into the camera a plate which prevented the area of the window being exposed on the negative. A second plate, permitting exposure of the negative only in the window area, was then used to record the train's arrival on the same strip of film. The technique is also apparent in a subsequent shot where the landscape can be seen to speed past an open door in a railway carriage. This technique, in more sophisticated forms, became one of the essential tricks for the creation of cinematic illusion.

Another fundamental technique was, and remains, the glass shot, again a common device in photography but apparently first used in a motion picture by Norman O. Dawn in his documentary *Missions of California* (1907). Dawn's speciality, as both a still and film photographer, was grand spectacles, and he used glass shots to reconstruct the former glories of ruined buildings. By carefully aligning, between camera and ruin, a sheet of glass on which was painted an impression of the complete building, he was able to combine in one frame, say, the base of a toppled arcade and a painted image of its upper parts.

A matte effect in Porter's The Great Train Robbery: *the train can be seen passing the window*

Glass shots were employed extensively in the following decades, not least because they saved the construction costs of the upper parts of vast sets. Instead of a complete cathedral or castle, the art director built only the base, and the spires and turrets were incorporated from a glass shot. A widely used variant of this technique involved painting only a black matte onto the glass, obscuring part of the negative; the frame was completed later by the superimposition of a painted image, shot under controlled circumstances. Yet another trick became known as the Schüfftan (or Shuftan) process, after the German cinematographer Eugen Schüfftan. This used a partly silvered mirror to combine, for example, a model of a building and actors moving in a full-size set of just part of the building. The negative mostly recorded the model but in one area, reflected in the mirror, it recorded the set and actors, which if the alignments were correct appeared to be integrated in the full-scale model. Many of the most spectacular shots in Fritz Lang's *Metropolis* were achieved in this way.

Travelling mattes were an obvious but complex extension of these techniques. There are many variants of this process, but they usually involve filming a model or human figure against a neutral background. The silhouettes of this element are then transferred, frame-by-frame, into individual mattes which obscure the background into which the element is to be introduced. When the background is filmed on the original negative, with these frame-by-frame mattes synchronised to the original figure, the two images should create a perfect fit.

Models and miniatures were one further staple of special effects from the earliest days of film. E. H. Amet claimed in 1898 to have filmed the American fleet's victory over the Spanish in Santiago harbour. In fact his shots, supposedly taken from a distance of six miles, were of model boats arranged according to newspaper accounts. A rather more legitimate use of models was in MGM's spectacular *Ben Hur* (1925). An elaborate miniature of the upper levels of the amphitheatre was hung between the camera and the lower levels, which had been built as a full-size set. The alignment was precise enough to allow the camera to pan across the tiered auditorium during the chariot race. And the miniature was equipped with rows of tiny spectators, mounted on rods, which could rise with the thousands of extras at the climactic moments.

The coming of sound

The introduction of sound forced producers back into the studios. Elaborate location filming became impractical, and special effects teams had to find new ways of creating the illusion of exteriors. The most popular technique was rear projection, which like many of the other basic effects had been utilised by 19th-century still photographers. Norman O. Dawn had explored its possibilities as early as 1913, but it proved difficult to achieve a sufficiently intense background image to match bright foreground figures. Farciot Edouart at Paramount is credited with resolving this problem by combining on the screen three separate images from three projectors.

Yet another technique known to still photographers, but not used by the cinema until after 1926, was optical printing. Essentially a combined, and synchronised, projector and camera, an optical printer throws a focused image on to a new negative. Manipulations of the process can produce fades and wipes, freezes, the appearance of zooms, and elaborate split-screen work. Linwood Dunn, head of photographic effects at RKO, is acknowledged as the master of the optical printer, which he used extensively in the making of *Citizen Kane*. Dunn estimated that as much as half of the film was optically manipulated in reprinting, including the final zoom in on the sled being consumed by the flames. Dunn also brought Katharine Hepburn and the leopard together in *Bringing Up Baby* (1938); in all but a few shots they were filmed separately, but the effect remains invisible.

Until the early 1950s each of the major studios had their own effects teams, and experienced professionals like Gordon Jennings, head of special effects at Paramount from the mid-1930s to 1953, were highly prized employees. When Jennings died during pre-production work on the Hollywood movie seen as the culmination of this studio tradition, Cecil B. DeMille's remake of his own *The Ten Commandments* (1956), Paramount turned to John P. Fulton, whose work at Universal in the 1930s had included supervising the aerial shots in John Ford's *Airmail* (1932) and the ingenious tricks of *The Invisible Man* (1933). For DeMille, Fulton created a splendid biblical tapestry, the highlight of which was the parting of the Red Sea. In the 1923 version, the towering walls of water had been slabs of Jell-O matted together with the fleeing Israelites. For the 1956 film, legend has it that the composite sequence took more than two years to achieve and cost more than $2 million. And the walls of water were photographed at the bottom of a specially built 32-feet high concrete dam.

With the dismantling of the studio system during the 1950s, there were to be few bravura displays of effects until the film widely recognised as a new watershed – *2001: A Space Odyssey* (1968). Indeed, during the 1960s there was a marked reaction against optical 'trickery'. Younger Hollywood directors, who had often come from television, preferred 'realism'. John Frankenheimer, for example, banned the use of process and matte shots from his motor racing spectacular *Grand Prix* (1966). Mechanical effects like explosions and car crashes were, of course, as popular as ever, if not more so, and the best stunt men and women continued to be in demand.

Space Odysseys

During the making of *2001: A Space Odyssey* for MGM in England, Stanley Kubrick assembled an effects team which included many of those who would transform special effects in the next two decades, including Con Pederson, Douglas Trumbull, and Colin Cantwell (a key designer for *Star Wars*), along with two veteran British technicians who had worked on the influential *Things to Come* back in 1936, Wally Veevers and Tom Howard. The finished film is a virtual directory of effects work. The opening sequence combines immaculate ape make-up with an elaborate and original front projection system. The space station was a model nine feet in diameter, orbiting in space by means of hand-drawn travelling mattes. But it was the celebrated Stargate Corridor which proved to be the most remarkable sequence, suggesting that the character played by Keir Dullea is travelling at tremendous speed between dazzling walls of light. It worked on the principle of filming moving art-work through a narrow slit, which was also moving, but in a different direction. The visceral impact of the finished shots was not to be matched for more than a decade.

After *2001*, Trumbull began to develop motion control cameras, which could be programmed to repeat exactly a complex move, thus permitting elaborate layering of the image. The idea had been around at least since 1914, when Edison's James Brautigan created ghostly apparitions using a block-and-tackle to repeat the required camera movements. Greater sophistication had been achieved in the early 1950s with systems that recorded camera movement on disc and on an optical film strip, but it was digital recording on tape that was to make possible the sophistication achieved in the 1970s. Trumbull began to explore its possibilities in effects work for *The*

The Stargate Corridor in Kubrick's 2001: A Space Odyssey

Andromeda Strain (1971) and his own directorial debut *Silent Running* (1972). At the same time the effects animator Robert Abel had teamed up with Con Pederson, and they were using similar techniques, linked to comparatively crude computer technology, for television commercials.

The most celebrated application of electronic motion control is that supervised by Trumbull's former protégé, John Dykstra, for George Lucas' *Star Wars* (1977). In the climactic dogfights within the Death Star trench, the film matched (and for many surpassed) Kubrick's achievements in *2001*. But by the time *Star Wars* was released, Paramount had one of its subsidiaries, the Future General Corporation, together with Douglas Trumbull, achieving comparably sophisticated effects work for Steven Spielberg's *Close Encounters of the Third Kind* (1977). Motion-control, mattes and front projection were all integral to the film, but the most remarkable moment, the appearance of the vast mother ship, is a composite shot featuring an animation-enhanced miniature some six feet in diameter.

After these box-office triumphs by Lucas and Spielberg, special effects movies were fashionable again, and a remake of *King Kong* (1976), *Superman: the Movie* (1978), *The Black Hole* and *Alien* (both 1979) soon followed. Industrial Light and Magic, the effects company set up by Lucas and Dykstra for *Star Wars*, created the motion-control work for the sequel, *The Empire Strikes Back* (1980), and also contributed centrally to Spielberg's subsequent films, although the latter's *E.T.: The Extra-Terrestrial* (1982) depended more on model work. But as traditional effects work became increasingly sophisticated, a new generation of effects was emerging, based on computer animation. This new technology (see Chapter 19) has the potential to create images 'miraculous' in ways previously undreamt of.

Further reading

Leon Barsacq, *Caligari's Cabinet and Other Grand Illusions*, Boston: Little, Brown & Co., 1976.

John Brosnan, *Movie Magic: The Story of Special Effects in the Cinema*, New York: St Martin's Press, 1974.

Mary Corliss and Carlos Clarens, 'Designed for Film', *Film Comment*, May-June 1978.

John Culhane, *Special Effects in the Movies*, New York: Ballantine, 1981.

Raymond Fielding, *The Techniques of Special Effects Photography*, London: Focal Press, 1965.

John Hambley and Patrick Downing, *The Art of Hollywood: Fifty Years of Art Direction*, London: Thames Television, 1979.

Charles Higham, *Hollywood Cameramen*, London: Thames and Hudson/BFI, 1970.

Joseph McBride (ed.), *Filmmakers on Filmmaking* (2 volumes), Los Angeles: J. P. Tarcher, 1983.

Todd McCarthy, 'Hollywood Style '84', *Film Comment*, March-April 1984.

Leonard Maltin, *The Art of the Cinematographer*, New York: Dover, 1978.

Carrie Rickey et al, 'Art Directors', *Film Comment*, January-February 1982.

Michael Webb (ed.), *Hollywood: Legend and Reality*, Boston: New York Graphic Society/Smithsonian Institution, 1986.

7
Animation

The principle of animation was being exploited long before the cinema. Throughout the 19th century the passion for scientific exploration and invention brought a variety of toys and gadgets, which by means of spinning, turning or flicking motions were able to produce the illusion of movement in a series of separately drawn images. The most sophisticated of these apparatuses was the Praxinoscope, whose moving belt of separately drawn slides created a simple narrative. But the process was laborious – even very basic stories required hundreds of separate frames – and it was the invention of the movie camera, which allowed the photographic recording of *pre-existing* movement, that spurred the development of cinema.

The histories of animation and live-action filming intertwine, but there is an essential difference in their operation. Since the live-action camera films a *moving* image, the movement is already inscribed within each film frame. To view a single frame is, as Roland Barthes has said, to observe 'the trace of the absence of time'. In mainstream live-action cinema the original movement is *re-created* through projection. The animation camera, in contrast, shoots a still image, so the illusion of movement is *created* through projection. Indeed, the principle of animation does not necessarily require a camera, and many interesting effects can be produced by, for example, drawing or scratching directly onto film.

The other commonly perceived difference results from live action's use of the photographic image, with all its cultural connotations of realism, and has led to animation, which usually uses a drawn or modelled image, being associated with 'fantasy'. The mistake in this is to equate the real with the photographable – and, by implication, to doubt the reality of what cannot be photographed. Recent studies have, on the contrary, concentrated on the psychic phantasies underlying much mainstream narrative realist film. And animation has frequently been used to narrate or re-create real-life events.

The American animated cartoon
Photographed animation was used by Edwin S. Porter in the titles for two films he made in 1905. The following year Porter included animated models

98

in his inventive fantasy *The Dreams of a Rarebit Fiend.* J. Stuart Blackton's more celebrated *Humorous Phases of Funny Faces* was released at about the same time, featuring letters, words and faces apparently scampering around the screen. Blackton's own increasing mastery of the technique was demonstrated in *The Haunted House* (1907). After this film had been shown in Paris, the film-maker Emile Cohl, recognising how the effects had been achieved, began to produce his own animations for Gaumont. Cohl later went to the United States to create the animated series *Snookums* (1913-14).

Early animation: Humorous Phases of Funny Faces, *made in 1906*

Animation's first characters came from the pen of the popular newspaper cartoonist and vaudeville performer Winsor McCay, who combined both skills in the presentation of his *Gertie the Dinosaur*, a partly live-action film of 1914 in which fellow newspaper cartoonists bet McCay that he cannot bring a dinosaur to life. An animated Gertie wins the bet for him. McCay used the film as part of his vaudeville act, in which he gave instructions to an animated Gertie projected onto a screen. Like his cartoon strips, McCay's films were beautifully drawn and astonishingly inventive. The use of overlapping editing to draw out the agony of the ship's sinking is one striking feature of his *The Sinking of the Lusitania* (1918), which aimed not only to document an event that had not been captured on film but also to make propaganda from it. But McCay's films were laborious and therefore expensive to produce, and, importantly, were dependent on his own outstanding drawing skills. It was left to others to develop the technical and economic means to allow animation to take its place in the now fully developed American film industry. Meanwhile individual film-makers in many parts of the world began to experiment with animation techniques, remaining independent of the mainstream trajectory which reached its climax in the Disney studio.

Gertie the Dinosaur

McCay's films were designed as one-offs, and it was John Randolph Bray who produced the first commercial series of cartoons, with *Colonel Heezaliar in Africa* (1913), a satire on Theodore Roosevelt's African safari. Unlike McCay, who usually redrew each frame as a whole, Bray broke frames down into components on different sheets, a method known as the slash technique. By keeping several components the same in any sequence, the process is consequently made far more efficient. The following year, the cartoonist Earl Hurd proposed using stationary backgrounds and drawing the moving characters on transparent sheets of celluloid. Hurd patented this technique, known as cel animation, and it has become the basis for all classic commercial animation.

The financial base, as well as much of the talent, for the early animation industry was provided by the newspaper industry. Newspaper magnates such as William Randolph Hearst found animated shorts a useful way of promoting their comic-strip characters. Hearst set up an animation studio in 1916 to produce a short cartoon every week, featuring characters such as The Katzenjammer Kids and Krazy Kat, to be shown in cinemas along with the Hearst newsreels. It was not until the 1920s that there appeared the first original animation character whose image and vitality added up to a

Felix the Cat in Felix Wins and Loses *(1925)*

From the Out of the Inkwell *series:* Koko Chops Suey *(1927) with Max Fleischer's pen*

Betty Boop

distinctive personality which became truly popular. Felix the Cat was owned and promoted by Pat Sullivan, and animated by Otto Messmer, and owed much to a close observation of Charlie Chaplin's screen tramp. Felix became the first star of animation, his image being exploited in one of the earliest merchandising and licensing operations, which included a subsequent newspaper strip. The campaign proved extremely lucrative, and it was only with the coming of sound that Felix's popularity was supplanted by an even more famous mouse.

Max and Dave Fleischer

In many ways, the Fleischers are a key link between the early years of commercial animation and the mature studio industry of the 1930s. Like so many of his contemporaries, the Austrian-born Max Fleischer was a graphic artist for newspapers and magazines until 1915 when, together with his brother Dave, he began to experiment with animation. One of his many inventions was the rotoscope, which projected live-action film frame by frame onto a drawing table so that live characters could be traced onto animation paper. The technique was used in the acrobatics of Koko the Clown in the *Out of the Inkwell* series. Each film began with a live-action Max, from whose pen Koko would appear. Dave Fleischer directed the films, and Koko's prankishness was the ideal vehicle for his talent for gags and surrealist invention, which together with technical invention was the studio's hallmark. In 1924 the Fleischers teamed up with Lee De Forest, a pioneer of film sound, to make the first sound animation, *Oh Mabel.* The American film industry was not yet prepared for the advent of sound, however, and the film was often shown in its silent version. After a successful run with a series of *Song Car-Tunes* featuring the original bouncing ball to encourage audiences to sing along, and a short-lived attempt to set up their own distribution company, the Fleischers began a long-term distribution arrangement with Paramount in 1927.

The continuing popularity of Fleischer cartoons into the sound era was ensured by Grim Natwick's creation, in 1930, of Betty Boop, initially a strange hybrid between woman and dog. Partly based on singer Helen Kane, Betty was a dizzy child-woman, simultaneously innocent and flirtatious; her large head, tiny body and wiggly hips were an animator's delight. Since Paramount also distributed the films of Mae West, they had on their hands two of the hottest female properties of the pre-Hays code cinema. Both Betty Boop and Mae West, however, had their disruptive powers curtailed by the strengthening of film censorship in 1934. Betty's skirt was lengthened below garter level.

Fleischer's other great heroine was the girlfriend of a character introduced into animation from his comic strip in 1933, Popeye the Sailor. Olive Oyl played a starring role in films such as *Olive for President* and *A Dream Walking* (1934), and with her streetwise Brooklyn accent she was a typical product of Fleischer's New York-based studio.

On the West Coast meanwhile the Disney style, with its barnyard fables, was proving popular. Pressure from Paramount to compete led to a softening of the Fleischer style in the feature film *Gulliver's Travels* (1939), made at the newly established Florida studio. But the film, like the Fleischers' second feature, *Mr Bug Goes to Town* (1941), could not match Disney's success. Now in serious debt, Max was forced to sell the studio to Paramount, with Dave staying on as creative director. The American film industry had now consolidated into a massive cartel. The creation of an animation studio which could compete financially and technically with the major live-action studios was the achievement of Walt Disney.

Walt Disney

Of all those who could be said to have shaped the way we understand our world, Disney must be one of the most influential. Generations of children have grown up watching Disney movies and TV shows, reading Disney books, playing with Disney toys. In the 1930s Disney enjoyed the admiration of fans as diverse as Eisenstein and Mussolini, and the distrust of Hitler, who had Mickey Mouse banned in Nazi Germany. In 1939 the critic Lewis Jacobs wrote of Mickey: 'His popularity out-ranks that of kings and dictators; he is the best known figure of the twentieth century.' And there is a story that Ray Bradbury once suggested to Disney that he should become a candidate for mayor of Los Angeles. 'Why should I run for mayor,' Disney replied, 'when I'm already king?'

Yet the man who is often thought of as the king of cartoons had himself given up animation by the time of his studio's first big success, *Steamboat Willie* (1928). His talents lay rather in entrepreneurship, showmanship, and a remarkable understanding and respect for popular taste. He began his career as a commercial artist in Kansas City after the First World War, breaking into animation with a series called *Laugh-o-Grams*. In 1923, with his brother Roy and fellow animator Ub Iwerks, he went to Hollywood, where his team produced a moderately successful series called *Alice in Cartoonland*, which combined a live-action Alice with drawn backgrounds. After animating Oswald Rabbit for Charles Mintz, the Disney studio introduced the new sound technology to a film featuring a character designed by Iwerks, Mickey Mouse. *Steamboat Willie* made lively use of music and effects synchronised to the naughty antics of Mickey, whose high-pitched voice was spoken by Disney himself.

Steamboat Willie: *Mickey Mouse's debut,* © *Walt Disney productions*

Heartened by the enormous public response, the studio started the *Silly Symphony* series, animated to music. *Skeleton Dance* (1929) was the first of these, a comic *danse macabre* and a brilliant orchestration of visual rhythm. In 1931 Disney joined United Artists, with very favourable terms for distributing his films, while a three-year contract signed in 1932 gave the studio exclusive animation rights to three-colour Technicolor, used for the first time in *Flowers and Trees* (1932).

The graphic films of the late 20s gave way in the next decade to cuddly naturalism and lavish production values. The 'barnyard humour' of the earlier films, objected to by the Hays Office, was supplanted by a sanitised view of nature, which even eliminated the udders from the cows in *The Old Mill* (1937). The films became vehicles for the atmospheric effects made possible by Technicolor, and by the efforts of the studio's technical department. Among other achievements Disney's craftsmen invented the multiplane camera, which separated the various layers of cel and background so that the animation camera could move about in apparently real space.

The Disney studio grew massively, and by the mid-1930s employed some 800 workers. Many new characters were created, including Donald Duck, Pluto and Goofy; and films like *Three Little Pigs* (1933), with its story of redemption through industriousness, chimed perfectly with the country's mood as it came to terms with Roosevelt's New Deal. To compete with the high profits of live-action films, Disney moved into feature production. The studio's first feature was *Snow White and the Seven Dwarfs*, begun in 1934 and released in 1938, soon after a profitable new distribution deal with RKO. More features were to follow, including *Pinocchio* (1940), *Dumbo* (1941) and *Bambi* (1942).

Production had by this time been rationalised into a factory system. Unlike earlier studios such as the one run by John Randolph Bray, where each animator had total responsibility for a whole sequence, making cartoons became divided into major functions, with a management led by Disney himself communicating with the workforce through an avalanche of pink slips. The new story department initiated a major development with the introduction of the storyboard, on which the entire narrative could be pre-planned. Characters were designed by another department, and turned out on model sheets for animators to work from, so that the appearance, movements and personalities of the characters would remain consistent. They had to be drawn by many people, so were reducible to standard proportions, circles and curves. The labour of animating itself was also divided. The most skilled animators concentrated on the key animation drawings. Others then supplied the 'in-between' drawings, which were 'cleaned up' by someone else, while yet another department traced and painted these onto cel. A separate department produced the backgrounds, another mixed the paints, and so on. The Disney division of labour remains the standard model for the commercial production of animation throughout the world, one of its attractions being that the efforts of a great many people can be convincingly subsumed under the authorial signature of a single 'artist', often the person who owns the studio. Having created an animation

Flowers and Trees, *in three-colour Technicolor,* © *Walt Disney productions*

Donald Duck tripled in Donald's Better Self (1938), © *Walt Disney productions*

factory, Disney had also produced a body of workers large enough to organise itself. During the unionisation of Hollywood, Disney resisted the overtures of the Screen Cartoonists Guild, and set up his own in-house union. A struggle for control ensued, which erupted into a strike in 1941, and eventually led to a number of Disney's best animators leaving the studio.

This was one of several factors which led to a growing disenchantment with Disney films among both critics and audiences. Disney's venture into middlebrow culture with the musical feature *Fantasia* (1940) had been less than successful. And his populism in the 1930s, which had endeared him to left and right alike, veered towards a nationalistic conservatism once the United States entered the Second World War. Offering the services of his studio to the war effort, Disney produced a number of propaganda films. After the war it proved increasingly difficult to repeat the success of films like *Snow White*, and the studio began to diversify into live-action productions like *Treasure Island* (1950), nature documentaries, merchandising, much work for television after 1954, and the Disneyland theme parks.

Fantasia, © *Walt Disney productions*

Tex Avery

The success of the Disney studio in the 1930s inspired companies like Warner Bros and MGM to set up their own animation studios. Disney had set a high standard and had the reputation for training the best animators, but the growing mawkishness of his films invited burlesque from a profession noted for its iconoclasm. No one was better at this than Fred ('Tex') Avery.

Avery made his name at Warners, where he was an animation director from 1936 to 1942. Warners had ventured into animation in 1930, releasing the *Looney Tunes* and *Merrie Melodies* series, made by Hugh Harman and Rudolph Ising and produced by Leon Schlesinger. In 1934 Warners set up, under Schlesinger, their own animation operation, known as 'Termite Terrace'. Many of Hollywood's finest animation talents were to work at Termite Terrace over the years. Frank Tashlin, later to be a live-action comedy director, made a major contribution to the bizarre, often almost abstract style which began to distinguish the Warners product, directing many of the Porky Pig series. Chuck Jones, who directed his first cartoon in 1937 and was with Warners until the animation unit closed in 1962, worked on several series, including those featuring Daffy Duck and Bugs Bunny. Perhaps his most enduring creation is the *Road Runner* series with its wordless conflict between the Road Runner and Wile E. Coyote, often expressed in violent action. Other members of the team included Bob

Chuck Jones' Daffy Duck

Clampett, Friz Freleng, musical director Carl Stalling, and Mel Blanc, who provided many of the voices.

At the centre was Tex Avery, whose bizarre, outrageous, dazzlingly orchestrated visual world defies adequate verbal description. Avery parodied Warners' gangster movies in *Thugs with Dirty Mugs* (1939) and travelogues and newsreels in *Believe It Or Else* (1939). He directed the first Bugs Bunny cartoon, *A Wild Hare* (1940), and created Porky Pig and Daffy Duck. In 1942 he left Warners for the MGM unit, where Joseph Barbera and William Hanna, creators of the hugely popular Tom and Jerry series, were already working. Avery did some of his best work at MGM, creating characters such as the lunatic Screwball Squirrel to subvert the tradition of Disney cuteness. Another characteristic Avery spoof was *Red Hot Riding Hood* (1943), which begins in saccharine sweetness before the wolf, Red Riding Hood and Granny demand from the animator a more sensational version of the tale. Red Riding Hood duly reappears as a nightclub stripper and the libidinous wolf sports a tuxedo. The overtly sexual formula proved so popular with American troops that it was repeated in several films.

Subverting Disney: Tex Avery's Little Rural Riding Hood (1949)

Alternative modes

Although the American animated cartoon dominated the international market for thirty years, there were distinguished animators in many countries during this period. These film-makers worked with a range of techniques, some of them mainstream – such as the cut-out or cel techniques used in Britain by the Anson Dyer studio and Anthony Gross and Hector Hoppin – and others more original, like the 'pinscreen' technique invented in France by Alexandre Alexeieff and Claire Parker and used to notable effect in their interpretation of Mussorgsky's orchestral suite *Night on a Bare Mountain* (1933).

Lotte Reiniger's The Adventures of Prince Achmed

In Germany, ten years before *Snow White*, Lotte Reiniger produced a magical animated feature film, *The Adventures of Prince Achmed* (1926), using backlit paper silhouettes. Reiniger had developed her art in the theatre, where she worked briefly with Max Reinhardt, whose theatrical lighting had also influenced German Expressionist cinema. Experimental film-makers Walter Ruttmann and Bertold Bartosch collaborated on the backgrounds of this tale of the Arabian Nights.

In the 1930s Reiniger worked for some time with the British GPO film unit under John Grierson, who actively encouraged government sponsorship of experimental animation. Also at the GPO unit was the New Zealand artist Len Lye, who made promotional films animated to music. Lye's *Colour Box* (1936), with a stencilled message promoting the parcel post, is painted directly onto film without the use of a camera. *Rainbow Dance* (1936) pioneered the use of an optical printer to produce multiple colour images of the same – originally live – action. And *Trade Tattoo* (1937) cuts to music images from the unit's documentary films, overpainted and stencilled. Another GPO film unit experimental animator was the Scot Norman McLaren, who while still at art school had made the powerful anti-war film *Hell UnLtd.* (1936) in collaboration with Helen Biggar. In one of McLaren's later films, *Love on the Wing* (1939), a lock and key, a spoon and a fork and other metaphors for love mesh against a background of clouds. The Postmaster General evidently found the film too 'Freudian', and it has the distinction of being the only GPO unit film to be banned.

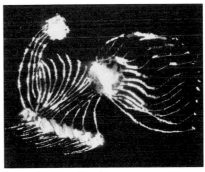

Animation without a camera: Norman McLaren's Begone Dull Care *(1949)*

When Grierson was invited to Canada to establish that country's National Film Board, he asked McLaren – who had meanwhile made several films in the United States using the technique of drawing directly onto celluloid – to set up the Board's animation unit. Under McLaren, the NFBC was to develop as a major world centre for non-commercial animation. McLaren also continued his own work, which included many experiments with camera-less animation, synthetic sound (drawn directly onto the sound-track), and a technique known as pixillation which involved the filming of live actors with an animation camera and was used to great effect in the 1952 film *Neighbours*. The NFBC has continued to provide funding for a number of outstanding animators, one of the most interesting being the American-born Caroline Leaf, whose *The Street* (1976) is painted on glass directly under the camera.

Grierson's original model for the production of animation to challenge dominant forms and engage with issues of cultural identity has continued to be influential in the Developing World. In India, for instance, government-sponsored animation units were established in the late 1950s in Bombay and at the National Institute of Design at Ahmedabad, where film-makers like Nina Sabnani are treating contemporary political issues as well as the problem of representation in films like *Happy Wedding,* which attacks the illegal dowry system.

Art and experiment

Histories of the cinema have often treated animation as a marginal practice, perhaps because the history of animation is full of individual film-makers who are not easily categorised. One such is the Russian Ladislav (or Wlady-slaw) Starewicz, who experimented with stop-motion techniques as early as 1911. A scientist by training, he discovered that models of insects and other small animals were easier to film than live ones, and he made a number of bizarre fables and parodies featuring these tiny models. *The Cameraman's Revenge* (1912), for instance, is the tale of two beetles who spy on each other's romantic encounters, one of them employing a film cameraman to record the evidence. Starewicz emigrated to France after the Revolution, where he continued to make moral tales, including an ambitious puppet film, *Le*

Puppet animation: Starewicz's Le Roman de Renard

Roman de Renard (1938), some sequences of which feature as many as seventy-five puppets in simultaneous motion.

Puppet animation has been a continuing European tradition, particularly

Animal Farm

in Eastern Europe. Hungarian-born George Pal worked in Germany in the early 1930s, and then in several European countries. His puppet commercials were developed into the 'Puppetoon' series when he emigrated to the United States, where he went on to become producer and special effects designer on feature films like *Destination Moon* (1950) and *The War of the Worlds* (1953). Pal's apprentice, John Halas, left Hungary for Britain, where in 1940 he set up his own animation company with his wife Joy Batchelor. Halas and Batchelor developed into one of the most successful British animation studios, producing many cartoons for the cinema and for television and in 1954 the first British animated feature, a version of Orwell's *Animal Farm*.

Another central figure in European animation is Jiri Trnka, a former puppeteer who in 1945 set up an animation unit at the Prague film studios. Trnka's puppet films, such as *The Emperor's Nightingale* (1948), *The Good Soldier Schweik* (1954) and the dark political allegory *The Hand* (1965), have earned him an international reputation. The surrealist flavour of some of Trnka's best work is more sharply echoed in the work of Jan Lenica and

Jan Lenica's Labyrinth

Walerian Borowczyk in Poland. Lenica and Borowczyk collaborated on films such as *Dom* (1958) and *Solitude* (1961) before going their separate ways. Lenica's bold graphic style, often using collage, was developed in films like *Labyrinth* (1962) and *Rhinoceros* (1963). Borowczyk's style is even bleaker. *The Theatre of Mr and Mrs Kabal*, made in France in 1967, portrays a disturbingly violent relationship, fuelled by mutual hatred and set in a dark, despairing world. The legacy of surrealism is also evident in the more recent films of the Czech Jan Svankmayer, whose bizarre work reveals influences ranging from Kafka to the 16th-century painter Archimboldo. The latter's paintings of faces composed of fruit and vegetables are the source for the aggressive animated confrontations in Svankmayer's *Dimensions of Dialogue* (1982). Svankmayer is also fascinated by the world of Lewis Carroll, and has recently made the feature *Alice* (1987).

Working in a different tradition were a group of Yugoslav animators who emerged in the 1950s and came to be known as the 'Zagreb school'. Film-makers like Zlatko Grgic, Dusan Vukotic and Vatroslav Mimica, reacting against Stalinism and the Cold War, emphasised the struggle of the individual against conformity and the concept of the universal man and of animation as a universal language.

The Zagreb animators adopted the low-budget, 'limited animation' tech-

106

nique pioneered in the early 1940s by a group of Disney employees who left Disney after the 1941 strike and set up the United Productions of America (UPA) studio. Among those involved were John Hubley, who helped create the Mr Magoo character first seen in *Ragtime Bear* (1949); Robert Cannon (the Gerald McBoing McBoing films); Stephen Bosustow, who made *Hell-Bent for Election* to support Roosevelt's 1944 Presidential campaign; and Ernest Pintoff, who was subsequently to set up his own studio. UPA looked for a more contemporary style in their work. Their drawing was freer, less straightforwardly representational than the Disney style, with the emphasis on background design, camera movement and the use of colour and line to create space and atmosphere. Their influence was considerable, and their sophisticated, often whimsical style was widely adopted.

The Zagreb style: Mimica's The Egg (1959)

It is not, of course, simply because it uses drawing and painting that animation has often been associated with the visual arts. This association has been most evident in the area of the avant-garde, where animation has been freely mixed with live-action techniques (see Chapter 8). Many experimental animators have also been painters and sculptors. Musical composition too has been an important source of inspiration — from the experiments of Viking Eggeling, Hans Richter, Walter Ruttmann and Oskar Fischinger in Germany in the 1920s, to the modern music videos of Zbigniew Rybczynski or Annabel Jankel and Rocky Morton.

Oskar Fischinger's work offers an interesting example of the crossover between art and popular culture. Fischinger's abstract silent films of the 1920s, employing techniques as diverse as charcoal drawing, cartoon and clay figures, and a specially designed wax-slicing machine, were often synchronised to phonograph records. He helped develop a new colour process in the advertising film *Circles* (1933), and his success in attracting such commercial commissions indicates how popular his films were with German audiences. Fischinger went to Hollywood in 1936, where he made *Allegretto* to a jazz theme, but his designs for the Bach 'Toccata and Fugue' sequence in Disney's *Fantasia* were considered too abstract. He subsequently returned to his own projects, his work becoming an important influence on avant-garde animators like Mary Ellen Bute and Norman McLaren.

Animation and television

In the early days of American television, animation was thought to be too expensive to produce especially for the new medium. Around 1957 several sales deals were struck with the major studios, and Popeye, Bugs Bunny and the rest became staple elements in the television schedules, just as several major animation studios, including the one at MGM, closed down. Filmmakers like William Hanna and Joseph Barbera turned to television, where they made the *Huckleberry Hound* series for Columbia's television subsidiary Screen Gems, and soon afterwards introduced the character of Yogi Bear. Primetime television was still closed to animation, however, until the ratings success of Hanna and Barbera's *The Flintstones* (1960-66) proved that there

Pop art: Yellow Submarine

was an adult audience for television animation. But although the idea of a cartoon sitcom in a stone-age setting was not without charm, the fast production schedule meant that the animation was flat and unsubtle.

Restrictive budgets were occasionally a stimulus to imaginative American television animation, but increasing costs have generally entailed a decline in standards, and the role of merchandising has become determinant. Toys, games and clothes associated with series like *My Little Pony* and *Masters of the Universe* have generated enormous revenue. Nowadays the toys are often designed first, and the series made to promote them.

In Britain, animation enjoys a lucrative outlet in television commercials. John Halas and Joy Batchelor contributed three of the first-night advertisements when commercial television began in 1955, and they have continued to work successfully in the field. Another animator with a first-night credit was Bob Godfrey, who for many years has combined work on T V commercials with films like his crude satire on suburban sex, *Kama Sutra Rides Again* (1971), and *Great!* (1975), an inventive biography of the Victorian engineer Isambard Kingdom Brunel which won an Oscar. The Canadian George Dunning also made some notable T V commercials, as well as films like *The Apple* and *The Flying Man* (both 1962) which were characterised by bold line, minimal backgrounds and strong but simple character design. In 1968 he had a commercial success with the feature film *Yellow Submarine,* which intriguingly related the colourful graphic styles of the period to the music of the Beatles.

The Quay Brothers' Street of Crocodiles

The company founded by Dunning, TV Cartoons, has been responsible for some of the most striking of British animation. Their version of Raymond Briggs' fantasy *The Snowman* (1982) won an Oscar, and the more sombre *When the Wind Blows* (1987), directed by Jimmy Murakami from another Briggs story, is one of the few animated features to engage with a serious contemporary issue – in this case, nuclear war. Both these films were co-produced by Channel 4 Television, which has provided financial support for a number of independent animators. Among them are the Quay Brothers, with their disturbing, fantastical puppet films like *The Cabinet of Jan Svankmajer* (1984) and *Street of Crocodiles* (1986). The latter film was co-produced by the British Film Institute, which also produced some of the films by Vera Neubauer, such as *Animation for Live Action* (1978). Neubauer's playfully inventive feminist films are one example of a growing political awareness among independent animators, ranging from the Leeds Animation Workshop, a feminist collective making agit-prop cartoons, to the political cartoonist Steve Bell, who has made several characteristically scabrous films for Channel 4.

Television has also fostered some adventurous animation for children, notably in the films made by the Thames Television subsidiary Cosgrove Hall, with series like *Dangermouse* (1980) and longer films such as *The Wind in the Willows* (1983). But it is the world of T V commercials which is increasingly the mainstay of many British animators. The Richard Williams

108

studio, for instance, has produced numerous commercials, including the Cresta Bear, Tic Tac, the 'fizzical' Corona bubbles and the rural idylls created for Ben Truman beer. Williams, a Canadian who has worked in Britain for many years, is also known for his credit sequences for films (notably the Pink Panther features and the 1968 *Charge of the Light Brigade*) and for occasional films of his own, like his version of Dickens' *A Christmas Carol* (1972) with its exquisite drawings in the style of 19th-century engravings. He has been working for many years on an ambitious animated feature based on a tale from 'A Thousand and One Nights'; and collaborated with Steven Spielberg and director Robert Zemeckis on *Who Framed Roger Rabbit?* (1988), an elaborate combination of animation and live action.

The Disney tradition survives, of course, and the studio itself has continued to re-release its classics, and to produce new features like *The Jungle Book* (1967) and the hugely expensive and hugely unsuccessful *The Black Cauldron* (1985). But the new generation of film-makers moves freely between techniques and technologies, ideas and ideologies. The new technologies offer almost unlimited visual possibilities. Animation is only just beginning to realise its full potential.

Richard Williams whimsy: Guinness at the Albert Hall (1966)

Further reading

Joe Adamson, *Tex Avery: King of Cartoons,* New York: Library, 1975.

Film Comment, January-February 1975. (This issue is devoted to studio animation in the United States and contains articles on, among others, the Fleischers and Walt Disney.)

Leonard Maltin, *Of Mice and Magic,* New York: McGraw-Hill, 1980.

Jayne Pilling (ed.), *That's Not All Folks!,* London: British Film Institute, 1984.

Alexander Sesonske, 'The Origins of Animation', *Sight & Sound,* Summer 1980.

Richard Schickel, *The Disney Version: The Life, Times, Art and Commerce of Walt Disney,* New York: Simon & Schuster, 1976.

Ralph Stephenson, *Animation in the Cinema,* Cranbury, New Jersey: A.S. Barnes, 1966.

Frank Thomas and Ollie Johnson, *Disney Animation: The Illusion of life,* New York: Abbeyville, 1982.

8
The Avant-garde Cinema

Throughout the history of the moving image, the commercial mainstream has been complemented by the separate, often ignored, but highly significant development of an 'avant-garde'. Cataloguing definitive limits for this tradition, which is also variously described as 'experimental', 'underground' and 'independent', is problematic. There are many avant-gardes and many independent cinemas, and their differences and contradictions are as significant as their similarities.

Avant-garde cinemas have often been explicitly oppositional to the commercial structures of production, distribution and exhibition, rejecting the forms, conventions and narrative principles of commercial films. Moreover, avant-garde films are usually seen as the creative achievements of particular *individuals,* who set themselves apart from studio-based production and identify themselves as artists. In many of the films there is also a close relationship with other arts, and especially with painting, music and dance. As the film-maker Stephen Dwoskin has suggested, 'They are personal works, individually motivated, like any other creative activity. The painters and poets have become film-makers.'

Until the 1970s experimental or avant-garde film-making largely spurned the mainstream structures, and its practitioners often argued that the tradition of the film-maker as artist was the only one of interest. But this view failed to recognise the connections and parallels between the different kinds of cinema. During the 1920s, for example, many central figures in the European avant-garde, including Dziga Vertov and Eisenstein in Russia, and Jean Epstein and Marcel L'Herbier in France, also contributed significantly to the 'commercial' cinemas of their time. Today, too, a film-maker like the American Jordan Belson can work consistently within Hollywood (creating special effects sequences) at the same time as pursuing his creative activities as an individual.

Painting and the cinema
The idea of a film avant-garde took shape when painters started to show an intense interest in the cinema from around 1910. They were attracted both

110

by its dynamism – here, finally, was an art of *moving* pictures – and by its potential for creating worlds of fantasy. Picasso, for instance, considered working with film in about 1912. Even earlier, Kandinsky had considered filming his collaboration with Arnold Schoenberg on the opera *Die glückliche Hand.*

The idea of bringing together painting and the cinema, to achieve a new synthesis to embody the spirit of modernist culture, was first explored in practical terms by the Futurists in Italy and Russia. An iconoclastic celebration of the modern age, Futurism rejected the styles and subjects of the past and embraced the new century's forms of speed, violence and power. Modern life, to the doctrine's adherents, was a thrilling aesthetic event, and war was its ultimate expression. For the acknowledged leader of the movement, Filippo Marinetti, the cinema held many exciting possibilities. But the achievements of the Italian Futurists as film-makers were limited, and the loss of most Futurist-inspired films, including their abstract hand-painted colour work, means that critical prominence has been accorded to the later avant-garde work from Germany and France. Marinetti, however, had no doubts about the significance of this work: 'The abstract film is an Italian invention,' he declared in 1926.

Before this, however, a group of Russian Futurist painters had made what they claimed as the first Futurist film, a parody of the horror genre called *Drama in the Futurists' Cabaret 13.* Also prominent among the Futurists was the charismatic young poet Vladimir Mayakovsky, who wrote a series of enthusiastic articles about the cinema in 1913. After the Revolution, Mayakovsky scripted and acted in three short films, but the directors with whom he collaborated were unsympathetic to Futurism, and he felt that his scenarios were 'mutilated'.

Europe in the 1920s

Soon after this, two painters working together in Berlin, Hans Richter and Viking Eggeling, also began to experiment with the graphic potential of film. Although both had earlier been associated with the anarchic Dada movement, from around 1917 they had been exploring how simple abstract shapes could be juxtaposed on canvas to create visual harmonies and rhythms which were directly analogous to music. By 1919 they were using long scrolls of paper to develop the patterns in continuous sequences, and film was an obvious next stage. With support from Ufa's animation studio, and after battling with numerous technical problems, Richter finished *Rhythm 21* (1921), which lasted for about one minute and animated a complex interplay of black, grey and white rectangular forms. He developed the technique in three further short films, but Eggeling wanted to achieve something closer to a true animation of the scroll drawings, an ambition he achieved in part with *Diagonal Symphony* (1924), his only finished film, in which flowing lines and curves are modulated in a complex tempo on the flat screen surface.

Richter and Eggeling's combination of painting and film in a form of

Viking Eggeling's Diagonal Symphony

'visual music' was the first of many such experiments. In Munich, the painter and violinist Walter Ruttmann was also making short abstract films with similar intentions. Later he was invited to develop his sense of 'optical music'

Composite of images from Berlin, Symphony of a Great City

in the editing of a film devised by the writer of *Dr Caligari*, Carl Mayer, and shot by the cameraman Karl Freund – *Berlin, Symphony of a Great City* (1927). Working with images from the life of the city, Ruttmann shaped them by largely abstract principles of pattern and movement (using a dawn-to-dusk structure), and created a film which was both popular and influential.

During and after the war in France there was also enormous interest in the cinema among artists and intellectuals. The important critical writing of Louis Delluc was one reflection of this; others were the establishment of a network of cine-clubs, and the exceptionally innovative work in the commercial cinema by directors like Abel Gance, Jean Epstein and Marcel L'Herbier. There were also numerous points of contact between these industry figures and the artistic milieu. The poet Blaise Cendrars worked on Gance's *La Roue* (1922), while René Clair could direct both an experimental film like *Entr'acte* (1924) and more conventional crowd-pleasing comedies.

Entr'acte was commissioned for the interval of a ballet designed by the painter Francis Picabia. Picabia himself wrote the script, Eric Satie composed the music, and the film features other significant figures of the time including Man Ray, Marcel Duchamp and Georges Auric. Initially a sequence of seemingly unconnected shots of fairgrounds, Paris boulevards in slow motion and a bearded ballerina, the film eventually resolves itself in a macabre chase after a runaway hearse. In the same year the painter Fernand Léger made *Ballet mécanique,* which used similarly carnivalesque images as well as hard-edged geometrical cut-outs in a dazzling extension of the possibilities of abstract cinema. The movements of humans and machines are juxtaposed in a film which is clearly a dynamic expression of many of the ideas in Léger's canvases. Marcel Duchamp was similarly attracted by film. For his *Anemic Cinema* (1926) he made a series of motorised discs decorated by spiral patterns. The discs, which create complex illusions of receding and advancing space, are interspersed by spiral-printed Dadaist punning sentences.

Although these films by Clair, Léger and Duchamp are close to the anarchic spirit of Dada, they are often also considered as contributions to the Surrealist cinema, along with films by Man Ray, Germaine Dulac and Luis

112

Buñuel. For the founder of the movement, André Breton, in Surrealism 'an attempt is made to express, either verbally, in writing or in any other matter, the true functioning of thought, in the absence of all control by reason, excluding any aesthetic or moral preoccupation'. Surrealism was thus concerned with expressing the hidden depths of the unconscious. Free association was an essential element, and great significance was attached both to dreams and to the play of unfettered desire.

In contrast to Delluc, Gance and their supporters, the Surrealists rejected any notion of a self-consciously 'artistic' cinema, and celebrated instead popular American movies and the serials of Feuill- ade. They would visit cinemas at random hoping to catch some chance expression of the bizarre. Chance was also important to films like *La Retour à la raison* (1923) and *Emak Bakia* (1927), both by Man Ray, which juxtaposed obliquely related images to achieve both poetic and disorienting effects. Direct 'rayogramming' on the filmstrip (with nails, pins, salt and pepper) in *Le Retour à la raison* expands into the stippled glass effect and dreamlike story of frustrated love in *Etoile de mer* (1926). Characteristically, Man Ray attacks conventional camera-lens perception to force film into unfamiliar – hence revelatory – image-making.

Man Ray's Les Mystères du Château de Dés

Overt opposition to narrative logic was taken to an extreme in *Un Chien andalou* (1928), made as a collaboration between Luis Buñuel, who had worked as Jean Epstein's assistant, and the painter Salvador Dali. The famous opening images of a cloud passing across the moon and a woman's eye being slit by a razor retain their power to shock, but the rest of the film – with its fragmented action and erotic tension – is also still mysteriously disturbing. Two years later Buñuel made the savagely anti-clerical satire *L'Age d'or* (1930), mocking bourgeois social conventions and celebrating the surrealist notion of 'l'amour fou'. Germaine Dulac's *La Coquille et le Clergyman* (1927), scripted by the poet Antonin Artaud, also has an erotic theme, this time the Oedipal triangle. All three films expose dark and threatening elements of the unconscious. Using free association of images, they also challenge received notions of plot and narrative structure.

Un Chien andalou

By the end of the decade Surrealism was losing its initial impetus, in part because of divisive political disputes. The private patronage on which many of the films depended became harder to find (their key patron, the Vicomte de Noailles, switched his allegiance to the Surrealists' enemy, the 'arch-aesthete' Jean Cocteau, whose allegorical work was to influence a later generation of American underground film-makers). By now there was throughout Europe a well-established film avant-garde. A European conference in Switzerland in 1929 was attended by many of the leading film artists. A year later the conference reconvened in Belgium. But political

113

One of the dream sequences from Jean Vigo's Zéro de Conduite *(1933). Vigo made only four films, including two short documentaries, but they are all marked by an entirely individual blend of surrealism and fantasy. His last film before his early death was* L'Atalante *(1934), in which Vigo transformed what might have been a conventional story about a newly married couple on a canal barge into a bizarre, dreamlike fantasy.*

issues were now being recognised as increasingly urgent. To many participants abstract films and self-conscious experiment no longer seemed as important as countering the growing threat of fascism.

The influence of this avant-garde work was nevertheless both significant and widespread. For Buñuel, it lasted throughout his long career as a director. Within the French film industry, it was important in the formation of Jean Cocteau, and exercised a more indirect effect on directors like Jean Renoir and Marcel Carné. For the British cinema, it was an important element in the ideas of the documentary movement of the 1930s. And both the films themselves, and their spirit, were to be taken to America by practitioners such as Hans Richter and Man Ray. In the post-war years American painting was to eclipse European art and achieve an international dominance. In a rather more modest way the avant-garde cinema was to experience a comparable shift.

American avant-garde

Perhaps the earliest film made in the United States self-consciously outside the commercial framework is *Manhatta* (1921), a rather static visualisation of a Walt Whitman poem, shot by Charles Sheeler and the photographer Paul Strand. Four years later Robert Flaherty directed *24 Dollar Island*, which also hymned the beauties of the New York skyline. Another noteworthy independent film is *The Life and Death of 9413 — A Hollywood Extra* (1927), a satire on the industry made by Slavko Vorkapich and Robert Florey, who were both Hollywood writers. And the true spirit of Surrealism was caught by *Rose Hobart* (also known as *Tristes Tropiques*, 1939), made by the artist Joseph Cornell. For this Cornell took the 1931 Columbia movie *East of*

Maya Deren in her own Meshes of the Afternoon

Borneo, radically re-cut it to around fifteen minutes in length, tinted it blue and replaced the soundtrack with Latin American dance music. Crammed with strange juxtapositions and unexplained, apparently obsessive actions, *Rose Hobart* is a delightful and disturbing 'found film'. But although there were several other examples of independent work, there was nothing in America which could be identified as an avant-garde group or movement until after the war.

Indeed, the history of the American avant-garde is usually dated from 1943, when Maya Deren and Alexander Hammid made *Meshes of the Afternoon*. This short subjective drama has the qualities of a dream, in which a young woman, played by Deren, is seen to repeat, with variations, a sequence of actions leading perhaps to a death, perhaps to a suicide. The critic P. Adams Sitney has argued that *Meshes of the Afternoon* defined the characteristics of the 'trance' film, which was to dominate the next decade of American experimental film-making. Deren herself elaborated on the form in *At Land* (1944), before developing a concentrated exploration of dance and ritual in *A Study in Choreography for Camera* (1945),

114

Ritual in Transfigured Time (1946) and *Meditation on Violence* (1948). Later to become an important theorist of the avant-garde and influential in establishing exhibition and distribution possibilities, Deren was at first an isolated figure. But as the war came to an end broader cultural possibilities began to open up for the American avant-garde. A number of key European figures, like Richter and Duchamp, were now in the United States (Duchamp was one of the several artists who collaborated on Richter's *Dreams That Money Can Buy*, 1946). The Museum of Modern Art was circulating the established experimental classics of the 1920s; and the new developments in American painting, led by Jackson Pollock, Willem De Kooning and others, were to encourage, however indirectly, a recognition of the plastic possibilities of film. Moreover, the demands of war photography had made 16mm film equipment far more widely available, and local television stations were to increase the number of trained film-makers working outside Hollywood.

Marcel Duchamp and his spiral discs in Dreams That Money Can Buy

Until the late 1960s the development of the American avant-garde was intimately connected with the growth of exhibition and distribution frameworks, and with the creation of new critical contexts and languages. In the early 1960s, new groups dedicated both to production and exhibition were set up, including the New York Film-makers Co-operative. Among the film-makers who extended the subjective impetus of Deren's cinema were Curtis Harrington, Sidney Peterson and James Broughton, and one of the avant-garde's most mysterious and controversial figures, Kenneth Anger. A child of Hollywood (he appeared in Max Reinhardt's 1936 *A Midsummer Night's Dream*) and subsequently a scabrous chronicler of Hollywood's dream factory, Anger began to make films at the age of eleven. His four essential creations are *Fireworks* (1947), *Eaux d'Artifice* (1953), *Inauguration of the Pleasure Dome* (1954) and *Scorpio Rising* (1962-3), films of magic and myth, and of Hollywood and homosexual fantasy.

Another key figure in the American avant-garde is Stan Brakhage. With *Anticipation of the Night* (1958), Brakhage began to explore the possibilities of a highly subjective cinema, exposing the film-maker as the first-person protagonist and endeavouring to replicate directly the intensity and the complexities of seeing. One major film in this form is *Dog Star Man* (later incorporated into the five-hour *The Art of Vision*, 1961-5), which uses a number of devices, from scratched film to optical distortions, to convey the totality of visual experience. Brakhage's films are often explicitly autobiographical, an intimate (for some, too intimate) examination of himself, his family and his friends.

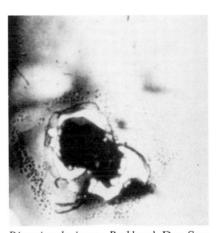

Distorting the image: Brakhage's Dog Star Man

Brakhage's films can be seen as both the culmination of the trance form and the key breakthrough into new areas. But alongside this work, and for the most part on the West coast, a distinct tradition had also been reaching maturity in the 1950s: that of graphic cinema. This American work can be seen as continuing the explorations of the European graphic cinema of the 1920s, and the work of animators like Oskar Fischinger and Len Lye. Like Lye, Harry Smith in the early 1940s experimented with the possibilities of

115

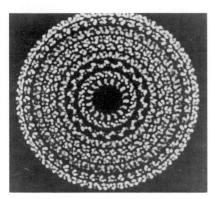

James Whitney's Lapis

painting directly onto film. John and James Whitney began to create films on the pattern of Fischinger's abstract animations, first in their jointly produced *Variations* series (1941-3), and then separately. John Whitney worked on a number of commercial projects (including, with Saul Bass, the credit sequence for Hitchcock's *Vertigo*) before investigating the potential of computer graphics. James Whitney concentrated on short, mystical graphic animations, including *Yantra* (1950-7) and *Lapis* (1963-6). Similar concerns can be seen in the work of Jordan Belson. Initially making films from painted scrolls, in 1957 Belson began to organise the influential series of Vortex Concerts at the Morrison Planetarium in San Francisco. These early examples of 'expanded cinema' used films, slides and various light sources, accompanied by electronic music, to create a complete sensory environment for the spectator.

The rise of independent cinema

By the late 1950s in America strong avant-garde traditions were established on many cultural fronts. Abstract Expressionism was soon to be complemented by the paintings of Robert Rauschenberg and Jasper Johns, the Beat generation was creating a new literature, John Cage and Merce Cunningham were making radical breakthroughs in music and dance, and The Living Theatre and La Mama were challenging theatrical conventions. In film there was a developing awareness of new possibilities for an independent cinema, seen as distinct from the experimental and avant-garde work of Brakhage and others. As with the 'new wave' in France, some American film-makers looked towards new forms of narrative, and to working on a scale unavailable to the individual artist. John Cassavetes made *Shadows* (1959), about alienated youth in Manhattan, whose grainy photography and improvised acting made it look very different from contemporary commercial cinema. *Pull My Daisy* (1959), by Robert Frank and Alfred Leslie, is a disjointed documentary about the Beat generation, with a soundtrack by Jack Kerouac. A central concern, shared by film-makers like Shirley Clarke, Lionel Rogosin, Ron Rice and Adolphas and Jonas Mekas and paralleled in the 'direct cinema' documentaries of Richard Leacock and others, was to capture a raw, spontaneous sense of reality.

In the early 1960s, this 'new wave' was one strand of an immensely varied independent film culture in America. Another distinct, although occasionally overlapping, group of work was what the critic and film-maker Jonas Mekas labelled 'Baudelarian cinema' and others have called 'New York Dada'. One central film was Ken Jacobs' bizarre meditation on myth, suicide and sexuality, *Blonde Cobra* (1963), constructed from footage originally shot by Bob Fleischner of both documentary scenes and fantasies enacted by the film-maker Jack Smith. Smith's own *Flaming Creatures* (1962) is a melancholy, bitter film that pays oblique homage to Hollywood in its central orgiastic fantasy and its 'exotic' stars, although its serious intent was largely obscured by a trial for obscenity. A third, related work, Gregory Marko-

116

poulos' *Twice a Man* (1963), more seriously engages with mythical arche-
types, re-presenting the classical story of Hippolytus in a fragmented,
elliptical narrative set in contemporary New York.

Much of this work was first celebrated by Jonas Mekas, whose writings
and organisation of the Film-makers Co-operative were significant contributions to the new cinema. Mekas is also a film-maker, and probably the
most distinguished exponent of the film diary. In *Diaries, Notes and Sketches*
(1964-9), *Reminiscences of a Journey to Lithuania* (1971) and *He Stands in the
Desert of his Life Counting the Years* (1985), Mekas offers a rough, improvisa-
tory, yet compelling personal chronicle.

Another avenue of enquiry was opened by Bruce Connor, who began to
make complex, witty collages of found footage as a development of his work
as a sculptor. The first of these, *A Movie* (1958), draws together disparate
fictional and documentary material to expose both the humour and the
violence of cinema. *Report* (1965) is even more pointed, using the technique
to look at media response to the assassination of President Kennedy. His
much later film *Mongoloid* (1978), cut to a song by Devo, reveals a striking
link to the British video clips of the 1980s and to the cut-up technique known
as 'scratch'.

Further connections with the visual arts are
apparent in the film work of Andy Warhol. Already
established as a painter, Warhol began to work with
film in 1963 when he made *Sleep*, a perhaps inten-
tional reversal and parody of the trance tradition,
consisting of six hours, and just half a dozen shots,
of a man asleep (technical problems cut it short of
the planned eight-hour length). Other unblinking
examinations of the image followed, each of which
repudiated the myths associated with the individual film-maker as artist. Gradually, however,
increasing formal sophistication, characters and
narrative appeared, and *The Chelsea Girls* (1966) is
a two-screen distillation of a New York sub-
culture, which combines a diaristic impulse with
many of the ideas which were to be associated with
structural film.

Andy Warhol in The Chelsea Girls

Structural film in Europe

In Europe, once the strong avant-garde tradition of the 1920s had been
dissipated, there was only sporadic experimental work until the mid-1960s.
One of the largely isolated figures working in Paris in the 1950s was Robert
Breer, who had trained as a painter, and who extended his interest in
geometric abstraction in a series of graphic animations, including a sequence of films compiled from single frames each of which was an independent image. Breer later returned to America, and developed his graphic work

117

with humorous cartoon-like films such as *Horse Over Teakettle* (1962).

Breer's influential work is often considered, along with the highly formal films of Kurt Kren and Peter Kubelka, as formative for what came to be known as 'structural film'. Both Kren and Kubelka began to work in Vienna in the 1950s. Although imagistic, their films can be seen as extensions of the graphic tradition of Eggeling and Richter, now stripped down to a pure essence. Kubelka's modest output comprises films which mostly use recognisable images but are essentially abstract in conception. Their dynamic derives from the articulation of sequences of frames and sound arranged according to mathematical principles. *Arnulf Rainer* (1958-60) is the most uncompromising, for in a little more than six minutes it uses only black and white frames combined with white sound and silence. Commissioned to document an African safari trip by wealthy Austrian tourists, Kubelka subverted the project by producing in *Unsere Afrikareise* (1966) a film whose rich fusion of sound and image, while it does celebrate the African landscape, also sharply deprecates its exploitation by the film's slaughter-happy patrons.

Abstractions: Peter Kubelka's Mosaik im Vertrauen *(1955)*

Abstraction is similarly important in the work of Kurt Kren, who also often combines brief, fragmentary shots in rhythmic patterns. The content of the images is subordinated to the system of ordering by which they are juxtaposed, repeated and superimposed, as in the interlaced branches of *Trees in Autumn* (1960), or the minimalist portrait of a changing dockside café in *TV* (1967), which uses five brief shots repeated in changing combinations. Along with such minimalist studies in time and space Kren has also documented the provocative neo-Dadaist 'action-art' performances of the Austrian artist Otto Mühl and his collaborators.

It was this interest in the material qualities of film that dominated much European, and especially British, avant-garde film-making between the mid-1960s and the late 1970s. This (and other) work was nurtured by a number of new production and distribution co-operatives, founded under the influence of American developments. In Britain, for example, the London Film-makers' Co-operative was set up in 1966, and soon established itself as a key focus for experimental work. Among the film-makers associated with it were Stephen Dwoskin, who began a series of intense, often erotic personal encounters on film such as *Times For* (1970) and *Dyn Amo* (1972).

Stephen Dwoskin's Times For

The dominant interest of the London Film-makers' Co-operative, however, was expressed in further explorations of structural film. As already suggested, such work is far more formal and less directly expressive than, say, American avant-garde work from the 1940s and 1950s. Rejecting all the illusionist elements of the cinema, it stresses film as material and as a set of

118

conventional assumptions, and by foregrounding the former quality endeavours to challenge and overturn the latter. One key exponent is Malcolm Le Grice, whose *Little Dog for Roger* (1967-8) was the product of refilming and reprinting a 9.5mm home movie so that dirt, splices, sprocket holes and so forth are made visible. Over the next fifteen years, Le Grice extended this form of investigation to explore the mechanisms by which viewers perceive and make sense of film. Another central figure associated with the London Film-makers' Co-operative is Peter Gidal, who remains the most determined polemicist for structural film. One of his most ambitious films is *Room Film 1973*, which consistently denies an image by offering only tentative, fragile glimpses of an interior.

At the same time American film-makers were also exploring structural interests. This is explicit in the title of George Landow's *Film in which there appear sprocket holes, edge lettering, dirt particles, etc* (1966), and can also be identified in work by Paul Sharits, Ernie Gehr, Joyce Wieland and others. Yet structural film in the United States, in contrast to the European tradition, has probably been less concerned with prescriptions of purity and less associated with polemic. Broad affinities with structural interests can be discerned in the work of a number of major film-makers, including both Brakhage and Warhol, but such a description does not exhaust the ideas and potential which they offer. In many respects Michael Snow's *Wavelength* (1987) is a seminal structural film, but it also refuses such categorisation. A staggered zoom shot (lasting, as seen, about 45 minutes) closes in on the far wall of an apartment. On four occasions a human action is registered, offering the most

Wavelength

oblique suggestions of a thriller narrative, but the only resolution is the final recognition of an image on the wall as a photographic seascape. His *Back and Forth* (1969) uses a camera which scans a room relentlessly from side to side. And *La Région Centrale* (1971) is a three-hour picturing of a mountain landscape by a camera mounted on an elaborate gyroscope which can be manipulated in all three planes.

Hollis Frampton, too, is often labelled as a structural film-maker, yet this gives little sense of the poetry, beauty and humour of his major work, *Zorns Lemma* (1970). Combining images and signs with related words in a complex sequence based on the alphabet, the film is labyrinth, game, mystical text, a challenge to the authority of language and much more. In the 1970s, Frampton's films included *(nostalgia)* (1971), an autobiographical mediation on his interest in both still photography and film, and the beginnings of his epic *Clouds of Magellan*, a cycle intended to last twenty-four hours and to contain a film for every day of the year. Sadly, his death in 1984 prevented the completion of the work.

'The avant-garde is dead . . .'

Despite such significant work by Snow, Frampton and others, from the mid-1970s there was a fundamental shift within the American avant-garde, as elsewhere. Part of this was an awareness of the growing richness of an experimental tradition being developed by artists using video technology, which was often more readily available and cheaper than film (see Chapter 17). Super-8 film, too, proved to enjoy comparable advantages, and its distinctive potential was fruitfully explored by artists like Brakhage as well as by a younger generation. The Kuchar brothers, George and Mike, had been making bizarre 8mm parodies of Hollywood movies since the late 1950s, but the greater possibilities of Super-8 sound cameras, introduced in 1974, stimulated much wider use. Alongside the punk underground in New York, Scott and Beth B. used the technology to produce crude, raw B-movies like *The Black Box* (1978) and *Letters to Dad* (1979). In Britain, John Maybury and Cerith Wyn Evans were among those younger film-makers who used technology to produce rather more lyrical images. But video and Super-8 were only two strands of an emerging pluralism within independent film-making, where a now enormously diverse range of work appeared to subsume any narrowly defined tradition of the avant-garde.

The impact of feminism was a major force in much of this new avant-garde work. Other political concerns had become increasingly central for many film-makers, as the cultural and intellectual upheavals of 1968 were analysed and assimilated. For many artists the primacy of formal concerns was supplanted by a new engagement with theory. The previously rigid boundaries between the avant-garde and art cinema no longer seemed so clearly defined, nor did those between the avant-garde and pop culture. Television, too, began to exert an influence, as institutions like Channel 4 in Britain and ZDF in West Germany made available some limited but nonetheless crucial funding to film- and video-makers who previously had been identified with the avant-garde.

In West Germany, a strong and diversified avant-garde movement grew from structural and film co-operative origins. Some film-makers, such as Wim Wenders, moved quickly into commercial production. Others worked on independent features as well as their own projects: Klaus Wyborny, for instance, shot the dream sequences for Werner Herzog's feature *The Enigma of Kaspar Hauser* (1974). In his own work Wyborny has moved from consciously 'primitivist' narratives like the semi-mythic *Birth of a Nation* (1972-3), through the avant-garde road movie *Pictures of the Lost Word* (1975), to a series of films which reflect, in highly personal form, western history. In this more recent work Wyborny uses a complex computer-based matrix, combining a structural script with intuitive handheld camerawork. Like Wyborny, Heinz Emigholz began as a structural film-maker in the late 60s, and his work continues to emphasise the materiality of film. A tilted camera in the feature-length *Normalsatz* (1981) acts as a distancing device, while the action recalls the edginess of performance art in its intense

120

depiction of daily life and the normality of paranoia in the jungle of the city.

In the United States, Yvonne Rainer's films are among the most significant feature-length films shaped by a feminist perspective, although Rainer has acknowledged that her earliest work, *Lives of Performers* (1972), owed far more to her experiences working with contemporary dance in New York than to consciously feminist or political concerns. In *Film About a Woman Who . . .* (1974) she presents conventional representations of emotional relationships, but fragments and makes explicit the ways in which narrative and spectator identification are set up.

Feminist theory, and particularly re-readings of Freudian psychoanalysis, were central to much of the most challenging criticism and practice of avant-garde film-making in the 1970s. In Britain films like *Penthesilea* (1975) and *Riddles of the Sphinx* (1977), both by Laura Mulvey and Peter Wollen, examined questions of female subjectivity, and asked how women can find a voice within a patriarchal language system. Sally Potter's *Thriller* (1979) presents a multi-faceted investigation of the heroine of Puccini's *La Bohème.* The Film Work Group's *Song of the Shirt* (1979) is an examination of history, fiction and reality centred on the lives of 19th-century seamstresses. Such films call atten-

Riddles of the Sphinx

tion to the processes of film-making, inviting the viewer to participate in the making of their meaning and challenging the conventional understandings of documentary and fiction films.

'. . . Long live the avant-garde'

Films like *Thriller* and *Song of the Shirt* do share certain features with the avant-garde tradition. Made outside the dominant structures of funding and distribution, they are also explicit challenges to the conventions of mainstream cinema. In the 1980s, however, the position is less clear, as film-makers previously identified with an avant-garde move in different directions. Sue Clayton and Jonathan Curling, two of those who made *Song of the Shirt*, produced the innovative documentary series *Commodities* (1986) for Channel 4 Television. Sally Potter made an ambitious feature, *The Gold Diggers* (1983), which starred Julie Christie and was also largely financed by Channel 4.

The Belgian film-maker Chantal Akerman is another who occupies a place somewhere between the political avant-garde and the art cinema. Her *Jeanne Dielman, 23 Quai du Commerce, 1080 Bruxelles* (1975) is a lengthy documentation of the life of a widow who supports herself by prostitution, the film-making precise and detached and in certain ways comparable to structural work. British film-makers like Derek Jarman and Peter Greenaway (see Chapter 15) and Americans like Lizzie Borden and Jim

Jarmusch have negotiated similar moves from the avant-garde to the art cinema and even the commercial mainstream.

To see the strategies of these film-makers as in any sense betrayals of their avant-garde heritage is of course an absurd simplification. The 1980s have offered new possibilities, and these film-makers have exploited them in the ways they feel are most appropriate. Beth B., John Maybury, Jim Jarmusch and others are making video promos. Film-makers once identified with the art cinema, like Jean-Luc Godard and Jean-Marie Straub and Danièle Huillet (see Chapter 14), are making some of the most formally and politically challenging work on both film and video. Techniques pioneered by the avant-garde are appropriated by television title sequences and by advertisements. In the late 1980s, the avant-garde's development is intimately entwined with the many other strands of the moving image's present and future. But then, in different ways, it always was.

Further reading

David Curtis, *Experimental Cinema*, London: Studio Vista, 1971.

Stephen Dwoskin, *Film is . . . The International Free Cinema*, London: Peter Owen, 1975.

Peter Gidal (ed.), *Structural Film Anthology*, London: British Film Institute, 1976.

Paul Hammond (ed.), *The Shadow and Its Shadow*, London: British Film Institute, 1978.

J. Hoberman et al, 'The Avant-Garde Now', *Film Comment*, May-June 1981.

Stephen Koch, *Stargazer*, Praeger: New York, 1973.

Standish D. Lawder, *The Cubist Cinema*, New York: New York University Press, 1973.

Malcolm Le Grice, *Abstract Film and Beyond*, London: Studio Vista, 1977.

P. Adams Sitney, *Visionary Film: The American Avant-Garde 1943-1978*, Oxford: Oxford University Press, 1979.

Parker Tyler, *Underground Film: A Critical History*, London: Secker & Warburg, 1971.

Gene Youngblood, *Expanded Cinema*, London: Studio Vista, 1970.

9
The Studio Era

Despite temporary difficulties during the Depression, the years between the arrival of sound and the end of the Second World War saw five corporations consolidate their joint position as the overwhelmingly dominant force in both the American and the international film industries. Paramount, Loew's with its production subsidiary MGM, Fox, Warner Bros and RKO — collectively known as the 'Big Five' — controlled both major production studios and the key distribution and exhibition networks not only in the domestic market but throughout the world. Net profits to the Five were more than $50 million in 1930, and comparable results were achieved fifteen years later. Together with the less significant 'Little Three' — Universal, Columbia and United Artists — these corporations produced close to 500 feature films each year. In 1937 their films, together with a handful made by independents or imported from abroad, attracted three-quarters of the country's expenditure on amusements, and in the following year, in the United States alone, they were pulling in 80 million admissions each week.

The key to the continued success of the Five throughout what is known as the 'studio era' was that they were not just remarkably efficient production factories. All five integrated their output of films with elaborate distribution systems and, most importantly, with exhibition outlets. This vertical integration stabilised the system and ensured that potential competitors remained marginal. Even the Little Three, because they drew their income largely from production and distribution, were unable to mount any effective challenge. The fortunes of each constituent company might rise and fall, but only a national economic crisis like the Depression of the early 1930s could dent the system's overall profitability. At the end of the decade overseas rentals, which brought in around half of an average film's earnings, were seriously disrupted by political events in Europe. But a wartime boom at home compensated for this, as did attempts to open up new markets.

The studio system
At the start of this period, Paramount was by far the most successful of the corporations. In 1930, at the height of the cinemagoing boom spurred by

sound, and despite production costs having doubled because of the new technology, Paramount's net profits were $25 million. In 1946, in the American cinema's best-ever box-office year, it was again the top-grossing studio. Yet in the fifteen years between Paramount's management had changed numerous times and on several occasions the corporation had only narrowly escaped bankruptcy. A central problem was the company's extension of its theatre holdings in the late 1920s. This meant that, like each of the other Big Five corporations, Paramount's profile throughout the 1930s was very much that of a theatre chain, which used its interests in production and distribution to supply its own houses. At first the many new exhibition sites pushed up the company's profits, but as audiences tired of the novelty of sound and as the effects of the Depression were felt, these additional cinemas became a financial burden.

For a competing company like Loew's, with its smaller exhibition circuit, the fall in admissions during the Depression was serious but more easily negotiable. Throughout the studio era, Loew's and its subsidiary MGM was Paramount's one serious rival. After the abortive merger with Fox in 1929-30, Loew's remained consistently successful through the next fifteen years and, unlike each of the other majors, did not report a net loss in any year. But the company's relatively small number of theatres meant that it was not in nearly as advantageous a position to benefit from the wartime boom. Exhibition, then, was the key determinant of each corporation's profits, and their activities in this area were boosted by the new Roosevelt administration's National Recovery Act (NRA) of 1933, which accepted the legitimacy of the Big Five's effective monopoly. The NRA, however, was declared unconstitutional by the Supreme Court in 1935, and three years later the first anti-trust suits were filed against the corporations. In 1940 they voluntarily accepted certain restrictions, but because of the war further action to separate exhibition from their other operations was delayed until the end of the decade.

For all the importance of exhibition, the studio lot remained the heart of a corporation. Since the early 1920s these lots had been as complex as small towns, and the largest ones employed several thousand people, organised into specialist departments. Ways of working were overwhelmingly uniform throughout the industry. The common comparison with factories is an apt one, and there were many similarities between the Hollywood studios and contemporary assembly-line manufacturing plants. Union jurisdiction, for example, had been recognised and stabilised in 1925-6, with five craft unions dividing the responsibilities of making motion pictures. But the following years were marked as much by inter-union squabbling as they were by collective action against the studios.

As for the bosses, the early 1930s witnessed a shift at most studios to what was known as the 'unit producer' system. Rather than a single central producer controlling the whole output, the new structure depended on a group of men who each supervised some six or eight films a year. In part, this was a reaction to the sense that new ideas were being suppressed, although the repetitive comedies and musicals of many unit producers suggested that there was only limited enthusiasm for originality.

Along with their cinemas and their studio lots, each of the Big Five also owned interests in a range of related operations, including film processing, real estate, the 'legitimate' theatre (a valuable source of potential screenplays) and radio and television. Loew's, for example, used their radio station WHN in New York to generate publicity in the market where half their theatres were sited. Music publishing, for the popular tunes featured in their films, was another significant source of revenue for each of the majors. Loew's controlled Robbins Music Publishing, which handled many of the songs featured in MGM musicals, and in 1947 the corporation released its first record on the MGM label, to promote *Till the Clouds Roll By*.

The Production Code

On the nation's cinema screens, Paramount, like the other studios, responded to the Depression by increasing the number of films with what was identified as salacious subject matter. Heroines were now more likely to be singers, chorus-girls and gold-diggers, such as Kay Francis and Lilyan Tashman in *Girls About Town*, and Tallulah Bankhead in *Tarnished Lady* (both directed by George Cukor in 1931). Equally popular was the cycle of tough gangster films which Warners initiated with Edward G. Robinson in *Little Caesar* (1930, directed by Mervyn LeRoy) and *The Public Enemy* (1931, William Wellman), which made James Cagney a star. At the same time Warners was producing a series of musicals spotlighting the spectacular choreography of Busby Berkeley. Often set backstage at a Broadway show, films like *42nd Street* and *Gold Diggers of 1933* (both 1933) were showcases for the lavish geometric patterns and rhythmic movements which Berkeley fashioned from rows of women's faces and bodies.

Little Caesar *(Edward G. Robinson, William Collier Jr)*

Quite different in tone, but seen as posing a similar challenge to 'family' values, were a group of films starring Marlene Dietrich and directed for Paramount by Josef von Sternberg. The director first worked with Dietrich on *The Blue Angel* (1930), a co-production with the German conglomerate Ufa. The Dietrich persona of sultry vamp was further refined in *Morocco* (1930), in which she plays a cynical cabaret singer who can ask her prospective husband, 'Every time a man has helped me there has been a price. What's yours?' In *Dishonored* (1931) she is a Viennese streetwalker turned spy, in *Shanghai Express* (1932) an oriental seductress, and in *Blonde Venus* (1932) she plies the trade in Paris. *Shanghai Express* made $3 million for Paramount, but this success was not to be repeated by either *The*

Marlene Dietrich (with Clive Brook) in Shanghai Express

Scarlet Empress (1934), with Dietrich as Catherine the Great of Russia, or *The Devil is a Woman* (1935). Each of these Sternberg-Dietrich films is an extraordinary creation of shadows and decor, hymning a mysterious and artificial exoticism and laced with a brooding sexuality.

A Production Code, established in 1930 and overseen by the Hays Office, was the industry's self-regulatory system intended to curb any unacceptable excesses. Many producers, however, attempted to buck its rules, and religious groups began to protest, the best organised group being the Catholic Legion of Decency for which eleven million people undertook to boycott offensive films. Direct economic pressure like this was readily appreciated by the companies, and in 1934 they greatly strengthened the provisions of the Code. Under Joseph Breen, a new body called the Production Code Administration was set up to approve each script and each finished film. No picture could secure effective theatrical exposure without the PCA's approval, and by 1937 it was seeing and passing 98 per cent of all the films shown in the United States. 'Family' values, which were assumed to represent the aspirations of the mass audience, became centrally enshrined as Hollywood's understanding of the world.

Ownership, executives and profits

Paramount's purchases at the end of the 1920s had locked the company into massive repayments, which caused a record deficit in 1933. Immediate production cutbacks were imposed, a studio in Long Island was closed, and management changes and financial restructuring became a central preoccupation. Paramount's internal affairs were chaotic until the end of 1936, when Barney Balaban, an exhibitor from Chicago who was to run the company until 1964, was invited to take charge. This boardroom manoeuvring was one indication of a fundamental shift in the ownership of Hollywood. A year before Balaban's appointment, Paramount Pictures Inc emerged in July 1935 from a major court-approved reorganisation. The corporation was now dominated by bankers, and the only men on the new board with direct experience of the film business were sales manager George Schaefer and founder Adolph Zukor.

Similar financial reconstruction was forced on other studios. The Fox Film Corporation also entered the 1930s with huge debts, and the inevitable refinancing both removed founder William Fox from control and created a corporation that only narrowly survived the next few years. In May 1935 it merged with the independent company Twentieth Century Pictures, itself a recent creation of Darryl Zanuck, formerly with Warners, and Joseph Schenck, previously head of United Artists. A stable and profitable decade followed with Zanuck overseeing production on the West Coast. Meanwhile, Schenck and Sidney Kent (previously with Paramount) co-ordinated distribution and exhibition from New York. In 1942 their roles were taken over by Spyros Skouras, formerly an executive in charge of Fox's theatres, and from 1944 unchallenged head of the whole corporation.

RKO, the newest of the majors, suffered its financial troubles earlier even than Fox and Paramount, and the courts spent almost seven years after 1933 trying to put together an appropriate financial structure. Profits remained elusive until the war, although RKO's cinema chain and the Pathé newsreel operation (acquired in 1931) both made money, and its management was in constant flux. Among those who tried to make the operation work were David Selznick, production chief for just over a year in 1932-3; George Schaefer, who came in as President in 1938 with a commitment to quality productions; and Dore Schary, formerly a writer and producer with MGM, who oversaw production in the final years but left when Howard Hughes purchased the studio in 1948.

In contrast to these upheavals, and like Loew's and MGM, Warner Bros was able to ride out the Depression without extensive reorganisation. Still a family firm, the company was run by the three brothers until Harry and Albert retired in 1951. Harry mapped out the overall strategy, Albert looked after distribution around the world, and Jack ran the production side. Riding high after its early successes with sound, Warners began the 1930s in a strong position, but with the financial pressures of the Depression the company found the inevitable mortgage repayments hard to meet. Operations were pared down to a minimum, almost half its theatres were closed, and budgets and salaries were cut to levels lower than the other majors. As a consequence the company's figures throughout the 1930s were solid but unspectacular, but by the 1940s the policy had paid off and the brothers oversaw a steady expansion. At the end of the decade Warner Bros was challenging the supremacy of Paramount and Loew's.

Paramount and MGM

For its audiences Paramount was invariably the guarantor of glossy light comedy, directed by craftsmen like Wesley Ruggles, Leo McCarey and Mitchell Leisen. Leisen worked regularly with writers Preston Sturges and Billy Wilder, and later in the decade they created together two of Hollywood's sharpest comedies, *Easy Living* (1937) and *Midnight* (1939). The studio was particularly successful in finding film vehicles for stars who had already established themselves in vaudeville or on radio. The Marx Brothers, Mae West and W. C. Fields were all well-known before they brought their talents to Paramount, and this policy of working with safely bankable names was later to prove most successful in the pairing of Bing Crosby and Bob Hope for the series of *Road* movies.

Elsewhere on the lot, Cecil B. DeMille continued to turn out lavish, invariably profitable epics,

Midnight *(John Barrymore, Claudette Colbert)*

including *Cleopatra* (1934), *The Crusades* (1935) and *The Plainsman* (1936). In contrast to M G M, the studio had only a small stable of dramatic stars, of whom the most prominent was Gary Cooper. But again unlike its main rival, Paramount had the reputation of granting a certain freedom to its writers, producers and directors and this proved attractive to men like King Vidor, Rouben Mamoulian and Ernst Lubitsch. Lubitsch, indeed, had a brief spell as head of production, as well as making polished artifices like *Trouble in Paradise* (1932), *Design for Living* (1933) and, with Dietrich, *Angel* (1937). Henry Hathaway was employed regularly as an action director for pictures like *The Lives of a Bengal Lancer* (1935), with Gary Cooper, and *The Trail of the Lonesome Pine* (1936), the studio's first film in Technicolor. William Wellman undertook a number of assignments, most notably *Beau Geste* (1939, also with Cooper); as did Lewis Milestone, whose best film from these years was *The General Died at Dawn* (1936).

The General Died at Dawn *(Madeleine Carroll, Gary Cooper)*

Paramount was disadvantaged by management instability and its lack of a production chief with the flair of Jack Warner or Darryl Zanuck. Loew's, by contrast, was run by the brilliant Nicholas Schenck, who had started with the company in 1906 and remained President until 1956. Under him, but with a significant degree of autonomy, was Louis B. Mayer, the highest-paid executive in America and the epitome of the quick-tempered tyrant who expected total obedience. Mayer's lieutenant, until he died in 1937, was the cultured Irving Thalberg. Mayer fashioned the company's pictures in a narrow but highly successful mould. Conservative and family-oriented, M G M's films during the 1930s and 1940s boasted 'more stars than there are in the heavens' and were usually distinguished by their elegance and high production values. The necessary capital came from an arrangement with the Chase National Bank. To achieve a consistent level of quality, Mayer introduced the 'unit producer' system, entrusting key projects to a handful

Hepburn and Tracy in Woman of the Year

of reliable executives like musical specialist Hunt Stromberg, who oversaw the Jeanette MacDonald-Nelson Eddy operettas, and Lawrence Weingarten, who produced the hugely popular Marie Dressler comedies and later the sparkling Katharine Hepburn-Spencer Tracy films like *Woman of the Year* (1942). Among the most expensive projects of all were those supervised personally by Thalberg, such as *Anna Christie* (1930) and *Mutiny on the Bounty* (1935).

For the public, M G M was a studio of stars — Garbo (with John and Lionel Barrymore, Joan Crawford and Wallace Beery) in *Grand Hotel* (1932), *Queen Christina* (1933), *Anna Karenina* (1935) and *Ninotchka* (1939); Norma Shearer in *The Barretts of Wimpole Street* (1934), *Romeo and Juliet* (1936) and *Marie Antoinette* (1938); Joan Crawford in *The Bride Wore Red* (1937, directed

128

by one of Hollywood's few women directors, Dorothy Arzner) and *The Women* (1939); and Jean Harlow in *Red Dust* (1932) and *Bombshell* (1933). In the later 1930s, MGM's male stars shone just as brightly — Clark Gable in *San Francisco* (1936), and Spencer Tracy in *Boys Town* (1938) and *Dr Jekyll and Mr Hyde* (1941).

MGM, however, was as dependent as the other studios on formula pictures, and various linked series were produced, including the *Broadway Melody* series, in 1936, 1938 and 1940, the *Andy Hardy* series with Mickey Rooney, and the continuing adventures of *The Thin Man*, begun in 1934 with William Powell and Myrna Loy as the husband-and-wife detectives. The closeness of these films to television series thirty years later is exemplified by the sequence begun by MGM's *Young Dr Kildare* (1938).

In the 1940s the studio found hits, and stars, rather harder to come by, although *Mrs Miniver* (1942) established Greer Garson as their most prominent female lead. Soon, however, MGM became identified with musical Technicolor spectacles, the first of which was *The Wizard of Oz* (1939). Louis Mayer had originally wanted Shirley Temple for the lead, but when Zanuck refused to release her, producer Arthur Freed began the process of moulding Judy Garland into a star. Several pairings with Mickey Rooney followed, before Judy Garland's first adult role, complementing Gene Kelly's debut in *For Me and My Gal* (1942). Freed, musical supervisor Roger Edens, director Vincente Minnelli and Garland subsequently collaborated on *Meet Me in St Louis* (1944), a turn-of-the-century tale of family life which, apart from MGM's release of *Gone with the Wind*, became the corporation's biggest-grossing film to date.

Fox, Ford and Hawks

In the early 1930s Fox had tried to combat the fall in audience figures with major films like *The Big Trail* (Raoul Walsh, 1930). *Cavalcade* (1933), a record of the London stage production shot by a Movietone News crew, was a big hit. But in the first half of the decade only the Will Rogers vehicles consistently turned in profits. From 1935 Zanuck rigorously controlled output, relying heavily on stars Alice Faye, Tyrone Power and Shirley Temple, who had her first feature hit at the age of six with *Stand Up and Cheer* (1934). He also made a star of the ice-skating champion Sonja Henie, who became a professional performer after the 1936 Olympics. Zanuck's invaluable assistant was producer and writer Nunnally Johnson, who oversaw a number of the company's prestige productions. Many of these were directed either by John Ford or by Henry King, who shot the early Technicolor feature *Ramona* (1936) as well as several of the historical dramas favoured by Zanuck, like *Lloyds of London* (1936) and *Stanley and Livingstone* (1939).

To cut costs, Zanuck frequently recycled plots from Fox films, and from the output of his rivals. But he ensured that Fox films made extensive use of Technicolor, and after 1941 the studio turned out a string of gaudy, and highly profitable, Betty Grable musicals. Fox also maintained a strong

Stars of MGM: Clark Gable (with Jeanette MacDonald) in San Francisco; *Greta Garbo in* Queen Christina; *Spencer Tracy in* Dr Jekyll and Mr Hyde; *Joan Crawford (with Phyllis Povah) in* The Women

129

Judy Garland and Gene Kelly in For Me and My Gal

B-picture production unit, overseen by Sol Wurtzel, which made series of films with the Charlie Chan character, with Peter Lorre as Mr Moto, and with the comics the Ritz brothers. But during the war, with profits assured, the studio concentrated on the more prestigious productions.

Throughout these years John Ford recognised Fox as his home lot, although he made several of his best films for other studios. *The Informer* (1935), a brooding tale of Irish Republicanism, was made at RKO. A self-consciously literary film, it won five Oscars and established Ford as a major director. Back at Fox, Zanuck kept Ford employed on standard offerings like *The Prisoner of Shark Island* (1936) and a Shirley Temple vehicle, *Wee Willie Winkie* (1937). Zanuck also turned down what was to become Ford's first masterpiece, *Stagecoach* (1939). Gary Cooper rejected it as well, so Ford made the film with Walter Wanger and United Artists, and with former B-Western star John Wayne.

Also in 1939 Ford directed *Young Mr Lincoln* and *Drums Along the Mohawk*, both for Fox, and marked out the territory he was to explore over the next three decades. His cinema places its characters not only against the vistas of Monument Valley, but against the history and development of the United States. From the frontiersmen of *Drums Along the Mohawk* to the Second World War sailors of *They Were Expendable* (1945), his films explore the social tensions, the values and morals of a nation. Even when he ventures outside America, to the Wales of *How Green was My Valley* (1941) for instance, Ford engages with ideas of community, of hearth, of history, and of personal responsibility, which bear directly on his chronicles of an emerging country.

Aside from maverick talents like Sternberg and Orson Welles, one of the very few Hollywood directors of comparable stature to Ford is Howard Hawks. After the success of the gangster film *Scarface* (1932), which he directed as well as co-produced with Howard Hughes, Hawks worked with which studios he chose and across the whole range of available genres. Comedies like *Twentieth Century* (1934), *Bringing Up Baby* (1938) and *His Girl Friday* (1940) alternate with studies of male camaraderie like *Only Angels Have Wings* (1939). The

John Ford's Stagecoach

closeness of his worlds of crazy humour and intense professionalism, and the clashes between them, contribute to a cinema which, for all its apparent simplicity, is the work of a master.

Warners and RKO

Throughout the 1930s, first under producer Darryl Zanuck and later with Hal B. Wallis, Warners turned out genre films cheaply, efficiently and consistently. Zanuck, who had started as a writer with the studio in 1924, brought into being the gangster pictures which, together with Busby Berkeley's musicals, kept the company afloat through the Depression. After 1935 Wallis initiated a cycle of romantic roles for Errol Flynn, like *The Charge of the Light Brigade* (1936), and *The Private Lives of Elizabeth and Essex* (1939), and a run of rather earnest 'biopics' with Paul Muni, including *The Story of Louis Pasteur* (1936), and *The Life of Emile Zola* (1937). Wallis even indulged himself with the occasional 'artistic' project like *A Midsummer Night's Dream* (1935), directed by the stage veteran Max Reinhardt and with James Cagney a creditable Bottom. Along with Flynn, Muni, Cagney and Edward G. Robinson, the other prominent stars associated with the studio were Bette Davis and, later, Humphrey Bogart.

Howard Hawks' His Girl Friday *(Cary Grant, Rosalind Russell)*

Of all the films produced during the studio era, those from Warners were the most socially engaged. Subjects treated seriously, although usually with a streak of cynicism, include the press (*Five Star Final*, 1931), prison (*I Am a Fugitive from a Chain Gang*, 1932; *20,000 Years in Sing Sing*, 1933), unionism (*Black Fury*, 1935) and racism (*Black Legion*, 1936; *They Won't Forget*, 1937). But it was an assembly-line operation, directed towards stability rather than box-office triumphs, and there was little room for innovation, or even for Technicolor. As a refinement of the same policy, the production of B-features was prolific, and occasionally an emerging actor like Bogart would cross over into the more expensive projects. After supporting roles in *The Roaring Twenties* (1939) and *They Drive By Night* (1940), Bogart first shared top billing (after Paul Muni, George Raft, Cagney and Robinson had all turned down the role) in *High Sierra* (1941).

Bogart (with George Raft) in They Drive By Night

When David Selznick was installed in 1932 as production chief at RKO, he brought in two important producers. One was Merian C. Cooper, who with Ernest Schoedsack made RKO's monster hit *King Kong* (1933). The other was Pandro Berman, who supervised the studio's Fred Astaire and Ginger Rogers musicals. Teamed briefly in *Flying Down to Rio* (1933), Astaire and Rogers first starred together in *The Gay Divorcee* (1934), and then made seven further films together. Selznick also introduced Katharine Hepburn to the studio, first for *A Bill of Divorcement* (1932), which was followed by other popular films. After Selznick was forced to resign early in 1933, heads of production came and went, while Berman and others continued working with their own semi-autonomous production units. But only the estimated half a million dollars profit from each Astaire and Rogers film, together with income from 'The Saint' series, ensured the studio's survival.

King Kong

Another management upheaval in 1938 established at the head of the studio George Schaefer, charged with finding prestige projects. Of these, the most celebrated is Orson Welles' *Citizen Kane* (1941). Welles was a boy-wonder who had already made his mark in the theatre and on radio, where he had masterminded a startling documentary-style adaptation of H.G. Wells' *War of the Worlds*. Working closely with theatrical colleagues like John Houseman and Joseph Cotten, and with the screenwriter Herman J. Mankiewicz, this film novice created an audacious, imaginative, technically dazzling portrait of a press tycoon, closely modelled on William Randolph Hearst. After repeated viewings, each set-up of the film remains fresh, every sequence continues to offer surprises. Much of this derives from Welles' remarkable creative innocence when faced with what he called 'the biggest electric train-set any boy ever had', but much was also due to cinematographer Gregg Toland, editor Robert Wise, and a production team which demonstrated the full potential of the studio system at its best.

Welles shot a comparably audacious follow-up, *The Magnificent Ambersons* (1942), but he could no longer depend on Schaefer's beneficence. Yet

Welles' The Lady from Shanghai

another new studio head ordered cut-backs, Welles' material was re-edited as a second feature while he was in South America working on a new film, and he began the unsettled odyssey which was to be the remainder of his career. As a director he would make unique thrillers like *The Lady from Shanghai* (1948) and *Touch of Evil* (1958), as well as rich and idiosyncratic readings of Shakespeare in *Macbeth* (1948), *Othello* (1952) and *Chimes at Midnight* (1966). As an actor he was to distinguish *The Third Man* (1949), *Moby Dick* (1956) and many lesser films which did not deserve him, nor he them. And for television he could make something as simple yet as breathtaking as the half-hour *The Fountain of Youth*, for Desilu's 'Colgate Theatre' on NBC in 1958.

Schaefer's regime at RKO was also responsible for quality pictures like *The Hunchback of Notre Dame* (1939), with Charles Laughton, and *My Favorite Wife* (1940), with Cary Grant. He supervised the company's important distribution contract with Disney and arranged for RKO to distribute the independent productions of Sam Goldwyn, who had fallen out with United Artists. This deal was to prove particularly important towards the end of the war, when Goldwyn turned in a number of big hits, including the Oscar-winning *The Best Years of Our Lives* (1946, director William Wyler). But after 1942 the newly installed Charles Koerner decided to concentrate on cheaply made, heavily promoted 'exploitation' films, like the cycle of superior horror films produced by Val Lewton, including *Cat People* (1943) and *I Walked with a Zombie* (1943). Jean Renoir (*This Land is Mine*, 1943)

Superior horror: Jacques Tourneur's I Walked with a Zombie, *produced by Val Lewton*

132

and Alfred Hitchcock (*Notorious*, 1946) also worked at the studio during this time.

Poverty Row and the 'Little Three'

Throughout the studio era the activities of the Big Five were complemented by three smaller companies (Universal, Columbia and United Artists), by leading independents like Samuel Goldwyn and David Selznick, and by the 'poverty row' producers such as Republic and Monogram. Created by pioneer Carl Laemmle, Universal had specialised during the 1920s in cheap, down-market product, but when Laemmle appointed his son, known as Junior Laemmle, general manager in 1929, the studio began to look for more prestigious productions. Chief among these was *All Quiet on the Western Front* (1930, director Lewis Milestone), but throughout the 1930s Universal's balance sheet recorded a loss. After 1939, and especially during the war, the company turned a profit and plans were made for a post-war expansion. A partnership in 1946 with the independent company International Pictures was briefly successful, but Universal-International was ailing when it was purchased by Decca Records in 1952.

All Quiet on the Western Front

Junior Laemmle's major legacy was the cycle of horror films begun with *Dracula* (1931), based on a Broadway play and starring the stage actor Bela Lugosi. Sets left over from *All Quiet on the Western Front*, director Tod Browning and German cameraman Karl Freund, gave the film a distinctive style, and its success prompted *Frankenstein* (1931, James Whale), *The Mummy* (1932, directed by Freund), *The Black Cat* (1934, directed by another German refugee, Edgar G. Ulmer) and *The Bride of Frankenstein* (1935, Whale). Later in the decade Universal relied heavily on the talents of Deanna Durbin, and subsequently on comedies starring W.C. Fields and the team of Bud Abbott and Lou Costello. The studio also specialised in serials, including Westerns with Buck Jones and Johnny Mack Brown and *Flash Gordon* (1936) and its sequels. But despite its impressive distribution network, once it had been forced to sell its remaining cinemas in 1933 Universal could hope for only modest profits.

A shoestring distributor and producer in the 1920s, Columbia was run until 1958 by founders Harry and Jack Cohn. The company expanded rapidly in 1927-9, but it did not purchase any cinemas and by comparison with the other corporations remained relatively prosperous through the 1930s. Costs and salaries, even executive ones, were kept low, and stars were not signed to long-term contracts. As head of production, Harry Cohn preferred to borrow stars from other studios, as with Clark Gable (from M G M) and Claudette Colbert (from Paramount) for *It Happened One Night*

(1934). The director of this spectacular success was Frank Capra who, with writer Robert Riskin, turned out a number of entertaining, socially conscious hits for the studio, including *Mr Deeds Goes to Town* (1936) and *You Can't Take It With You* (1938). But when Cohn tried to pass off another director's film as by him, Capra parted company with Columbia. Cohn had to rely increasingly on series of B-pictures, including those featuring 'Blondie' (28 in all) and 'Crime Doctor' (10), although during the war he had hits with several Rita Hayworth features, and afterwards with *The Jolson Story* (1946) and its sequel. Columbia had also profitably turned over numerous B-Westerns, many featuring Gene Autry, serials like *The Shadow* (1940) and *Batman* (1943), animation, and comedy shorts with, among others, the Three Stooges.

Capra's populism: James Stewart (with Claude Rains) in Mr Smith Goes to Washington *(1939)*

You Only Live Once *(Sylvia Sidney, Henry Fonda)*

Of the original partners at United Artists only Chaplin remained active in the later 1930s, making *Modern Times* (1936) and his parody of Hitler, *The Great Dictator* (1940). Despite a first successful year, a relationship with Twentieth Century Pictures, formed in 1933 to produce films for United Artists, went sour when the board was unwilling to take on the new company as a full partner. Twentieth Century founders Joseph Schenck and Darryl Zanuck sought a more profitable marriage with Fox, and the independent productions of Walter Wanger (such as Fritz Lang's *You Only Live Once*, 1937), of Samuel Goldwyn and of David Selznick became increasingly important to the company.

Goldwyn and Selznick were undoubtedly the most prominent independents during the studio era. Many such individuals and companies had continued to operate during the 1920s, but their prospects had been seriously damaged by the coming of sound and the consolidation of the Big Five. Most of those without a corporate relationship with a distributor could no longer expect to get their films into first-run cinemas, and they consequently found financing harder to secure. But as double features became more common around 1931, the demand from second- and subsequent-run cinemas increased, and by 1936 one estimate suggested that between 25 and 30 producers were each making between three and ten films a year.

Monogram and Republic were the largest of these companies. With both a small studio lot and a national distribution network, Monogram (founded in 1929 by producer W. Ray Johnston) could sell widely their second features, which where made in about eight days on budgets of around $20,000. Debts allowed the Consolidated Film Laboratory to take over the original Monogram, but Johnston re-formed the company, continued to turn out numerous B-Westerns, and during the war made decent profits. The Consolidated Film Laboratory had also set up Republic Pictures, which became known for its cheaply produced Westerns with John Wayne and Gene Autry, and its serials like *Dick Tracy* and *The Lone Ranger*.

Samuel Goldwyn located himself firmly at the other end of the market, making glossy features for first-run theatres. While he was working with United Artists, Goldwyn established a fruitful relationship with director William Wyler, who was granted considerable autonomy on projects like *Dodsworth* (1936), *The Westerner* (1940) and *The Little Foxes* (1941). Goldwyn, however, became frustrated in his own attempts to buy out the company's founders, and he eventually threw in his lot with RKO. Selznick built a comparable profile for his work, relying on Technicolor romances like *A Star is Born* (1937, director William Wellman). He also tempted Alfred Hitchcock to Hollywood, where the British director made his American debut with *Rebecca* (1940).

Selznick's masterpiece, however, is undoubtedly the film which more than any other Hollywood production is recognised as the creation of its producer, *Gone with the Wind* (1939). Its production, and the intense search for the right stars, has been more thoroughly chronicled than that of any other movie. And it has become clear that much of the credit for the film's visual sweep and power must be ascribed to the art direction of William Cameron Menzies, whose detailed sketches guided, in turn, directors George Cukor, Victor Fleming and Sam Wood. Selznick had bought the book before its 1936 publication for the then huge sum of $50,000. The final budget was over $4 million, and to secure Clark Gable and part of this money he had had to agree that MGM distribute the film, and split the profits down the middle. These were soon considerable, and have remained so. In 1978 the film's 20-year lease to television in the United States cost $20 million, and in 1980 the BBC paid £4.4 million in a package deal which secured the screening rights over a ten-year period. For all its creakiness as drama, *Gone with the Wind* remains a monument to the studio era, and to the power of a producer.

Goldwyn gloss: Bette Davis in The Little Foxes

In the cinemas

Back in the Depression, the owners of many of the smaller cinemas had begun to tempt audiences with the offer of two films for the price of one, and the double-bill became increasingly popular in the early 1930s. Even the larger cinemas affiliated with the Big Five, which had mostly dropped live shows after the introduction of sound, took up the practice. Gifts and games, like bingo and screeno, were also introduced after 1931, but the National Recovery Administration prohibited these after 1933. When the NRA was revoked two years later, these audience lures were reintroduced. An evening at the cinema became far more than just the featured attraction.

In a Big Five cinema, and in many non-affiliated ones, a full programme would often include, as well as one or two features, a short film featuring a vaudeville act (particularly popular in the early days of sound) or later a big band, extended trailers like Paramount's *Hollywood on Parade* series, an edition of a general interest film magazine, a newsreel and an animated short. Most of the large studios produced all of these, or distributed exclusively a supply from an independent producer. Loew's, for example, distributed comedy shorts from producer Hal Roach in the early 1930s. MGM subsequently began to produce its own shorts, often using them as training grounds for potential stars (like James Stewart and Judy Garland) and directors (Fred Zinnemann and Joseph Losey started this way). MGM even made a curious series with Pete Smith, a former studio press agent whose short films became popular by mixing feature-type items with camera tricks like running footage backwards or upside down.

The financial problems of the corporations in the early 1930s meant that they no longer had the money to spend on lavish decor for cinemas, or even on the upkeep of the exotic surroundings which had become common in the 1920s. Air-conditioning, however, became an added attraction in a number of houses. Balaban and Katz had installed it first in 1917 in their Chicago cinemas, but it was not until the introduction of a cheaper system in the 1930s that it came within the reach of most of the Big Five houses, together with some of the independent ones. One other innovation was the sale of food and drink in cinemas.

The war effort

In the years prior to the Second World War the closure of markets in Germany and the Far East, together with tighter restrictions on imports to Italy and on currency exports from Britain, contributed to a decline in Hollywood's foreign earnings. New production arrangements in Britain (see Chapter 10) were one response, but it was the wartime boom in audiences at home which was to compensate for the lost revenue. The war years produced the best American domestic box-office figures in history, in part accounted for by the need for entertainment and reassurance, and in part by buoyant incomes and restricted opportunities for spending them. Shortages of both personnel and of raw stock meant that fewer films were made, and production costs rose, but the crowds came anyway and the corporations cleared record profits.

After Pearl Harbor all the studios embraced the war with some enthusiasm, but even before that a number of films had been creating American sympathy for the Allied cause. Alfred Hitchcock's *Foreign Correspondent* (1940) ends with a rallying-call to the still neutral Americans. The theme was taken on even earlier by Warners, where Jack Warner demonstrated a particular concern for the dangers of Nazism. *Confessions of a Nazi Spy* (1939) is a rather overheated crime melodrama, but its robust patriotism was matched later at the studio in musicals like *Yankee Doodle Dandy* (1942) and gung-ho combat films, with Raoul Walsh directing Errol Flynn in *Desperate Journey* (1942) and *Objective Burma* (1945).

Elsewhere, wartime production included MGM's hands-across-the-ocean drama *Mrs Miniver* (1942), set in a never-never England of rural idyll and stiff upper lips. The studio was also responsible for such English-inflected syrup as *Lassie Come Home* (1943) and *National Velvet* (1944). Several studios offered all-star music revues, while MGM's enthusiastic portrait of the Soviet Union, *Song of Russia* (1943), was subsequently to prove an embarrassment to the anti-communist zealot Louis B. Mayer. Sam Goldwyn produced a similarly fulsome tribute to gallant Russia in *The North Star* (1943). Only in the final year of the war did the film industry produce some more reflective accounts of the fighting, like Ford's *They Were Expendable* (1945) and Wellman's *The Story of G.I. Joe* (1945).

The post-war years, and especially the 1948 anti-trust case, were to bring down the curtain on the studio era. Hollywood was never to be the same again, although many of its films would demonstrate only minimal awareness of a changing world. Among much else, however, the immediate post-war years produced a cycle of films which later became known as *films noirs* and which have been seen as reflecting the uncertainty, paranoia and disillusionment of these years. Films like *Crossfire* (1947, director Edward Dmytryk), Nicholas Ray's *They Live By Night* (1948) and Jacques Tourneur's *Out of the Past* (1947), all produced under Dore Schary's characteristically brief regime at RKO, presented a world which was dark, troubled, full of doubt. After Dachau and Hiroshima, so was the world in which they were seen.

The shadowy world of film noir:
Out of the Past

Further reading

David Bordwell, Janet Staiger and Kristin Thompson, *The Classical Hollywood Cinema: Film Style and Production to 1960,* London: Routledge & Kegan Paul, 1985.

Edward Buscombe, 'Notes on Columbia Pictures Corporation 1926–41', *Screen,* Autumn 1975.

Bosley Crowther, *The Lion's Share: The Story of an Entertainment Empire,* New York: Dutton, 1957.

John Douglas Eames, *The MGM Story: The Complete History of Over Fifty Roaring Years,* New York: Crown, 1976.

Philip French, *The Movie Moguls,* London: Weidenfield and Nicolson, 1969.

Clive Hirschhorn, *The Universal Story,* New York: Crown, 1983.

Richard Jewell with Vernon Harbin, *The RKO Story,* New York: Arlington House, 1982.

Todd McCarthy and Charles Flynn (ed.), *Kings of the Bs,* New York: E.P. Dutton, 1975.

Roy Pickard, *The Hollywood Studios,* London: Frederick Muller, 1978.

Nick Roddick, *A New Deal in Entertainment: Warner Brothers in the 1930s,* London: British Film Institute, 1983.

Murray Ross, *Stars and Strikes: Unionization of Hollywood,* New York: University of Columbia Press, 1945.

Andrew Sarris, *The American Cinema,* New York: E.P. Dutton, 1968.

David Shipman, *The Story of Cinema,* (2 vol), London: Hodder and Stoughton, 1982.

David Thomson, *A Biographical Dictionary of the Cinema,* London: Secker & Warburg, 1985.

10
The International Cinema
1930-1945

Sound inevitably brought major changes to the developed film industries outside the United States. Hollywood too was forced to reassess its relationship with these cinemas, in order to maintain its international dominance of exhibition and distribution. But as sound was introduced, the industries in Britain, France and Italy sought ways to overturn their economic subservience to Hollywood. The German film industry, in contrast, had been sufficiently strong in the later 1920s to continue to resist Hollywood successfully, and after 1933 this position was consolidated by the Nazi regime, which quickly set up a rigid, ideologically directed control of the cinema. Italian Fascism regarded the medium rather differently, and was content to provide state support for a domestic industry which concentrated on Hollywood-style entertainments. Elsewhere, the Soviet Union was effectively closed off from Hollywood, and was assimilating the new aesthetics of 'Socialist Realism'. And in Japan a distinctive industry developed alongside an extensive exposure to Hollywood. But much of this changed with the Second World War, which in Britain brought a box-office boom and new creative confidence, but which was eventually all but to destroy the Italian and German industries.

A British quota
The British film industry after the First World War was an unimpressive collection of small companies. Hollywood films occupied most of the screens most of the time, and the few successful British producers, like Herbert Wilcox and Michael Balcon, prospered by making Hollywood-style features, sometimes with Hollywood actors. Of the 748 long films released in 1926 just 34 were British, and the transatlantic imbalance began to cause concern beyond those directly involved in the cinema. Manufacturers saw American products enjoying valuable advertising advantages, while many politicians identified this foreign cinema as one of the main threats to traditional British values.

The British features that were produced often derived from the theatre, the transition to the screen amounting to little more than the replication of the stage action. The more imaginative productions mostly came from Balcon's company Gainsborough, for which directors like Graham Cutts and the young Alfred Hitchcock made impressive versions of West End hits. Balcon, like his competitor Herbert Wilcox, also exploited the possibilities of Anglo-German co-productions: Hitchcock made his first two films as a director in Munich.

As a response to the industry's widely perceived crisis the government introduced the 1927 Cinematograph Films Act, which imposed on distributors and exhibitors an annual quota of domestic productions. But with no stipulations about the budgets or quality of these films, the legislation's main effect was simply to promote the production of cheap 'quota quickies', made by both British and American-controlled companies with the sole purpose of exploiting the privileged access to screens. Lacking Hollywood skills and production values, these films proved unpopular with everyone except their producers.

The expansion prompted by the Films Act, coupled with the upheavals of sound, resulted in a major reorganisation of the industry. Two large, vertically integrated concerns emerged, both of which looked to the banking institutions for capital. Scottish businessman John Maxwell brought together his ABC circuit of cinemas with a new production company, British International Pictures (BIP). Acquiring sound patents from RCA, Maxwell financed the building of studio sound stages at Elstree, where rising star Alfred Hitchcock was hired at considerable expense to make films like *Blackmail* (1929), with its innovative sound effects. Maxwell was careful to keep his budgets under control, so that he at least stood a chance of recouping a film's costs from a domestic release alone. BIP's output through the 1930s, however, was largely undistinguished. The other major group, in which the American Fox Corporation held an interest, was the Gaumont-British Picture Corporation, forged from an alliance of Balcon's Gainsborough Pictures and the old Gaumont company.

Rome Express

With new production facilities in Shepherd's Bush in London, Balcon produced the first internationally successful British sound film, *Rome Express* (1932, director Walter Forde). In the early 1930s Gaumont-British made some twenty films a year, many of them directed by Walter Forde or Victor Saville, who guided the musical star Jessie Matthews through five hit films.

Films like *Evergreen* (1934) and *It's Love Again* (1936), both Jessie Matthews vehicles, typify one important strand of British cinema in the 1930s. These are innocent showcases for a stage talent; and although both films have a glossy, art deco style, they are directly comparable to productions set lower down the social scale with Northern music-hall stars like

Gracie Fields, George Formby and Will Hay. The world in these films is a bright, happy place, filled with stoical optimism, and neither the decade's mass unemployment nor international events like the Spanish civil war or the 1938 Munich crisis is allowed to intrude. In part, this was the result of a rigorous system of censorship, which not only prevented the screening of foreign films like *Battleship Potemkin*, apparently because the Admiralty feared a naval mutiny being depicted on screen, but which also applied tight constraints on the depiction of sexual immorality and political events.

Jessie Matthews in Evergreen

The decade's most consistently distinctive work is associated with Alfred Hitchcock, who directed a remarkable sequence of thrillers for Gaumont-British. Films like *The 39 Steps* (1935) and *The Lady Vanishes* (1938) created his reputation as 'the master of suspense' and led to David Selznick's offer to work in Hollywood. Hitchcock's features are crammed with novel ideas. Elsewhere the achievement of the British cinema in these years is a modest one, based on solid craftsmanship rather than originality.

Although Hollywood continued to extract the lion's share of cinema revenues, both sound and the 1927 legislation encouraged the American corporations to make new links with the British industry. The Films Act had not specified that 'British' companies had to be British-controlled; indeed, at least later in the decade, the Board of Trade welcomed what it saw as foreign investment in the film industry. So at the turn of the decade, to circumvent the quota restrictions, both Warners and RKO initiated production programmes in the United Kingdom. Paramount, too, struck production deals with Herbert Wilcox, and with a producer new to Britain who had worked for them in Hollywood, Alexander Korda.

The 39 Steps

Alexander Korda

Two years after he came to Britain, trailing a colourful career in his native Hungary, in Germany, Hollywood and France, the producer-director Alexander Korda enjoyed a huge success with his film *The Private Life of Henry VIII* (1933). Made by his own company, London Films, this feature was consciously aimed at the international market with which Korda was already familiar. Released in America through United Artists, it generated enormous revenues and quickly won him a co-production deal, and later a partnership, with the Hollywood company. This triumph appeared to indicate that prestigious British films could earn profits abroad, and with little more security than this illusion Korda assembled an impressive package of

140

financing from, among others, the Prudential Assurance Company. He began a rapid expansion programme, including many new productions and the construction of lavish new studios at Denham, soon staffed by a broad range of cosmopolitan talent. René Clair, Jacques Feyder and Josef von Sternberg, together with many others, came to work for him, but his casts and most of his stories were deeply British.

The Private Life of Henry VIII

Among Korda's most interesting productions were two costly films from stories by H.G. Wells – the science-fiction spectacular *Things to Come* and *The Man Who Could Work Miracles* (both 1936). He was also successful with three exotic Imperial epics – *Sanders of the River* (1935, with Paul Robeson), *The Drum* (1938) and *The Four Feathers* (1939). All this activity spurred an industry-wide boom in both production and studio construction, although during 1937 the boom started to look like one further phase of the crisis. Despite his links with United Artists, Korda encountered enormous problems in the United States, and other producers soon recognised that their expensive films would not recover their costs across the Atlantic. With rare exceptions, the films simply did not appeal to American audiences. In addition, producers were consistently hampered by the attitudes of the American distributors. In 1938, under threat of bankruptcy, Korda had to surrender Denham to the Prudential.

Looking to profit from problems at Gaumont-British, in 1936 John Maxwell tried, unsuccessfully, to take over the company. But the former duopoly was also being challenged by two other significant forces. One was Oscar Deutsch's Odeon circuit, which by 1937 numbered about 200 cinemas and which enjoyed access to Korda's output. The other was the emerging J. Arthur Rank empire, which included General Film Distributors and new studios at Pinewood. After 1938 Rank also acquired Denham, but the company's serious interest in production did not begin until the final years of the coming war. 1938 also brought new government legislation, which altered the quota system by insisting that any film submitted under it must have a minimum budget of £7,500. Higher budgets would also qualify for greater quota assessments. And such support for quality production helped sustain American interest in prestige projects. Columbia started a co-production deal with Korda, and MGM commissioned Carol Reed's *Climbing High* (1938) and Hitchcock's *The Lady Vanishes* (1938) from Gaumont-British. But after one more film, Hitchcock was not to work in Britain again until 1972. Sailing off to work for Selznick, Hitchcock left behind an industry once more beset by financial problems and a country beginning to accept the inevitability of international conflict.

The Second World War

In the early days of the war all British cinemas were closed because of the fear of air-raids. But their value for morale was recognised and they were soon operating again. Over the next six years the industry was to move from depression, during which Rank continued his programme of acquisitions, to

141

record box-office figures and a programme of films which demonstrated a new confidence and maturity. The first years of the war were disruptive, however, with the requisitioning of studios for storage space and the call-up of personnel leading to a sharp drop in the number of features made. Increased taxation, including big rises in an Entertainment Tax, was also onerous. The quota was suspended in October 1942; but by now British films were more acceptable in the United States, and adequate foreign distribution was secured with the help of the Ministry of Information.

British audiences too responded to the efforts of domestic producers, even though there were only 46 new releases in the worst year, 1942 (compared with 228 in the boom-time of 1937). Simply going to the cinema was a form of social relaxation, since there were few other leisure activities available. By 1945 the average weekly attendance was over 30 million. The Ministry of Information recognised the cinema's fundamental importance and, as well as assisting and encouraging producers, exercised a degree of guidance which has subsequently been described as an 'informal pre-censorship of projects'.

The war prompted distinguished documentaries (considered in Chapter 11) and a number of successful features, like Pat Jackson's *Western Approaches* (1941), which based low-key dramas on the experiences of men at war. The documentary influence was also felt in the commercial studios, most particularly at Ealing where former GPO Film Unit directors like Alberto Cavalcanti and Harry Watt were employed by producer Michael Balcon. Portrayals of the war at home, such as *Millions Like Us* (1943) and *Waterloo Road* (1944), the former written and directed by Frank Launder and Sidney Gilliat and the latter by Gilliat alone, also extended this impetus, offering sympathetic portraits of working-class families.

The home front: Eric Portman, Anne Crawford in Millions Like Us

The outstanding wartime films – those from Ealing, those produced by Gainsborough, and those made by Michael Powell and Emeric Pressburger – are treated in Chapter 15, along with the later work which made the 1940s probably the British cinema's richest decade. 1946 saw the highest annual total of admissions, and an ambitious plan by J. Arthur Rank to succeed where Korda had failed a decade before. Having taken over in 1941 as chairman of both Gaumont-British and the Odeon cinema circuit, Rank had quickly become by far the dominant figure in the industry. Now he intended to take on the American market, and to challenge Hollywood's control of international distribution and exhibition.

142

The film industry in France

The conversion to sound brought burdens as well as benefits to the French film industry. Effectively tripling production costs, sound seriously restricted the sources of finance available to new projects. Less powerful producers also found themselves squeezed out by the patents battle between the American companies and the German Tobis-Klangfilm system. The result was the consolidation, comparable to that in Britain, of two large, vertically integrated combines: Gaumont-Franco-Film-Aubert (GFFA) and Pathé-Nathan. Both embraced sound production with enthusiasm, but the national financial crisis in 1934 coupled with bad management brought both close to bankruptcy. After this, film production splintered among numerous small companies, which often existed only to make a single film. Despite these problems, audience resistance to subtitling and dubbing, together with quota restrictions introduced in 1932, meant that domestic production retained a significant share of the market. French films were also newly popular in countries which shared the language. As in Britain, fears about the dominance of the American cinema were widely expressed, but in the later 1930s the French industry maintained a level of production which averaged around 100 features a year.

Co-financing and co-production arrangements added numerous complexities to the industry's production profile. In 1930, for example, in a doomed attempt to dominate the European market, Paramount took over the Joinville studios to make low-budget films in several languages. Of the more than one hundred films made here in a hectic year one of the most interesting is Alexander Korda's version of Marcel Pagnol's stage drama *Marius* (1931). French-language films were also made in Hollywood, and in Berlin. Indeed, there was constant interaction with Germany, and several of René Clair's best films were made for Tobis-Klangfilm at their sound studios in Epinay. French producers needed capital as badly as German financiers wanted to earn foreign currency, and this relationship was little affected by the rise to power of the Nazis. Film-makers like Julien Duvivier and Jean Grémillon worked in the Ufa studios in Berlin, but such a migration was reversed in later years as Paris became a home to many film industry personnel who fled Nazi Germany.

The fragmented, often chaotic production sector after 1934 was paralleled by the systems of distribution and exhibition. Outside the capital, family firms controlling only a few films or one or two cinemas were the norm. But they could rely on a large regular audience, admission was cheap, and after the social reforms of 1936 workers had more leisure hours to fill. This audience was primarily interested in the farces, romances and melodramas which accounted for the overwhelming majority of features at this time, but it also supported the innovative work of directors like Carné and Renoir. Despite detailed consideration of the industry in 1936-7 the state did not intervene in the cinema, either to support domestic companies or to encourage quality productions. Even so, the fact that writers and directors were working outside the constraints of large-scale studio production, together with the security of a guaranteed audience, meant that France produced a richly diverse cinematic culture in these years.

The films which stand out from the commercial cinema are now usually identified as the creations of their directors, but they must also be seen as collaborations with a unique group of scriptwriters, designers and stars. The writer Charles Spaak, for example, was a central figure, collaborating regularly with Jacques Feyder, with Julien Duvivier on *La belle équipe* (1936), and with Jean Renoir on several of his best films. Another key writer was Jacques Prévert, who made a group of major films with Marcel Carné. The art director Alexandre Trauner and actors like Raimu, Jean Gabin and Arletty were also central to this period of French cinema.

The label 'poetic realism', which is attached to a number of the most distinctive films of the decade, is an imprecise term, used to link the work of Duvivier and Grémillon, the regional drama of Marcel Pagnol, and especially the films of Carné and Renoir. Working for small, independent producers, these directors enjoyed far more freedom than they would have been granted in Hollywood, but their limited budgets inevitably imposed restrictions on the subjects and the scale of their films. Elements common to the features of 'poetic realism' include a concern for working-class characters and everyday dramas, and naturalistic speech and settings. But

Poetic realism: Carné's Quai des brumes, *written by Jacques Prévert, designed by Alexandre Trauner*

these are heightened by strands of stylisation, in the dialogue and in the art direction, by a scattering of symbols, and in particular by a moody fatalism.

It is the films of Marcel Carné which are most readily associated with 'poetic realism'. Carné had been an influential critic and an assistant to Clair and Feyder before he made his debut with *Jenny* (1936). There followed *Drôle de drame* (1937) and *Hotel du nord* (1938), but it is *Quai des brumes* (1938) and *Le Jour se lève* (1939) which are considered as his major pre-war films. Both star Gabin as a proletarian outsider, and both were scripted by Jacques Prévert; and unlike many contemporary French films, they are

144

works of cinema which owe nothing to the stage. They also exhibit a profound despair, suggesting that life is lived in an irrational and indifferent world, and imbued with a pessimism reflecting what came to be regarded as the essential mood of a country about to be overwhelmed by war.

The Popular Front and Jean Renoir

In May 1936 a Popular Front government came to power in France, uniting the parties of the left under Léon Blum. Although this government lasted only just over a year there was a widespread sense of a new beginning, which was particularly important in encouraging artists and intellectuals on the left to search for new forms capable of expressing the politics of the moment. The cinema was particularly important to these debates, at the centre of which was the work of the key film-maker of the period, and indeed of French cinema in the 1930s, Jean Renoir.

The son of the painter Auguste, Renoir had started in the industry in 1923, and in 1926 had directed a remarkable version of Zola's novel *Nana*, much influenced by Stroheim's *Foolish Wives* and an early example of how brilliantly he could weave together tragedy and comedy. Renoir worked on further adaptations, before *Toni* (1935), made for Pagnol in Marseilles, brought to the fore an explicit concern with contemporary political and social issues. Its tale of love and murder among local labourers has since been seen as a precursor of Italian neo-realism.

Le Crime de Monsieur Lange (1936), a political comedy in which class tensions culminate in murder, was made with a left-wing theatre group. Next Renoir supervised the production of *La Vie est à nous* (1936), a documentary-based survey of France, sponsored by the Communist Party and released just before the elections which brought the Popular Front government to power. At the same time a workers production co-operative called Ciné-Liberté was founded, with Renoir as its secretary. During 1937, as the dreams of the moment turned to disillusionment, the society raised funds by subscription and began production on Renoir's *La Marseillaise* (1938). In this tale from the French Revolution can be found all the complexities and contradictions of a heady, but doomed, political struggle.

Renoir's other work at the end of the decade includes a powerful adaptation of Zola's *La Bête humaine* (1938, written with Charles Spaak) and two immensely rich studies of national and class conflict. *La grande illusion* (1937, also scripted with Spaak) is a First World War story about a group of French officers held in a German castle and their different attitudes towards the Prussian aristocrat commandant. *La Règle du jeu* (1939) takes place during a country-house weekend and constructs an elaborate counterpoint out of the affairs of masters and servants. Generally regarded as masterpieces of cinema, both are films of profound insight into the disintegration of an old social order, exposing the follies of their characters but always retaining a sympathy for them.

During the Vichy period exile from France was the choice of a number of

Jean Renoir (with Nora Gregor) in his own La Règle du jeu

145

the industry's most prominent figures. Clair, Renoir, Duvivier and Feyder, as well as actors Jean Gabin and Louis Jouvet, all elected to work abroad. Jews could no longer be employed; and many of the key works of 'poetic realism' were withdrawn. But under German control, and stimulated by the ban on foreign films, domestic production flourished. With fewer companies, with financing regularised by a number of government measures, and with record attendances, the system was more stable than it had been in the previous decade. Political themes were forbidden, but fantasy and the spectacular were particularly popular, notable examples being Marcel Carné's *Les Visiteurs du soir* (1942) and his theatrical epic *Les Enfants du Paradis* (1943-5), written by Jacques Prévert and designed by Alexandre Trauner. The uncertainties and contradictions of this period also found form in, for example, Henri-Georges Clouzot's thriller *Le Corbeau* (1943), in which a small town is terrorised by poison-pen letters. And a working-class drama like *Le Ciel est à nous* (1944), directed by Jean Grémillon and adapted by Spaak, could be publicly praised for its support of Vichy values and yet used as a symbol of resistance by the underground press.

Les Enfants du Paradis *(Jean-Louis Barrault)*

Germany under the Third Reich
At the end of the 1920s Hollywood set up a range of distribution and co-production agreements with German companies. These deals were intended to increase the German film industry's reliance on foreign capital, and consequently to curb its considerable power. But the country's largest production group, Ufa, was rescued in 1927 from an unfavourable arrangement with Paramount and Universal by the newspaper magnate Alfred Hugenberg. Hugenberg was subsequently to be appointed as the Nazi Minister of Economic Affairs, and well before Hitler was established as Chancellor in January 1933 the film industry's sympathy towards the National Socialists was encouraged by this powerful friend.

At the Ministry for Popular Enlightenment and Propaganda Hitler installed Dr Joseph Goebbels, who was made responsible for 'all tasks of spiritual direction of the nation'. Goebbels immediately set about establishing direct state control of the film industry. Scripts had to be approved before government-aided financing was made available, the industry was ruthlessly purged of Jews and other 'decadent artists', the state was able to encourage the production of 'good' or approved films by the use of tax legislation, and in 1936 all art criticism, including anything but 'descriptive' writing about films, was outlawed as negative and destructive.

During 1937 and 1938 Goebbels effectively nationalised the film industry by buying up and refinancing the major production companies, none of which was financially strong enough to resist. In 1939 these state-controlled companies accounted for 60 per cent of feature film production; two years later the figure was 70 per cent. At the same time the German conquest of Europe created a huge new monopoly exhibition structure for the domestic industry. Now the problem was the production of sufficient films to meet the

146

increased demand; and in 1942, to ensure a satisfactorily high level of output, full state ownership of the industry was consolidated in the giant new combine, Ufa-Film GmbH, or Ufi.

Goebbels had expressed his hopes for the new German cinema in an important March 1933 speech. 'The film can only be re-established on a healthy basis,' he said, 'if German nationality is remembered in the industry and German nature is portrayed in it . . . The only possible art is one which is rooted in the soil of National Socialism.' A cinema enthusiast (he greatly admired Eisenstein's *Battleship Potemkin),* Goebbels rejected Hitler's crude notion of film as 'an instrument of propaganda' and believed fervently in the idea of 'invisible' propaganda. 'The best propaganda,' he maintained, 'is that which works as it were invisibly, penetrates the whole of life without the public having any knowledge at all of the propagandist initiative.' His views were vindicated by the popular success in 1933 of *Hitlerjunge Quex,* which was less overtly political than other approved films of the time, and 'invisible propaganda' became his guiding principle for the next twelve years. A film which well illustrates this is *Friedrich Schiller* (1940, directed by Herbert Maisch), which relates the problems of the young Schiller at his military academy. Numerous other Nazi films exalted a historical 'genius' in a similar fashion, including *Robert Koch* (1939), *Andreas Schlüter, Rembrandt* (both 1942) and *Paracelsus* (1943). In a way, these men were to be seen as projections of the Führer, and Nazi ideas are written into the films. Genius is an inherent quality, derived from race, and is not to be constrained by the petty concerns, including the laws, of those who make up the mass.

Other clearly identifiable cycles within Nazi cinema include no less than ten films about the Prussian leader Frederick the Great; dramas which feature a hero's return to an idealised Germany; and numerous films which construct a unified national community, untroubled by the complexities of class or history. Several of these films look back to an innocent, pre-capitalist era, located either in the medieval world of *Paracelsus* or in a timeless rural homeland, which is the setting for Veit Harlan's *Carnival* (1943).

The characteristics of the Nazi cinema, however, should not be attributed solely to Goebbels' control of the industry. Siegfried Kracauer's influential book *From Caligari to Hitler* argues that many of the themes which mark films in the Third Reich are present in the German cinema of the 1920s. Mountain films, for example, like *The White Hell of Pitz Palü* (1929, directed by Arnold Fanck and G. W. Pabst) or Leni Riefenstahl's *The Blue Light* (1932), were popular throughout the decade. Kracauer identifies in these films a pantheistic impulse which was visible in many later Nazi films, not least the spectacular documentaries of Leni Riefenstahl (see Chapter 11).

Paracelsus, *one of many films made in Nazi Germany which looked back to inspirational figures of the past. Paracelsus was directed by G. W. Pabst, whose curious career extended from the disenchantment of* Die freudlose Gasse *(1925, with Asta Nielsen and Greta Garbo), through the heady eroticism of* Pandora's Box *(1929, with Louise Brooks) and the internationalism of* Kameradschaft *(1931), to post-war films like* The Trial *(1948) and* The Jackboot Mutiny *(1955, about the plot to assassinate Hitler). Why Pabst, having exiled himself from Germany in 1933, decided to return when war broke out has never been satisfactorily explained.*

Anti-semitism: Jud Süss

Alongside the 'invisible propaganda' films, German cinemas screened many straightforwardly propagandist documentaries and newsreels. Their overt messages were underlined by crude and explicitly political features like *Jud Süss* (1940, directed by Veit Harlan), one of a number of films which propagated hatred towards a target identified as the source of all misery. Both the Bolsheviks and the British (in *Ohm Krüger,* 1941) were singled out in this way, but the most virulent attacks, inevitably, were against the Jews. *Jud Süss,* set in the mid-18th century, portrays the Jewish race not only as physically repellent but also as criminal, utterly unscrupulous, eager to ravish pure Nordic maidens, and above all bent on world domination. The film was immensely popular, and reportedly prompted demonstrations and attacks against Jews. 1940 also saw the release of two other major anti-semitic films, *Die Rothschilds* and the virulent *Der ewige Jude,* and all three films played throughout Germany as mass deportations to the concentration camps were stepped up.

Entertainment in Italy

The Italian cinema was particularly hard hit by the aftermath of the First World War. Production slumped and by the early 1920s the Americans, with exciting films and a vigorous and effective export policy, had acquired up to 90 per cent of the Italian market. The distribution of American imports was largely in the hands of one company, the Società Anonima Stefano Pittaluga (S A S P), which also ran the country's largest exhibition chain. S A S P was not interested in film production and Stefano Pittaluga was quoted as saying, 'Whoever wants to make films in this country is either a hero, a philanthropist or a cretin.' But when in 1926 the Americans, alarmed at the success of German films in European markets, decided to create their own distribution network in Italy, bypassing S A S P, Pittaluga decided to enter production on his own account.

This was the first stage of an attempted resistance to Hollywood which would occupy the Italian industry until the Second World War and beyond. The motives were largely commercial, but partly cultural. The Fascist government, which had come to power in 1922, had at first no policy towards the cinema, but it allowed itself to be persuaded by Pittaluga of the economic advantages of a system of support to the industry which would make Italy less dependent on American imports. Pittaluga's policy was to compete with the Americans at their own game. He had studio stages constructed to take advantage of the opportunity provided by the coming of sound and the public's demand for Italian talkies. The company, however, remained dependent for its profitability on the distribution of American product and, with the successful introduction of dubbing, the Hollywood film regained its popularity and the American stranglehold on the Italian industry remained in place.

When Pittaluga died in 1931, there was an attempt to establish an artistic cinema inside the remains of the S A S P empire. But films like *Acciaio (Steel,*

1933), directed by the German documentarist Walter Ruttmann from a story by Luigi Pirandello, proved unsuccessful at the box office. At the same time the state indicated its interest in seeing other, smaller producers flourish alongside the SASP monopoly, but in an economy badly hit by the world depression few were able to survive. In 1934 the government, as part of a general economic restructuring, decided to take the film industry under centralised control, a process which was completed by 1938. Under the leadership of Luigi Freddi, the restructured industry concentrated on the commercially and culturally safe genres of comedy and domestic melodrama. Production levels steadily increased, until by the time of the overthrow of Fascism in 1943 some 120 features a year were being made.

The white telephone era: Il signor Max

Many of the comedies had society and aristocratic settings, and came to be known as 'white telephone' films – after the object which was regarded as the height of luxury and modernity. The director most closely associated with these films was Mario Camerini, who frequently worked with the actor (subsequently to become the neo-realist director) Vittorio De Sica, as in *I'll Give a Million* (1935) and *Il signor Max* (1937). Films like these, with their very mild social criticism, offered tacit support for the regime. Only a handful of dramas and adventure films openly acted as vehicles for Fascist policies and ideas. Carmine Gallone's *Scipione l'Africano* (1937) is particularly interesting for its attempt to derive Fascist lessons from a reading of Ancient Roman history. Scipio, the hero, is chosen by popular acclaim to be Rome's leader in the struggle against Carthage. Rome is seen as a model for Fascism while Carthage is insidiously oriental and barbarian. Coming at the time of Italy's invasion of Abyssinia and subsequent censure by the League of Nations, the film's message was obvious.

Ancient Roman: Scipione l'Africano

The most interesting director of the period, however, was Alessandro Blasetti. A convinced Fascist, he had campaigned vigorously if unsuccessfully in the 1920s for an understanding of the cinema as an art form, drawing heavily on ideas from France and Russia. His film *Sole* (*Sun*, 1929), about the draining of the Pontine marshes, was described by Mussolini as 'the dawn of the Fascist film'. On the whole, though, the regime showed little interest in Blasetti and his ideas, preferring to allow the cinema to develop as a commercial entertainment. In spite of universal discouragement, Blasetti persevered. His remarkable drama, *1860* (1934), which tells the story of a Sicilian peasant's encounter with Garibaldi and his army, is clearly ideologically in line with official interpretations of the Risorgimento, but it is certainly not facile propaganda. In its editing and its concern for the choice of faces it bears the distinct influence of the Russian revolutionary cinema, and because it was shot on location with a largely non-professional cast it looks forward to post-war neo-realism. With the failure of his next film, *Vecchia Guardia* (1935), Blasetti became disillusioned with Fascism. In 1941 he made the distinctly unpolitical studio-produced fantasy *Corona di ferro*, and the following year returned to the streets to make *Quattro passi fra le nuvole* (*Four Steps in the Clouds*, 1942), a clear forerunner of neo-realism.

When Italy entered the war in 1940, feature films set against the conflict were quickly put into production. Francesco De Robertis' *Uomini sul fondo* (1941), shot on a submarine with a non-professional cast, is a semi-documentary comparable in many ways to a British war film like *Western Approaches*. De Robertis also collaborated with Roberto Rossellini on *La nave bianca* (1942), and Rossellini made two further films in support of the war, *Un pilota ritorna* (1942) and *L'uomo dalla croce* (1943). But as Rome was occupied by the Germans in 1943 and liberated by the Allies in the following year, the infrastructure of the film industry crumbled. A few films were produced under the short-lived Republic of Salò in 1944 and 1945, but in Rome and elsewhere the Americans effectively dismantled whatever had escaped the bombing. Hollywood was eager to offer itself as a replacement. But the signs of a new Italian cinema were already apparent, in Visconti's *Ossessione* (1942) and in Rossellini's *Rome Open City*, which was released in the autumn of 1945.

Japan

Like the popular German and Italian cinema of the 1930s, much of the decade's output from Japan is little known. Indeed almost forty years after its supposed 'introduction' in the West, when Akira Kurosawa's *Rashomon* won the Grand Prix at Venice in 1951, the Japanese cinema as a whole is still relatively inaccessible to audiences in the West. A handful of names are familiar: Kurosawa of course, and the actor associated with many of his earlier films, Toshiro Mifune, together with the directors Mizoguchi and Ozu. But the extraordinary richness of the Japanese cinema remains sparsely documented in English.

Both Kenji Mizoguchi and Yasujiro Ozu began to work in the film industry in the early 1920s, when Japan was achieving more success than most countries at withstanding Hollywood's aggressive export policies. The well-established Nikkatsu company owned 350 of the 600 main theatres, and both a government tax on imports and censorship restrictions were additional barriers. Nonetheless numerous foreign films were screened, and one element in certain Japanese films of the time is an intriguing balance of domestic and foreign styles and concerns. Both Ozu and his colleague Heinosuke Gosho remembered their excitement at seeing American films, and both recognised this influence on their own work. Ozu included American film posters in many of his early films, and his silent film *That Night's Wife* (1930) is a thriller with obvious American affinities.

Imports had begun as early as 1897 when both the Lumière company and Edison had organised screenings in Japan. Along with straw boaters, specta-

150

cles and other Western products, films became immediately fashionable, and new views of the Occident were eagerly awaited. Early domestic production included local actualities but was dominated by films made in collaboration with traditional theatre companies, the Shimpa troupes. Theatrical conventions were also carried over into the actual screenings of films, which were invariably accompanied by a *benshi*, or narrator, who explained in great detail what was happening on screen. The *benshi* were popular enough with audiences to stop early experiments with synchronised dialogue.

Prior to the First World War Japan's own industry was dominated by the Nikkatsu company, which owned the two main studios and a string of theatres. Nikkatsu had been formed by the country's four main producers as an equivalent of the Trust in the United States, but 1914 saw the formation of the rival Tenkatsu company, which soon proved to be more adventurous in the film-making techniques it adopted. Theatrical conventions dictated the norms until they were overturned by, among others, the director Norimasa Kaeriyama. Soon the influence of the American cinema was recognisable in a broad range of films. A new production company, Shochiku, began to specialise in such films, although they often met resistance at the box-office. In 1923, American imports were boosted by the earthquake which devastated Tokyo and much of the domestic film industry. Hollywood films were more widely seen in the months after the disaster, but within a year Nikkatsu and other strong, vertically integrated companies had won back a significant share of the market.

In the years after the earthquake the most significant genre was known as *jidai-geki*, or traditional tales of period drama. Critics identify the late 1920s and early 1930s as a golden age for these period films, and single out the work of the directors Masahiro Makino and, particularly, Daisuke Ito. Ito's films, like *Servant* (1927) and *Man-Slashing, Horse-Piercing Sword* (1930), are distinguished by their violent realism, often featuring a heroic samurai whose actions expose the inequalities of feudal society. Another master of the period film, albeit a rather idiosyncratic one, was Teinosuke Kinugasa, who began directing in 1922 and set up one of Japan's few independent production companies in 1926. His contemporary subject film *A Page of Madness* (1926) uses fast intercutting, expressionistic camerawork and a confusion of time periods in a strikingly experimental manner.

Along with the popular historical dramas were films with a contemporary setting (*gendai-geki*), including what have been called 'tendency' films which focus on a social issue. Partly a response to economic depression, these films explored the problems of the lower middle-class and the proletariat. Mizoguchi's films *Street*

Japanese experiment: Kinugasa's A Page of Madness

Sketches (1925) and *A Paper Doll's Whisper of Spring* (1926) can be seen as part of this movement, as can *Tricky Girl* (1927) directed by Heinosuke Gosho. The introduction of sound was far from smooth, partly because of technical inadequacies, partly because of resistance from the *benshi*, and partly because of a suspicion of the technology by established film-makers. Gosho's 1931 film *The Neighbour's Wife and Mine* showed that sound could be used creatively, and find a wide audience. It also established its production and exhibition company, Shochiku, as the foremost producer of the time. In the middle of the decade Shochiku's position was challenged by the new Toho Corporation. Shochiku expanded and endeavoured to organise an exhibitors' boycott of Toho, but in the ensuing bitter and occasionally violent tussle it was Toho which established itself at the head of the industry, consuming a number of other independents along the way.

Many of the most notable films from the 1930s are *shomin-geki*, contemporary tales of middle-class life, some with a melodramatic inflection, others intentionally comic. Gosho was prominent in the genre, as was Mikio Naruse, whose 1935 film *Wife! Be Like a Rose!* was even successfully screened in America. Naruse's subject, to which he returns again and again, is the impossibility of family life, and he treats this theme through both comedy and serious drama. Detail, honesty, an almost obsessive scrutiny of emotional sterility – these are the qualities which mark out his work. Another director whose work was until recently virtually unknown in the West is Hiroshi Shimizu, whose films – often about children – reveal an innovatory camera style distinguished by extended travelling shots.

Shomin-geki comedy is probably most closely associated with Yasujiro Ozu. Working for Shochiku in the early 1930s, he extended that company's exploitation of comic domestic drama, but unlike many of his contemporaries he created films which entirely avoided sentimentality. His plots are usually though deceptively spare, as is the distinctive shooting style which he was to refine over the years. Donald Richie has described it as 'a series of scenes in which the camera is always at the same height, that of a person seated on the *tatami* matting of the Japanese room; the camera never pans and rarely dollies; the scenes are connected only by the simple cut.' This style (in fact rather more subtle than Richie implies) was already formed when Ozu made *Tokyo Chorus* in 1931, a film which reveals a darker side beneath the comedy in its story of an unemployed man forced to carry a sandwich board to support his family. The film also features the actor Chishu Ryu, who appeared in many of Ozu's films. The next year Ozu directed *I Was Born, But . . .*, a critical view of a man as seen by his two young sons. Like Naruse, Ozu consistently explored in his films the complexities of family life.

During the 1930s Kenji Mizoguchi also directed a number of significant *shomin-geki* films, including *Osaka Elegy* and *Sisters of the Gion* (both 1936). Although it would be misleading to suggest that Mizoguchi's work is more committed than that of Ozu to social analysis, these films do present their

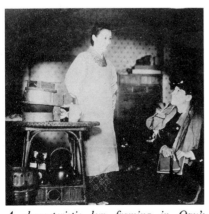

A characteristic low framing in Ozu's Woman of Tokyo *(1933)*

characters reacting to society's financial and moral pressures. *Sisters of the Gion* is a study of two sisters who are both geisha; one has 'modern' attitudes, the other clings to tradition. Their clash is set against an atmospheric portrait of the Gion district of Kyoto.

The Japanese cinema was largely unprepared for the conflict with China, since the contemporary war film had been almost entirely absent from its history. The earliest responses to the intensification of the war were a number of low-key, realist films made in 1939, of which the most interesting is Tomotaka Tasaka's *Five Scouts*. Its downbeat tale of a group of infantrymen bewildered by the fighting is quite different from the individual heroics which Hollywood was later to celebrate. Throughout 1938 and 1939 the government imposed new regulations on the industry, encouraging the production of 'positive' films about contemporary events. After 1940 'national policy' films were made under the direction of the Office of Public Information, and oppositional voices were almost completely silenced, although Heinosuke Gosho drained the 'national policy' elements from the scripts he was expected to film, making their wartime settings far less significant than their foreground romance. After Pearl Harbor ultra-nationalism and a stress on the importance of sacrifice became increasingly dominant features of the Japanese cinema.

Sacrifice was equally important to the films set on the home front. Ozu made two domestic dramas – *The Brothers and Sisters of the Toda Family* (1941) and *There Was a Father* (1942) – which some critics have seen as extolling the virtues of traditional patriarchy and the Japanese national spirit. And Akira Kurosawa's second film, *The Most Beautiful* (1944), is a typical home front tale about young women working in a military factory. Kurosawa's two other wartime features suffered at the hands of censors, and the originality of his work was not to become apparent until the years of the Occupation. Mizoguchi's work mostly escaped such attention, in part because he avoided

Jidai-geki: Mizoguchi's The 47 Ronin (1941)

153

the issues of the day and concentrated on tales of the Kabuki theatre in the Meiji era, like his remarkable *The Story of the Late Chrysanthemums* (1939).

In 1941 the government imposed a major restructuring of the Japanese film industry. The ten major companies were reorganised into three, built round Shochiku, Toho and Nikkatsu. Production was cut back, and as hostilities intensified many of the larger theatres were forced to close. But the war also made the industry more aware of the possibilities beyond its own shores. A number of (mostly unsuccessful) co-productions with Germany were initiated, and there was a push for expansion into other Asian markets. In a sense, the war made an important contribution to revitalising the industry, although it was to be battered again by the pressures of Hollywood during the Occupation.

In Britain the war had also brought new life to the cinema. In France, too, the industry was to make a relatively smooth transition to peacetime conditions. Hollywood, however, was poised to reclaim its hold on the Axis countries. In Germany, where Ufi was quickly dismantled by the Allies, the production and distribution infrastructure was effectively destroyed. As it was, to an even greater degree, in Italy. For the film industry in Rome, as for Italian society as a whole, 1945 was 'Year Zero'. But it was from these ruins that the most vigorous of post-war national cinemas was to emerge.

Further reading

Joseph L. Anderson and Donald Richie, *The Japanese Film*, New York: Grove Press, 1959.

Roy Armes, *French Cinema*, London: Secker & Warburg, 1985.

Raymond Durgnat, *Renoir*, London: Studio Vista, 1975.

James Hay, *Popular Film Culture in Fascist Italy*, Bloomington and Indianapolis: Indiana University Press, 1987.

Siegfried Kracauer, *From Caligari to Hitler: A Psychological History of the German Film*, Princeton: Princeton University Press, 1947, rev. ed. 1973.

Erwin Leiser, *Nazi Cinema*, London, Secker & Warburg, 1975.

Pierre Leprohon, *The Italian Cinema*, London: Secker & Warburg, 1972.

Rachael Low, *The History of the British Film 1929-1939: Film making in 1930s Britain*, London: Allen & Unwin, 1985.

Joan Mellen, *The Waves at Genji's Door: Japan Through its Cinema*, New York: Pantheon Books, 1976.

Julian Petley, *Capital and Culture: German Cinema 1933-45*, London: British Film Institute, 1979.

S.S. Prawer, *Caligari's Children: The Film as Tale of Terror*, New York: Oxford University Press, 1980.

Jeffrey Richards, *The Age of the Dream Palace: Cinema and Society in Britain 1930-1939*, London: Routledge & Kegan Paul, 1984.

Ginette Vincendeau and Keith Reader (ed.), *La Vie est à nous: French Cinema of the Popular Front 1935-1938*, London: British Film Institute, 1986.

11
Documentaries, Newsreels and the News

In the immediate post-war years the documentary form seemed to many to be – at least temporarily – exhausted. For more than two decades a single impetus had united, despite many differences, the films of Robert Flaherty, of Dziga Vertov, of the British directors working under John Grierson in the 1930s, and of those who had chronicled the war. But now that impetus appeared to have dissipated. Distinctive creative achievements were rarer, and sponsorship was increasingly hard to secure. 1951 brought the end of *The March of Time*, for sixteen years the unrivalled leader of the regular newsreel magazines. And a year later Britain's Crown Film Unit, which had assumed the mantle of the social documentary movement, was pronounced uneconomic and closed down.

In retrospect, the pessimism and uncertainty of this time can be seen as reflections of a period of transition. Since Lumière, both newsreel and documentary had been nurtured, albeit often grudgingly, by the cinema; but soon both would be developed almost exclusively by television. This new medium was now increasingly the way by which people were coming to see and understand the world around them. Television news, for example, at first depended on footage supplied by newsreel companies, but this reliance was quickly superseded by its own more flexible cameras and by the possibility of 'live' coverage. Nonetheless, for all the potential of the new medium, the tradition of the classic documentary was to remain a potent influence on television practitioners.

It has always been problematic to find a definition to encompass the diverse techniques and approaches, in both cinema and television, to which the word 'documentary' has been applied. John Grierson initially used the term for 'all films made from natural material . . . where the camera shot on the spot'. Later he was to offer a more famous definition: 'the creative treatment of actuality'. But the essential point about documentary, as Grierson recognised, is that no variant of the form can provide any kind of unmediated 'reflection of reality'. Whatever is recorded on celluloid or videotape is always, and in many different ways, a construction. It is influenced and shaped by politics, social forces, aesthetic choices, economic

155

constraints and the available technology. Any viewer actively interprets this construction in particular ways, shaping and supplementing it according to conventions and prejudices, to arrive at one individual sense of the 'reality' being shown. So there is never a single meaning for a film; moreover, the meanings available change over time, and are read differently by different audiences. Documentary is not 'objective'.

Early actualities

Although its pre-history could be held to include newspaper engravings and photography, the documentary film inevitably begins with Louis Lumière's first 'actualities'. These single, fixed framings presented fragments of middle-class French life in and around Lyon, and they and their many imitators dominated early cinema programmes. Within months of his Paris premiere in December 1895 Lumière's cameramen were travelling widely to film new subjects and to set up screenings of actuality material. In 1896, for example, Lumière programmes featured not only *Coronation of Nicholas II* from Russia, but also *Melbourne Races*, shot in Australia. Other film-makers were soon competing with Lumière. In the United States Thomas Edison's assistants shot scenes such as *Pile Driving — Washington Navy Yard* and *Pennsylvania Avenue, Washington DC*. British pioneers produced actualities showing railways, streets and beaches. Movement alone was a sufficient attraction, and spectacles like waves breaking on a shore were popular. Then, as the early grammar of film was developed, a number of different shots of the same scene were assembled together, and the camera was moved on cars and trains.

Television in its early days was to transmit its own versions of these actualities. Early in the BBC's experimental transmissions during 1936 a camera was pushed out onto a balcony, simply to take in the view. More elaborate outside broadcasts followed, the most successful of which was the six-camera coverage of George VI's Coronation procession in May 1937. Since the early days of both film and television, royal and state occasions have been particularly popular. In 1986 the wedding of an English prince could draw an international television audience of hundreds of millions.

Early newsreel: artillery on the move in the Boer War, February 1900. Filmed by the pioneer news photographer and film-maker Joseph Rosenthal, whose prodigious news coverage extended over many parts of the world.

156

Sport, too, was a staple both for early film-makers and for a new television service like the BBC, which was soon presenting coverage of Wimbledon, the Boat Race, and in 1938 a Test Match against Australia. Natural disasters, travel and exploration were also popular subjects for the first patrons of the movie houses, and these subjects retained their appeal after the interest in general actualities began to fade at the end of the cinema's first decade. Audiences were increasingly attracted by drama and comedy, but a particularly remarkable achievement could still command attention. Herbert Ponting, a photographer and cinematographer, had accompanied Captain Scott's expedition to the Antarctic. In 1911 his first footage reached London and the shots of vast frozen landscapes made an enormous impression. Comparable exploration films remain a staple element in television schedules around the world.

Recording man

In 1910 the young explorer Robert Flaherty began a series of expeditions prospecting for mineral deposits around Hudson Bay in Canada, and on his later trips he became increasingly interested in filming the Eskimos with whom he made contact. Over a period of sixteen months he filmed the Inuit people, in particular the exploits of the renowned hunter Nanook. *Nanook of the North* opened in New York cinemas in June 1922, to immediate acclaim. Despite the Inuits' regular contact with the traders and miners who were beginning to exploit the area, Flaherty chose to ignore these contemporary problems, focusing instead on traditional activities like hunting and igloo-building. Like all his subsequent work, *Nanook* is elemental and romantic, stressing a timeless struggle for survival in a battle against hostile Nature.

Flaherty's Nanook of the North

In both *Nanook* and *Moana* (1926), about Samoa in the South Pacific, Flaherty constructed a view of his subject that corresponded to a framework which his audiences could immediately understand and assimilate. Such misrepresentation has been a persistent problem in the work of European and North American film-makers who have chosen to work in cultures other than their own. Following Flaherty's success, features about 'primitive' peoples were particularly popular throughout the 1920s, when producers Merian C. Cooper and Ernest B. Schoedsack (later to create *King Kong*) made *Grass* (1925) in Turkey and Persia, and *Chang* (1927) in Siam.

To accuse such work of misrepresentation is not to suggest that there exists a single, ideal representation of any subject. Nonetheless, the problem of finding appropriate and responsible images of other cultures is one which has long preoccupied ethnographic film-makers. Pioneers in this tradition were Gregory Bateson and Margaret Mead, who in the late 1930s worked on a series of documentaries in Bali and New Guinea. A comparably influential figure was Jean Rouch, who began recording African rituals and dances in the immediate post-war years. Working with a second-hand Bell and Howell 16mm camera, Rouch achieved a remarkable closeness to his subjects. In the controversial *Les maîtres fous* (1955) he also introduced an explicitly political

Rouch's Les maîtres fous

framework – recognising the repressive powers of colonialism – into what had previously been regarded as an academic discipline untouched by such concerns.

As with many other variants of the documentary, ethnographic film-making underwent a radical change after the introduction around 1960 of lightweight cameras which could also record synchronous sound. Previously, the dominant style had been that of the illustrated lecture; now it was possible to work more closely with a group, and to allow them to be far more involved in the filmed representation of their lives. Among the most successful initiatives of this kind has been the television series *Disappearing World*, begun by the Granada TV producer Brian Moser in 1969.

While Flaherty and others were filming subjects far removed from their own contemporary realities, a group of film-makers in the Soviet Union were directly engaging with the political turmoil which surrounded them immediately after the Revolution. From June 1918 the film editor Dziga Vertov and his colleagues produced the compilation newsreel *Kino-Nedelia* ('Film Weekly'), and from 1922 the monthly *Kino-Pravda* ('Film Truth'). These newsreels featured scenes of everyday life, but were shot and edited not simply as a record but as a new way of seeing the world. Vertov saw the camera as an 'eye', better equipped than the human eye to perceive and interpret the realities of daily life and the connections between events. The ideas were developed in documentaries like Vertov's *One Sixth of the World* (1926) and *The Eleventh Year* (1928), and these films were widely seen abroad.

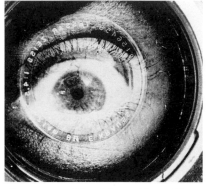

Camera eye: The Man with a Movie Camera

Zuyderzee, *made in 1933 by the Dutch documentarist Joris Ivens, whose film-making career extended over fifty years and a wide range of subjects, from* Rain *(1929) to* Spanish Earth *(1937, about the defence of Madrid) and* How Yukong Moved the Mountains *(1975), a cycle of films about life in China*

The culmination of this work is *The Man with a Movie Camera* (1929), which integrates shots of everyday life with an elaborate reflection on the role of the documentary camera. A cameraman makes frequent appearances, and the film's self-reflexive quality is heightened by split screens, superimpositions (a huge camera and operator tower above a crowded street) and animation (a model camera and tripod take a bow). Vertov and his cameraman and brother Mikhail Kaufman continued their work after the coming of sound, with the more lyrical *Enthusiasm* (1931) and *Three Songs of Lenin* (1934), but their experiments were increasingly at odds with the approved doctrines of 'socialist realism'.

Although coolly received in the Soviet Union, where even Eisenstein was concerned about its 'formalism', *The Man with a Movie Camera* became a key film for the developing avant-garde cinema in Europe. Searching for blends of painting, poetry and music with film, other pioneers were pushing forward the documentary film's expressive potential. In Germany, Walter Ruttmann made *Berlin: Symphony of a Great City* (1927), forging a rhythmic portrait of urban life by organising shots in the form of a musical composition. Alberto Cavalcanti's *Rien que les heures* (1926) attempted a similar project, portraying a day in the life of Paris. And Jean Vigo's *A Propos de Nice* (1930), made in collaboration with another of Vertov's brothers, Boris Kaufman, is a view of the town and its upper-class society that is both poetic and satirical.

158

Grierson and state sponsorship

The idea of film as art, as evidenced by the films of Ruttmann, Vigo and others, was to exercise a deep influence on the British documentary film-makers of the 1930s. But as their mentor and guru John Grierson later wrote, 'The British documentary group began not so much in affection for film *per se* as in affection for national education . . . its origins certainly lay in sociological rather than aesthetic ideas.' A passionate advocate of the ideal of democracy, Grierson was less optimistic about its prospects in the modern world. But in film he saw the possibility of informing and engaging the citizen, so that he or she could participate more fully in society. Awakened to this idea by a visit to the United States, Grierson in 1927 lobbied the Empire Marketing Board, a government organisation for promoting trade, and eventually unlocked the money to produce a film about the herring industry.

Grierson's *Drifters* was premiered in 1929 at the London Film Society in the same programme as Eisenstein's *Battleship Potemkin*. Its success prompted the establishment of an EMB Film Unit, which expanded rapidly. Grierson encouraged, cajoled, instructed, bullied and inspired a young and inexperienced team which included Edgar Anstey, Arthur Elton, Basil Wright and Paul Rotha. Cavalcanti was brought in from France, and Flaherty invited over from the United States. After three years the EMB was dismantled and the film unit was attached to the General Post Office.

Throughout the 1930s this group of film-makers produced numerous documentaries profiling public institutions and exploring social problems. *Night Mail* (produced by Grierson, directed by Harry Watt and Basil Wright, 1936) is a lyrical portrait of the work of the London to Scotland mail train. Films like *Industrial Britain* (Flaherty, 1931), *Shipyard*

The British documentary movement: Cavalcanti's Coal Face

(Rotha, 1935) and *Coal Face* (Cavalcanti, 1935) consider aspects of Britain's labour force. And *Housing Problems* (Anstey and Elton, 1935) looks at conditions in the slums and the work of the British Commercial Gas Association (which sponsored it) in aiding the clearance of the worst areas.

In retrospect the achievement of these documentaries is a complex and contradictory one. They did responsibly expose social concerns, not least by the simple but unprecedented technique of putting on the screen working-class people speaking about their problems. They also developed the technical possibilities of the documentary, especially in the creative use of sound. Cavalcanti, who was to take over as the unit's director after Grierson left in 1937, was particularly influential in exploring new techniques. And young artists from other disciplines were sometimes brought in to make their own

159

distinctive contributions: *Night Mail*, for instance, has music by Benjamin Britten and a verse commentary by W.H. Auden. Yet the films were always somewhat constrained by the sponsor. Basil Wright's poetic, mystical montage *Song of Ceylon* (1934-5, made for the Ceylon Tea Propaganda Board) ignores the harsh life of the plantation workers. And as one forthright critic observed, 'The scandalous working conditions in the GPO are not mentioned in the films. . . Mr Grierson is not paid to tell the truth but to make people use the parcel post.'

Alongside the Grierson group's films, however, a distinct and significant tradition of 'oppositional' documentary was developing in Britain. In the early 1930s Workers' Film Societies began to screen Soviet films, although they were often dogged by censorship problems. They also initiated some small-scale production of films like *Bread* (1934) and *March Against Starvation* (1936) which challenged the middle-class, consensual views of domestic issues. To provide films for union and other workers' groups, two distribution organisations were set up, Kino and the Progressive Film Institute (PFI). Under Ivor Montagu, the PFI was particularly active in production,

The River

making a number of films on the Spanish Civil War and, at the request of the Communist Party of Great Britain, *Peace and Plenty* (1939), an angry and effective attack on the failures of the Chamberlain government.

Responding to what they saw as the lies of the official newsreels, left-wing groups in the United States also began to document the miseries and rural poverty of the Depression. And after President Roosevelt's accession in 1932 such work received wider support. Two films in particular crystallised this impetus, and forced the commercial cinema to take note: *The Plow that Broke the Plains* (1936), about the farmers of the dustbowl, and *The River* (1937), about the Mississippi. Both were directed by Pare Lorentz, who worked in each case with a distinguished team of still and film cameramen, including Ralph Steiner, Paul Strand and Leo Hurwitz. Both were scored by the composer Virgil Thomson, and both were surprising commercial successes.

A rather different relationship between documentary-makers and the state emerged in Germany, where in 1933, at Hitler's request, the former dancer, actress and feature film director Leni Riefenstahl was commissioned to make a short film of the annual Nazi Party rally. The following year Riefenstahl martialled vast resources to make the extraordinary *Triumph of the Will*. In the opening shots the Führer's plane descends through the clouds over Nuremberg, before he emerges to receive the town's adulation and later to lead and inspire the spectacular and carefully choreographed celebration of National Socialism. Although it is recognised as a formal masterpiece, the film's relentless power and its glorification of Nazism means that viewing it today is an uneasy experience. Like Riefenstahl's subsequent two-part *Olympia* (1938), a grandiose record of the 1936 Berlin Olympic Games, it remains a problematic classic in the history of documentary propaganda.

Grandiosity: Riefenstahl's Olympia

The cinema newsreel

For most audiences in the 1930s, their primary exposure to documentary film-making was in the weekly newsreels included in the programmes at their local cinemas. In 1909 Charles Pathé had launched a weekly magazine which brought together a number of different actuality scenes. Gaumont and others soon followed, an American edition of Pathé's magazine began in August 1911, and in 1914 Pathé even tried a short-lived daily version. Exploiting to the full their offices across the world, Pathé created a model of local production coupled with rapid and extensive distribution and exhibition, which was to serve it and other companies for some fifty years. The Hearst News Organisation started a newsreel service in 1914, and during the First World War several other newsreel operations were launched. On both sides of the Atlantic during the war newsreels showed the power and fascination of footage from the front, but they also demonstrated the limitations of a technology still without sound. There was far less enthusiasm for the attempts at portraying the more prosaic politics of the early 1920s, and many companies went out of business. Those that survived worked by and large with low standards of journalism and film-making, producing bland features and official spectacles.

Then in April 1927 Fox created a sensation with its Movietone sound newsreel, and throughout the 1930s this was the most extensive of the five studio-affiliated services. Among many who welcomed a new era of mass communications was Benito Mussolini, who said of Movietone, 'Your talking newsreel has tremendous possibilities, let me speak through it in twenty cities in Italy once a week and I need no other power.' *The March of Time*, launched by Louis de Rochemont for Time Inc in 1935, added significant dimensions of research and analysis to the newsreel form, and for sixteen years its punchy style and strident narration proved extremely popular. Modelled on a successful radio series, and distributed to cinemas first by RKO and after 1942 by Fox, it at first included several stories in one edition; but after 1938 it increasingly opted for a single focus, allowing time for detailed consideration of an issue. Reconstruction was recognised as a legitimate technique, and justified by Henry Luce, head of Time Inc, as 'fakery in allegiance to the truth'. Deliberately provocative, the series often adopted a strong editorial line, including early opposition to Hitler.

'U.S. Dustbowl', A March of Time *film*

The success of *The March of Time* was recognised both by its special Academy Award in 1937 and by Orson Welles' loving parody in *Citizen Kane*. A number of comparable projects were launched, including the monthly *This is America,* begun by RKO in 1942 after the termination of its contract with Time-Life. The constant demand for information during World War Two further strengthened the newsreel, but after the war its appeal gradually diminished, and high production costs were increasingly difficult to justify. *The March of Time* and *This is America* both came to an end in 1951. Movietone, *Pathé News* and some other newsreels (like *Gaumont-British News* in Britain, which ended in 1956) staggered on for some years; but with television providing 'live' news daily, cinema audiences no longer needed the newsreels and their bland view of the world.

The Second World War

In most countries the coming of war in September 1939 imposed tight limits on the creative opportunities for documentary-makers. Strident morale-boosting newsreels and plain public service information films were the requirements now. This was as true in Germany, where Fritz Hippler made powerful tributes to the Nazi war machine like *Campaign in Poland* (1940) and *Victory in the West* (1941), as it was in the Allied countries. Remarkable exceptions to such imperatives were the films of Humphrey Jennings, who began working with the Grierson group in 1934 (and followed them into the Ministry of Information's Crown Film Unit

Jennings' Fires Were Started

during the war) but whose work has always been seen as distinct from the mainstream tradition.

A poet, a modernist, a Surrealist artist, Jennings has been described by Lindsay Anderson as 'the only real poet of the British cinema'. (Grierson characteristically regarded him as something of a dilettante.) His distinctive style can be seen in two films made in 1939 for the GPO unit. *Spare Time,* shot in peacetime, is an associative montage about forms of working-class leisure in Britain. *The First Days* (made with Harry Watt and Pat Jackson) shows London's preparations for war. Barrage balloons and sandbags transform familiar scenes and, with the paintings transported to safety, the National Gallery is hung with empty frames. Jennings' films are built on observation and association. They emerge (often from a close partnership with the editor Stewart McAllister) out of a complex interplay of picture and sound, which often includes poetry and music. The bizarre qualities of daily life frequently make quiet intrusions, and there is always respect for people's stoical response to threat. *London Can Take It* (co-directed with Harry Watt, 1940) and the wordless *Listen to Britain* (made with McAllister, 1942) show a nation surviving, partly by drawing on a deep, shared tradition of resistance. Similarly, his feature-length drama about the Auxiliary Fire Service, *Fires Were Started* (1943), remains a moving affirmation of personal courage and of quieter human virtues. Jennings' final wartime film, *A Diary for Timothy* (1945), is a darker piece, uncertain about the challenges of a post-war world.

Mainstream documentary production during the war was usually the work of the newsreel cameramen who accompanied fighting units and whose footage was often later assembled in distinguished compilations. In the United States, where the armed services allocated significant resources to film-making, Frank Capra was drafted in from Hollywood to make the celebrated *Why We Fight* series (1942-5). Capra and his team (which included Hollywood figures like Walter Huston and Dimitri Tiomkin as well as Robert Flaherty and the Dutch documentarist Joris Ivens) used footage from both Allied and enemy sources, together with bold graphics and emotive narration, to create seven inspirational documents. These proved enormously influential both at home, where they were mostly shown to military audiences, and abroad. Other feature directors enlisted for the war effort included John Ford, who made an account of the victorious naval engagement in the Pacific, *The Battle of Midway* (1944); William Wyler, who shot *Memphis Belle* (1944), a graphic record of a bombing raid; and John Huston, who made three outstanding films, including *The Battle of San Pietro* (1945), with its sympathetic concern for the ordinary fighting man.

The newsreel compilation was further developed in Canada in the series *The World in Action* (1941-5), made under the supervision of Stuart Legg by the recently established National Film Board (NFB). With John Grierson at its head, the NFB had been set up to project a positive picture of Canada to the nation itself and to the world. But the requirements of the war brought about this further refinement of front-line footage, in a series which was notable for its analytical approach and its interest in broad questions of strategy and policy. After the war the NFB continued to fund a wide range of documentary work, much of it clearly marked by Grierson's influence. In many ways the NFB was to act as a model for the development of documentary units in other countries.

The post-war world and television
One important legacy of the maturity which the documentary form had demonstrated throughout the war was its influence on fiction film-making. In different forms, this can be recognised in the films of Italian neo-realism like Roberto Rossellini's *Rome Open City* (1945), in a French feature such as

René Clément's Resistance story *La Bataille du rail* (1945), in dramas from Britain's Ealing Studios, and in the thrillers which *March of Time* producer Louis de Rochemont made for Fox. Another newsreel legacy to the post-war world was the almost unbearable film footage of the German concentration camps, assembled by units working with the advancing Allied armies. This and other footage was to be used as documentation of war crimes at the Nuremberg trials. Partly stimulated by a desire to understand what had happened in the past decade, there was a new interest in film as historical evidence and a number of compilation films were made.

In the early 1950s television also began to produce compilations. NBC had an early success with the 26-episode *Victory at Sea* (1952-3), about naval operations during the war. Ten years later the BBC produced *The Great War*, a series combining archive film and interview which set new standards of historical research. In 1974 Thames Television and series producer Jeremy Isaacs made *The World at War*, the most ambitious television history to that date. Thames subsequently developed the compilation form in two other important series, *Palestine* (1978) and *The Troubles* (1981). As this work developed, both historians and producers increasingly recognised the problems and responsibilities of handling archive material. Too often, for example, compilation documentaries on television subsume the archive material under a narrator's voice which constructs a single smooth narrative out of disputed events, and outside the interpretations and contradictions which are the stuff of any responsible history. A series like *The Troubles* indicates its awareness of these problems by including clearly articulated viewpoints from different political positions, and often revealing how, for whom and for what purpose the footage was originally shot. Marcel Ophuls' film *The Sorrow and the Pity* (1970) adopts a more personal focus to similar ends, in its methodical probing of France's memories of the Nazi occupation and its challenging of the popular myths about that time. And recently film-makers in the United States have begun to use archive material to confront their own history, as in the hilarious *Atomic Café* (1982) about Cold War attitudes to the Bomb, and *The Life and Times of Rosie the Riveter* (1980), which looks at working women in the Second World War and how they were shepherded back into the home after the war.

Confronting history: Atomic Café

In the late 1940s most television news in the United States had been supplied by cinema newsreel teams. NBC had a deal with Fox Movietone, which supplied *Camel News Caravan* with 35mm pictures, and for the pictures in *Television News with Douglas Edwards* CBS contracted with Telenews, a 16mm unit associated with the Hearst-MGM operation. Then in the early 1950s each network built its own news film staffs, often employing those who had worked in cinema newsreels. But from the beginning television's preference for dramatic pictures, and its disinclination to show anything which could not be made visual, skewed the medium's news values. In 1951 the distinguished radio correspondent Edward R. Murrow and producer Fred Friendly started *See it Now* on CBS, which was intended to provide analysis and background to the news. Their programmes criticising McCarthyism in 1953-5 (see Chapter 13), together with other courageous investigations, established an influential strand of television documentary; but after 1958 the commercial growth of the networks squeezed such programmes out of the schedules.

Television news in Britain

On 30 September 1938 the BBC transmitted a live broadcast of Prime Minister Neville Chamberlain's arrival in Britain after his mission to Munich. Richard Dimbleby described the events as Chamberlain held up his paper promise from Hitler that he would not go to war. The item was exceptional, for the pre-war outside broadcast units concentrated almost exclusively on more frivolous events. Nor was the Corporation developing an aggressive news operation. Both before and after the war television news was bound to a radio format, with an invisible announcer reading a bulletin over a caption card on screen. To complement this, a Television Newsreel unit was established which began to provide feature items for a nightly programme. In 1954, under a new Director-General and with a commercial competitor in sight, the BBC combined the two operations as *Television News and Newsreel*, but only reluctantly introduced in-vision newsreaders, who in any case remained anonymous, even after the introduction of a regular *News Bulletin* in 1955.

Eager to establish their respectability, the first four companies of the new ITV system agreed to set up a news-gathering organisation, Independent Television News. As its first Editor they appointed an experienced journalist and respected BBC presenter, Aidan Crawley, who recognised the weaknesses of the BBC's news output. His innovation of using strong personalities, like Robin Day and Christopher Chataway, as 'newscasters' was immediately successful, as was the more aggressive interviewing style and the sharper use of cameras to make the news more direct and immediate. The BBC needed to respond. In early 1957 producer Donald Baverstock, working under the formidable executive Grace Wyndham Goldie, launched the *Tonight* programme, an informal mix of news, comment, serious features, entertainment and quirkiness. The programme hired the best journalists from the photomagazine *Picture Post*, which was wound up in May 1957, and soon presenters like Fyfe Robertson and Trevor Philpott were teamed with young directors like John Schlesinger and Jack Gold.

Tonight: *Alan Whicker interviews*

Tonight was quickly successful, and its style influenced much of British television's documentary output over the next three decades. The long-running series *Whicker's World* is typical of the presenter-oriented mix of anecdote and reflection which is still the most widely accepted documentary form in today's schedules. It produces lively, occasionally astonishing films, like the one that is almost a national folk memory in which Alan Whicker visits the eccentric millionaire who invented 'cats' eyes'. But too often the work is superficial, lacking any precision or focus. British television only rarely supports film-makers seeking a more analytical style.

Cinéma-vérité

There is a shot in *Primary* (1960) which follows Senator John Kennedy into a building, down a corridor, up some stairs and out on to the stage of a political rally, where he is greeted by enthusiastic applause. The camera is close behind him, and the wide-angle lens captures all the excitement of the moment. More than any other, this one shot demonstrates the breakthrough in documentary technique which the film achieved. But *Primary* also includes intimate, unguarded moments of Kennedy and his rival Hubert Humphrey as they campaign in the Democratic primary in Wisconsin. Dziga Vertov had written about the documentary ideal of 'Kino Pravda' – camera-truth or *cinéma-vérité* – and for many practitioners and commentators *Primary* was its first authentic manifestation.

A number of rather loose terms have been used to identify this style and its techniques, most commonly *cinéma-vérité* and, for films made with the least possible intervention and influence by the film-makers, 'direct cinema'. What Vertov saw as 'Kino Pravda' remains a useful first definition: 'Photographing people without make-up from angles that take them unaware, and getting them with the camera-eye at a moment when they are not acting and letting the camera strip their thoughts bare.' Many film-makers were convinced that the obstacles to achieving this were primarily technical. Working as a cameraman on Flaherty's *Louisiana Story* (1948), Richard Leacock was frustrated by the bulky and inflexible equipment needed to record synchronous sound. A decade later Leacock tackled this problem with Richard Drew, a photo-journalist who had been commissioned by NBC to create a television style comparable to the candid photography featured in *Life* magazine. Together with a small team which included Albert and David Maysles and Don Pennebaker, they studied the potential of the most advanced lightweight cameras, tape recorders and fast film stock, and in early 1960 they shot *Primary*.

Financed by Time Inc, and with limited support from the ABC network, Drew, Leacock and their colleagues went on to produce a dozen further films over the next three years. Among the most significant were *The Chair* (1962), about a prisoner on Death Row, and *Crisis* (1963), in which cameras observe Attorney General Robert Kennedy dealing with the court-ordered integration of the University of Alabama. In all these films, *vérité* techniques are combined with notions of characters, structure and action drawn from fiction, and extracted from the situations under observation. The films employ what has become known as a 'crisis structure', and are organised so as to build towards moments of high drama. Inevitably, for all their concern with 'truth' these documentaries are as much constructions as any other.

The Maysles brothers left Drew Associates before the filming of *Crisis*, and Leacock and Pennebaker soon followed them. In different ways each of the film-makers felt the problems and limitations of this approach, and endeavoured to avoid them in their subsequent, de-dramatised work. Another influential American exponent of direct cinema (although he is cautious about the term) has been Frederick Wiseman. A former lawyer, Wiseman began directing films with *Titicut Follies* (1967), about life inside a hospital for the criminally insane. Since then he has dissected the workings of many other public institutions, as in *High School* (1969), *Hospital* (1970) and *Basic Training* (1971, about an army training camp). Wiseman's films have no narration and avoid concentrating on individuals. By building a mosaic of interconnected scenes, he is concerned to reveal the complexities of these organisations, and to develop through selection and juxtaposition an argument which encourages the viewer to engage with and evaluate the way they work.

Frederick Wiseman's Basic Training

In the past three decades *cinéma-vérité* techniques have been employed by many film-makers. Particularly notable are the films of the Canadian director Allan King, who made *Warrendale* (1966) about a Canadian treatment centre for emotionally disturbed children, and *A Married Couple* (1969), a close-up view of domestic tensions. The film-maker most closely identified with direct cinema in Britain is Roger Graef, whose television series *The Space Between Words* (1972) observed the communication processes within various institutions, including a family. Graef, cameraman Charles Stewart and a regular team of collaborators went on to make influential series like *Decision* (1976) and *Police* (1982).

'Fly on the wall': from Roger Graef's series Police *(note the sound recordist)*

The 'fly on the wall' approach to documentary film-making has been much debated. Is the camera an unseen, 'objective' observer, or does its presence influence the events it records? Such questions were prompted by one of the most elaborate undertakings in this field when in 1974 producer Paul Watson and director Franc Roddam made *The Family*, a BBC documentary serial about a working-class family which seemed at times to cross the borderline between close observation and the manipulation of real life as 'entertainment', even as soap opera when a wedding in the family became a national event. The success of *The Family* ensured that the documentary serial became a staple of BBC output in the late 1970s. But although series like *Sailor* (1976) used elements of *cinéma-vérité*, they began increasingly to rely on narration, music and other devices to stress drama and develop audience involvement in character.

Such problems were first revealingly confronted by the film-maker Jean Rouch. Dissatisfied with his anthropological work, which was increasingly being rejected by the subjects of the films as exploitative, Rouch began to challenge what would later become the conventions of observational film-making. In *Moi, un noir* (1958), a documentary about destitute casual labourers on the Ivory Coast, he records the poverty and oppression of these lives, but also encourages his subjects to improvise their fantasies, which turn out to be drawn from the Hollywood cinema. Rouch recognised that by inviting a subject to explore his or her relationship with the camera, insights and truths which would otherwise remain hidden could be brought to the surface. With the sociologist Edgar Morin, he made the camera into an acknowledged participant in *Chronique d'un été* (1960), which looks at 'the strange tribe that lives in Paris'. The camera as a catalyst has been an approach adopted subsequently by many directors.

The American director Emile De Antonio also uses the camera as participant, but his important political studies of the United States offer a rather different critique of *cinéma-vérité*. Since *Point of Order* (1963), which re-cut and re-ordered television coverage of the Army vs McCarthy hearings of 1954, De Antonio has examined the Kennedy assassination (*Rush to Judgment*, 1966), American involvement in Vietnam (*In the Year of the Pig*, 1969), and the career of Richard Nixon (*Millhouse*, 1971). In each film he explores the exercise of power and how this depends on the control of images, in both their methods of exhibition and in the way in which they are received by audiences. In De Antonio's work the 'neutral' observation of *cinéma-vérité* is exposed as a myth, and a dangerous one.

Emile De Antonio's Millhouse

Personal cinema

De Antonio's films can be seen as personal essays, expressing an individual response to a complex issue. In a sense, many if not most documentaries are 'personal'; but only certain strands of film-making acknowledge, in the narration, in the structure or in 'poetic' or formal devices, the film-maker's attempts to come to terms with the material. In Britain a significant tradition of this more personal work has developed, much of it influenced by the wartime films of Humphrey Jennings. One important manifestation of this was the 'Free Cinema' screenings held at the National Film Theatre between 1956 and 1959. Actually a range of disparate work, Free Cinema drew attention to the individuality of young directors like Lindsay Anderson, whose *O Dreamland* (1953) is a disenchanted portrait of an amusement park, and Karel Reisz and Tony Richardson, with their film of a teenage jazz club, *Momma Don't Allow* (1956). These were fresh, personal responses to everyday events, echoed in work for television by Denis Mitchell with films like *Morning in the Streets* (1959), a carefully structured impression of the sights and sounds of the city of Manchester.

Free Cinema: Karel Reisz's We are the Lambeth Boys *(1959)*

Two other important directors who have created a personal cinema within the institutions of British television are Philip Donnellan and Mike Grigsby. Donnellan began making films for the BBC in 1958 with *Joe the Chainsmith*, and continued to compose sympathetic profiles of working men and women.

His controversial *Gone for a Soldier* (1980) is a powerful, partisan look at the life of the British soldier from 1815 to 1979 which uses diary extracts, letters and songs. Grigsby also started by recording industrial experience, with *Enginemen* (1959), shown in the last Free Cinema programme. Later films for Granada Television, like *A Life Apart* (1973) and *A Life Underground* (1974), profiled deep-sea fishermen and miners, and were shot in Grigsby's distinctive manner, using long, reflective takes which encourage those to whom power is denied to find their own voice. Another major figure in this tradition was Robert Vas, who came to Britain after the collapse of the 1956 Revolution in his native Hungary. His impressions of a new land became the subject of his first film, *Refuge England* (1958), and the passion apparent within it indi-

My Homeland, *by Robert Vas*

cated how his work would develop until his death in 1978. Tackling a wide variety of subjects for the BBC, including the General Strike (*Nine Days in '26*, 1974) and Hungary again (*My Homeland*, 1976), Vas extended Humphrey Jennings' legacy into a form of personal documentary driven by intense moral commitment.

Drama-documentaries

Alongside traditions of observational film-making and the personal essay, television also fostered an even more controversial form of the documentary, known as drama-documentary or documentary drama. The legitimacy of integrating dramatic and documentary techniques remains a much-disputed question. The debate usually depends on the (misconceived) assumption that there is a clear distinction between 'fact' and 'fiction' and that the two should not be mixed. A more important question is the precise status of any filmed material, and the standards of historical or journalistic research which have been employed during its creation. Documentaries do not offer any unmediated access to the real world. Rather they present a view, an argument, which can be assessed on the basis of various contextual elements. Films which make a responsible use of dramatic elements should be considered in the same way. Drama can tend to impose certain structures and

169

constraints, but many styles of documentary are also inflected by these concerns, and drama-documentary can offer new insights closed to conventional documentaries.

Dramatic reconstructions featured within the documentary tradition from the very beginning. In 1898 Edward H. Amet reconstructed the naval battle of the Bay of Santiago in a bathtub with miniature boats. Flaherty restaged purportedly spontaneous events, and scenes in Grierson's *Drifters* supposedly shot at sea were actually filmed in a cabin built on the shore. Reconstruction had been recognised as legitimate by the makers of *The March of Time*, and many feature films were based on a synthesis of historical events. But drama-documentary has really flourished as a television form. One early American example, developed from a radio show, was CBS's *You Are There* (1953-7), which reconstructed how television news might have covered events like the fall of Troy or the Gettysburg Address. The combination of historical events and television conventions was later used in Britain by Peter Watkins to make *Culloden* (1964). And one of the most controversial of all drama-documentaries, *Death of a Princess* (1979, directed by Antony Thomas), used the structuring device of a film-maker's research to make explicit the constraints of television documentary production.

Since *You Are There*, television in the United States has produced many films based on historical and contemporary records. Particularly distinguished is the consistently intelligent work of producer Herbert Brodkin,

The War Game

who in 1954 produced as a live drama *The Last Days of Hitler*, and has made many other examples of 'faction', including *Pueblo* (1973) and *The Missiles of October* (1974). In Britain as early as 1946 producer Robert Barr made a television version of his radio project *I Want to be an Actor*, which like his later dramatised documentary work such as *Barrister at Law* (1952) used studio cameras and dramatised scenes to explore subjects which the cumbersome film cameras of the day found difficult to present in documentary form. After *Culloden* Peter Watkins made *The War Game* (1965), which dramatised the effects of a nuclear attack on Britain to such effect that the BBC stopped its transmission and – although it was shown in cinemas – it was not seen on television until 1985. Ken Russell's film biographies of artists and composers also broke new ground by introducing actors in dramatised sequences. After the success of *Elgar* (1962), Russell went on to make increasingly flamboyant films such as his baroque portrait of the dancer *Isadora Duncan* (1966), and *Song of Summer* (1968), about the last years of Delius.

Another variant of the dramatised documentary form in the 1960s is the *social drama of director Ken Loach and producer Tony Garnett. Cathy Come Home* (1966) used documentary conventions in its angry demonstration of the problems of homelessness, and Loach and Garnett continued to use a controversial mix of drama and documentary-style reconstructions in work like *Days of Hope* (1974) and *Law and Order* (1978, directed by Les Blair).

Drama-documentary was also encouraged at Granada Television, where a number of films were shaped out of detailed research and framed within dramatic conventions. *The Man Who Couldn't Keep Quiet* (1971) adopted the techniques of drama because its story, about a prominent Russian dissident, could not be filmed as documentary. Subsequent films from the same director, Leslie Woodhead, were *Three Days in Szczecin* (1976), about a shipyard strike in Poland, and *Invasion* (1980), which related the Soviet invasion of Czechoslovakia as seen by one prominent Czech official.

Now you see it. . .

In the early 1960s documentaries were all but squeezed out of the primetime schedules in the United States. The coverage of each of the main network news shows, however, was extended to thirty minutes in 1963, in part because satellite transmissions were offering a wider range of international pictures. 1963 also saw America and the world united by television in a quite unique way. On 22 November President Kennedy was shot and killed in Dallas. For days afterwards television created a ritual drama of grief, intensified by the shooting on camera of the alleged assassin Lee Harvey Oswald.

The end of the decade was to see a television event of comparable impact when in July 1969 pictures of Neil Armstrong stepping onto the moon's surface were transmitted live around the world. By then the United States was experiencing another television drama, the war in Vietnam, shown every night in close-up colour on the news broadcasts. Yet although Vietnam was 'the first television war' and the continuous exposure undoubtedly influenced American public opinion, the networks largely adhered to the government line and broadcast little which questioned why American soldiers were in Vietnam. *Morley Safer's Vietnam* (1967) aspired to a strict objectivity, but its interview with a helicopter crew exultant after a 'kill' was a rare glimpse behind the official smokescreen. *Inside North Vietnam* (1968) by the independent director Felix Greene, shown on the Public Broadcasting System, was one of the few accommodations the medium made to the viewpoint of the North Vietnamese. Elsewhere, however, films like Joris Ivens' *17th Parallel* (1967) were documenting wartime life in the North. A CBS film, *The Selling of the Pentagon* (1971), did make a major impact with its revelations about the relationships between the Pentagon and arms suppliers. But it was left to the cinema, more than a decade later, to offer American audiences a different experience of Vietnam.

Stasis and new directions

In the early 1970s, the excitement generated by, say, the first editions of

Granada Television's weekly current affairs programme *World in Action* seemed more difficult to achieve. Documentary and news programmes settled into efficiency, and small refinements to now established forms. In the mid-1970s there was an earnest debate about what was said to be British television's 'bias against understanding' in its coverage of complex issues. And when Britain's Channel 4 began in 1982, ITN started an hour-long news and analysis programme, *Channel 4 News*, which has successfully extended the depth and range of television news coverage.

British television documentaries have seemed even more constrained by established conventions. Alongside the debased forms of *cinéma-vérité* and the presenter-oriented feature, the blockbuster series established itself after the worldwide sales of the BBC's *Civilisation* (1969), in which Kenneth Clark undertook a lecture tour of cultural landmarks. The prestige status of such projects, their uncontroversial nature and the ease with which they brought in co-production monies or foreign sales, made them an increasingly attractive option for budget-conscious broadcasters.

Reacting against the blandness of most documentary work at the time, independent film-makers began to re-examine the fundamentals of the form. The work they produced was made outside, and often in opposition to, the existing structures of cinema and television. This new oppositional spirit echoed the upsurge of political radicalism in the late 1960s. The Paris 'events' of 1968 prompted radical newsreels and the 'counter-information' films of the SLON group; and the impetus for change was also felt in Britain, where groups like Cinema Action, the Newsreel Collective and the Berwick Street Collective began to make 'alternative' document-

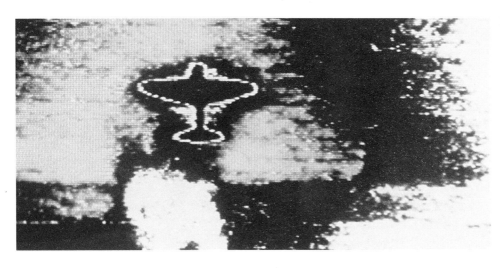

Chris Marker's Sans Soleil

ary films. Such films as the Berwick Street Collective's *Nightcleaners* (1975) or Cinema Action's *Film from the Clyde* (1977, documenting a workers' occupation of shipbuilding yards) set out to challenge received notions of documentary 'objectivity' by constructing arguments which were intended to provoke discussion among the working-class audiences to which they were addressed.

Much of the impetus of this new work came from the emergence of radical political attitudes which rejected the consensus view. Feminism, racial and national consciousness, gay liberation and environmental concerns in

172

formed many of the most stimulating films (and, increasingly, videotapes) of the later 1970s and the 1980s. In the United States work like the oral history of *Union Maids* (1976), or *Before Stonewall* (1984), which constructs a history of the American gay movement, and in Britain films like *Territories* (1984), about representations of race, all spoke with an urgent alternative voice.

Many of these films were made by young film-makers, exploring and questioning the conventions of the documentary form. One film-maker who has done this consistently over a long career, and whose work is an unclassifiable blend of documentary and personal essay, is the French director Chris Marker. Constructing an elaborate counterpoint of image and sound, external event and private reflection, Marker's idiosyncratic films range from the notebook observations of *Letter from Siberia* (1957), through the impressionistic collage of *Le joli Mai* (1963), to the astonishing *Sans Soleil* (1983). This feature-length work eludes adequate description, its cascade of images bringing together traces of San Francisco, shots from Hitchcock's *Vertigo*, an imaginary science-fiction movie, an intense scrutiny of Japan and its moving image culture, and much else besides. It is a poetic and absorbing reverie, and as much an analysis of the processes of film-making as Vertov's *Man with a Movie Camera*. Its dazzling montage is far from the classical documentary tradition of the Grierson school. Yet Grierson himself might well have responded with enthusiasm. 'The documentary idea,' he wrote, 'demands no more than that the affairs of our time shall be brought to the screen in any fashion that strikes the imagination and makes observation a little richer than it was.'

Further reading

Erik Barnouw, *Documentary: A History of the Non-Fiction Film*, Oxford: Oxford University Press, rev. ed. 1983.

A. William Bluem, *Documentary in American Television*, New York: Hastings, 1965.

Geoffrey Cox, *See It Happen: The Making of ITN*, London: Bodley Head, 1983.

Raymond Fielding, *The American Newsreel: 1911-1967*, Norman: University of Oklahoma Press, 1972.

Forsyth Hardy (ed), *Grierson on Documentary*, London: Collins, 1946.

Lewis Jacobs (ed), *The Documentary Tradition*, New York: Norton, 2nd ed. 1979.

Mary-Lou Jennings (ed), *Humphrey Jennings: Film-maker, Painter, Poet*, London: BFI Publishing, 1982.

Alan Lovell and Jim Hillier, *Studies in Documentary*, London: Secker & Warburg/ BFI, 1972.

Eva Orbanz, *Journey to a Legend and Back: The British Realistic Film*, Berlin: Edition Volker Spiess, 1977.

Alan Rosenthal, *The New Documentary in Action*, Berkeley: University of California Press, 1971.

Paul Rotha, *Documentary Film*, 3rd ed. London: Faber & Faber, 1952.

Elizabeth Sussex, *The Rise and Fall of British Documentary*, Berkeley: University of California Press, 1975.

Norman Swallow, *Factual Television*, London: Focal Press, 1966.

Dai Vaughan, *Portrait of an Invisible Man: The Working Life of Stewart McAllister, Film Editor*, London: BFI Publishing, 1983.

12
Post-war Hollywood

Cinema in the United States emerged from the war at a peak of power and confidence. 1946 box-office returns topped any previous year and, allowing for inflation, have remained unchallenged ever since. But the industry was soon hit by a series of near-fatal blows. Attendances dropped off rapidly, at the same time as production costs were spiralling. A Supreme Court decision in 1948 ended the companies' control of domestic exhibition, television established itself as a serious rival, and major social changes meant that there was no possibility of reconstituting the pre-war audiences. Moreover, the industry was torn by Cold War scare-mongering and there were many cases of blacklisting.

Hollywood responded on many fronts, and by the early 1960s there were signs that a testing transitional period had been negotiated, with due account taken of shifts in entertainment patterns. The most significant change was a new relationship with television, but since domestic box-office receipts rose between 1963 and 1968 even the much-depleted cinema circuits seemed relatively healthy. The new optimism was illusory, however, and by the end of the decade all the majors were once again engulfed in a financial crisis. A round of corporate takeovers resulted;

Hollywood defiant

the names remained the same, but the film industry was fundamentally restructured. The big companies retained their dominance, but they were now elements, and often minor elements, in multi-national empires just as interested in parking lots and funeral parlours as in movies.

174

Post-war crisis

The crucial factor in post-war Hollywood was that attendances were falling and costs rising. In the decade after 1947 weekly attendance declined by about a half. Between 1946 and 1956 annual box-office receipts fell almost 23 per cent, and many film theatres were forced to close. By 1951 the sharp fall in cinema attendances was being blamed on television. In those cities in which the new medium was now well established, its rise could be clearly matched against the fall in cinema admissions, whereas in television-free areas films continued to attract just as many patrons. The equation, however, was not quite so simple, for the availability of television did not alone account for the public's apparent preference for it.

The post-war decade saw a fundamental shift in America's population. As servicemen came home and the birth rate boomed, families moved out of the cities into the rapidly expanding suburbs. The new home became of paramount importance, and any spare dollars were spent on the modern domestic appliances, including television sets, now pouring off assembly lines released from armament manufacture. Other domestic leisure activities were also being introduced, including the new long-playing records, first marketed in 1948. The population remained film consumers, but the film theatre was no longer a central focus in their lives. When television brought stars into the home, sitting in a darkened cinema began to seem a less attractive option.

As attendances fell, post-war production costs were rising rapidly, in parallel with the nation's inflationary economy. A series of strikes and contested wage deals in 1946 pushed up budgets even further. Sharp cutbacks in production were necessary, particularly at the major studios with their high, fixed payrolls and overheads. Many long-term contracts were terminated, executive salaries were reduced, and Warners even shut down production for a period. 1947 saw the collapse of the small Producers Releasing Corporation, which only five years earlier had been making one low-budget feature a week. United Artists, too, almost went under. Recognising the industry's instability, Wall Street was reluctant to advance money for reinvestment. Although a minor studio like Columbia, with lower fixed costs, remained relatively healthy, employment overall in the industry fell from 24,000 in 1946 to only just over half that a decade later.

The 1948 Supreme Court anti-trust decision fuelled this economic crisis. Anti-monopoly proceedings had been irritants for the vertically integrated majors ever since the early 1920s. Independent exhibitors resented the majors' control of the key first-run theatres. They were also bitterly opposed to the widespread practices of block-booking and blind-selling, which forced theatres to take the whole of a studio's output regardless of quality or box-office appeal. Charged with enforcing the Sherman Act of 1890, which outlawed unfair business monopolies, the Anti-trust Division of the Department of Justice intensified the pressure on the industry with a suit filed in July 1938. The eventual case two years later forced only minor concessions, but new moves were begun at the end of the war. After much legal wrangling, the Supreme Court handed down its historic judgment in 'US vs Paramount Pictures Inc.', and the majors were forced to recognise that their unquestioned control of exhibition was at an end.

In the wake of the court's decision, a series of 'consent decrees' were negotiated specifying how each corporation's exhibition structures were to be divested from the production and distribution elements. RKO and Paramount were immediately conciliatory, but the rest of the 'Big Five' – Loew's, 20th Century-Fox and Warners – dragged out the process with appeals and delaying tactics until well into the mid-1950s. Indeed MGM did not fully emerge from the Loew's nest until 1959. Nonetheless competition at the exhibition level was significantly increased, especially as minor distributors could now more easily enter the market.

On a broader political front, as the uneasy wartime accommodation with the Russians was transformed into the Cold War, anti-Communist sentiments spread throughout American society. In Congress, the House Un-American Activities Committee (HUAC) became a zealous force in the exposure of 'subversion', and in 1947 it began investigations into alleged Communist infiltration of the film industry. The story of HUAC's relationship with Hollywood is an ugly one. The Committee held public hearings in October and November 1947, at which first 'friendly witnesses' testified to the extent of alleged Communist infiltration, and then ten of the defendants – soon to be known as the Hollywood Ten – charged that the investigation infringed their rights under the Constitution's First Amendment, which guaranteed freedom of speech. The Ten, who included the writers Dalton Trumbo, Ring Lardner Jr and John

The Hollywood Ten (from Hollywood on Trial, *1976)*

Howard Lawson, and the director Edward Dmytryk, were imprisoned for contempt of Congress.

Many of the film industry's intellectuals had belonged to the Communist Party in the 1930s. But it was less any pro-Communist sentiment in specific films than the cinema's more general liberal humanism to which the right-wing Congressmen were reacting. Nonetheless their highly publicised investigation generated panic, and the studios cravenly co-operated with HUAC and those who shared its views. A blacklist was initiated, many distinguished writers and directors were no longer offered work, and an atmosphere of distrust and betrayal infected the whole community.

Further HUAC hearings were held in 1951-2, at which witnesses were encouraged to denounce colleagues for Communist sympathies, and the blacklist remained in operation for a decade. Some of its victims, like Joseph Losey, Jules Dassin and Carl Foreman, were forced into exile in Europe;

others like Dalton Trumbo only worked with the disguise of an alias. Finally, the 1956 screenwriting Oscar was awarded to 'Robert Rich' for *The Brave One*, who was revealed to be Trumbo, and in the first open defiance of the blacklist Otto Preminger hired him in January 1960 to script *Exodus*. The following December, despite a boycott by the American Legion, the film opened to exceptional business and the grip of the blacklist was broken. Even so, the industry's morale and self-confidence had been significantly weakened, at just the point when the economic crisis should have put a high premium on these qualities.

Hollywood responds

The film industry's responses to the perceived pressures and changes of the post-war period were complex. Television spurred both competition and compliance. A boom in independent production complemented the business-as-usual attitude which, despite serious cutbacks, prevailed at many of the major studios. As for the films themselves, the two post-war decades saw a rich and varied output, a brief survey of which will obviously be less than complete.

During the war many of the most prominent Hollywood directors had worked with newsreel and documentary units. For some, slick escapism was no longer an adequate response to a world in change. William Wyler returned home to make *The Best Years of Our Lives* (1946), about the problems of servicemen's readjustment, which was seen at the time as a harsh portrait of contemporary America. *The Lost Weekend* (1945, directed by Billy Wilder) and *The Snake Pit* (1948, Anatole Litvak) also took on contemporary problems, respectively alcoholism and mental illness. A comparable sense of social concern can be seen in the work of Elia Kazan, who came to Hollywood with a distinguished record in the theatre. His *Gentleman's Agreement* (1947) tackles anti-semitism, and *Pinky* (1949) has a similarly self-conscious approach to race. *Viva Zapata!* (1952), *On the Waterfront* (1954) and *East of Eden* (1955) continued the parade of his liberal conscience (especially ironic given that he was among the 'friendly' witnesses before HUAC), and were films which brought to Hollywood 'method actors' like Marlon Brando and James Dean, trained in New York for the theatre by Lee Strasberg.

On the Waterfront *(Marlon Brando, Eva Marie Saint)*

The styles of documentary film-making and of Italian neo-realism were other influences in the post-war years. Location shooting became more common, and was facilitated by new cameras and lights and by faster film-stock, all of which had been developed for military purposes. Location filming was also encouraged by hard-pressed studios being no longer as willing as they were to construct elaborate sets. Thrillers like *The House on 92nd Street* (1945), *13, rue Madeleine* (1946) and *Call Northside 777* (1947), all directed by Henry Hathaway for 20th Century-Fox, made especially effective use of urban sites. In 1948 Jules Dassin's *The Naked City*, which used 107 different New York locations, was a big hit for the struggling

Universal. Rain-washed city streets at night became a dominant motif in the style later to be identified as 'film noir'.

If the post-war American cinema is seen in terms of genres, it is clear that the Western entered a golden period, beginning with John Ford's *My Darling Clementine* (1946). Ford's engagement with the genre continued and deepened through films like *She Wore a Yellow Ribbon* (1949), *Wagon Master* and *Rio Grande* (both 1950), and reached a peak in the extraordinary *The Searchers* (1956). Howard Hawks made some similarly elegiac Westerns, like *Red River* (1947) and *Rio Bravo* (1958). Other directors adopted the Western for more explicit social commentary, most notably Fred Zinnemann, working from Carl Foreman's script for *High Noon* (1952), widely interpreted as an anti-McCarthy parable. Parallel to this new liberalism, American Indian culture was treated more sympathetically than before in a cycle of films begun by Delmer Daves' *Broken Arrow* (1950). And reflecting the darker mood of the post-war years were a number of 'psychological' Westerns, like Raoul Walsh's *Pursued* (1947), Nicholas Ray's *Johnny Guitar* (1954) and Anthony Mann's *The Man from Laramie* (1955).

Elegy: John Ford's The Searchers

Perhaps the best-loved group of films from the post-war years are the MGM musicals, especially the distinguished productions of Arthur Freed. In 1938 Freed had initiated MGM's first colour feature, *The Wizard of Oz* (which, far from being an instant success, lost $1 million on its first release), and during the war he oversaw the development of its child star Judy Garland into a mature actress. With Garland, with the actor and later choreographer Gene Kelly, with directors like Vincente Minnelli and Stanley Donen, and with a host of regular collaborators, the Freed unit presented a string of Technicolor spectaculars, including *The Pirate* (1948), *On the Town* (1949), *An American in Paris* (1951) and *Silk Stockings* (1957). And – perhaps the best of them – *Singin' in the Rain*, directed in 1952 by Kelly and Donen, whose account of the arrival of sound in Hollywood remains one of the most sharply satirical of the industry's self-portraits.

On the Town *(Vera-Ellen, Gene Kelly)*

No other studio hosted such a distinct group of productions, although certain trends and emphases can be observed in each studio's output. Under Darryl Zanuck at 20th Century-Fox, directors like Elia Kazan, Joseph Mankiewicz and Henry King were encouraged to tackle serious themes.

178

Paramount meanwhile continued its successful exploitation of light comedy, especially in the hugely profitable series of films with Bing Crosby and Bob Hope. In general, however, comedy was poorly served by post-war Hollywood, particularly as formerly quick-witted directors like Preston Sturges and Frank Capra seemed unable to recapture their earlier form. Capra, though, did make his masterpiece, *It's a Wonderful Life* (1947), which conjures up a deeply sentimental yet marvellously effective picture of small-town life, and reassures James Stewart's character that his modesty and warm-heartedness is the essential foundation-stone of his country's greatness.

Warners had both Bette Davis and Humphrey Bogart under contract, and they used such assets brilliantly. Davis played in films like *A Stolen Life* (1946) and *Winter Meeting* (1948), cementing an association between the studio and 'women's pictures' to which other key stars like Joan Crawford and Barbara Stanwyck also contributed. Bogart played in *The Big Sleep* (1946) and *Dark Passage* (1947), before forming his own company in 1947, and the following year making *The Treasure of the Sierra Madre*, with John Huston directing. Huston was one of a generation of directors who had learnt their craft writing for the studios in the 1930s, and who were now ready to make their mark as major directors. Others were Fred Zinnemann and Billy Wilder, who found his talent for black comedy appreciated at Paramount, where he made *Sunset Boulevard* (1950) and *Ace in the Hole* (1951). More established directors who continued to work at a high creative level included Alfred Hitchcock (with films like *Notorious*, 1946; *Strangers on a Train*, 1951; *Rear Window*, 1954), Fritz Lang (*Rancho Notorious*, 1952; *The Big Heat*, 1953), and Max Ophuls (*Letter from an Unknown Woman*, 1948).

Gloria Swanson, William Holden in Wilder's Sunset Boulevard

Hitchcock's Rear Window *(Grace Kelly, James Stewart)*

Independent production

Humphrey Bogart's decision in 1947 to establish his own company was indicative of a wider trend within the industry. For alongside – and often working with – the major studios, a new Hollywood figure was coming to prominence: the independent producer. In the 1930s independents like Samuel Goldwyn and David Selznick had been well established, but their ambitions had often been frustrated by the monopolistic exhibition structures. Now more than ever films had to compete individually, both for the attention of the theatre owners and for that of prospective patrons. An independent like Hal Wallis or Walter Wanger, it was argued, could shape films more successfully for these market conditions. In addition, extended runs of studio hits were no longer so common; so theatres needed more and different product, which the economising studios were unable to provide from their own production rostas.

Working without fixed studio overheads made independent production more efficient. The tax laws, too, made it advantageous for a writer, director or star to work for their own production company. As early as 1943 the trade papers noted that, among others, James Cagney was operating in this way. Soon the majors were leasing out their facilities, and as distributors were picking independent projects. United Artists was particularly successful in this respect, releasing nearly fifty films a year from 1953 to 1957. A struggling concern still controlled by Chaplin and Mary Pickford, UA was taken over in 1951 by two lawyers, Arthur Krim and Robert Benjamin. They oversaw the company's successful consolidation in these years, functioning without a studio's physical plant and simply providing financing and distribution, and their example did much to stimulate independent production. By 1958 it has been estimated that 65 per cent of Hollywood movies were made by independents.

Independent production and the new realism:
Marty *(Ernest Borgnine, Betsy Blair)*

One demonstration of the independents' central importance was the film version of the Paddy Chayevsky television drama, *Marty,* directed in 1955 by Delbert Mann as a low-budget independent production. Garnering four Oscars and the Grand Prix at Cannes, it encouraged a generation of new directors – Arthur Penn, Sidney Lumet, John Frankenheimer, Robert Mulligan – to move from the small screen to the large. *Marty's* low-life 'realism', which would have been anathema to a studio project a decade before, was also an indication of the greater freedom of expression which independent productions achieved. In addition, a 1952 Supreme Court decision declared that the Constitution's guarantee of free speech applied as much to movies as to the press, which meant that many local censorship boards had to become significantly more tolerant. And by this point the power of the central Production Code Administration had been weakened by the ending of exhibition monopolies. Films like *The Moon is Blue* (1953) and *The Man with the Golden Arm* (1955, about drug addiction), both directed by Otto Preminger, were successfully produced and distributed, even though their (now commonplace) subject matter meant that they were denied PCA approval. New exhibition practices and this new freedom of expression also encouraged the import and screening as 'art cinema' of foreign films which had no reason to respect traditional Hollywood taboos.

Adjusting to television

The adult language and subject matter now permitted in the cinema was to become one element in the large screen's competitive tussle with the small. Other attractions loudly trumpeted as unique to the cinema were the newly introduced technologies of 3-D and widescreen. But Hollywood was not simply interested in competing with the new medium. From the first the studios had endeavoured to create business relationships with television, and if possible to control it. At the end of the war Warners, 20th Century-Fox and MGM all made bids for television stations.

In the 1930s it had been Paramount that had shown the keenest interest in the new medium. With its significant investment in the television manufacturer and station-owner DuMont, the company was involved in four of the first nine stations to be established. But in the anti-trust atmosphere leading up to the 1948 Supreme Court decision, the Federal Communications Commission (FCC) discouraged film company acquisitions, and ruled that no single corporation could own more than five stations. In the meantime, the established radio interests were able to take up the bulk of the key licences. After the anti-trust case, however, Paramount broke into two: Paramount Pictures Corporation and United Paramount Theatres. By 1951 the latter company was negotiating a merger, ratified in 1953, with the ABC network. The deal provided ABC with the capital to establish it on more equal terms with NBC and CBS.

Another strategy seriously considered as early as 1938 was the introduction of television into film theatres. This could be done for a relatively modest outlay, and it was felt that both newsreels and live sporting events would prove attractive to audiences. 1947 saw a number of experimental screenings, mostly using projection systems of which one was developed by RCA and the other underwritten by Paramount. In 1949 screenings of World Series baseball were immensely popular in New York, Boston and Chicago. Prospects looked good, and each of the majors became involved. But despite well over a hundred theatres being equipped, the increased returns were never substantial enough to recoup the initial costs. The FCC refused to authorise exclusive broadcast channels, and operators had the choice of either duplicating what audiences could see at home or renting AT&T coaxial cables to distribute programmes. The cost of this was prohibitive, and by 1953 it was clear that theatre television was not going to fulfil its promise, and attention turned to 3-D and CinemaScope.

In retrospect, an obvious move for Hollywood was to start production specifically for the new medium. But at first it was assumed that television would take over production practices from radio, and that most of it would be live transmissions. For some years after the war the large stations produced almost everything in this way, including the increasingly popular episodic drama series. Subsidiary stations with few production resources, however, soon needed other material to fill the screen and in 1948 Columbia – well-established as a producer of B-pictures – formed a subsidiary, Screen Gems Inc, to produce commercials and short films for the small screen.

Dragnet

In 1951 Lucille Ball and her husband Desi Arnaz began to *film* their television comedy show *I Love Lucy,* employing the veteran German cinematographer Karl Freund and three cameras in a small Hollywood studio. This audacious move was soon vindicated: within a year the series was high in the all-important Nielsen ratings. The police drama *Dragnet* adopted the technique in 1952, as did a former live series, *Man Against Crime,* which was now shot in an Edison studio in New York. Apart from Columbia, however, the major studios held off from such productions, in line with their policy not to sell to television. The studios were hoping to achieve better exploitation from their output through pay television, although their plans were frustrated by the FCC. Several of the majors still had significant exhibition interests, and those that did not were wary of threats by independent exhibitors of a boycott of studios who embraced the new medium too eagerly. Smaller companies had no such qualms. Hal Roach Productions, Ziv Television and Revue Productions were all soon supplying television stations with product. The first sale to television of a film series made by an independent producer was agreed in 1948. Numerous series followed, although the networks were wary and budgets and production values were rock bottom.

But the major studios could not delay for much longer. In 1954 Walt Disney agreed to make a series for ABC, and the potential of this lucrative deal persuaded Jack Warner that his studio should follow suit. To create the highest profile for the studio the series was called *Warner Brothers Presents,* and featured storylines based on three of the studio's pictures – *Casablanca, King's Row* and *Cheyenne.* The *Cheyenne* stories were a great success, and many more Western series followed, including *Maverick.* By 1960 Warners was earning $40 million from television production, compared with its total revenue in 1959 from all other sources of just $90 million.

Soon after the Warners success, *MGM Parade* (1955-6, ABC) and *Twentieth Century-Fox Hour* (1955-7, CBS) followed suit. Each series adopted a different strategy to distance the programmes themselves from the ordinary run of television, and to assure audiences that it was the film companies which could supply them with quality entertainment. *MGM Parade* went inside the studio, explained the film-making process and interviewed the stars. 20th Century-Fox adopted a variant of the Warners approach, but produced new, or almost new, versions of the studio's hits. A further series, *Screen Directors Playhouse* (1955-6, NBC and ABC), from the

Hal Roach Studios, featured telefilms by among others John Ford, George Marshall, Allan Dwan and Rouben Mamoulian. Capra, Hitchcock and Welles also made work for the new medium in these years.

Alongside the studios, there was a new entrant in the game which quickly established itself as perhaps the dominant player. Revue Productions was a subsidiary of the leading talent agency MCA. With the demise of the studios and the phasing out of contract players, MCA had become increasingly involved in 'packaging' feature films. Now it saw television as a natural extension of its activities, and by the end of the 1950s Revue Productions was supplying some forty hours a week of network programming, including *Wagon Train* (1957-65, NBC and ABC), *Alfred Hitchcock Presents* (1955-65, CBS and NBC), and *This is Your Life* (1952-61, NBC). In 1959 the company purchased the backlot of Universal Studios, and later Universal Pictures itself. Its power, perceived by many as an effective monopoly, also regularly attracted the attention of anti-trust investigators.

Wagon Train: *Ward Bond leading*

In October 1960 ABC premiered *The Untouchables*, produced by Quinn Martin at Desilu, and the immediate success of the series consolidated the network's challenge to its two rivals. Despite growing fears about the violence in such shows, 'action adventure' series were now central elements in the schedules, and their producers were key men in a Hollywood which, within five years, had happily adjusted to the small screen. The re-run potential of these shows was now acknowledged, as was their strength in areas of the schedule, like daytime and late evening, previously regarded as marginal. Moreover, by 1962 the rest of the world had caught up with the United States in numbers of television sets, and there were many new markets for telefilm series. By the early 1960s Hollywood dominated primetime television.

Selling features to television

Although it was clear that television could also prove to be a new market for motion pictures, the majors initially refused to sell or license films to the small screen – and their stars were usually prohibited from appearing on television. As a fledgling, underfunded industry, the new medium could not compete with prices set by the theatrical market. Television did, however, begin to screen movies, for from 1948 British producers like Ealing, Rank and Korda, still effectively barred from theatrical exposure in America, were happy to make their product available. Alexander Korda was particularly

183

intrigued by television's potential, and was to part-finance his last production, Laurence Olivier's *Richard III* (1956), by a pre-sale to NBC. The small domestic film producers like Monogram and Republic were also keen to deal with television. But it was not until 1955 that a major broke ranks.

In 1948 the eccentric industrialist Howard Hughes had purchased a controlling interest in RKO. By 1954 the studio was deep in debt, and Hughes was forced to buy out the remaining shareholders. Within a year he had unloaded the company and its assets to the General Tire & Rubber Company, which closed down production, sold the studio lot to Lucille Ball's Desilu company, and started to license the catalogue of films to its own New York television station and elsewhere. The immediate profits from this move impressed the other studios and in 1956 Columbia, Warners, Fox and MGM made similar arrangements for the use of their pre-1948 features. MGM even secured $1 million for a single screening of *The Wizard of Oz*. No longer were the majors concerned about a possible boycott of their theatrical product by exhibitors, since the power of the theatres was by now significantly reduced. And suggestions that colour television was not far away reinforced their concern to maximise returns on black-and-white movies.

Richard III, *part-financed by a sale to US television*

Paramount held off until 1958, when it sold its pre-1948 library to MCA. The price was $50 million, but as MCA picked up outright control they were soon able to turn this to substantial profits. By 1965 they had grossed more than $70 million, without even exploring sales to the networks. The profits from this financed MCA's purchase of Universal and consolidated its place among the major media conglomerates. In later years the companies were to regret selling their films outright. Warners had sold their pre-1948 library for $21 million. By 1982 it was reported that they were trying to buy back the films, for what was regarded as the bargain price of $95 million.

After 1955 the networks used the newly available movies as special attractions in the schedules, but it was not until 1961 that NBC introduced a weekly series of features, including many made since 1948. Not the least of their reasons for such an innovation was that colour movies helped sell new television sets made by NBC's parent corporation RCA. ABC brought in a movie slot in 1962, CBS followed in 1965. Primetime schedules became increasingly dependent on features, and consistently solid ratings inevitably pushed up the prices for screenings. From an average of $10,000 per movie in the first RKO package, fees had risen to $200,000 in the early 1960s, and in 1966 ABC paid Columbia $2 million to show *The Bridge on the River Kwai*.

The supply of movies 'suitable' for television was nevertheless limited, particularly given the increasingly adult content of films in the 1960s. The obvious move was for suppliers to produce features to be premiered on television. The licence fee for such a screening would cover low-budget production costs, and the producer could then exploit the film in other markets afterwards. The first such production was to have been *The Killers*, a two-hour thriller made by Don Siegel for Universal in 1964. But ironically it was considered too violent for the small screen and was released in theatres instead. A few similar projects were shown in 1964 and 1965, but it was *Fame is the Name of the Game*, premiered in November 1966, which initiated the first full series of made-for-TV movies, or telefilms as they were to become known. This remake of the 1949 Alan Ladd movie *Chicago Deadline* was subsequently developed into a prime-time series, *The Name of the Game*, which ran from 1968-71. Trying out series ideas in pilot films like this was to become common practice.

Too violent for television: Ronald Reagan and Angie Dickinson in Don Siegel's The Killers

Made-for-TV movies quickly established themselves as staples both for the producers and the networks. With their low budgets and fast schedules, they were frequently compared with the B-features of the 1940s. A number of writers (most notably Richard Levinson and William Link) and directors (Steven Spielberg, Buzz Kulik, Boris Sagal, Paul Wendkos) have shown themselves proficient exponents of the form. By the late 1960s the cinema and television industries, which had once seen each other as dangerous rivals, were bound by many mutual interests.

Exploitation and blockbusters

In the production sector still working primarily for the theatres, it had been recognised for years that it was no longer worthwhile for the majors to make B-pictures for the bottom half of double-bills. In the early 1950s, after the anti-trust decrees, the new uncertainties of exhibition encouraged the majors to concentrate on top-flight films, and even low-budget specialists Republic and Monogram (which changed its name to Allied Artists) found profits increasingly elusive.

An exception to this trend and one of the decade's distinctive success stories was American International Pictures, which in 1955 began to make low-budget productions for new markets. With lurid advertising, sensational titles and subject-matter, these films often played as double-bills in down-market theatres and drive-ins. *The Day the World Ended* (1955, directed by AIP's foremost film-maker Roger Corman), *Hot Rod Girl* (1956), *I Was a Teenage Werewolf* (1957) and many more attracted a young audience dissatisfied with both conventional movies and the domestic offerings of television. AIP and Roger Corman went on to produce a distinguished cycle of horror films in colour, based on the stories of Edgar Allan Poe.

Roger Corman's The Day the World Ended

Many of these exploitation films worked within a genre which had not really established itself within the American cinema, but which now proved increasingly popular: science-fiction. A number of the films, like *The Thing* (1951) and *Them!* (1954), displaced the fears and fantasies of 'subversion' and Communist takeover onto extra-terrestrial invasion. Among the most effective is Don Siegel's *Invasion of the Body Snatchers* (1955), in which the aliens reproduce themselves as replicants of seemingly normal human bodies.

Through the 1950s the major studios, often working with independents, continued to produce a wide range of genre pictures, adding to the accepted formulas both sci-fi and 'youth pictures' like *Rebel Without a Cause* (1955, directed by Nicholas Ray) and *Blackboard Jungle* (1955, Richard Brooks). But the box-office pressures were towards greater differentiation of each film – by the stars, or the director, or the concept – and an increasing emphasis on the first-run theatre audiences. The consequences of this included a move towards the more 'respectable' parts of the market, as well as the production of ever more expensive blockbusters. As each film now had to sell itself, the tendency was to improve production values, with the inevitable increase in budgets.

186

An appeal to youth: James Dean in Nicholas Ray's Rebel Without a Cause

An increasingly important factor for both studio and independent was a 'property' which had already proved itself in another market. This could be a best-selling book, like *The Caine Mutiny* (1954, Edward Dmytryk), *From Here to Eternity* (1953, Fred Zinnemann) or *Exodus* (1960, Otto Preminger). A hit stage show would serve just as well: if it had already made money in one medium, the theory was, it would make money in another. The producer found such projects easier to sell to financiers, and often to the public. One of the most successful entrepreneurs to work in this way was Mike Todd, who had already proved his worth as a Broadway producer. In 1955 he mounted the wide-screen Todd-AO spectacle based on Rodgers and Hammerstein's musical *Oklahoma!* (director Fred Zinnemann). The following year he repeated its commercial triumph with *Around the World in Eighty Days* (director Michael Anderson). Far-flung locations and countless guest-stars allowed Todd to exploit the film as a 'road-show' attraction, with higher seat prices and attendant ballyhoo, just as forty years earlier D.W. Griffith had first shown *The Birth of a Nation*.

Much of the film industry followed Todd's lead, especially as it was felt that the blockbuster (after the discredited 3-D, and along with colour, scope and 'adult' subject-matter) was yet another riposte to television, which with its black-and-white screen and as yet limited finances could not possibly compete. Subsequent Rodgers and Hammerstein hits included *Carousel* and *The King and I* (both 1956, for 20th Century-Fox), *South Pacific* (1958) and in 1965 *The Sound of Music* (director Robert Wise, for Fox again). The extraordinary success of *The Sound of Music* suggested to the industry that the musical blockbuster was the profit machine of the future.

The other popular blockbuster form was the historical spectacular, preferably set in the ancient world. The advantages of shooting in Europe –

cheaper labour and the opportunity to use blocked funds – encouraged such productions, and the cycle attracted directors as distinguished as Nicholas Ray, with *King of Kings* (1961) and *55 Days at Peking* (1962); and Anthony Mann, with *El Cid* (1961) and *The Fall of the Roman Empire* (1964). But 20th Century-Fox's *Cleopatra* (1963, directed by Joseph Mankiewicz) was at $37 million both the most expensive film ever made and one of the most colossal failures.

Blockbuster: 55 Days at Peking

Ever more insistent profit demands prompted an increasingly desperate attempt to reconstruct the family audience, despite the box-office evidence that this was illusory. The corporations also became more and more interested in capitalising on all the music, publishing and merchandising possibilities of a blockbuster. So the pattern was to be repeated, again by Fox, which was almost bankrupted by its musical follow-ups to *The Sound of Music*. The $24 million *Hello Dolly* (1969, director Gene Kelly), the $18 million *Doctor Dolittle* (1967, Richard Fleischer), even the $10 million *Star!* (1968, Robert Wise), all of which had seemingly the right ingredients, failed to perform at the box office. Compounding their folly, Fox put $25 million into the Pacific war spectacular *Tora! Tora! Tora!* (1970), hoping to achieve a hit comparable to their 1962 success *The Longest Day* (produced independently by Darryl Zanuck). The mass family audience could still be attracted, but only very occasionally. In 1969-70 the company admitted losses of just over $100 million.

The 1960s were an uneasy time for the majors. There was a recognition that the industry was witnessing the death throes of the studio system, and neither Paramount nor MGM maintained their profiles of earlier decades. Buoyed by the success of their television series, Warners appeared more

188

stable, and the studio participated in a number of the more interesting independent productions of the time, including *Who's Afraid of Virginia Woolf?* (1966, Mike Nichols) and *Bonnie and Clyde* (1967, Arthur Penn). But mostly studios and independents alike were chasing the big movies, and consequently leaving themselves vulnerable. With more and more theatres closing down, steady distribution profits were no longer available as a cushion. The bank rate soared, and although television-related revenue disguised the true precariousness of many companies, few of the supposedly sure-fire cinema hits justified the faith of their producers.

By the end of the decade, the industry was experiencing its worst ever financial crisis. Between 1968 and 1971 the overall losses of the 'Big Five' were close to $500 million, at a time when both production and exhibition costs, particularly for the increasingly necessary mass advertising campaigns, were once again spiralling. The companies no longer appeared viable in their traditional form, and by the end of the 1960s each of the majors had either been absorbed into a conglomerate or diversified themselves towards conglomerate status. Universal had in any case been part of Decca Records since 1951, and after 1962 both were elements of the MCA empire. Now, within three years, the whole structure of Hollywood was to change.

In 1967 Jack Warner, recognising the problems to come, sold his interest in what was still essentially a family concern to Seven Arts, a company formed by two brothers, Eliot and Kenneth Hyman, who had been successful packagers. Two years later they in turn were bought out by Kinney National Service Inc, and Warner Communications Inc was formed. Along with movies, the new conglomerate was involved with parking lots, funeral parlours, *Mad* magazine, a lucrative Coca Cola franchise, and several record labels. Also in 1969 Transamerica Corporation, which made most of its money from insurance, took over United Artists, and the oil-based Gulf + Western Industries swallowed Paramount. In 1970-1 Fox, Paramount and Warners all cut back production to a fraction of previous levels. Studio lots were sold off and, just as in the post-war period, job losses were acute. MGM was taken over by Kerk Kerkorian, who sold off parts of the lot and the props department to finance new hotel building. In 1973 MGM pulled out of distribution completely, and supported only a marginal film production operation. Fox and Columbia, in similar difficulties, began parallel operations, and to diversify. The impact of their decisions was to become clearer in the next decade.

The financial logic of such corporate moves was clear. Excess profits from the handful of hit movies could be invested in a range of more stable industries, the steadier returns from which were intended to support production activities during leaner times. This was the shape of the much-discussed 'New Hollywood', although in 1969 a single movie seemed to point towards another interpretation of the phrase. *Easy Rider,* starring Peter Fonda and Dennis Hopper and made on a low budget, attracted a massive young audience – much to the surprise of Hollywood. For a moment, it was seen as the way towards a profitable future. As was later to become clear, the film's significance was less for its financial formula than for what it indicated about narrative, characters and the form of Hollywood films to come.

Further reading

Lawrence Alloway, *Violent America: The Movies 1946-64*, New York: Museum of Modern Art, 1971.

Rick Altman (ed), *Genre: The Musical*, London: Routledge & Kegan Paul/BFI Publishing, 1981.

Peter Biskind, *Seeing is Believing: How Hollywood Taught us to Stop Worrying and Love the Fifties*, New York: Pantheon, 1983.

Larry Ceplair and Steve Englund, *The Inquisition in Hollywood: Politics in the Film Community 1930-60*, New York: Doubleday, 1980.

Michael Conant, *Antitrust in the Motion Picture Industry*, Berkeley and Los Angeles: University of California Press, 1960.

Jim Cook and Alan Lovell (eds), *BFI Dossier 11: Coming to Terms with Hollywood*, London: British Film Institute, 1981.

John Gregory Dunne, *The Studio*, New York: Farrar, Straus, 1969.

Jane Feuer, *The Hollywood Musical*, London: Macmillan/BFI Publishing, 1982.

Christine Gledhill (ed), *Home is Where the Heart Is: Studies in Melodrama and the Women's Film*, London: BFI Publishing, 1987.

E. Ann Kaplan (ed), *Women and Film Noir*, London: British Film Institute, 1978.

Jim Kitses, *Horizons West*, London: Secker & Warburg/British Film Institute, 1969.

Colin McArthur, *Underworld USA*, London: Secker & Warburg/British Film Institute, 1972.

Hortense Powdermaker, *Hollywood: The Dream Factory*, Boston: Little, Brown, 1950.

Thomas Schatz, *Hollywood Genres*, New York: Random House, 1981.

13
Television Takes Over

In the years after the Second World War television began to establish itself as the dominant medium for both entertainment and information. In the United States a vigorous commercial system developed, which became increasingly controlled by three national networks. In the early 1950s the all-important mid-evening schedule on these networks – primetime – featured a wide range of programming including variety shows, documentaries and single dramas. Much of the output was live and distributed to the affiliate stations of each network from New York, and a significant proportion of it was produced by advertising agencies. By 1960, however, primetime was crammed with episodic series made on film in Hollywood, and the networks had asserted their power to ensure that neither agencies nor affiliates could exercise any significant control.

In Britain the BBC's monopoly was broken, its ethic of public service broadcasting complemented by an advertising-financed system which began operations in 1955. After a difficult start, the regionally based Independent Television was soon attracting a majority of the audience and was profitable enough for one of its executives to liken it to 'having a licence to print your own money'. The BBC responded with management and programme changes which by the early 1960s had brought about a rough parity in audiences. Elsewhere during the 1950s new television services were set up as variants of these commercial and public service broadcasting models. By 1958 some 26 countries had started television broadcasting.

Post-war America
Regular television broadcasts had continued in the United States until 1941. Small stations spread across the country, but the centre of the industry remained in New York, where both NBC and CBS were finally granted commercial licences for their stations on 1 July 1941. The government's regulatory body, the Federal Communications Commission (FCC), determined that television signals should be broadcast on the relatively narrow VHF section of the waveband, a decision which limited future expansion and led to the industry's dominance by the three (briefly four)

networks. This post-war network system began in a nascent form when, just prior to the official start of a commercial service, NBC New York started to feed programmes, on AT&T co-axial cables, first to the General Electric station in Schenectady and then to the Philco station in Philadelphia. The war curtailed transmissions, although experimental work continued and some new licences were granted, including one in 1944 to DuMont Laboratories for a third commercial station in New York.

As hostilities ended, the electronics manufacturers now wanted to use their wartime assembly lines to turn out television sets. The many restrictions of the war had forced savings on consumers, who were soon persuaded to buy the domestic luxuries considered necessary for a new home. The television set was one of these luxuries, and it was also the most effective medium for the aggressive advertising of other household products. NBC and DuMont began to extend their networks, sending live signals to East Coast affiliates and supplying stations in the mid-West and on the West Coast with tele-recordings or kinescopes, which were records of electronic broadcasts filmed from a screen. Central to the development of the networks was the handful of regular series which began to attract audiences beyond those intrigued simply by the novelty of the new medium. Foremost among these was NBC's variety show *Hour Glass*; another pioneering series was the prestigious *Kraft Television Theater*, which began in 1947 on NBC.

In 1943 government anti-trust measures had forced NBC to sell its Blue Network of two television stations (with part ownership in a third, plus a number of radio stations), and this was picked up and transformed into the American Broadcasting Company (ABC) by Edward J. Noble, the maker of Life Savers Candy. At first without a New York flagship, ABC bought time on other stations and prepared for a more elaborate network operation, which it initiated in 1948. The fourth player in the game, CBS, had been experimenting during the war with an early colour system, and it endeavoured, without success, to have this adopted as a standard by the FCC. Instead, the position of NBC's parent corporation RCA was strengthened by further FCC decisions, and as servicemen returned home NBC quickly had improved black-and-white sets on the market. NBC's coverage of the 1947 World Series baseball games finally convinced CBS that it needed to compete on its rival's terms. Within a year it too was feeding black-and-white programmes to a small network.

The 1947 World Series demonstrated the mass audience potential of the new medium. The following year, however, worried about problems of signal interference, the FCC stopped issuing new licences. The list of a hundred or so stations already in existence was not extended until 1952, by which time many of the institutional structures and programme patterns were firmly in place. NBC and CBS were able to consolidate their positions during this 'freeze', whereas both ABC and DuMont faced escalating losses. And in 1948 Mutual, Philco and Paramount all dropped plans to begin their own network operations. The freeze also facilitated comparative studies of those markets with and without television, and it became clear that television was not only effectively promoting the sales of advertised products, but was capturing large parts of the audiences traditionally attracted both to the movies and to sports events.

In these early years the network schedules contained a broad mix of programming, but they were dominated by the immensely successful variety series. Milton Berle launched *Texaco Star Theater* (later *The Milton Berle Show*, 1948-69) and Ed Sullivan hosted *Toast of the Town* (later *The Ed Sullivan Show*, 1948-71). 1949 saw the successful debut of what later became *Your Show of Shows*, with Sid Caesar and Imogen Coca providing ninety minutes of live comedy on a Saturday night. Both Milton Berle and Sid Caesar were engaged by NBC, and their series used a wide range of the radio talent attached to the company. CBS meanwhile ran a vigorous campaign to attract top performers, and set up a range of tax deals which secured far better remuneration for the artistes. Jack Benny, George Burns and Gracie Allen were among those tempted to switch allegiances, and by the mid-1950s CBS was the leading network, a position which it retained until the end of the 1960s.

Your Show of Shows *(Carl Reiner, Imogen Coca, Jack Palance, Sid Caesar)*

Cold War scaremongering, already affecting the film industry, also began to blight television following the publication in 1947 of a report which purported to identify Communists within the business. Bowing to the pressure, the networks instituted blacklists similar to those operating in the film industry. In October 1953 the reporter Ed Murrow and his producer Fred Friendly confronted the issue – and the vocal anti-Communist Senator Joseph McCarthy – in their CBS current affairs series *See It Now*. A study of the case of a dismissed Air Force lieutenant, the programme was a rare challenge to McCarthyist demagogy. In March 1954 the series focused on McCarthy himself and, using mostly film of his speeches, produced a devastating report. A month later ABC carried in full the Congressional hearings of a dispute between McCarthy and the Army. Again McCarthy's flimsy arguments were exposed to wide scrutiny, and by the end of the year he was a discredited figure. ABC, which had taken the hearings largely for reasons of economy, won impressive ratings.

Ed Murrow in an edition of the CBS *current affairs series* See It Now

The 'Golden Age'

Following the model of NBC's *Kraft Television Theater*, the dramatic anthology series found a central place in all the network schedules. Produced live, and mostly in New York, series like *Studio One* (1948-58, CBS), *U.S. Steel Hour* (1953-63, ABC and CBS) and *Goodyear Television Playhouse*

Marty, *produced for the Philco Goodyear Theatre in 1953 (Joe Mantell, Rod Steiger)*

(1951-60, NBC) each week featured a different play. Many of the subjects, and the dominant aesthetic, reflected the naturalism which ruled the post-war American stage. The theatre also provided new stars like Paul Newman, Rod Steiger and Joanne Woodward and young directors such as Delbert Mann, Arthur Penn and Sidney Lumet. Between 1953 and 1955 the potential of this original form generated considerable excitement, especially after the production of Paddy Chayevsky's *Marty*, broadcast in May 1953. This low-key contemporary tale of an unattractive young butcher in the Bronx finding love touched audiences and critics, and influenced many aspiring writers looking to put onto the small screen what Chayevsky called 'the marvellous world of the ordinary'.

New works by writers like Chayevsky, Gore Vidal, Reginald Rose and Rod Serling were mounted in consistently imaginative studio productions. In 1956 CBS introduced television's most ambitious live drama series, *Playhouse 90*, which staged shows of considerable complexity: John Frankenheimer's production of Serling's *Requiem for a Heavyweight* (1956), for example, remains a remarkable achievement, both as powerful drama and as a triumph of live television logistics. Yet even as CBS was planning the series, changes in programming policy and in patterns of sponsorship were already contributing to the decline of what has been called the 'Golden Age' of American television.

NBC and CBS had hoped to avoid a repetition of what they regarded as a mistake in radio development, which had allowed agencies to gain control of production and often to reserve favoured slots in the schedule. But with the new medium short of cash, the agencies and sponsors were able to duplicate previous arrangements. From 1950 the networks wanted to reassert their control, in part so as to build schedules more effectively and also so as to contract talent directly rather than be dependent on a sponsor's wishes. Production costs were in any case rising rapidly, and often beyond a level acceptable to an individual sponsor. The types of sponsor and their needs were also changing. At first car and electrical goods manufacturers had been eager for corporate identification, but as consumer goods combines began to advertise specific products, like food and toiletries, a spread of coverage became more valuable and the move towards first participation and then 'spot' advertising, introduced by the hungry ABC network, more closely matched the sponsors' new requirements.

Film series, which proved their ratings power in 1952 when *I Love Lucy* became the number one show, similarly suited both networks and sponsors. The former could use them to assert their control, the latter could more efficiently reach the audiences they were looking for. ABC in particular was attracted by the potential of film series, because at this point it had fewer affiliates and many of these could not be fed live shows from a central source. In addition, NBC and CBS had a monopoly of the existing talent, and film series might more easily make new stars who would be harder for the others to poach.

194

All these changes made a major impact on the live anthology drama series, presaged by ABC's cancellation in 1955-6 of all its drama slots in favour of Hollywood-produced film series. Sponsors themselves were also becoming disillusioned with the often downbeat subject matter of contemporary drama. And writers were being submitted to increasing interference and censorship by sponsors. The most famous case was the removal from a 1958 drama about the Nuremberg war crimes trials of all references to the use of gas chambers by the Nazis: the sponsor was the American Gas Association. In the rapidly changing broadcasting economy live drama series no longer satisfied either network or sponsor.

BBC Television returns

In Britain, a BBC committee under Lord Hankey had since 1943 been considering the Corporation's future relationship with television, and in March 1945 it recommended that after the war the television service should be reinstated as before. Operations began again on 7 June 1946, in time to relay pictures of the next day's Victory Parade in London. A schedule of plays, lectures and variety followed, including the new children's show *Muffin the Mule*. But despite the BBC's distinguished record during the war, there were many who felt that a wide-ranging review of its operations should be instituted. In 1946 the new Labour government extended the Charter by only five years, instead of the hoped-for ten, and June 1949 saw the first meeting of a government commission, chaired by Lord Beveridge, with a wide brief to advise on the future of both sound and television broadcasting.

The Beveridge Committee's report was published in January 1951, and in general it approved of the BBC's operations and plans. Most of its

Muffin the Mule, *with Annette Mills*

attention was devoted to radio, but it also included a good deal of the submitted evidence arguing for the break-up of the Corporation's monopoly. The committee as a whole rejected this, but a minority report by the Conservative MP Selwyn Lloyd called for the establishment of commercial radio and television. Although there were many who pointed to the market-led American model and feared advertising's deleterious effects in Britain, Selwyn Lloyd's ideas seemed appropriate to the year which saw the Festival of Britain, the official end of post-war austerity and, in October, a new Conservative government.

Over the next three years there was a vigorous debate in Parliament, and elsewhere, about the possibilities of a second television service. The arguments for another broadcaster were primarily political, although there were active lobbies from both the electronics industry and from the larger adver-

195

tising agencies. Conservative MPs in particular attacked the concentration of power in the BBC, and pointed out that this increased the danger of the Corporation being subjected to direct government control. Unlike the BBC's garlanded radio services, television had just a brief record to defend, and in the early 1950s the Corporation was in any case demonstrating only a half-hearted commitment to the younger medium. Moreover, as relative affluence replaced austerity (in 1951 there were 1 million sets in Britain, in 1955 over 5 million), it became almost inevitable that the monopoly would be broken.

Panorama: *Richard Dimbleby and the radio and television pioneer Marconi*

The first indication of the change was contained in a White Paper in May 1952, which accepted the desirability of 'some element of competition'. In November 1953 a second White Paper proposed a compromise between the monopoly and the market. A parallel authority to the BBC would be established to oversee a commercial television system. This body, the Independent Television Authority (ITA), came into being in July 1954, and for the next twenty-five years British television was to be controlled by what was now a dual monopoly.

Although the Corporation's predominant interest remained sound broadcasting, and the new medium was consequently starved of resources, BBC Television's first post-war decade did demonstrate a growing confidence. Television's coming-of-age is widely acknowledged as the triumphant live coverage of the Coronation in June 1953, when some 56 per cent of the population watched the service in Westminster Abbey. New programmes which gained respect were the current affairs magazine *Panorama*, hosted by Richard Dimbleby, and the popular *Sportsview*. Nigel Kneale's *The Quatermass Experiment* (1953) was a compelling science-fiction serial and the Drama Department mounted an average of three single plays each week, including classic productions like Ibsen's *Peer Gynt* and an adaptation of Orwell's *Nineteen Eighty-Four* (1954). The early 1950s were the last years in which sound broadcasting played the central role, although on the evening of ITV's arrival in 1955 it was a radio show which stole much of the thunder from the new service. The producers of the radio serial *The Archers* chose that night to kill off a central character, whose demise was felt to have overshadowed the debut of the upstart service.

Nineteen Eighty-Four, *made by the BBC's Drama Department*

Independent Television
The ITA first met in August 1954, under the chairmanship of Sir Kenneth Clark, and the commercial service began in London just a year later, on 22

196

September 1955. At their first meetings the Authority devised a regional system, with contractors competing against each other for the supply of programmes. Also quickly settled on was a framework of restrictions and obligations placed on each contractor, including that of producing a 'proper balance' of programmes. Three stations were to be put in place – one in London, one in the Midlands, and one in the North – and these were initially shared between four contractors: Associated-Rediffusion (A-R), backed by Associated Newspapers and the Broadcast Relay Service; ATV, effectively controlled by a show business consortium which included the leading talent agency the Grade Organisation; Granada Television, a wholly-owned subsidiary of Granada Theatres, run by the Bernstein family; and ABC, a subsidiary of the film production company Associated British Picture Corporation, in which Warner Bros held a 37½ per cent interest. The fifth programme contractor, Independent Television News (ITN), was to be owned jointly by the others.

Programmes on the first night included coverage of a banquet at London's Guildhall, a short performance by the Hallé Orchestra, a variety show from the Wood Green Empire – and the first commercials, for Gibbs SR toothpaste, a drinking chocolate and a margarine. These bright, unrestrained advertisements were to set the tone of commercial television. One of those involved in setting up ITV, Bernard Sendall, later wrote: 'It was believed by many people that the object of the BBC was to improve the viewer; and feelings of alienation, however unjustified, were certainly widespread. Along came ITV with their brash new programmes seeking the "mass audience", and challenging the accepted standards of broadcasting … ITV set out to be popular – to achieve the common touch.'

Immediate popularity, however, eluded the new service, partly because only a small proportion of households could receive the programmes. In November 1955 A-R made significant changes to its schedule, moving cultural items to a later slot and introducing the American Western series *Gunsmoke*. Even so, the first ITV contractors began to fear far greater financial losses than expected, and possibly a complete collapse of the system. One strategy to counter this was the frequent exchange of programmes between contractors, and this developed into a core of network programmes taken by all or most of the companies. Signs of better prospects appeared around April 1956, and by the end of the year it was clear that the ITV companies did indeed have what the new franchise-holder in Scotland, newspaper magnate Roy Thomson, called 'a licence to print your own money'.

Programmes were initially provided in three groups throughout the day. Children's programmes in the late afternoon were followed by the period of closedown known as the 'toddlers' truce' (also observed by the BBC), which was invaded in early 1957 by the ATV serial *Emergency – Ward Ten* and by the BBC's *Tonight* programme. Evening offerings included quiz shows like *Take Your Pick* and *Double Your Money*, as well as American series such as *Dragnet*.

Armchair Theatre: The Thug, *directed by Philip Saville in 1959 (with Sheila Allen, Alan Bates)*

Face to Face: *John Freeman's interview with Gilbert Harding, which provoked controversy when Harding was seen to break down*

The variety show *Sunday Night at the London Palladium* (1955-65) soon became a fixed feature, as did further imports like *Wagon Train* and *Maverick*. Another noteworthy network contribution was A-R's *Armchair Theatre* (1956-68), overseen after 1958 by the Canadian producer Sydney Newman, which produced contemporary social dramas and introduced to television a number of new writers including Harold Pinter and Alun Owen. The best current affairs work came from Granada, with its ground-breaking election coverage and the *Searchlight* series of documentaries.

Parallel to the regional growth of I T V, the B B C extended the spread of its transmissions, so that by August 1958 80 per cent of the population could receive both B B C and I T V programmes. But the B B C's share of the audience was falling rapidly, reaching a low point of just 28 per cent late in 1957. And this was not the Corporation's only problem. Many trained engineers and programme-makers were leaving for more highly paid jobs in I T V, where rising profits meant higher programme budgets. The B B C made a spirited response to the challenge, creating in particular the irreverent, fast-moving current affairs magazine *Tonight* (1957-65). The public service tradition was also well served by programmes like John Freeman's in-depth interviews *Face to Face* and the arts magazine *Monitor*, under the imaginative editorship of Huw Wheldon. Both Jack Good's *6.5 Special* pop music show and the comedy series *Hancock's Half-Hour* indicated that commercial television did not have a monopoly on enter-

Hancock's Half-Hour: The Cold *(February 1960, with Tony Hancock, Sid James)*

tainment, and soon after its introduction in 1958 *Grandstand* was pulling a huge Saturday afternoon sports audience. I T N's bulletins also stimulated sharper B B C news coverage. Then in January 1960 Hugh Carleton Greene was appointed as the B B C's new Director General, and he was to do more than anyone to shape British broadcasting in the coming decade.

American networks and ratings 1955-70

In the United States meanwhile there were more than 500 stations by 1956, and the annual total of advertising sponsorship was almost one billion dollars. In programming, the newest craze was for quiz shows. These attractions had long featured in the schedules, but the prizes remained modest until 1955 when the cosmetics agency Revlon sponsored *The $64,000 Question* (C B S). High ratings, increased lipstick sales and carbon-copies of the show all followed. Then in 1959 a hugely successful contestant on the quiz series *Twenty-One* (N B C) admitted that he had been provided with the answers in advance. In a Senate investigation it also emerged that sponsors had dictated which contestants were regarded as sufficiently attractive to win. The exposés rocked the networks, and caused the virtual

198

disappearance of quiz shows. For a brief period the networks' collective conscience brought documentary series back into primetime, although they were soon replaced by further telefilm series. But the scandal meant that direct production by sponsors was now largely discredited.

In the later 1950s, although family-comedy telefilms continued to find audiences, the big attractions were crime and action-adventure series, including Westerns. Physical action and violence became increasingly common and prompted the first of many expressions of concern about its effects. The popularity of *The Untouchables* in 1960 confirmed this trend; and when a Senate subcommittee on juvenile delinquency focused on television violence in 1961, the networks took notice and introduced more socially responsible dramas, like *The Defenders* (CBS) and *Dr Kildare* (NBC).

Throughout the 1960s ratings became increasingly important to the networks. The Nielsen company had started their measurements of audience levels across the country in 1950, and advertisers had come to accept these figures as Holy Writ. A statistical sample of over 1,000 households had a recorder wired into their television set, and viewing patterns were aggregated to give a picture of national habits. The higher a programme's rating, the higher the price a network could charge an advertiser to buy into it. In 1950 it took six weeks to assemble the figures, but by 1973 it was possible to measure results overnight. Every ratings point was fought over, and both stock market prices and careers rose and fell along with a network's ratings.

As the price for spots increased in the mid-1960s, the networks began to milk the areas of the schedule which had previously been undervalued. Saturday morning, when children were watching, became important for toy manufacturers. Late-night television became more attractive, particularly after Johnny Carson took over NBC's *The Tonight Show* in 1962 (he still hosts this nightly programme). Daytime television became another revenue earner, especially once the radio form of the daily 'soap opera' was adapted for the visual medium. And in 1961 NBC overhauled *Today*, which had started ten years previously, for the breakfast-time audience. The early 1960s also marked the development of television's obsession with sport. CBS paid $28 million for the 1964 and 1965 rights to the National Football League games, and immediately recouped their investment with huge advertiser deals. 'Instant relays', exploiting the immediate playback potential of videotape, were first used in coverage of a football game on 31 December 1963 and did much to increase the popularity of televised sport.

Primetime television in the mid-1960s was infiltrated by a cycle of spy series, initiated by *The Man from U.N.C.L.E.* (NBC). Influenced by the James Bond movies, this show and others like it (*I Spy*, NBC; *Mission: Impossible*, CBS) offered a comforting negotiation both of America's internal social changes (positing unity against an external threat) and of revelations about the intelligence services' actions in Cuba and elsewhere. The upheavals of 1968, however, were significant enough even to make some dents in the cocooned fantasy-world of network television, where men boldly went to

Fantasy: from a 1966 episode of Star Trek

the outer galaxies (*Star Trek*, NBC) and a woman could wiggle her nose and magically restore domestic harmony (*Bewitched*, ABC). Post-1968 the networks wanted 'relevance', which found form in shows like *Mod Squad* (ABC) about three 'hippie cops' working undercover.

CBS achieved the highest overall rating in the 1968-9 season, as it had done for the past thirteen seasons. But NBC came close to overturning the CBS dominance, and the challenger now began to pay close attention to the 'demographics' of their ratings. In the past, overall totals had been all-important, but advertisers were increasingly interested in the specific segments of the audience which were the heaviest consumers. Time-buyers began to look for programmes which could attract young, urban adults, especially women; and NBC argued that their audiences contained a higher proportion of these target groups. CBS recognised that their top-rating shows, comedies with rural settings like *The Beverly Hillbillies* and *Petticoat Junction* and Westerns, were popular largely with older, non-urban audiences, and in the 1970-1 season these shows were phased out and replaced by short-lived youth-oriented and city-based series like *Storefront Lawyers*. Such demographic calculations were to be central to the medium throughout the next decade.

1970 was also the year in which the FCC announced a new set of rules, intended in part to curb the increased power which the networks had accrued in the shift from sponsored programmes to the selling of spot advertising. Indeed, there were clear parallels with the anti-trust legislation following the Paramount case in 1948, which had broken the monopolistic hold of the Hollywood majors on distribution and exhibition. The networks were now barred from participating in profits made by programmes in domestic syndication (that is, the marketing of programmes to individual stations, usually after a primetime run) or foreign distribution. Nor could they own or part-own programmes made by their suppliers. And, in an attempt to encourage new sources of programme supply, the Prime Time Access Rule restricted the networks to three hours of programming each night, obliging affiliate stations and even those owned and operated by the networks to fill one of the hours between 7pm and 11pm.

The BBC in the 1960s

One of the first responsibilities of the BBC's new Director-General, Hugh Carleton Greene, in 1960 was the preparation of the Corporation's evidence to the Pilkington Committee, set up to advise the government on the future of broadcasting. Published in 1962, the committee's report praised the BBC's 'professionalism' and its commitment to public service broadcasting. The Corporation's bid to start a third channel was accepted, and advertising on the BBC was ruled out. ITV, in contrast, was extensively criticised. 'Those who say they give the public what it wants,' the report suggested, 'begin by underestimating public taste and end by debauching it.' It was recommended that the ITA's direct control be extended.

The Pilkington Report was widely attacked as 'elitist' and many of its specific recommendations were not taken up, but the BBC was delighted. Among the first fruits of what seemed to be a new confidence was the start, in November 1962, of the late-night satirical programme *That Was The Week That Was*, which introduced to television an unexpectedly irreverent and occasionally openly hostile attitude to the great and the good. There was considerable opposition to the show in Parliament, but for Greene it was exactly what was needed to give the BBC a younger and more contemporary image, and it ran successfully until taken off the air, amid some controversy, in November 1963. This new, questioning attitude distinguished much of the Corporation's output in the 1960s, and seemed to match the political promise offered by a new Labour government and the broader social and cultural changes of the decade. But even in this new climate there were still limits, in television if not elsewhere, as when in 1965 the BBC stopped the transmission of *The War Game*, Peter Watkins' graphic account of a nuclear attack on Britain.

BBC television drama in the early 1960s included the popular *Maigret* adaptations, and the prestigious *An Age of Kings* (1960), eight of Shakespeare's history plays produced by Peter Daws as a 15-part serial. But it was with the new realism of *Z Cars* (1962-78), a series based on the work of the Lancashire police which overturned the cosy world of the earlier police series *Dixon of Dock Green*, that a truly contemporary look was introduced to BBC television drama. Commercial television's *Armchair Theatre*, however, was still seen as the most socially aware dramatic series, and in 1962 the BBC poached its pioneering producer, Sydney Newman. In 1963 Newman initiated the children's science-fiction adventure series *Dr Who*, which soon won a huge following, and he began to shape *The Wednesday Play* in the mould of his earlier success. Among the controversial portraits of contemporary Britain produced for the series were *Up the Junction* (1965) and *Cathy Come Home* (1966). The comedy series *Steptoe and Son* (1964-73), written by Ray Galton and Alan Simpson, and *Till Death Us Do Part* (1964-74), by Johnny Speight, also won praise – and some vocal criticism – for their clear-eyed but affectionate portraits of older characters refusing to accept the new realities of the 1960s.

BBC 2 went on the air on 20 April 1964. Its early pattern of scheduling similar programmes on one night each week was soon abandoned, but its profile as an up-market, special interest and cultural

The new realism: an early episode of the police series Z Cars

channel was successfully developed. Among its early successes were the documentary series *The Great War*, a major archive-based history of the First World War, and the comedy *The Likely Lads*. In 1967 a mammoth adaptation of Galsworthy's cycle of Edwardian life, *The Forsyte Saga*, found both a huge audience and an appreciative critical response. Two years later the channel produced a similarly ambitious project, in the shape of the 13-part documentary series *Civilisation*. Lauded around the world, both series mixed middlebrow culture and popular presentation in ways which have since proved enormously influential.

ITV after Pilkington

ITV was stung by the unexpected criticisms made by the Pilkington Committee. The report's recommendation of a thorough restructuring of the system was not acted on by the Conservative government, but certain more modest changes were made. A new Chairman of the ITA, Lord Hill, appointed in 1963, endeavoured to increase the Authority's direct supervision of the schedules. In August 1966 the ITA asked each of the contractors to look at the make-up of their primetime schedules and to try 'to whet the appetites of the more intelligent viewers by providing more variation from the standard fare'. One indirect result was *News at Ten*, a half-hour broadcast from ITN each weekday night.

This Week, *reporting on a famine in Africa*

The ITV schedules in the mid-1960s were far from a commercial wasteland, and included cultural series like ABC's arts magazine *Tempo* (1961-8) and a wide range of documentaries and dramas. Both *This Week* (A-R) and *World in Action* (Granada) developed distinctive styles of current affairs reporting. In entertainment programming, the success story of these years was the string of popular series turned out for ATV by Lew Grade's ITC subsidiary. In the late 1950s ITC had made half-hour period swashbucklers like *The Adventures of Robin Hood*; later they made international thrillers such as *OSS* and *Danger Man*. Each of these enjoyed as much success abroad as they did at home, and with later series like *Department S* and *The Persuaders* they remain British television's most profitable initiative in international sales. One of the most quirky of these ITC offerings, *The Prisoner* (1967-8), was even sold to the CBS network. The brainchild of former *Danger Man* star Patrick McGoohan, the series featured a secret service agent trying to escape from a bizarre fantasy village. Twenty years on, it retains a cult interest.

In 1967 Lord Hill announced a number of fundamental changes to the ITV system. A certain resentment had been building over the by now enormous profits being made by the larger contractors. A shake-up was expected, and the ITA determined that the regional patterns would be considerably altered and that one of the smaller contractors, Television West and Wales (TWW), would simply lose its licence. For many commentators the changes presaged an improvement in the quality of programmes. But London Weekend Television (LWT), a new contractor awarded the weekend franchise in the capital, found it harder than expected to make good its promises and was soon in serious financial trouble. Commercial television in Britain was still searching for an optimum balance between the public's perceived tastes and public service.

Television around the world

Every broadcasting system finds a balance between the concerns of the state and the interests of the market. And as countries set up their television systems after the war, a few models emerged as feasible expressions of this balance. In the United States the market was submitted to only minimal governmental control; a similar freedom was permitted to the commercial stations in Japan. In Russia, however, state control remains paramount, and the power of the State Committee for Radio and Television Broadcasting is enormous. Between these poles lie two other basic structures. There are public corporations, as in Britain, which usually enjoy considerable autonomy; and there are private corporations, in which the state may be a commercial partner. France, West Germany and Belgium have operated variants of the former model. The Italian, Swedish and Swiss television services were set up with the latter framework.

Before 1950 only France and Russia, in addition to the United States and Britain, had started regular television services. In August that year, the BBC carried its first cross-channel broadcast, with Richard Dimbleby introducing a programme from Calais, and in July 1952 a more elaborate London-Paris link was set up for a week of programmes seen in both England and France. Japan, Switzerland and Belgium all started television services in 1953. Italy and Denmark followed soon afterwards, and a Eurovision link-up brought together signals from eight countries. In 1956 the first television station in the Middle East opened in Baghdad.

As these countries chose their television structures and organisations, the problems of the various models – and some solutions to them – became apparent. The dangers of a state-dominated public corporation, for example, are well illustrated by developments in France. Pre-war commercial radio there was felt to have been too easily manipulated by political groups, and legislation enacted in 1946 nationalised broadcasting and set up the state-controlled Radiodiffusion et Télévision Française (RTF). Available resources were mostly committed to radio, and the television service grew slowly. RTF was directly responsible to the Ministry of Information, and rigorous government supervision was more or less accepted as routine, especially after General De Gaulle became President in 1958. The General astutely used television to by-pass conventional government channels and to appeal directly to the nation. Partly as a result of this political interest, budgets and resources for television were increased and a second network was begun in 1964. But critics of the country's role in the Algerian war found no opportunity to put across their views on television: between 1956 and 1959 French television did not carry a single programme about the conflict.

In 1962 De Gaulle used television to argue for his amendments to the Constitution, which strengthened the office of the Presidency. Criticisms of the blatant political bias eventually led to legislation in 1964, which set up the autonomous Office de Radiodiffusion-Télévision (ORTF) and provided for greater, although still limited, independence. Searching treatment of domestic politics was extremely limited, and during the strikes and riots of May 1968 ORTF at first almost ignored the events. When journalists defied the management and mounted broader coverage, government officials intervened and stopped the transmission of three programmes.

If countries had been able to follow the patterns of radio organisation there is little doubt that more services would have been established as government monopolies, but the costs of developing and maintaining a television operation meant that many governments had to reach an accommodation with commercial interests. In Italy, for example, television and radio were operated after 1956 as a monopoly by RAI, a private company largely owned by the government. Finance was (and still is, although the system has changed greatly in recent years) derived from a combination of a licence fee and advertising.

Television in Japan had started in the late 1940s when a group of businessmen requested permission from the occupying Americans to begin

Japanese television: a programme about national folk dances

a commercial service. In 1950 the authorities allowed a challenge to the government-sanctioned Nippon Hosai Kyokai (NHK) radio service, and two years later a commercial television station was licensed. At this stage both NHK's television broadcasts and the Nippon Television Network (NTV) were available to only a few domestic sets, but NTV erected large public screens in Tokyo and other cities to create an audience. By 1960 Japan had a booming consumer economy, to which electronics was making a major contribution, and some 7 million television sets were served by 128 stations. Approximately half these stations were attached to NHK, and offered what might be called a BBC-style service mixing entertainment and enlightenment. The commercial stations, however, unrestrained in their quest for ratings, aggressively scheduled domestic entertainment along with American imports.

Few of the new television services which began in the 1950s were backed with resources adequate to finance large-scale domestic production. Station operators had no choice but to turn to Hollywood for relatively cheap attractions which could more or less guarantee healthy ratings. And the suppliers, having mostly cleared costs at home, could afford (at least at first) to set competitively low prices. Action series translated more easily, and more cheaply, than dialogue-heavy domestic dramas, and this international acceptance gave additional support in these years to the production of Western and adventure series.

The situation clearly paralleled Hollywood's relentless takeover of international feature film exhibition in the 1920s. And as before, some countries endeavoured to introduce quotas, although only Britain's strictly enforced level of 14 per cent non-Commonwealth origination was really effective. But this time, television programming was just one element in a more fundamental economic strategy. For alongside the export of American series came subsidiaries of American companies, looking now to expand internationally rather than to compete in the increasingly tough domestic market. As Eric Barnouw has written, 'Television, like missionary expeditions of another era, seemed to serve as an advance herald of empire. Implicit in its arrival was a web of relationships involving cultural, economic and military aspects, and forming the basis of a new kind of empire.'

Further reading

Tim Brooks and Earle Marsh, *The Complete Directory to Prime Time Network TV Shows, 1946—Present*, New York: Ballantine, 1979.

Les Brown, *Television — the Business Behind the Box*, New York: Harcourt Brace Jovanovich, 1971.

Fred W. Friendly, *Due to Circumstances Beyond Our Control*, New York: Random House, 1967.

Alvin H. Marill, *Movies Made for Television: The Tele-feature and the Mini-series 1964-1979*, Westport, Conn.: Arlington House, 1980.

Dennis Norden, with Sybil Harper and Norma Gilbert, *Coming to You Live!*, London: Methuen, 1985.

Bernard Sendall, *Independent Television in Britain: Origin and Foundation 1946-62*, London: Macmillan, 1983.

——*Independent Television in Britain: Expansion and Change 1958-68.* London: Macmillan, 1983.

Max Wilk, *The Golden Age of Television: Notes from the Survivors*, New York: Delacorte Press, 1976.

H. H. Wilson, *Pressure Group: The Campaign for Commercial Television*, London: Secker & Warburg, 1961.

14
The International Art Cinema

Since 1945 world cinema has witnessed several groups of films – Italian neo-realism, the French 'new wave', the 'New German Cinema', and so on – which can be loosely categorised as 'art cinema'. These films, for all their many differences, can be seen to share certain characteristics. The forms of criticism applied to them are similar, and they are marketed in distinctive ways. They have their own audiences and they circulate within the same areas of exhibition, which are parallel to but distinct from those of mainstream cinema. And behind the emergence of each of these cinemas there are related institutional and economic determinants.

The art cinema took its earliest form in the French *films d'art* of the cinema's first decade. After the First World War, as the urgency of resisting Hollywood became apparent, cinemas developed in both France and Germany which self-consciously recognised their practice as art. But it was only after the Second World War, as the dominance of Hollywood was challenged in America by the anti-trust action and by television, that art cinema became a really effective strategy. New possibilities appeared for distributors of foreign films in the United States, and exhibitors everywhere were looking for distinctive attractions with which to compete with television.

In the wake of the war, national cinemas were also considering how best to restructure their industries. New production strategies, which absorbed the changes brought by television, created the openings for both the French new wave and the New German Cinema. Such cinemas were then presented to the world through the magazines and film festivals which had blossomed after the war. The Cannes festival, established in 1947, and all the gatherings which emulated it, reflected and promoted a greater awareness of other cinema traditions. Since the early 1970s these traditions have also depended to a large degree on quite another form of accommodation with television. Many of the art cinema's offerings in the past two decades have been fully financed, or more commonly co-funded, by broadcasters. The Italian service RAI was the first to commit large-scale funds to directors like Bernardo Bertolucci, Roberto Rossellini and Francesco Rosi, and this example has since been followed in West Germany, France, Britain and elsewhere.

The recognisable characteristics of art cinema include a rejection of the traditional narrative conventions of Hollywood. Action is suppressed and character, rather than plot, is stressed. Conflict is most likely to arise out of an individual's internal psychological tussle, and the outcome to be some form of judgment on 'modern life'. Social forces are usually significant for their direct impact on characters, and only a minority of art films develop a political analysis of society. Ambiguity is frequently central, and open endings are so common as to have become virtually a cliché. Hollywood's traditional visual transparency is also rejected, and there is often a celebration of visual style. Most importantly, all these elements are seen as expressions of the vision of an individual author, who is invariably the director. The director, indeed, comes to be regarded rather like a novelist, and the cinema is seen to offer pleasures comparable to those of literature.

Italian neo-realism

The Italian cinema was the first to impress international audiences in the immediate post-war years. Roberto Rossellini's *Rome, Open City* (1945) was widely admired for its stark portrait of Italian resistance to German occupation. Filmed in part while the Germans were still in Rome, its story of individual responses to oppression is told with amateur actors, with the city's devastated streets as locations, and with technical values which were from necessity the opposite of studio polish. And these were the elements which came to define the essential features of 'neo-realism'. Due account was rendered at the time to one significant precursor of the neo-realist style, Luchino Visconti's *Ossessione* (1942), which treats its rural drama with a despairing fatalism. More recently, critics have identified a continuing realist tradition within the Italian cinema: Alessandro Blasetti's work in the 1930s is often cited.

Neo-realism: Visconti's La Terra Trema

Rossellini followed *Rome, Open City* with *Paisà* (1946), a series of vignettes set against the background of the Allied liberation of Italy. Both here and in *Germany Year Zero* (1947) Rossellini established an essential counterpoint between individuals and landscapes, a theme he was to return to constantly. Vittorio De Sica's *Shoeshine* (1946) and *Bicycle Thieves* (1948) combined the neo-realist style with sentiment and more traditional narratives, and perhaps because of this these films were far more widely seen than Visconti's neo-realist masterpiece *La Terra Trema* (1947), which chronicles a young fisherman's attempt to break away from exploitative wholesale dealers. Shot on Sicilian locations (by a team which included Francesco Rosi and Franco Zeffirelli) and with an amateur cast speaking their own dialect, *La Terra Trema* is nonetheless a stylised work.

207

These films were made in the immediate wake of the Allied military occupation, and the imposition by American trade representatives of an exhibition policy which allowed Hollywood's products to swamp the market. For several years the domestic industry struggled to reassert its own monopolistic structure, and it was in this period of confusion and openness that neo-realism was able to establish itself. It also benefited from the relatively consensual politics of the time. Then in 1949 the Italian government introduced a law which both supported domestic production and severely limited the subjects thought suitable for film-makers to tackle. Explicitly aimed at curbing neo-realist work, legal restrictions could now deny an export permit, and hence foreign earnings, to any film which did not present a 'positive' view of Italy. At the same time influential critics on the Left, bowing to the precepts of Stalinist aesthetics, were also attacking neo-realism for not being 'positive' about the working classes. In the improving economic climate of the early 1950s the major neo-realist directors began to search for ways to transcend verisimilitude.

For Rossellini this involved a spiritual quest, which animated his extraordinary trilogy of contemporary dramas — *Stromboli* (1949), *Europa 51* (1951) and *Journey to Italy* (1953) — each of which contrasts solitude and emotional barrenness with an abstracted search for religious meaning. Visconti's later work is equally rich, encompassing both the powerful contemporary melodrama *Rocco and his Brothers* (1960), about Southern immigrants in Italy's industrial North, and sumptuous historical narratives which embed epochal changes in stories of operatic passion. Both *Senso* (1954) and *The Leopard* (1963) are set during the Risorgimento of the 1860s, and express a nostalgic regret at the arrival of the new modern order. Yet both also question how the revolutionary impulses of the late 19th century were contained by conservatism and reaction. For all the lush pictorial pleasures which it offers, Visconti's cinema is far from comfortable or reassuring. Traces of his privileged background clash with intellectual leanings to the Left, and these contradictions are further complicated by many reflections of the social and political confusions of post-war Italy. It is in this very uneasiness that the continuing power of his films lies.

The new Italian cinema
Of the 393 films released in Italy in 1948, 274 were American productions, and only 13 per cent of the gross returns went to Italian producers, compared to 77 per cent which went to Hollywood. And as the political restrictions of the 1949 law came into effect, genre films reasserted their popularity. After the Cinecittà studios were re-opened in 1947 mythological epics and historical blockbusters, often co-produced with American money, were the core of domestic production, along with horror films (some of them, notably those made by Riccardo Freda and Mario Bava, distinctively baroque) and, later, the so-called 'spaghetti Westerns'.

As a consequence, during the 1950s only a very few established directors were able to produce individual films. And those who made their debuts in this period were documentary film-makers like Michelangelo Antonioni, or scriptwriters like Federico Fellini (who had collaborated on several of the central neo-realist films). Fellini's earlier films, like *I Vitelloni* (1953) and *La Strada* (1954), showed the continuing influence of neo-realism. By the time of the baroque conceit of *8½* (1963) Fellini had refined the mix of poetic fantasy, nostalgia and autobiography which was increasingly to mark his films. Antonioni was also making highly individual films, though of a very different kind. 'Film,' he had written in 1942, 'should link its method of representation to the external appearance of nature and individuals because it is through this appearance that their interiority reveals itself.' And from his first feature, *Cronaca di un amore* in 1950, his work has been unswervingly devoted to revealing this interiority through an intense scrutiny of appearances. His films are distinguished by a highly formal style which incorporates lengthy sequence shots and often geometrical framing. In *L'Avventura* (1959) a man and a woman search for the man's missing fiancée and in the process begin to discover truths about themselves. Antonioni treats their relationship with a distanced objectivity, placing it within landscapes which suggest the characters' internal contradictions. *La Notte* (1961), *The Eclipse* (1962) and *Red Desert* (1964) continue this exploration of emotional sterility in an alienating physical world.

Fellini's 8½: Marcello Mastroianni as the director's alter ego

An alienating world: figures in a modern landscape in Antonioni's Red Desert *(Richard Harris, Monica Vitti)*

By 1961 Visconti, Fellini and Antonioni were widely recognised as major figures in world cinema. But this year also saw the emergence of a new generation of Italian film-makers. The country's economy was growing rapidly, and the film industry prospered. The 1949 law had been amended, the French new wave had made a strong impact, and producers began to look for new talents and new subjects. The financiers were rewarded by increased foreign sales; even the domestic market was healthy, for television was not to make a significant impact until the end of the decade.

In this new climate younger directors like Ermanno Olmi and Francesco Rosi were encouraged to make more personal statements; and others, including Pasolini, Bertolucci and the Taviani brothers, were able to set up their debut features. A former documentary director, Olmi was greatly influenced by neo-realism, as is clear in early films like *Il Posto* (1961) and in his finest achievement, *The Tree of Wooden Clogs* (1978), a recreation of peasant life at the turn of the century. A simple, direct film of great beauty, it concentrates on daily events but always recognises the broader frameworks of religion and politics. Francesco Rosi, a former assistant to Visconti, first attracted widespread attention with his account of the Sicilian bandit *Salvatore Giuliano* (1961). Here, as in a number of his later films, Rosi produced

The price of power: Rosi's Illustrious Corpses *(1975)*

one of the cinema's most satisfying films about power. Perhaps his most original film is *The Mattei Affair* (1972), a cinematic investigation of the mysterious death in 1972 of Enrico Mattei, President of Italy's state-owned oil company.

Well established as a poet and scriptwriter, Pier Paolo Pasolini made his debut feature with *Accattone* (1961). For the next fifteen years he was a controversial figure in Italian culture and politics, not least because of the authorities' persecution of his celebrations of his homosexuality. The range of his films is remarkable, from *Accattone*'s chronicle of the life of a thief and pimp in the shanty towns on the edge of Rome, through his highly personal, symbol-crammed studies of moral corruption, *Theorem* (1967) and *Pigsty* (1969), to his final savage tale of Sadean sexuality set during the final days of Italian fascism, *Salò, or the 120 Days of Sodom* (1975).

Pasolini's Accattone, *with Franco Citti*

Through each of Pasolini's films run the two dominant currents of Italian intellectual life, Catholicism and Marxism, and these are also the forces with which Bernardo Bertolucci's films attempt to come to terms. His debut, *The Grim Reaper* (1962), is based on a story by Pasolini, for whom Bertolucci had worked as an assistant on *Accattone*. *Before the Revolution* (1964) is a semi-autobiographical exercise in style about a young man's attempts to renounce his upper middle-class background. Later, the *succès de scandale* of *Last Tango in Paris* (1972) allowed Bertolucci to embark on his ambitious epic *1900* (1976), which maps Italian political and social history in the first half of the century through the relationship of the son of a rich landowner and the son of a peasant.

In the early 1970s American producers stopped using the Italian industry as a production base, and domestic attendances fell off sharply as television finally made its impact. Production declined, and an Italian art cinema survived largely because of the state television organisation, RAI, which financed many of the decade's significant films. The impact of this funding became clear when *Padre Padrone*, a small-budget film for television directed by Vittorio and Paolo Taviani, won the Grand Prix at Cannes in 1977. From their first features in the late 1960s, the Taviani brothers had set out to challenge the social fabric. In *St Michael had a Rooster* (1971) and *Allonsanfan* (1974), they use historical settings as metaphorical arenas for contemporary debates within the Italian Left. And *Padre Padrone*, about the education of an illiterate Sardinian shepherd, is both an extension of the neo-realist tradition and a poetic and political fable.

The most remarkable group of films funded by RAI were Rossellini's historical dramas. In *The Rise to Power of Louis XIV* (1966), Rossellini worked with non-professional actors, using long, exploratory camera shots and innovative special effects work to create period settings. Driven by a desire to understand the social and political dimensions of history, his subsequent films for RAI like *Socrates* (1969), *Blaise Pascal* (1971) and the three-part *Cosimo de Medici* (1972) are revelatory works, which offer a radical counterpoint to the cosy costume dramas of most television.

210

Sweden and Ingmar Bergman

Before and during the First World War the Swedish film industry had enjoyed a strong international reputation, with the films of Mauritz Stiller and Victor Sjöström being widely respected. But in the 1920s these directors, together with stars like Greta Garbo, were tempted to Hollywood. Sound proved to be a further blow to the industry, effectively preventing exports; but Sweden's neutrality in the Second World War disrupted Hollywood's invasion, and this stimulated domestic production. The theatre director Alf Sjöberg made *Frenzy* (1944), from a script by Ingmar Bergman, who the following year made his own debut as a director with *Crisis*. Both Sjöberg and his younger colleague worked consciously within the tradition established by Stiller and Sjöström (the latter had now returned to Sweden). A decade later Bergman was to mark a debt to the director that was both personal and professional when he asked Sjöström to play the leading role in *Wild Strawberries* (1957).

Bergman's first real international success was his sixteenth film as director, the comedy of sexual manners *Smiles of a Summer Night* (1955), but his next success, *The Seventh Seal* (1957), more accurately indicated the metaphysical concerns which are central to his work. In the early 1960s he made a trilogy of spare, despairing films centred on God's absence from the modern world: *Through a Glass Darkly* (1961), *Winter Light* (1963) and *The Silence* (1963). A further trilogy – *Persona* (1966), *Hour of the Wolf* (1967) and *The Shame* (1967) – explores variations on the theme of an artist's moral and emotional paralysis. Another recurring preoccupation is the family, which Bergman invariably sees as authoritarian and patriarchal. In both *Wild Strawberries* and *Cries and Whispers* (1972) it is an impending death which forces a reassessment of filial and generational relationships. *Scenes from a Marriage* (1974), made for television, is a painful dissection of a couple's difficult relationship. But his skill with a repertory company of actors and, particularly, actresses ensures that Bergman's work rarely succumbs to sterile debate. Time and again, he demonstrates a humanity which relieves the otherwise dark and painful implications of most of his films.

Throughout his career Bergman has remained as interested in stage direction as in the cinema, and the theatre recurs constantly in the films. It is nowhere more apparent than in the triumphant *Fanny and Alexander* (1982),

Victor Sjöström in Bergman's Wild Strawberries

211

a family drama with a theatrical background, set at the end of the 19th century. Here his visual style is a sedate naturalism, created with flowing camerawork and sumptuous art direction. But he has also explored elliptical and fragmented forms of narrative. In *Persona,* supposedly a psychological study of an actress, self-referential shots of the process of film-making are inserted into a fictional construction in which images are related more by dream-logic than by conventional story-telling.

Despite Bergman's international popularity, domestic production in Sweden in the early 1960s was minimal. To counter this, a comprehensive system of state support was established, financed by a levy on admissions and administered by the newly founded Swedish Film Institute. New directors were encouraged, including Bo Widerberg, who made the period romance *Elvira Madigan* (1967), and the former cameraman Jan Troell. And as elsewhere, the problems of the industry were greatly alleviated in the mid-1970s by new accords with television. Bergman, in fact, had begun to work for Swedish television in 1969, with *The Rite,* and much of his most interesting work since then, including *The Lie* (1973), *Scenes from a Marriage, The Magic Flute* (1975) and *After the Rehearsal*(1984), has been made for the small screen.

France and the 'new wave'

Most of the French film-makers associated with what came to be known as the *nouvelle vague,* or 'new wave', had begun their professional lives as critics. The children of the post-war cine-clubs, they were also the spiritual progeny of the theorist André Bazin and of the French Cinémathèque's wayward director Henri Langlois. United in their championing both of Hollywood cinema, which was flooding back into Paris in the late 1940s, and of the French cinema of the 1930s, they passionately rejected the products of the post-war domestic industry. François Truffaut was particularly outspoken, attacking with venom the 'cinéma du papa' which he, Jean-Luc Godard, Claude Chabrol and others intended to overturn.

Wartime restrictions had protected the domestic industry, and after the war limited quotas and some government support ensured that, unlike in Italy, the French cinema did not experience a 'Year Zero'. Nonetheless there was a huge influx of American movies, to which the conservative industry endeavoured to respond with glossy 'quality' films. Until the late 1950s the French cinema was consequently dominated by the tasteful, well-crafted works of directors like Jean Delannoy and Claude Autant-Lara.

For Truffaut and his peers these films lacked all trace of distinctive personal expression. As critics, they recognised no signs of that paramount quality of 'authorship', to the analysis of which their writing was wholly committed. They also saw these films as little more than books or plays transposed to the screen; for the aspiring directors of the hugely influential and iconoclastic film journal *Cahiers du Cinéma,* hooked on the baroque visuals of Nicholas Ray and Sam Fuller, the French mainstream of the 1950s was ignorant of all the most exciting possibilities of film. Nonetheless it is too easy to forget that directors as significant and as individual as Clouzot, Melville, Bresson and Tati, as well as older figures like Renoir and Max Ophuls, produced some of their finest films in the years after the war.

Both Henri-Georges Clouzot (with films like *Les Diaboliques*, 1954) and Jean-Pierre Melville (*Bob le Flambeur*, 1955), for example, demonstrated their pre-eminent skill with the genre conventions of the thriller at the same time as creating individual cinematic worlds. The last four films directed by Max Ophuls – *La Ronde* (1950), *Le Plaisir* (1952), *Madame de . . .* (1953) and *Lola Montès* (1955) – are among the most intense yet also the most disenchanted romances in the cinema's history. Ophuls choreographs the camera through dazzling and elaborate moves, circling and entrapping his hapless characters. And Renoir's

Ophuls' Lola Montès *(Peter Ustinov, Martine Carol)*

late films, like *French Can-Can* (1954) and *Le Déjeuner sur l'herbe* (1959), are colourful fantasies of great beauty, addressed (like so much of Renoir's work) to the differences between the theatre and life and imparting a sense of nostalgic serenity. For the French cinema at this time Renoir was a key transitional figure, working within the mainstream tradition yet also a constantly innovative director for whom the new wave iconoclasts felt boundless admiration. They also respected two other highly individual directors, Robert Bresson and Jacques Tati.

Even in his first feature, *Les Anges du Péché* (1943), set within a Dominican convent, Bresson created a spare, elliptical style of singular concentration, which he has put at the service of spiritual dramas of redemption ever since. His *Diary of a Country Priest* (1951) is a searching exploration of a young priest reaching towards an understanding of his God. *Pickpocket* (1959), in contrast, is set in the world of petty crime, from which only salvation through love provides an escape. And Bresson's most recent film, *L'Argent* (1983), returns to the mechanics of criminality to map out another environment drained of spirituality. Tati's world of gentle humour, combining visual gags with an inventive use of sound in its mockery of the impersonal gadgetry of

Jacques Tati in his own Playtime

the modern world, has been seen as offering as rigorous an alternative as Bresson's to conventional narrative cinema, in films like *Monsieur Hulot's Holiday* (1953) and *Mon Oncle* (1958). Tati's fragmented narrative style and virtual abandonment of conventional dialogue were refined in his later films, *Playtime* (1967) and *Traffic* (1971), with their often almost abstract visuals counterpointed by amplified natural sounds.

A 1953 law reinforced the system of state aid for film production. Financial support was linked explicitly to aesthetic quality, a criterion which bolstered the 'cinéma du papa' but which also ensured the making of low-budget features by new directors like Louis Malle and Claude Chabrol later in the decade. The law also made provisions for short films, and it was in this form that Truffaut, Godard and others were to gain their first experience behind the camera. Directors like Alain Resnais, Georges Franju and Chris Marker made a number of major short films, not least among them Resnais' powerful meditation on the Nazi concentration camps, *Night and Fog* (1955).

Figures at the domestic box office stayed high, with audiences reaching a peak in 1957, after which the spread of television began to be felt. Along with state support, however, came political intervention, aimed especially – with France engaged in the Algerian war – at keeping off the screen expressions of anti-colonialism. At the same time there was a sense of stagnation in the cinema. Producers recognised that the old formulas for commercial success were no longer attracting audiences, and there was consequently an openness to innovation. The commercial success of Roger Vadim's lively low-budget film *Et Dieu créa la Femme* (1956), with Brigitte Bardot, suggested new possibilities.

The interest of enlightened producers like Pierre Braunberger (who was to finance early films by Resnais, Rouch, Rivette, Godard and Truffaut) and Georges de Beauregard was complemented by political initiatives and technological innovations. André Malraux, Minister of Culture from 1959, extended state support for distribution and exhibition as well as for production. And the availability of smaller, lighter cameras, together with new fast film stock, meant that location-based films could be made on shorter schedules and on relatively small budgets. Among those to take advantage of this was Bresson's former assistant Louis Malle, with *Les Amants* (1958) and *Zazie dans le Métro* (1960).

The loose grouping of film-makers that was to benefit most from these new opportunities were by now well established as critics. As Godard said in 1962, 'All of us thought of ourselves as future directors . . . Writing was already a way of making films . . . We were thinking cinema and at a certain moment we felt the need to extend that thought.' Godard made his first documentary short in 1954, and each of his colleagues had soon followed the example. Chabrol was the first to raise a feature budget, for his intense rural melodrama *Le Beau Serge* (1958), financed by a family inheritance left to his wife. The following year both Truffaut's *Les Quatre cents coups* (also paid for with family money) and Resnais' *Hiroshima mon amour* won prizes at Cannes. For all their differences – the one an unsentimental and strongly auto-biographical portrait of contemporary childhood, the other a philosophical meditation on time and memory – the films seemed to share an energy and originality alien to the stagnant domestic industry. Journalists, looking for signs of cultural renewal under De Gaulle's newly established Fifth Republic, began to create the 'new wave'.

Resnais' Hiroshima mon amour

Over the next four years more than a hundred French directors made their first feature. For many it was to be their only film, but Truffaut's subsequent work established him as a dominant figure, along with Godard, whose audaciously free-wheeling *A bout de souffle* was released in 1960. Truffaut's films are personal, intimate, with an ironic attitude to the grand themes – apart, that is, from love. There are broad strokes of autobiography, notably in the cycle of films which follow the sentimental education of Antoine Doinel (played by Jean-Pierre Léaud), and in his celebration of the act of film-making, *La Nuit américaine* (1972), in which Truffaut himself plays the harassed director. There is a passionate love of cinema: *Tirez sur le pianiste* (1960) is a pastiche gangster movie, *Jules et Jim* (1962) a love story, *Fahrenheit 451* (1966, made in Britain) science-fiction. At the same time there is a deep appreciation of literature, in *Fahrenheit 451* where there is a painful scene of books burning, but also in the

Gangster pastiche: Truffaut's Tirez sur le pianiste

sensitivity of his adaptations from Henri-Pierre Roché – *Jules et Jim*, *Les Deux anglaises et le continent* (1976) – and from a Henry James story, *The Green Room* (1978). Above all, there is a fascinated preoccupation with the pleasures and the pains of everyday life.

Godard's cinema, in contrast, is a cinema of analysis. More than any of his contemporaries, Godard is a film-maker (and more recently a video-maker) who interrogates. Like Truffaut, he may adopt the classical genres – the musical in *Une Femme est une femme* (1961), the war film in *Les Carabiniers* (1963), a gangster thriller in *Bande à part* (1964), science-fiction in *Alphaville* (1965) – but always and only to go beyond their conventions and their limits, and to ask more of them than they have offered directors in the past. Again like Truffaut, many of his early films are love stories. But the personal dimension alone is never enough for Godard: his characters are alive in a society and a culture which assaults them with images and slogans and posters and films and roles and memories and languages.

One of the most frequent criticisms of the new wave films was that they lacked a significant social dimension. Truffaut's films, and those of directors like Jacques Demy (*Lola*, 1961; *La Baie des Anges*, 1963) mostly maintain a

Demy's Les Parapluies de Cherbourg *(1964, with Catherine Deneuve)*

strict distance from politics. They capture a sense of contemporary France, but the immediate worlds of their characters exhaust the films' canvases. The new production possibilities also permitted Eric Rohmer and Jacques Rivette, both *Cahiers* critics, to make their first features. But neither *Le Signe du lion* (1959) nor Rivette's ambitious and convoluted *Paris nous appartient* (1960) was received with enthusiasm. Alain Resnais, a member along with Chris Marker and Agnès Varda of what was known as the Left Bank group, had more success. Along with Resnais' *Hiroshima mon amour*, Varda's *Cléo de 5 à 7* (1962) – about a woman confronting the possibility of death – and the political, poetical film essays of Marker can be entered as evidence of a social dimension in at least some strands of the new wave. So too can the features made at the time by the anthropological film-maker Jean Rouch, *Moi un noir* (1958) and *Chronique d'un été* (1961).

Each of these film-makers has since created a distinctive and significant body of work. Collectively, they had more influence on film cultures around the world than any other group since. They established unequivocally a cinema of authors, and validated the idea that a film could be as personal as a novel. Using lightweight cameras on location (like both the neo-realists before them, and contemporary television reportage and *cinéma vérité*), they demonstrated that studios, stars and the rest were no longer necessary to create cinema. Shooting fast, and often improvising, they overturned the script-dependence of the 'literary' cinema, while at the same time, in collaborations with Marguerite Duras and Alain Robbe-Grillet, forging new links with contemporary literature. And they brought low-budget, independent film-making into the mainstream, thus encouraging producers in the United States, Italy, West Germany and elsewhere.

Many of the films, inevitably, were commercial failures, and even the most successful were confined to art-house circuits. But their example helped older directors like Bresson and Tati to find new audiences and production finance. What they were unable to do was to change the framework of the popular cinema, and their success as art cinema only served to perpetuate what is still seen as the gap between commerce and culture. The structures of the film industry in France stayed much the same, and in the later 1960s comedies and thrillers reasserted themselves as the dominant elements. Production controls were also tightened, and the level of required capital investment was raised considerably, as a deterrent to casual production. Union requirements, too, were more strictly enforced. Ironically, the success of the new wave eventually made it harder to make a debut feature in France. The important legacy of these film-makers is the radical break in the style of cinema which they initiated. Fragmenting, improvising, often dispensing with the rules of cinematography or with strict continuity editing, directors like Godard, Truffaut and Resnais extended the languages of the cinema, at the same time as demonstrating its specificity as a medium. Inevitably, much of this was used as no more than superficial stylistic tricks by many subsequent, and lesser, directors, and traces continue to appear in commercials and music videos. But the achievement was real, and the cinema is richer for it.

No film-maker demonstrates this enrichment more clearly than Godard, whose work from the past three decades is the most stimulating and provocative body of films produced by any director, at least since the war. Taken as a whole, it is an unparalleled investigation of the moving image, and of sound. In *Les Carabiniers*, Godard set out consciously not only to make a war film against war, but to reinvent the cinema. In *Le gai savoir* (1968), a character talks of the necessity of getting back to zero. And with every Godard film or videotape there is a sense of beginning again, and of tentatively setting off in a new direction.

Godard's films during the mid-1960s illustrate an increasingly sophisticated political understanding, and a growing awareness of the urgency of finding appropriate forms for this understanding. *Made in USA* (1966) can be seen as an attempt to make visible the politics of Hollywood's conventions. As the commentary tells us, 'We were certainly in a film about politics: Walt Disney plus blood.' In retrospect, *La Chinoise* (1967) is remarkably prescient in its depiction of a group of young people living together as a Maoist cell. The following May police action against students at the Sorbonne led first to widespread street fighting in Paris, and then to a wave of strikes across France. The political and cultural impact of these 'events' was far-reaching: not least they prompted a radical reappraisal of both the theory and practice of cinema. Godard, unsurprisingly, was at the centre of this thinking anew. The problem was now 'not to make a political film, but to make films politically'.

Le gai savoir is the first full expression of this reappraisal. Proposed to French television as an adaptation of an 18th-century text on education, it in fact brings together in an empty studio Jean-Pierre Léaud and Juliet Berto, who in a series of dialogues consider language, education and the sounds and images of our everyday lives. Godard's analysis of the languages of the moving image continued in *British Sounds* (1969), commissioned (but not shown) by London Weekend Television, in which he asks how the politics of a country might be represented. Four subsequent collective creations, credited to the Dziga-Vertov group, and two collaborations with Jean-Pierre Gorin, continued this questioning, as has all Godard's work since, including that for television. As an analysis of fundamentals, it is of supreme importance in our understanding of the moving image.

Making films politically: Godard's La Chinoise

Russia: 'socialist realism' and beyond

Questions of political cinema are raised in a different form by film-making in Russia and Eastern Europe. Each of the art cinemas considered so far is framed by varying degrees of resistance to the economic and aesthetic dominance of Hollywood. In Russia and Eastern Europe, however, although foreign films are screened and circulated, the imperatives which have shaped art cinema have been quite different. The Russian cinema has been nationalised since 1919, and the industries of each of the other main film-producing countries – Poland, Hungary, Czechoslovakia – adopted the same stategy after the Second World War. Film workers in these countries accepted (or were obliged to accept) the cultural programme of 'socialist realism', first proclaimed in 1934. Perhaps even more than in the West the visions of individual directors, their distinctive narrative and visual styles, and the psychological journeys of their protagonists have always to be understood within historical traditions and present-day political realities.

Kozintsev's King Lear

The post-war cinema in Russia cranked out celebrations of victory, adulatory biographies and tales of worker-heroes. Only after Stalin's death in 1953 and Khrushchev's speech at the 1956 Party Congress were cracks permitted to appear in the monumental edifice of culture. There followed a period of greater freedom, which coincided with a significant increase in film production. Perhaps the most notable films of this period were Mikhail Kalatozov's lyrical *The Cranes Are Flying* (1957), which acknowledged the influence of the pre-Stalinist avant-garde of the 1920s, and Grigori Chukhrai's *Ballad of a Soldier* (1959). The 'thaw' at least made literary adaptations, especially of the Russian classics, acceptable; and it was generally these films, such as Josef Heifitz's *Lady with the Little Dog* (1960), which were made available for export. With *Don Quixote* (1957) Grigori Kozintsev began a distinguished group of adaptations, which later included *Hamlet* (1964) and *King Lear* (1971).

Tarkovsky's Andrei Roublev

Contemporary Soviet literature was also recognised as a legitimate source, and Andrei Tarkovsky made his feature debut with *Ivan's Chilhood* (1962), taken from a respected short story. This film's expressionist elements – criticised by the bureaucrats – indicated the path Tarkovsky's cinema was to follow. He made just four more features, including the monumental fresco *Andrei Roublev* (1966) and the densely textured *Mirror* (1975), before he was forced to work abroad. Tarkovsky died at the end of 1986, just as the Soviet Union was entering a period of openness which might have allowed him the freedom to go on working in his homeland.

218

Polish cinema and Andrzej Wajda

Every aspect of Polish life had been devastated by the Nazi occupation, and this national tragedy was to dominate much of the post-war Polish cinema. Film production had ceased during the war, and only gradually was what had once been a thriving industry resurrected. Film-makers mostly accepted the rigid principles of socialist realism, until Andrzej Wajda's *A Generation* (1954), which relates the exploits of a group of young Communist resistance fighters. With its romanticism and intense symbolism (which were to mark much of the director's later work), the film reflected the growth of new ideas; it was released soon after a conference of film workers had publicly attacked the stultifying effects of socialist realism. At the same time, in the wake of Stalin's death in 1953, intellectuals were beginning to question the authoritarian power of the Workers' Party.

These feelings culminated in a month of strikes and demonstrations in October 1956, when Soviet tanks were sent to surround Warsaw. Hopes of a broad democratisation were soon seen as illusory. The tensions of that year are apparent in Andrzej Munk's *Man on the Track,* a fragmented investigation of the life of an engine driver. The following year Munk made *Eroica,* an ironic black comedy attacking the myths of heroism. Wajda's *Kanal* (1956), set during the Warsaw uprising against the Germans, similarly attempts to come to terms with the memories of the resistance, as does his *Ashes and Diamonds* (1958) in which, on the first day after the war, a resistance hero (played by Zbigniew Cybulski) is ordered to kill a Communist official. But events during 1957 brought the end of the relative intellectual freedom which had allowed such films to be made.

Zbigniew Cybulski in Wajda's Ashes and Diamonds

In an attack on his country's cinema in 1963 First Secretary Gomulka singled out for criticism both Wajda's *Innocent Sorcerers* (1960), about the dreams of youth, and *Knife in the Water* (1962), the feature film debut of the director Roman Polanski. Co-written with Jerzy Skolimowski, *Knife in the Water* is a bitter analysis of contemporary Poland, cast as a triangular relationship between a married couple and a student. A year later, Polanski left his homeland, to work first in Britain and later in Hollywood. Wajda too worked briefly abroad, but it was in Poland that he made *Everything for Sale* (1968), a tribute to the actor Cybulski (who had died in a train accident) as well as a work of self-analysis about a director making just such a film. Dull literary adaptations dominated the approved mainstream during these years, relieved occasionally by a strange, quirky production like Wojciech Has' *The Saragossa Manuscript* (1965), which is structured as an infinite regression of ever more improbable and fantastical tales. Skolimowski, however, managed to direct a loose trilogy of films (*Identification Marks: None,* 1964; *Walkover,* 1965; *Barrier,* 1966) which see the Poland of the day through the eyes of a dissatisfied young rebel. But his subsequent *Hands Up* (1967) was banned, and he followed his friends abroad.

Political changes in 1971 offered a new chance of cultural innovation. The film units, which had been established in 1956, won further independence,

The new resistance: Skolimowski's Barrier

219

and more challenging work was encouraged, like the rigorously intellectual cinema of Krzysztof Zanussi. *Illumination* (1972), for example, is as much philosophical reflection as it is autobiographical narrative. Towards the end of the decade Wajda's film *Man of Marble* (1977) was the first sign of the far-reaching social changes which came after the 1976 strikes and anti-government demonstrations. An investigation of the life of a Stakhanovite bricklayer, a forgotten hero of the Stalinist 1950s, the film is a powerful study of the recent past and of contemporary attitudes towards it. Wajda had waited for years for official permission to start shooting. A companion piece, *Man of Iron* (1981), portrays the excitements and upheavals of the months leading up to the government's historic recognition of the trade union movement Solidarity in 1980. These films, together with others by Zanussi and by younger directors like Krzysztof Kieslowski and Feliks Falk, acted as a kind of national conscience, questioning at a time of great uncertainty the moral and political implications of different courses of action.

The imposition of martial law in December 1981 once again stifled a period of fruitful creativity. Interesting films have been completed since, including Zanussi's *A Year of the Quiet Sun* (1984), about the immediate aftermath of the war. But Wajda, Zanussi and others have mostly chosen to work abroad. The debate between film-makers and society in Poland seems to have been adjourned.

Cinema in Hungary and Czechoslovakia

When the critically acclaimed neo-realist film *Somewhere in Europe* (director Geza Radvanyi) was shown at Cannes in 1948, it was welcomed as a hopeful

Landscape and power: Jancsó's The Round-Up

sign of new life in the Hungarian cinema. But in the same year the industry was nationalised, and not until the mid-1950s was there a significant challenge to official orthodoxy, in films by Zoltán Fábri and Félix Máriássy, a shift that paralleled the revolution, both political and intellectual, which was ended by the arrival of Russian tanks in late October 1956.

In the late 1950s Hungary under Janos Kádar began the slow, limited integration of elements of Western economics and culture into Soviet Communism. One reflection of this was the appearance in 1962-3 of several films which seemed to harbinger a renaissance for the Hungarian cinema:

220

Cantata (1962), about a doctor's relationship with his peasant father, directed by Miklós Jancsó; István Gaál's *Current;* and István Szabó's *The Age of Daydreaming* (both 1963).

Jancsó's films over the next decade were marked by a particularly individual authorial style, which he and his regular collaborators put at the service of variations on the theme of oppressor and oppressed. In *The Round-Up* (1965) the conflict is between prisoners captured during the abortive 1848 revolution and their guards; and in *The Confrontation* (1969) the protagonists are a group of young Hungarian communists in 1947. Jancsó choreographs the action of his films like a ballet, weaving his camera through groups of characters in extended sequence shots. His setting is often the vast Hungarian plains, on whose landscape he gives form to symbolic representations of power and rebellion; as in *Elektreia* (1975), a meditation on the nature of tyranny in which a very few shots contain an elaborate accumulation of detail.

Gaál and Szabó have also continued to produce interesting work. Gaál's most striking film perhaps is *The Falcons* (1970), a rich allegory set in a training school for birds of prey. Szabó has attracted international attention for his two remarkable studies of the effects of political pressure on personal relationships: *Mephisto* (1981), set in Germany during the rise of the Nazis; and *Colonel Redl* (1984), an epic account of an officer's life in the final days of the Austro-Hungarian empire.

Unlike those of its Eastern European neighbours, Czechoslovakia's economy and its liberal cultural traditions emerged from the war in (relatively) robust health. The film industry was nationalised in August 1945, but after the Communists took power in 1948 they began to impose the political and cultural line formulated in Moscow. With the installation of a more liberal party presidium in 1963, there were indications of greater cultural freedom. And a new generation of film-makers, trained at the Prague Film Academy, were ready to exploit this opportunity. Among them were Vera Chytilová, Jaromil Jires and Milós Forman, each of whom made their debut feature in 1963.

Forman's *Peter and Pavla* is a deceptively simple tale of everyday life, about a young man, his first job and a relationship with a girl. Like his subsequent *A Blonde in Love* (1965) and the black comedy *The Firemen's Ball* (1967), it is a film of gentle satire, a bitter-sweet observation of human frailty. Jaromil Jires' *The Cry* shares similar concerns, touching lightly on the expectations and evasions of everyday life as a television engineer awaits the birth of his child. And Vera Chytilová had made several observational documentaries before *Something Different* (1963), which paralleled the lives of two women.

Black comedy: Forman's The Firemen's Ball

221

Chytilová's later films, like *Daisies* (1966), were marked by the vein of surrealist fantasy which is never far from the surface of Czech cinema.

Forman's scripts were written by Ivan Passer, who himself directed *Intimate Lighting* (1965), a study of the sense of futility shared by two intellectuals which largely dispenses with plot in favour of a reflection of only apparently inconsequential truths. A darker and more stylised world of allegory and metaphor was revealed in Jan Nemec's *The Party and the Guests* (1966). A satirical, surreal attack on totalitarianism, which bears the clear influence of Kafka, the film was not released until 1968. The films of Evald Schorm, like *The Return of the Prodigal Son* (1966), share Nemec's more explicit engagement with political and moral dilemmas.

Each of these directors was supported by a system of production groups which in the mid-1960s gained increasing autonomy from the centralised mechanisms of control. Further liberalisation in the months leading up to the 'Prague Spring' made possible, among other films, the critique of Stalinist bureaucracy which is the not so hidden subtext of *The Firemen's Ball*. This film opened just three weeks before Alexander Dubcek and his reformist Communism were installed in power at the beginning of 1968. The new regime abolished censorship and granted full autonomy to the film workshops. But most of the productions which took advantage of this new climate remained uncompleted when the Warsaw Pact troops entered Prague in August. Although Forman has pursued his career in the United States, Jires, Chytilová and others have continued to work in Czechoslovakia. But despite occasional signs of life, the promise of the Czechoslovak cinema of the 1960s seems to have been muffled by the tanks of 1968.

The New German Cinema

The Oberhausen Manifesto of 1962 is generally taken as the moment of renaissance for the post-war German cinema. A rather vague call for a 'new German feature film', the document was drafted and signed by twenty-six aspiring film-makers during the Oberhausen festival. Inspired by the success of the 'new wave' in France, the signatories to the Manifesto then began a process of lobbying which led to a broad framework of support for domestic productions. This provided the opportunities for Werner Herzog, Rainer Werner Fassbinder, Wim Wenders and others to make their first films. But the story is far more than a triumphant progress by individual film-makers. As elsewhere, events were shaped by the confluences of broader social, cultural and economic forces.

After the war the German film industry was restructured in line with American demands. Production was dispersed, in part to prevent the kind of political control imposed by the Nazis. At the same time, Hollywood's domination of distribution was ensured, not least by a ban on the imposition of an import quota. Within this framework vain attempts were made throughout the 1950s to lessen the dependence on foreign films and to strengthen the position of German producers. A system of state aid did

Cinema in Yugoslavia: Dusan Makavejev's Switchboard Operator *(1967). The post-war Yugoslav cinema was dominated by films about the wartime partisans and (apart from the Zagreb animation) was little seen abroad. Towards the end of the 1960s, however, some more individual work began to emerge, notably from Aleksandr Petrovic (*I Have Even Met Happy Gypsies, *1967) and from the iconoclastic Dusan Makavejev, who went on to make eccentric and sporadically brilliant films like* Innocence Unprotected *(1968) and* WR: Mysteries of the Organism *(1971), but who has since worked abroad.*

222

operate, but it worked largely to deny opportunities to new film-makers, and it was also an effective means of repressing politically or socially contentious films. Audiences remained high until the middle of the decade, but in the later 1950s television contributed to a sharp decline. The industry shrank rapidly, so that in 1961 there were only 69 domestic productions and German producers controlled only just over a quarter of the market.

This was the state of things to which the Oberhausen Manifesto was addressed. In its wake a new Film Institute was set up at Ulm, under the supervision of Alexander Kluge and Edgar Reitz, and a programme of lobbying, co-ordinated by Kluge, eventually led in 1965 to the 'Kuratorium junger deutscher Film'. The Kuratorium was a programme of federal funding, in the form of interest-free loans for the production of first features. Both Kluge, with *Yesterday Girl* (1966), and Reitz, with *Mealtimes* (1967), were early beneficiaries. Their work won festival prizes and international acclaim; and also attracted approval from the Film Assessment Bureau, set up in 1955 to reward 'films of merit' with significant tax relief. With the simultaneous critical success of films by Volker Schlöndorff (*Young Törless*, 1966) and Jean-Marie Straub (*Not Reconciled*, 1965), a New German Cinema could be promoted in the press and at foreign festivals.

Jean-Marie Straub's The Chronicle of Anna Magdalena Bach *(1968)*

West Germany's commercial producers remained unimpressed, however, and lobbied successfully for the 1968 Film Promotion Law, the provisions of which established the principle of future subsidies being financed from a levy on box-office returns. Although there was some limited recognition of the importance of supporting 'quality' films, the new legislation mostly reinforced the continued production of formula pictures, including a large number of sex films. Nonetheless, the newly established Film Development Board and additional, though strictly limited, subsidies from the Ministry of the Interior brought about a striking increase in low-budget productions between 1969 and 1971, including a number of original films like Wim Wenders' *The Goalkeeper's Fear of the Penalty* (1970). Many of those who benefited were, like Wenders, recent graduates from the new state-funded film schools in Munich and Berlin.

What was becoming clear, however, especially after the Kuratorium's initial funds had been spent, was that the films of the New German Cinema could find only a small domestic market. Neither distributors nor exhibitors – and consequently audiences – showed much interest. Responding to this, the Ministry of the Interior and the Kuratorium began to subsidise a number of cinemas in 1970, and in 1971 supported the distribution of specific 'quality' films. There was a similar recognition on the part of the film-makers, including Wenders and Fassbinder, who set up the 'Filmverlag der Autoren' as a production collective in 1971. By 1973 the energies of the Filmverlag were being directed to distribution.

Television's role in the shaping of the New German Cinema was an ambivalent one. From the early 1960s television companies had worked with a large pool of freelancers, and had supported some independently made programmes. By the early 1970s television was an important co-producer, as well as one of the few conduits between new films and an audience. Television also recognised, in a way that the commercial film industry did not, the cultural imperatives behind subsidising original film-makers. But the available co-financing deals usually limited a new film's distribution in cinemas. The position was eased in November 1974 with the signing of the Film/Television Agreement which made new co-production funds available, and under better terms. Along with further grants for the production of first-time scripts, the Agreement provided an important fillip to the financing of the New German Cinema; and once Fassbinder's *Fear Eats the Soul* was lauded at Cannes in 1973, the reputation of the New German Cinema began to be consolidated internationally.

From the beginning, the New German Cinema was seen as a cinema of authors, which meant a director's cinema. Rejecting the previous decade's commercial, producer-oriented output, the campaign which followed the Oberhausen Manifesto stressed the importance of the individual director. Kluge's Department of Film-making at Ulm was set up to 'train young directors for a cinema of *Autoren*', and this idea was enshrined in the structure of the Kuratorium. 'Quality' and 'art', both of which the Kuratorium were to encourage, was understood to result from an individual film-maker's unconstrained self-expression. German television also found 'authorship' useful, since using the ideas of independent film-makers was one way of ensuring the plurality of views required by the West German constitution.

Although the New German Cinema may be seen as a radical break from the past, it should also be recognised that many of its directors were reworking the traditions of Germany's cinema history. Rainer Werner Fassbinder's early exercises in *film noir* obviously explore the Hollywood style, but they also reveal the legacy of Fritz Lang. Expressionism runs deep in the films of Werner Herzog, as he acknowledged in his remaking of *Nosferatu* (1979). And several directors have engaged with potent forms of the so-called *Heimatfilm*, notably Edgar Reitz in his monumental series *Heimat* (1984), largely funded by television.

Obsessions: Herzog's Fitzcarraldo (1982), *about a man who wants to build an opera house in the Amazonian Jungle*

The three film-makers who were most to impress themselves on international audiences were Herzog, Fassbinder and Wenders. Herzog's *Aguirre, Wrath of God* (1972) encapsulates much of what he was to explore in his later films. A portrait of a ruthless fanatic, a 16th-century Spanish soldier determined to find El Dorado, the film is fascinated with power and with the metaphysics of obsession. The *conquistador* is in part a self-portrait; as are the

224

characters in the films Wenders made in the early 1970s. *Alice in the Cities* (1973), *The Wrong Move* (1974) and *Kings of the Road* (1976) are all studies in contemporary urban alienation, deeply marked by the post-war shadow of America. This is most apparent in *Kings of the Road*, in which two men travel across Germany and through the recent history of their country – and especially of its cinema's colonisation by the United States.

Fassbinder's films too are often about America, and about obsession, sexuality, money, power and exploitation. A theatrical *enfant terrible*, Fassbinder established his 'anti-teater' group in 1969 with several of those who were to form the stock company for his subsequent films, including Hanna Schygulla and Kurt Raab. His first feature in 1969 was financed with private capital; his second, *Katzelmacher* (1969), was made very cheaply. Continuing to work in the theatre, he began a prolific outpouring of films, initially with many autobiographical elements. His characters are often working-class, sometimes gay, sometimes petty criminals, and the films are marked by a fatalistic melancholy. After his ninth film, *Beware of a Holy Whore* (1970), about the difficulties of a collective making a film, he increasingly assimilated the forms of Hollywood melodrama, particularly as represented in the work of Douglas Sirk.

Fassbinder's later melodramas, like *Martha* (1973) and *Fear of Fear* (1975) – both made for television – are often provocative and confrontational, and the emotional pitch of his films is invariably extreme. Often with only oblique references to politics, they are nonetheless powerful challenges to bourgeois values. Although he himself scripted many of his films, Fassbinder also demonstrated a remarkable ability to reveal his world in material drawn from other sources, like Fontane's novel *Effi Briest* (filmed in 1974) or Alfred Döblin's *Berlin Alexanderplatz*, shot as a television serial in 1979-80. In just thirteen years, Fassbinder produced a remarkably varied range of films.

Fassbinder's later films, like *The Marriage of Maria Braun* (1979), are mature reflections on Germany and on the legacies of Nazism. A quite different approach to these questions is found in the shadow plays of Hans-Jürgen Syberberg's films, especially his *Hitler: A Film from Germany*

Fassbinder's The Bitter Tears of Petra von Kant *(1972, with Margit Carstensen)*

(1977), which mounts a theatrical extravaganza before elaborate back projections in an ambitious attempt to understand the origins of the dictator within the German consciousness. A comparable confrontation, but with the immediacies of the present, is expressed in the collectively produced film *Germany in Autumn* (1978). Made by Fassbinder, Kluge, Reitz, Volker Schlöndorff and others, it was an instant response to the actions against the state by the Baader-Meinhof group, reflecting the confusions and paranoias

225

of the moment and the moral and political debates which they provoked.

The end of the 1970s saw the New German Cinema increasingly dependent on adaptations of classics and contemporary novels, and on international co-productions. In the charged atmosphere of 1976-7, which culminated in the kidnapping and killing of a leading German industrialist, works with a literary pedigree were regarded as less contentious investments than original, contemporary scripts. Fassbinder's *Despair* (1977), written by Tom Stoppard from the novel by Nabokov and with Dirk Bogarde heading the cast, was an early indication of new attempts to appeal to international audiences. Herzog's *Stroszek* (1977), partly filmed in the United States, and Wenders' *The American Friend* (1977) were similar moves in the same direction. And in 1980 Wenders moved to America to work on *Hammett* (1982). By the time of Fassbinder's death in 1982, there was little of its original life left in the New German Cinema.

Coppola's The Godfather II *(Robert De Niro)*

The New Hollywood

In Billy Wilder's *Fedora* (1978) an ageing Hollywood director ruefully acknowledges that 'the kids with beards have taken over'. His reference is to a new generation of film-makers, including Steven Spielberg, George Lucas, Martin Scorsese and Brian de Palma, who by the end of the 1970s dominated the American industry. These directors saw themselves as unquestionably the authors of their films, and were so regarded by many critics. At the same time the studios had been fundamentally restructured (see Chapter 18), and producers were searching for new ways to appeal to new audiences. In this 'new' Hollywood films began to explore visual styles and narrative forms quite different from those of the 'classical' Hollywood feature of the 1930s and 1940s. Just as the silent cinema had borrowed from the European avant-garde, elements of the American cinema of the 1970s were clearly marked by the influence of art cinemas.

Films like *McCabe and Mrs Miller* (1971) and *Three Women* (1977), directed by Robert Altman; Francis Coppola's *The Conversation* (1974) and *The Godfather II* (1974); and most obviously Woody Allen's tributes to Bergman (*Interiors*, 1978) and Fellini (*Stardust Memories*, 1980), are all marked by techniques and conventions identified with the art cinema. Fragmented and elliptical narratives, for example, are a notable feature of these films, as they

226

are of Arthur Penn's *Mickey One* (1965) and *Night Moves* (1975) and Bob Rafelson's *Five Easy Pieces* (1970). Scorsese's *Taxi Driver* (1976) is just one of the many psychologically ambiguous studies of an aimless and alienated protagonist. Open endings became relatively common after Stanley Kubrick's *2001: A Space Odyssey* (1968). And self-conscious references to the cinema's past dotted American films of the 1970s, in Brian De Palma's virtual re-makes of Hitchcock (*Sisters*, 1972; *Obsession*, 1975), for instance, and in Lucas and Spielberg's futuristic throwbacks to B-Westerns and Republic serials.

Stylistic devices drawn from the art cinema also entered the Hollywood film-maker's vocabulary. Although occasional precedents existed in 'classical' Hollywood, jump-cuts, freeze-frames and discontinuous sound now became far more common. The austere framings of Bresson were adapted by Paul Schrader for the 'look' of *American Gigolo* (1980). Such a distinctive and self-conscious visual style, which took different forms in other films, seemed to demonstrate little concern for the traditional 'transparency' of the classical Hollywood cinema; and contributed to what one critic has identified as a new flaunting of a film's narration, which finds its most extreme aspect in portrayals of the director-as-creator, as in the sequence which features Coppola himself as a news cameraman in *Apocalypse Now* (1979).

Scorsese's Taxi Driver *(Cybill Shepherd, Robert De Niro)*

Each of the key directors of the new Hollywood is a movie buff, and many of them went to film school in the 1950s and 1960s when the creativity and freedom of the art cinema appeared peculiarly seductive. But the extent of the art cinema's influence needs to be accounted for by more than personal experience. To collapse a complex argument, it can be seen as a (late) response to the 1948 separation of exhibition from production and the loss to television of a guaranteed audience. Hollywood was looking for new audiences, who were generally younger and better educated than previously. As increasingly important elements in independent 'packages', directors were able to use their contracts to institutionalise their creative control. At the same time the social changes of the 1960s, the counter-culture, Vietnam and later Watergate prompted a radical reassessment of American values, for the expression of which the fragmentations and ambivalences of the art cinema seemed highly appropriate.

But did the integration of art cinema's styles and forms bring about a fundamental change in the Hollywood cinema? Any assessment of the past two decades would have to reject the idea of a major shift. The broad parameters of the classical style have in fact survived unchanged, and the conventions of the traditional genres have had to widen only marginally to accommodate diluted variants of the art cinema's narrative forms. Hollywood's conventions have by and large remained stable, capable as before of taking in outside influences but resisting any fundamental disruption.

227

Further reading

Don Allen, *Truffaut*, London: Secker & Warburg/British Film Institute, 1974.

Stig Bjorkman, Torsten Manns, Jonas Sima, *Bergman on Bergman*, trans. New York: Simon and Schuster, 1973.

David Bordwell, 'The Art Cinema as a Mode of Film Practice', in *Film Criticism*, vol. 4, no. 1, 1979.

Sylvia Harvey, *May '68 and Film Culture*, London: British Film Institute, 1978.

Jim Hillier (ed), *Cahiers du Cinéma: The 1950s — Neo-realism, Hollywood, New Wave*, London: Routledge & Kegan Paul/British Film Institute, 1985.

———*Cahiers du Cinéma: The 1960s — New Wave, New Cinema, Re-evaluating Hollywood*, Routledge & Kegan Paul/British Film Institute, 1986.

Robert Phillip Kolker, *The Altering Eye: Contemporary International Cinema*, New York: Oxford University Press, 1983.

Mira Liehm, *Passion and Defiance: Film in Italy from 1942 to the Present*, Berkeley and Los Angeles: University of California Press, 1984.

Colin MacCabe, *Godard: Images, Sounds, Politics*, London: Macmillan/British Film Institute, 1980.

Tom Milne (ed), *Godard on Godard*, London: Secker & Warburg, 1972.

James Monaco, *The New Wave: Truffaut, Godard, Chabrol, Rohmer, Rivette*, New York: Oxford University Press, 1976.

Geoffrey Nowell-Smith, *Visconti*, London: Secker & Warburg/British Film Institute, rev. ed. 1973.

Richard Roud, *Jean-Luc Godard*, London: Thames and Hudson/British Film Institute, rev. ed. 1970.

John Sandford, *The New German Cinema*, London: Oswald Wolff, 1980.

R. T. Witcombe, *The New Italian Cinema: Studies in Dance and Despair*, London: Secker & Warburg, 1982.

15
Britain's Moving Images

François Truffaut once opined that there is 'a certain incompatibility between the terms "cinema" and "Britain"'. At the same time it has been said that Britain has produced perhaps the best — certainly the 'least worst' — television in the world. Ironically, the 'New British Cinema' that is now being celebrated around the world owes its genesis and its continuing existence in large part to television. Both television and this 'new' cinema have inherited, to a degree, the 'old' traditions of British film-making. At the heart of these traditions is a vein of social realism, derived from the meshing during the Second World War of documentary concerns from the 1930s with the literary conventions of narrative drama. The continuing influence of this tradition can be seen in the 'new wave' films of the early 1960s and in a great deal of subsequent television drama. And to a large extent it has shaped the way cinema is thought about in Britain.

Literary heritage has been comparably significant. The post-war decade alone produced numerous adaptations, from Shakespeare, Dickens, Shaw, Noël Coward, Graham Greene and Terence Rattigan. Most of these films demonstrated a quiet respect for their source, just as the majority of television dramas do today. And linked with the cultural validation imparted to a film by a pre-existing novel or play is the importance to the British cinema of the 'quality' film. This is a complex idea, but it includes a recognition of cinema's potential for enlightenment, its possibility of engaging with universal truths — its value, in essence, as art. Much of this discourse is familiar from the Reithian aspirations for broadcasting (see Chapter 4).

Many generalised dismissals of the British cinema are motivated by the understanding that the nation's film-making, and to a large degree its television, is realist, literary and concerned above all with quality. Yet there are a number of vital strands which cannot be comfortably housed within this model. The dominant strand and the several alternative ones within Britain's moving images are present in many ways, often within the same groupings of films, and sometimes contesting individual movies. Much of the vitality of (some) recent television and (some) new British cinema derives from the continuing contention of these traditions.

Rank

The central figure of the British cinema in the 1940s was the industrialist J. Arthur Rank who, by a number of rather haphazard investments, had built up a commanding film empire. At the end of 1941 he not only controlled studios at Pinewood and Elstree, he was also the chairman of both Gaumont-British and of Odeon Cinema Holdings, and consequently ruled two out of three major exhibition circuits. (The Associated British Picture Corporation held on to the third.) The wartime boom at the box office boosted the value of all these holdings; and despite his own admission that he knew little about production, the Rank empire financed the bulk of the decade's prestige films. At their busiest Rank companies were responsible for more than thirty features per year, as well as animations, the newsreel *This Modern Age*, productions for children and a series of religious films for non-commercial distribution.

Many of Rank's wartime hits were brought to the corporation by the producers Gabriel Pascal and Filippo Del Giudice. The association with Pascal began with a version of *Pygmalion* (1938), a quintessentially literary film; and the producer's subsequent mounting of another Shaw play, *Caesar and Cleopatra* (1945), was Rank's most lavish production during these years. But it is a dull, stolid film, and the elaborate sets and costumes, together with constant production problems, more than doubled the initial budget, contributing significantly to Rank's post-war problems. Del Giudice secured Rank's backing after his production *In Which We Serve* (1942, directed by David Lean) had brought good returns at the box office. His production company Two Cities then made a number of films with the three directors — Anthony Asquith, Carol Reed and David Lean — whose work is usually taken as epitomising the literary cinema of the later 1940s.

Asquith's films of the late 1920s and 1930s were often visually inventive, but his work with Two Cities, and later films like his Rattigan adaptations

Carol Reed's The Third Man *(Alida Valli, Joseph Cotten)*

The Winslow Boy (1948) and *The Browning Version* (1950), show him as a conservative, essentially theatrical director. Carol Reed's work, including *Odd Man Out* (1947) and *The Third Man* (1949), both shot for Alexander Korda's London Film Company, is more visually flamboyant. Lean's films, too, are always grounded in strong writing, by Noël Coward for *Blithe Spirit* and *Brief Encounter* (both 1945), or after Dickens in *Great Expectations* (1946) and *Oliver Twist* (1948). His skill lies in the transformation of words into cinema, whether the setting is the trains, smoke and repressed sexuality of *Brief Encounter* or the wide-screen vistas of epics like *The Bridge on the River Kwai* (1957) and *Lawrence of Arabia* (1962).

Del Giudice was also instrumental in bringing a

number of other interesting talents to Rank in the mid-1940s. The brothers Roy and John Boulting, for example, followed wartime documentary achievements with a series of films tackling social issues, like juvenile delinquency in *Brighton Rock* (1947) and education in *The Guinea Pig* (1948). And it was Two Cities who produced Laurence Olivier's major contribution to the war effort, *Henry V* (1944). This remarkable Technicolor spectacle, with a visual style drawn partly from medieval manuscripts, combines a recreated Elizabethan production of the play with scenes in perspective sets and on a battlefield. Such a sophisticated fantasy resists as well as celebrates the dominant British filmmaking tradition, yet its credentials and its patriotic fervour ensured that it was accepted as a 'quality' film.

By the middle of the decade the mood of confidence within the industry had encouraged a number of those who had worked under the Two Cities banner to set up separate production units, linked to Rank through a group called Independent Producers. The Archers, the company formed by Michael Powell and Emeric Pressburger, was one member, and Individual was another. Individual was Frank Launder and Sidney Gilliat,

Henry V

who had scripted sprightly thrillers during the 1930s and made home-front dramas like *Millions Like Us* (1943) and *Waterloo Road* (1944). Their post-war work includes many entertaining if largely conventional thrillers like *Green for Danger* (1947) and *State Secret* (1950), together with Alastair Sim comedies in the 1950s and 1960s. But after Rank's financial crisis in 1948-9, the Archers, Individual and Cineguild (David Lean and others) went to work for Korda at London Film Productions.

Throughout the 1940s Rank's profits came not from the various production programmes but from the company's extensive exhibition interests. Poor investment decisions, including the commitments to *Caesar and Cleopatra* and the million-pound musical flop *London Town*, were setbacks, but with assets of more than $200 million the organisation was still comparable in scale to any of Hollywood's Big Five studios. Yet if the ambitious production plans were to prove profitable Rank, like the Korda operation a decade before, could not rely on domestic returns alone. The all-important American market had to be opened up. In the mid-1940s Rank had a better chance of doing this than any previous British producer. Initially at least there was considerable pro-British sympathy across the Atlantic. British films were better, and more efficiently produced than before the war. Moreover, along with the organisations taken over at the end of the 1930s, Rank had acquired financial links with 20th Century-Fox and United Artists as well as a controlling interest in Universal.

The tie-up with Universal secured a relatively favourable distribution pattern, and United Artists had some success releasing *Henry V* and *Caesar and Cleopatra*, but the theatres of the majors mostly remained inaccessible. Rank was enjoying an all-time high at the domestic box office, and was undertaking an expansion programme elsewhere in the world. But while *The Red Shoes* and *The Seventh Veil* were also popular in the United States, there was still considerable resistance from both the public and exhibitors, especially in rural areas. Many felt that British films were simply too esoteric.

In June 1947 the Labour government imposed an onerous tax on the import of semi-luxury goods, including foreign films. Although American exhibitors denied that they were making reprisals, Rank's returns from the American market fell rapidly. Nonetheless, at the end of the year Rank announced an ambitious production programme to fill the gaps on British screens now that new Hollywood product was not coming in. Then just three months later the imposition of duty was revoked and Hollywood's output flooded back. Despite the introduction of a 45 per cent British quota in October 1948 (up from just 17½ per cent) Rank productions proved disappointingly unprofitable through the winter and the company's losses for the year were over £4.5 million. The assault on the transatlantic market was at an end. Throughout the next decade Rank films, often those from Ealing, enjoyed modest art-house success in the United States, and in 1957 the corporation leased a number of cinemas to showcase its product more prominently. But little came of this venture, and Rank was never to compete seriously with Hollywood.

Ealing

Ealing Studios was built for Basil Dean's Associated Talking Pictures in 1931, but by 1938 ATP (like the rest of the British industry) was in trouble. Dean resigned and Michael Balcon, tired of battling with MGM as a co-producer, was invited to become head of production. For the next twenty years he ran a small, stable business which, partly because of Rank's backing from 1944 to 1955, was successful in the domestic market and in a modest way abroad. Ealing's distinctive films are those with which the British post-war cinema, and to a degree the national culture of these years, are most often identified.

Initially Balcon continued Basil Dean's production programme with the comedian George Formby and others, but early in the war the studio began work on films like *Next of Kin* (1942, directed by Thorold Dickinson) which was a War Office commission intended as a warning against careless talk. Subsequently, as the confidence of both Ealing and the nation grew, Balcon initiated a number of semi-documentaries, including Charles Frend's *San Demetrio, London* and Basil Dearden's *The Bells Go Down* (both 1943), in which a small, closely-knit team heroically but unostentatiously carry out wartime duties, respectively shipping oil into Britain and fire-fighting during the Blitz. There is a strong sense of community in these films, which both reflected the national mood and heralded what was to become a recurring feature of Ealing productions.

By 1943 there was a small team of directors at Ealing who, together with the writer T. E. B. Clarke, would create most of the studio's key films over the next decade. Balcon's model, as well as several recruits (including Alberto Cavalcanti and Harry Watt), came from John Grierson's team of documentary-makers in the 1930s. Like Grierson, he expected loyalty from his staff, and the resulting close collaborations contributed to the remarkably consistent Ealing approach. Balcon, however, retained final control, and often clashed with the more idiosyncratic of his directors, Robert Hamer and Alexander Mackendrick, who felt constrained by the tight budgets and schedules.

The energies of this team were consciously directed to making films for Britain. Balcon later wrote of 'the building up of a native industry with its roots firmly planted in the soil of this country', and his hopes of 'making British film a viable and significant part of our national life'. Unlike the far larger Rank combine, he could afford more or less to ignore the American market, and hold to his belief that 'a film, to be international, must be thoroughly national in the first instance'. But these 'national' qualities reflected the views and ideas of only part of the nation. As Balcon later admitted, 'We were middle-class people brought up with middle-class backgrounds and rather conventional educations. . . We voted Labour for the first time after the war; this was our mild revolution.' Mild revolution, often incarnated in eccentricity, was to a be a characteristic feature of many Ealing films.

Immediately after the war there was a sense of the studio casting around for an identity. A costume drama adaptation of *Nicholas Nickleby* (1947), directed by Cavalcanti, was premiered in the same year as two contemporary 'social problem' films, Basil Dearden's *Frieda* and Robert Hamer's *It Always Rains on Sunday*. *Hue and Cry*, a comic film about boys outwitting criminals, was also released that year; but it

Ealing eccentricity: Alec Guinness as the murder victims in Kind Hearts and Coronets *(Valerie Hobson is the odd woman out)*

was with the appearance in 1949 of *Passport to Pimlico*, directed by Henry Cornelius, *Whisky Galore!*, directed by Mackendrick, and Hamer's *Kind Hearts and Coronets* that Ealing came to be identified with its own particular form of comedy. These, together with the later *The Lavender Hill Mob* (1951, Charles Crichton) and *The Ladykillers* (1955, Mackendrick), are the classic Ealing films, remembered with affection for their gentle humour, their controlled eccentricity, their decency and wholesomeness.

Yet the Ealing legacy is more complex than that. Intimations of another world, one of sexuality and violence, are present elsewhere in the films, most notably in Robert Hamer's section of the 1945 supernatural omnibus film *Dead of Night*. Here a couple's shallow but stable relationship is disturbed by the man's visions when he stares into an antique mirror: the power of these images, it is suggested, comes from the sexual jealousy of a previous owner who murdered his wife. Sexuality is also central to *Kind Hearts and Coronets*, the darkest of the Ealing comedies. Built round a series of murders told in flashback, the film can be seen as an elaborate expression of frustrated desire within an examination of the class structure of British society. It is an enigmatic film, yet as in *Dead of Night* it is the interaction of realism and fantasy, calm and disruption, that produces its truly disturbing qualities.

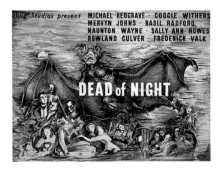

Poster by Leslie Hurry for Dead of Night. *Ealing commissioned a number of artists to design their posters, including John Piper, Edward Bawden, John Minton, Mervyn Peake, Edward Ardizzone and Ronald Searle.*

In the early 1950s it was the comforting currents within Ealing which ran stronger. A whimsical comedy like *The Titfield Thunderbolt* (1953) bears little sign of the dark undercurrents in *Kind Hearts and Coronets*, although Mackendrick's *The Man in the White Suit* (1951) does offer a troubling analysis of the changes within British society and of the tensions between old and new.

Basil Dearden's *The Blue Lamp* (1950) is centred on a similar opposition, with order restored after its violent disruption by a young criminal. Dearden went on to collaborate with producer Michael Relph on a sequence of tortured social problem pictures for Rank, including *Sapphire* (1959), *Victim* (1961) and *Life for Ruth* (1962).

Social problem pictures· Basil Dearden's Sapphire

By the early 1950s the energies of Ealing, along with those of much of British culture, were dissipated. Quaintness replaced any connection with contemporary events, and a prevailing mood of emotional and sexual repression, witnessed in a film like the war story *The Cruel Sea* (1953), closed down the possibilities suggested by earlier films. When the arrangement with Rank came to an end in 1955, the studios were sold to BBC Television, and Balcon and the Ealing company moved to Borehamwood as part of MGM's enterprise. But there was little vitality left; and the most interesting of the last films is *Dunkirk* (1958), a look back to a moment of unity and purpose from which both the nation and Ealing had drawn so much.

Alternative forms

In recent years a good deal of writing about the British cinema has been devoted to uncovering a 'hidden' line of work which resisted the dominant realism of the mainstream: a parallel but undervalued vein of fantasy which explores just those forces of sexuality and violence that threaten to undermine Ealing's project. The central characters in this alternative vein are Michael Powell and Emeric Pressburger, whose films were invariably regarded with suspicion by critics concerned with 'quality' British filmmaking. This came to a head with the outraged response to Powell's uncompromising Freudian fantasy, *Peeping Tom* (1959), in which a young murderer films the death of his women victims as he spears them with a camera tripod. More recently, the Powell and Pressburger films have been re-evaluated, and Technicolor restorations of several of them have been undertaken by the National Film Archive.

Powell and Pressburger's wartime films have already been noted (Chapter 5) as triumphs of art direction, and they are uninhibitedly, often extravagantly *visual* movies, marked by streaks of the fantastic and the supernatural but always balanced by a strong sense of England's past and present. *The Life and Death of Colonel Blimp* (1943) traces a dizzying historical progression through the early years of the century. *A Matter of Life and Death* (1946) begins with a plane crashing into the sea, before following the pilot to heaven. The ethereal realms are shot in black and white while the scenes on earth burst into Technicolor, and the film is replete with such visual inventiveness.

Powell and Pressburger's The Tales of Hoffmann

After the war Powell and Pressburger made simmering melodramas like *Black Narcissus* (1947) and the baroque musical extravaganzas *The Red Shoes* (1948) and *The Tales of Hoffmann* (1951). These are films of grand romantic passion, which clearly refuse both the cosiness of Ealing and the realism of most British cinema. The work of other individual film-makers has been

Thorold Dickinson's Queen of Spades *(Anton Walbrook, Edith Evans)*

Gainsborough melodrama: Margaret Lockwood as The Wicked Lady, *with James Mason*

similarly claimed as offering a potent alternative to the mainstream, perhaps most notably the films of Thorold Dickinson. Certainly his striking version of Pushkin's *Queen of Spades* (1949) shares many qualities with the style of Powell and Pressburger, as does his powerful thriller *Secret People* (1952). Much of the critical analysis of anti-realism, however, has been centred on two studio operations: Gainsborough, identified with a cycle of popular post-war melodramas; and Hammer Films, usually associated with films of horror and fantasy.

Gainsborough had been founded in 1924 by Michael Balcon, and during the 1930s had turned out low-budget pictures for Gaumont-British and a handful of higher-profile Hitchcock films and Will Hay comedies. In 1941 it came under Rank control, and two years later collected significant profits from Launder and Gilliat's level-headed realist feature *Millions Like Us* and from the costume melodrama *The Man in Grey*, directed by Leslie Arliss and starring Stewart Granger, Margaret Lockwood and James Mason. Studio head Maurice Ostrer went on to repeat the successful melodrama formula with *They Were Sisters* and *Madonna of the Seven Moons* (both 1944, both directed by Arthur Crabtree) and with Mason and Lockwood together again in *The Wicked Lady* (1945), also directed by Arliss. Each film made handsome profits for a modest outlay, as did the contemporary melodrama *The Seventh Veil* (1945).

These films were clearly directed at a female audience, and express the confused expectations about a woman's place in the post-war world. The hostilities had disrupted the family, and the intensity of events had encouraged active expressions of emotion. Women had also been needed in the work-force; and while concern at the end of the war about a falling birth rate prompted the reassertion of traditional family values, it was no longer possible to assign women to their former passive role. The Gainsborough formula was one way in which these contradictions could be expressed in a popular form. Sexuality and its suppression were central to these conflicts, as is demonstrated by Margaret Lockwood's pursuit of excitement and seduction in *The Wicked Lady*. There was also a recurring emphasis on brutality and sadism, as with James Mason's cruel jealousy over his young ward in *The Seventh Veil*. Margaret Lockwood as a gypsy girl is also the emotional centre of *Jassy* (1947), attacked by the critics for its enthusiastic depiction of 'torture, flogging and bloodshed'. Sexuality and violence also run through *Good Time Girl* (1947), although here in a contemporary social problem framework.

These Gainsborough films were not, however, rejections of the literary traditions of British cinema. Producer Sydney Box defended them by noting that films like *Madonna of the Seven Moons* were adapted from respected novels. Rather, Gainsborough was seeking a strategy for differentiating its dramas from contemporary Hollywood films, to appeal to audiences at home and abroad. A quite distinct strategy with a similar aim, and showing a comparable disregard for the expected realism and restraint of the British cinema, can be seen in the work a decade later of the Hammer studio.

After seven years of turning out unremarkable low-budget dramas, Hammer released in 1955 a film version of a BBC television serial *The Quatermass Xperiment*. Its immediate success prompted the company to rush two further science-fiction movies into production. A year later Hammer embarked on a lavish variation of the Frankenstein legend, *The Curse of Frankenstein*, directed by Terence Fisher. The studio had found a successful formula to sustain it through the next two decades. A host of low-budget exploitation pictures followed, made in and around an old house at Bray by a repertory company of actors, writers and directors.

Critics attacked *The Curse of Frankenstein* and its successors in much the same terms that they had rejected Gainsborough films. More recently the Hammer oeuvre has been seen as expressing a tradition of the fantastic which stretches back more than two centuries in British culture, a 'Gothic' tradition which has given form to the macabre and the unexplained, and indeed to the darker regions of sexuality, at least since Horace Walpole's 1764 novel *The Castle of Otranto*. Hammer films like *Dracula, The Revenge of Frankenstein* (both 1958) and *The Mummy* (1959) extend these concerns in a form appropriate to the twentieth century. They were concerns, however, which were quite at odds with the ideas and aspirations of a group of films soon to be hailed by just those critics who turned away in disgust from the myth and magic of Hammer.

Hammer horror: The Mummy, *directed by Terence Fisher in 1959*

The British 'new wave'

In contrast to the 'never had it so good' bullishness of Prime Minister Harold Macmillan and most of the population, the mainstream British film industry in the later 1950s appeared to be in terminal decline. Between 1951 and 1960 annual admissions dropped from 1,365 million to 501 million. Television, inevitably, had made an enormous impact, especially after the advent of ITV in 1955. Exhibitors even endeavoured to buy up the television rights to British films to prevent them reaching the small screen, and to boycott producers who made their movies available to the rival medium. Throughout the decade Rank and the Associated British Picture Corporation intensified their duopoly control of distribution and exhibition, and it was the independent cinemas which suffered most from the crisis. An onerous entertainment tax was a further burden, and neither Rank nor ABPC demonstrated any real commitment to a sustained domestic production programme.

A limited form of state support had been introduced in 1949 with the setting up of the National Film Finance Corporation, which was intended to supplement, not supplant, the industry's own capital. Soon afterwards the Eady levy was introduced, modelled on similar schemes in France and Italy. A proportion of each ticket sold was diverted to a central fund, which was subsequently shared among British – or at least notionally British – producers. But this did not prevent American majors forming subsidiaries which could benefit from the in any case limited funds available. Encouraged in part by Eady monies, and attracted by lower costs and by government restrictions on the proportion of a film's earnings which could be remitted back to the United States, American producers worked increasingly in London throughout the 1950s. Lavish 'international' films like John Ford's *Mogambo* (1953) and Gene Kelly's *Invitation to the Dance* (1956) were shot at Borehamwood by MGM. Columbia and Fox also made films in England; and Warners used Elstree to make a number of films, including John Huston's *Moby Dick* (1956). And an independent producer like Sam Spiegel could use British and American talent to make British-based, location-shot, internationally successful films like Huston's *The African Queen* (1951) and David Lean's *The Bridge on the River Kwai* (1959).

War films, perhaps inevitably, occupied a great deal of British screen time throughout the 1950s. Dramas like Jack Lee's *The Wooden Horse* (1950) and Michael Anderson's *The Dam Busters* (1955) present an almost cosy view of the war, and despite an occasional troubled undertone are generally marked by nostalgia for the uncomplicated goals of the conflict. Society was experiencing rapid social change, adjusting to a post-Imperial role abroad and recognising the loosening of class loyalties at home, but most mainstream cinema turned its face from these concerns. By the end of the decade a 'new wave' might be breaking, but family audiences could only be counted on to turn out for the latest Norman Wisdom comedy, for a new feature in the *Doctor*... or *Carry On*... series, or perhaps for a Cliff Richard musical.

Paralleling changes in Hollywood a decade earlier, a number of smaller, independent productions emerged, often driven by the initiative of actors and directors. Allied Film Makers was formed, with backing from Rank, by Richard Attenborough, Bryan Forbes and others in late 1959, and was soon enjoying a major success with Basil Dearden's polished thriller *The League of Gentlemen* (1960). The Bryanston company also began operations in the same year, with connections to the Twickenham studios and the distributor British Lion, and the involvement – now that Ealing's uneasy deal with MGM had come to nothing – of Michael Balcon. The independence of these ventures, however, was to be curtailed by continuing dependence on Rank and ABPC, both for distribution guarantees and for access to theatres. Neither Allied Film Makers nor Bryanston survived beyond the mid-1960s.

A third new company was Woodfall, founded by Tony Richardson and John Osborne, respectively director and writer of the play *Look Back in Anger*. First seen at London's Royal Court in 1956, this drama was recognised as the symbol of a significant cultural shift. A challenge to what its leading character called the 'stifling atmosphere of socially deferential conservatism', it expressed many of the confusions attendant on the country's recent social and political changes. With producer Harry Saltzman, support from Warners, and assistance from the NFFC, Woodfall made a film version of *Look Back in Anger* (1959), and then a further Osborne adaptation, *The Entertainer* (1960). Neither film scored at the box office, but Woodfall's third feature, *Saturday Night and Sunday Morning* (1960), was much more success-

The new social realism: Albert Finney in Saturday Night and Sunday Morning

ful and established the company, along with its policy of artistic independence, as a credible production force.

Woodfall's first productions, together with Jack Clayton's *Room at the Top* (1959), began a cycle of films with working-class settings which was to distinguish the British cinema for the next three years. Richardson made two further key contributions, *A Taste of Honey* (1961) and *The Loneliness of the Long Distance Runner* (1962). Karel Reisz directed *Saturday Night and Sunday Morning*, and then produced Lindsay Anderson's debut feature *This Sporting Life* (1963). These three film-makers had organised the Free Cinema documentary initiative in the mid-1950s; and this new cycle of films reflected the persistence of the realist tradition in British cinema. Anderson's subsequent work, however, which includes *If...* (1968), *O Lucky Man!* (1973) and *Britannia Hospital* (1982), combines social realism with elements of fantasy.

Lindsay Anderson's If ...

The extent to which these 'new wave' films, as they were soon dubbed, were an authentic representation of working-class life, or simply the romantic views of middle-class radicals, has been much debated. Nonetheless, this new cinema was seen as serious and committed, addressed to contemporary realities, and a distinct break from the escapist offerings of most cinema and television of the period. Ironically perhaps, it was the small screen to which this realist impetus was soon to shift, while the film-makers associated with it began to seek an escape from its confines. In 1961 Jack Clayton made a stylish ghost story in *The Innocents*. Two years later John Schlesinger, who had made the determinedly realist *A Kind of Loving* in 1962, introduced fantasy into *Billy Liar*. Tony Richardson secured financing from the newly established London office of United Artists for his bawdy version of Fielding's 18th-century novel *Tom Jones* (1963), whose picaresque tale proved immensely popular and was to contribute in a fundamental way to the changes about to occur in British cinema.

'Hollywood England'

As well as *Tom Jones*, United Artists financed the first of the James Bond films, *Dr No*, and a low-budget musical called *A Hard Day's Night*, with a rising pop group called The Beatles. By mid-1964 it was clear that the company had three major international hits. Not only did *Tom Jones* and *Dr No* express a growing acceptance of sexual openness, and translate this into box-office profit, but along with The Beatles they came from a culture which was soon to be at the centre of the world's consciousness.

The Beatles in Richard Lester's Help! *(1965)*

The director Richard Lester had conjured up a loose, free-wheeling energy for *A Hard Day's Night*, and he combined this with an oddball surrealism in *The Knack* (1965), which can be seen as the first of the 'Swinging London' films (although *Time* magazine was not to coin the phrase until April 1966). John Boorman's lively pop musical *Catch Us If You Can* and John Schlesinger's caustic morality tale *Darling* (both 1965) followed soon afterwards, all three directors bringing to features a freshness which could be attributed to their training in documentaries and television.

Performance

1965 also saw the establishment of production programmes in London by several of the larger American companies. Attracted both by United Artists' success and by the cultural excitement increasingly associated with the city, these companies financed wholly or in part two-thirds of the films made in Britain in 1965. 20th Century-Fox poured money into Joseph Losey's comic-strip thriller *Modesty Blaise* (1966), and Columbia was to make millions from the comedy *Georgy Girl*. Foreign directors like François Truffaut (*Fahrenheit 451*) and Michelangelo Antonioni (*Blow Up*; both 1967) were attracted to London. The Polish exile Roman Polanski made *Repulsion* (1965), *Cul de Sac* (1966) and *Dance of the Vampires* (1967) in Britain. The work of each of these film-makers entered the worlds of sexuality and fantasy that were alien to British realism, and in ways that were closed to most British directors.

Universal Pictures arrived in London in 1966, and over the next three years financed more than a dozen films. Not only was the international appeal of London attractive, so was the range of acting and directing talent nurtured by British theatre and television. Moreover it was simply cheaper to make a movie in Britain. By 1968, just under 90 per cent of the films made in Britain had American money in them. Few of Universal's films made money, however, and by 1969 the balance sheets of a number of American companies were looking far less healthy than had been hoped. Tony Richardson's *The Charge of the Light Brigade* (1968) cost United Artists $6.5 million, and flopped. Paramount's expensive musical *Half a Sixpence* (1968) was also a failure. Although a handful of increasingly expensive productions continued to be made, including United Artists' *The Battle of Britain* (1969) and MGM's *Goodbye, Mr Chips* (1969), the glamour of production in Britain had disappeared. The American companies, pressed by escalating debts at home, pulled out. In 1969 American investment in British films was £31.2 million; by 1971 it was just £8.3 million.

Of those films made in the production boom at the end of the 1960s only Nicolas Roeg's *Performance* (1968, co-directed by Donald Cammell, and financed by Universal), and perhaps the features made by Joseph Losey such as *Accident* (1967) and *Secret Ceremony* (1968), can be seen as significant challenges to the dominant strand of British cinema identified above. A former cinematographer, Roeg is one of the few consistently challenging British film-makers of the past two decades. *Performance* is a dark, hippie gangster movie, featuring a powerfully sinister performance from Mick Jagger. Its games with perception and identity are echoed throughout Roeg's subsequent work, which includes the supernatural thriller *Don't Look Now* (1972) and the enigmatic drama *Bad Timing* (1980). Meanwhile, by the late 1960s the social realism of the 'new wave' had re-entered the cinema from television.

Television drama
Until the end of the 1950s British television drama remained in thrall to the

240

theatre. Most plays were adaptations of stage works, mounted and shot in the studio as televised theatre. This began to change when the ABC-TV company brought over from Canada the producer Sydney Newman, who immediately began to implement a policy of original plays by contemporary dramatists, written for the medium and concerned with issues of the day. Contemporary with the early stage work of Osborne and others and the 'new wave' cinema of Woodfall, this strategy shared similar concerns and a number of the same writers.

Following his move to the BBC in 1963 as Head of Drama, Newman encouraged producers like Tony Garnett and James MacTaggart to concentrate on 'the turning points of English society'. Garnett's collaborations with Ken Loach on filmed dramas like *Up the Junction* (1965) and *Cathy Come Home* (1966) were the first evidence of an influential strand of work which continued with television films like *The Big Flame* (1969) and *Rank and File* (1971), about trade unionism, and *Days of Hope* (1974), a controversial reconstruction of the events of the 1926 General Strike. Productions like these shared some of the concerns of the 'new wave' film-makers: the wish to break out of the studio, and to reflect working-class life not in an artificial way, but in actual locations. 16mm film cameras, offering for the first time the chance to make television drama in this

Days of Hope, *written by Jim Allen, produced by Tony Garnett, directed by Ken Loach*

way, were beginning to be widely used by documentary film-makers, including some like Jack Gold and Kevin Billington who moved first into drama and later into feature films. Film was regarded as being a more subtle and creative medium than the constricting electronic videotape of the studios. And with the impetus of filmed dramas and documentary-based series like *Z Cars*, social realism came to occupy centre stage in the best television drama.

It has continued to do so into the 1980s. The popular twice-weekly serial *Brookside*, for instance, which began on Channel 4 in 1982, is a conscious attempt to integrate the social realist tradition with the conventions of soap opera. But this strand has by no means displaced the other central tradition of British film-making: the 'quality' literary adaptation. Among many television productions in this vein have been Granada's two acclaimed adaptations *Brideshead Revisited* (1981) and *The Jewel in the Crown* (1985).

At the same time British television, like British cinema, has provided ample evidence of alternatives to these dominant traditions. Ken Russell's dramatised profiles of artists and musicians are one example from the 1960s of a challenge to the primary conventions of television production. The innovative videotape productions of Philip Saville — in particular his direction of Alan Bleasdale's series *Boys from the Blackstuff* in 1985 — also show a clear break from the conventions of social realism. The plays of Dennis

241

Potter, culminating in the extraordinary serial *The Singing Detective* (1986), are equally iconoclastic, the work of an author committed to writing for television as a distinctive medium, and with an unmatched appreciation of its potential.

Cinema in the 1970s and 1980s

When the Americans pulled out in 1969-70, the British film industry's weaknesses were cruelly exposed. Money for new features was scarce throughout the next decade, although both the independent distributor British Lion and the media conglomerate EMI (which had purchased a controlling interest in ABPC in 1969 and begun a production programme) continued to flirt with the financing of movies. EMI set up a co-production arrangement with MGM in 1970, but this came to an end in 1973 when MGM cut back its film-making operations. The conglomerate had also expanded the number of ABC screens which it now controlled, in large part by splitting cinemas into several small auditoria. Then in May 1976 EMI purchased British Lion, and began an ambitious production programme — but mostly of American films made in Hollywood. Two years later the group was in deep financial trouble. By 1979 it had accepted a takeover bid by Thorn Electrical; and although production has continued, neither a consistent creative policy nor significant profits have been achieved.

Another concern which became involved in feature production during the 1970s was Lord Grade's ITC group. Lew Grade had run a successful talent agency in the 1930s and an exceptionally successful company producing television film series in the 1950s and 1960s, but he failed spectacularly with feature films, in part brought down by the box-office sinking of the $34 million *Raise the Titanic* (1979). Rank also returned to feature production in 1977, but the corporation's former sure touch now eluded it. Towards the end of the decade the British industry's main production facilities at Pinewood and Elstree were largely occupied by Hollywood-based blockbuster features such as *Star Wars* (1977) and *Superman* (1978). Attracted both by lower costs and by the skills of British technicians, large-scale productions like these have kept alive what remains of the mainstream industry in Britain.

The mid-1970s were the bleakest of times for the British cinema. The *Carry On. . .* series carried on, the American Film Theatre shot some classic dramas with British directors and casts, and there were a handful of television comedy spin-offs. But as the cliché of the moment expressed it, the British cinema was alive and well and living in television. Developing the work begun in the mid-1960s by Loach, Garnett and others, writers and directors working mostly for the BBC were creating small-scale but striking film dramas. Stephen Frears directed work like *Last Summer* (1976, Thames), *Long Distance Information* (1978, BBC) and *Saigon — Year of the Cat* (1983, Thames). The playwright David Hare wrote and directed *Licking Hitler* (1977) and *Dreams of Leaving* (1979, both BBC), and later made *Wetherby* (1985) as a feature. Roland Joffé made *The Spongers* (1978) and

Films for television: Stephen Frears' Saigon – Year of the Cat *(Roger Rees, Judi Dench)*

242

United Kingdom (1980; both from scripts by Jim Allen), and it was the latter which led to the invitation to direct *The Killing Fields* for the cinema. Gavin Millar, Michael Apted, Waris Hussein, Giles Foster, John Mackenzie and Malcolm Mowbray followed a similar path towards feature film-making.

Apart from the sources already noted, a producer's only realistic possibility for financing a feature film in the 1970s was as an individual 'package', always dependent on a distribution guarantee from the United States. One producer who proved peculiarly adept at this was David Puttnam. After making two distinctive stories centred on British pop music — *That'll Be the Day* (1973, director Claude Whatham) and *Stardust* (1974, director Michael Apted) — he produced the successful gangster film pastiche *Bugsy Malone* (1976), with all the parts played by children. The director was Alan Parker, who had proved himself as an outstanding commercials director with a flair for parody, and who went on to make a number of intense dramas like *Midnight Express* (1979) and *Birdy* (1985).

Bugsy Malone

To make *Bugsy Malone* Puttnam secured £200,000 from the National Film Finance Corporation, on condition of a distribution guarantee of $300,000. Paramount and Rank provided the rest, apart from the final £50,000 that had to come from new mortgages on both Puttnam and Parker's houses. Within a couple of years the prospects for film financing were a little easier, as companies recognised the possibilities of tax shelter schemes. The producer Don Boyd, for example, was able to put together a package of five low-budget features in a deal which involved twenty-six individuals contributing a total of around £370,000. For this they were able to claim tax losses of some £1.5 million.

Another new company which emerged in 1978 was Handmade, set up by former Beatle George Harrison and his financial adviser Denis O'Brien. Good box-office returns from the Monty Python team's supposedly blasphemous religious satire *Life of Brian* (1979) encouraged them to continue with relatively low-budget features, including Terry Gilliam's fantasy *Time Bandits* (1981). Goldcrest was another recently established and small concern, whose initial modest results attracted finance (half of which came from 20th Century-Fox) to make David Puttnam's project *Chariots of Fire* (1981, directed by Hugh Hudson). When this won the Best Film Oscar in 1982 Goldcrest was expanding rapidly, with Richard Attenborough's *Gandhi* (1982) about to prove another major success and a productive relationship with the new Channel 4 Television.

Richard Attenborough's Gandhi

Further large-scale projects followed, including *The Killing Fields* (1984), produced by Puttnam and directed by another graduate from television, Roland Joffé. But the company's increasingly ambitious programme faltered with the disappointing results of the musical *Absolute Beginners* (1985), and fell apart after the box-office failure of *Revolution* (1986), Hugh Hudson's grandiose epic about the American War of Independence.

As Goldcrest prospered, and talk of the British cinema's 'renaissance' began, the government continued to demonstrate its lack of interest in the industry, and when intervention did come it was largely negative. The quota was suspended in early 1983, and the following year tax shelter financing was ended by new legislation. The NFFC, which since 1949 had contributed to well over 700 films, received little encouragement; and in 1985 it was abolished, together with the Eady levy, and replaced by the British Screen Finance Corporation, a private consortium backed by Thorn-EMI, Rank, Channel 4 and the British Videogram Association.

Channel 4 and 'New British Cinema'

After more than a decade of debate about the structure of a new British television channel, Channel 4 Television went on the air in November 1982. An astute compromise between the pressures of commercialism and the public service system, the new channel was established under the Independent Broadcasting Authority. The ITV companies were to fund Channel 4, in return for the right to sell advertising in their individual regions. But they would have no direct control of the schedule, which was to be independently programmed.

The 1977 Annan Committee, set up by the government to review the future of broadcasting, had recommended that a new channel act as a 'publisher' of programmes, and Channel 4 was directed to put this idea into practice. It now commissions or purchases work from the ITV companies and from hundreds of small and medium-sized independent producers, as well as from abroad. Moreover, the legislation bringing Channel 4 into being required the new service to provide programmes for audiences not previously well served by television (subsequently interpreted to mean women, ethnic groups and young people) and to 'encourage innovation and experiment in the form and content of programmes'. This statutory requirement has ensured that Channel 4 has sought out new ideas for television.

By now it is clear that Channel 4 has immeasurably enriched Britain's moving image culture. The range of subjects tackled by television, and the approaches taken to them, is far more diverse than before. Many individuals and groups have begun programme-making, often expressing the views of groups previously disenfranchised by television. Channel 4's diversity of programming has ranged from Brazilian soap operas and African cinema to European productions like *Shoah*, Claude Lanzmann's nine-hour documentary about the Nazis' attempted extermination of the Jews. And there is a successful multi-cultural output, an innovative policy towards arts programming, new television sports like American football, and much else which has refreshingly broadened the range of British television.

One of the channel's most important decisions was to fund or co-fund a

244

number of feature films each year, which it was hoped would be shown in cinemas before being seen on the small screen. 'Film on Four' contributed monies to some twenty films in its first year, and has continued a bold policy ever since. The early emphasis was on financing low-budget British features, including films like Neil Jordan's Northern Ireland story *Angel* (1982) and his fantasy *The Company of Wolves* (1984) and Richard Eyre's clinical dissection of the state of Britain at the time of the Falklands War, *The Ploughman's Lunch* (1983). More recently the channel has begun to contribute to more international productions, such as Wim Wenders' *Paris, Texas* (1984) and Andrei Tarkovsky's final film *The Sacrifice* (1986).

A number of the films financed by Channel 4 and others have begun to be seen and marketed abroad as representing a 'new British cinema'. Stephen Frears' *My Beautiful Laundrette* (1986; originally intended only for television) has been a substantial art-house success in the United States and elsewhere, as has the same director's *Prick Up Your Ears* (1987), Neil Jordan's *Mona Lisa* (1986) and the low-budget *Letter to Brezhnev* (1985). Channel 4 has also funded the work of several film-makers who consciously reject the post-war conventions of British cinema. Chris Petit, for instance, has directed four features, including *Radio On* (1979), whose aesthetic is closer to that of Wenders and the New German Cinema. *Radio On* was part-funded by the British Film Institute Production Board, which has been an important source of finance for work on the edges of the mainstream. The Board has also consistently supported the idiosyncratic films of Peter Greenaway and Derek Jarman.

Jarman alternates experimental work in Super-8 with distinctly unconventional 35mm features: *Sebastiane* (1976), a gay fantasy of Roman Britain with dialogue partly in Latin; *Jubilee* (1978), a punk portrait of contemporary Britain; and a startling version of *The Tempest* (1979). His most elaborate film is *Caravaggio* (1986), made for Channel 4. Greenaway's films are intricate fantasies which play Borges-like games with language and categorisation. One of Channel 4's first feature successes was his *The Draughtman's Contract* (1982), a teasingly enigmatic elaboration of a 17th-century sexual conspiracy, and the channel has since part-funded three more Greenaway films. It is in large part thanks to Channel 4 that British cinema now embraces a wider range of options and possibilities than perhaps ever before.

Peter Greenaway's The Draughtsman's Contract

Further reading

Sue Aspinall and Robert Murphy (eds), *BFI Dossier 18: Gainsborough Melodrama,* London: British Film Institute, 1983.

Martyn Auty and Nick Roddick (eds), *British Cinema Now,* London: BFI Publishing, 1985.

Michael Balcon, *Michael Balcon Presents: A Lifetime of Films,* London: Hutchinson, 1969.

Charles Barr, *Ealing Studios,* London: Cameron & Tayleur/David & Charles, 1977.

Charles Barr (ed), *All Our Yesterdays: 90 Years of British Cinema,* London: BFI Publishing, 1986.

George W. Brandt (ed), *British Television Drama,* Cambridge: Cambridge University Press, 1981.

James Curran and Vincent Porter, *British Cinema History,* London: Weidenfeld and Nicolson, 1983.

Raymond Durgnat, *A Mirror for England: British Movies from Austerity to Affluence,* London: Faber and Faber, 1970.

Jane Fleugel (ed), *Michael Balcon: the Pursuit of British Cinema,* New York: Museum of Modern Art, 1984.

John Hill, *Sex, Class and Realism: British Cinema 1956-1963,* London: BFI Publishing, 1986.

Stephen Lambert, *Channel Four: Television with a Difference?,* London: BFI Publishing, 1982.

David Pirie, *A Heritage of Horror: The English Gothic Cinema 1946-1972,* London: Gordon Fraser, 1973.

Alexander Walker, *Hollywood, England: The British Film Industry in the Sixties,* London: Michael Joseph, 1974.

———*National Heroes: British Cinema in the Seventies and Eighties,* London: Harrap, 1985.

16
Alternatives:
Asia, Africa, Latin America

The bias, in this book as in our culture as a whole, towards Hollywood and its familiar dependents is not of course accidental. Hollywood has dominated the world's moving images since the 1920s. The cinemas treated in this chapter are alternatives to Hollywood, and are the expressions of cultures either, as with China and India, largely cut off from the United States and its associates, or concerned to preserve an independent identity. This cultural resistance may have parallels with military and political conflict, or it may be one element of a reaction to the economics and ideologies of neo-colonialism.

The danger of recognising each of these distinct moving image cultures as alternatives to Hollywood is that spurious parallels and connections, or even a quite inappropriate unity, may be suggested. There are certain clear relationships, especially among the cinemas of countries which experienced degrees of colonialism by European powers and which are now developing nations with market economies. But an encompassing label like 'Third World Cinema' must be treated with caution. What remains paramount, as in any exploration of moving images, is to see and understand films and television programmes within the range of political, industrial, social and economic contexts appropriate and specific to those images. Thus an understanding of the ways in which the Japanese cinema offers an alternative to Hollywood involves quite different concerns from an awareness of the interactions between Hollywood and the various Latin American cinemas.

Post-war Japan

With Japan under American occupation at the end of the Second World War, Hollywood movies enjoyed easy access to cinema screens, although domestic productions still drew a larger audience overall. Certain subjects were prohibited to film-makers, and more than two hundred wartime films were banned by the Americans. Period films were not welcomed by the authorities, depictions of feudal societies being deemed anti-democratic. A rather different engagement with the West came in 1951 when Akira Kurosawa's *Rashomon* won the main prize at the Venice Festival. Three years later

Kinugasa's *Gate of Hell* won both the Cannes Grand Prix and an Academy Award. The richness of the Japanese cinema began to be seen abroad.

Throughout the war the leading Japanese studio had been Toho, but it soon ran into trouble during the Occupation. Labour unions were formed for the first time within the industry, and disputes occurred at Shochiku, Daiei and the smaller companies. Toho, which had employed among others the directors Mikio Naruse and Akira Kurosawa, was torn apart by a bitter strike. By the early 1950s Daiei was the most prominent concern, and in the wake of its domestic and international success with *Rashomon* it developed a strategy designed to appeal both to a broad audience at home and to a more specialised but still significant market overseas.

The hold of the large studios was weakened during the 1950s, as many independent companies were formed. Admissions rose steadily throughout the decade, as did production, which reached a peak in 1956 when 514 films were made. A new company, Toei, earned large profits with a calculatedly commercial policy, and with an extensive production programme launched in 1956 of films shot in widescreen processes, which were then quickly adopted by all the main studios. And film companies found that not only was 'art' welcomed in the West, but that fantasy exploitation movies like *Godzilla* (1954) and *The Mysterians* (1957) could make significant returns.

Once the Americans had left in 1952, the Japanese cinema began a rigorous reassessment of recent history. Examinations of the war and of what was seen as the subsequent spiritual decline motivated many of the decade's best films. Keisuke Kinoshita's popular *Twenty-four Eyes* (1954), for example, looks at the 1930s through the eyes of a provincial schoolteacher. His *A Japanese Tragedy* (1953), a sympathetic portrayal of a woman who humiliates herself to raise a family alone during the 1940s, offers a bleak view of an unremittingly materialist society, with no place even for filial love. Masaki Kobayashi's three-part *The Human Condition* (1958-61) takes up similar issues with a broader sweep, examining the response of one Japanese soldier to the appalling realities of war. Shohei Imamura's films offer a more contemporary protest against militarism. His *Pigs and Battleships* (1961) is a polemic against the continuing presence in Japan of American naval bases. *History of Postwar Japan as Told by a Bar Hostess* (1970) is more subdued but no less effective, intercutting an interview with a bar owner who works alongside an American base with newsreels from 1945 onwards.

Alongside the post-war generation of Kon Ichikawa and Kinoshita and younger directors like Imamura, veterans such as Mizoguchi, Ozu, Naruse and Gosho continued to make distinguished films. Ozu's most achieved response to the post-war years was *A Hen in the Wind* (1948), which develops the relationship between a man and his wife as a metaphor for the disillusionment of the Occupation. As in so many of his films, Ozu's attitude appears to be one of resignation, a recognition that things are as they are and cannot be changed by individual action. Most of his final films, from *Late Spring* (1949) to *An Autumn Afternoon* (1962), confront the problems of the

Rashomon

248

family in this empty world with an increasing melancholy.

Mizoguchi was to make in his last years what for many critics are his finest films. In his post-war dramas he continued to engage with the problems of women within Japanese patriarchy, and prostitution is a key image of oppression. *The Life of Oharu* (1952) opens with a prostitute in the 17th century relating her story to her friends; her fall, the film suggests, prompted only by an act of love, is the inevitable outcome of feudalism. Over the next two years Mizoguchi made three further period films, *Ugetsu Monogatari* (1953), *Sansho Dayu* (1954) and *Chikamatsu Monogatari* (1955), each of which sets a love story against the background of feudalism. In these late films, aided by the exquisite cinematography of Kazuo Miyagawa, Mizoguchi achieved a painterly sense of composition, which he was able to integrate with his celebrated technique of shooting important sequences in a single take, with the camera always slightly distanced from the action.

Mizoguchi's Ugetsu Monogatari

Seen against the disillusioned mood of much post-war Japanese cinema, Akira Kurosawa's films seem more positive than those of his contemporaries. Not that he avoids contemporary problems. *Drunken Angel* (1948) sets an alcoholic doctor against the problems of slums. *Record of a Living Being* (1955) is an anti-nuclear drama, about a factory owner's fear of another bomb being dropped on Japan. In *Ikiru (Living,* 1952) a middle-aged man discovers that he has terminal cancer and resolves to carry out one meaningful act before his death; his personal protest is soon recuperated by the system.

Kurosawa's preoccupation with extending the possibilities of the cinema is apparent in *Rashomon* (1950), which relates the same incident in four subjective versions, none of which is to be taken as 'true'. His subsequent films are distinguished by their technical innovations, such as the use of telephoto lenses to create an almost claustrophobic intimacy in *Seven Samurai* (1954). But in his best work the stylistic virtuosity is matched by profound psychological insight. *Throne of Blood* (1957) is a revelatory version of Shakespeare's *Macbeth*, while *Yojimbo* (1961) and *Red Beard* (1965) are engrossing examinations of individuals battling with the social forces of their respective worlds. The humanity of these films is perhaps overwhelmed by visual pyrotechnics in his later feudal epics like *Kagemusha* (1980) and *Ran* (1984).

Kurosawa's Ran, *an epic retelling of King Lear*

By the early 1960s the rapid growth of Japanese television was beginning to be reflected by a sharp fall in cinema admissions, and the major studios came increasingly to rely on formula pictures, with Toei for example turning out numerous *yakuza* (or gangster) films. One independent producer, the Art Theatre Guild, offered an important alternative by financing a range of low-budget art-house films, including productions by the Japanese director whose work in the past two decades has enjoyed the highest profile in the West, Nagisa Oshima.

Oshima began directing 'youth films' for Shochiku in the late 1950s. Since *Night and Fog in Japan* (1960), after which he set himself up as an independent, he has undertaken a radical engagement with the forms of narrative cinema, and rather like Jean-Luc Godard has sought a new film-making practice for the exploration of political concerns. *Violence at Noon* (1966) constructs its case history of a sex criminal from hundreds of short shots edited together with the rigour of classical Russian montage. *Death by Hanging* (1968) is an angry, multi-faceted assault on capital punishment and the 'problem' of Japan's Korean minority. *Boy* (1969) and *The Ceremony* (1971) are more conventionally constructed but nevertheless incisive satires on Japanese society. And in a pair of films which were to gain international notoriety, *In the Realm of the Senses* (1976) and *Empire of Passion* (1978), Oshima uncompromisingly confronts our accepted representations of sexuality and violence.

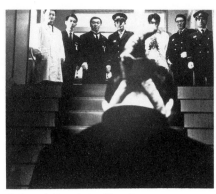

Oshima's Death by Hanging

Cinema in China

Travelling showmen first brought films to China in 1896, and domestic production, mostly of extracts from the theatre and opera, began around 1905. Cinemas were at first largely confined to the West's treaty ports, with distribution and exhibition dominated by American and European companies. Studios, mostly located in cosmopolitan Shanghai, were dependent on foreign equipment and stock. Hollywood's control of the major screens become almost total.

In the 1920s, when the country was torn by internal conflicts, financing of films was precarious and companies often short-lived; but in 1922 the producer Zhang Sichuan set up the Mingxing Film Company, which was to enjoy both commercial and creative success for the next fifteen years. Its output included comedies, melodramas, the first Chinese sound film *Sing-Song Girl Red Peony* (1929), and a martial arts serial, *The Burning of Red Lotus Monastery* (1928-31), which eventually fell foul of the censors. The comparably prosperous Lianhua Film Company was started in 1930, and these rivals produced the bulk of Chinese features until the industry was effectively shut down by the Japanese invasion of Shanghai in 1937. Hollywood's products retained their position in the early 1930s. But as in India, increasing industrialisation swelled the potential urban audience, and domestic production levels were high.

After the Japanese had first bombed Shanghai in 1932, both Mingxing and Lianhua began to produce strongly patriotic features. At the same time young intellectuals from the Communist Party started to infiltrate the Shanghai industry. Political censorship by the nationalist government was strict; but, particularly at Mingxing where the prominent writer and director Xia Yan was employed, the Left's influence was strongly felt. *Street Angel* (1937, director Yuan Muzhi) is perhaps the most impressive of several films

250

set among the city's poor; the interference of the censors was avoided by the incorporation of only oblique references to contemporary political events. Fired from Mingxing in 1934, Xia Yan joined Lianhua, and after 1936 that company also produced features which were politically aligned with the Left.

After the war Lianhua was started up again by a group of left-wing artists who continued to challenge the dictates of the Kuomintang, now involved in civil war with the Communists. The two-part *The Spring River Flows East* (1947, directors Cai Chusheng and Zheng Junli) is a chronicle of recent history centred on the moral downfall of its anti-hero. In the immediate aftermath of the Communist victory in 1949, the studio — now reorganised as the Kunlun Film Company — produced *Crows and Sparrows* (directed by Zheng Junli), an anti-Kuomintang tale set in Shanghai. The five independent studios allowed to continue production after the Liberation were absorbed into the new state film industry in 1952-3, after several independent productions were pronounced 'ideologically dubious'. The Beijing Film Studio's *Dragon Beard Ditch* (1952, director Xian Qun) is typical of the time, using an approved play to show the state of things before and after the Liberation. In the first half of the film, storms hang over a squalid slum; in the second, sunshine beams down on a sparkling courtyard.

The 'Hundred Flowers' campaign of 1956-7 (which was soon to be reversed by the anti-rightist campaign in the summer of 1957) encouraged a number of older film-makers to re-enter the cinema. The veteran Shen Fu, for example, made a biographical feature about the father of Chinese herbal medicine, *Li Shizen, The Great Pharmacologist* (1956). At the same time regional film studios were established; there were twelve in operation at the start of the Cultural Revolution in 1965. Production levels were forced up in the 'Great Leap Forward' campaign of 1958-9, but quality suffered. In the early 1960s the 'ultra-leftists' gained power within the industry, before the Cultural Revolution closed down film production entirely. A handful of 'model revolutionary works', like *Taking Tiger Mountain by Strategy* (1970), were recorded on film between 1970 and 1976; but the industry was decimated, and the slow process of reconstruction only began in 1977 after the 'Gang of Four' had been ousted.

Li Shizen, The Great Pharmacologist

In the mid-1980s films by directors recently graduated from the Beijing Film Academy have been widely seen outside China. They include Chen Kaige's stunningly photographed *Yellow Earth* (1985), made at the Xi'an Studios, as were Kaige's military drama *The Big Parade* (1985), and Huang Jianxin's gentle satire of office life, *The Black Cannon Incident* (1985). The West has only just begun its acquaintance with the old and the new Chinese cinema, but there is clearly both a rich tradition and the work of a vital modern industry waiting to be explored.

Chen Kaige's Yellow Earth

The Indian industry

The first film show in India, at Watson's Hotel in Bombay, was organised in July 1896. As elsewhere in the world it was given by a Lumière representative, and was followed within months by presentations by Vitagraph and other competitors. Domestic production by enthusiastic individuals began soon afterwards. H. S. Bhatvadekar filmed a wrestling match in Bombay in 1897, and before the turn of the century Hiralal Sen in Calcutta was photographing scenes from the theatre. These first Indian films were shown in tents or in the open air by itinerant projectionists travelling by bullock cart.

The first Indian feature was produced by Dadasaheb Phalke. After a trip to England to buy equipment, he embarked on *Raja Harischandra* (1913), which he based on the ancient folk epic *The Mahabharata,* and which was such a success that Phalke was soon able to set up a prosperous studio. Over the next two decades he made a hundred films, many of which extended the mythological genre. Other prominent directors who began their careers during the silent era were Dhiren Ganguly, who specialised in lively comedies, and Debaki Bose. In the 1920s the social dramas of Chandulal Shah, like *Gun Sundari* (*Why Husbands Go Astray*) and *Typist Girl* (both 1925), also made a considerable impact.

During and after the First World War, however, Hollywood began to penetrate the Indian market. Universal set up a distribution agency in 1916, and was soon profiting from the many American features which, because their costs had usually been covered in the home market, could be made available to exhibitors at a price far below the budget of a new Indian production. By 1927 some 85 per cent of feature releases came from abroad, most of them from Hollywood.

As in certain European countries, the coming of sound acted to restrict imports and provided an important stimulus to domestic production. The first Indian talkie, *Alam Ara* (1931), was hugely successful, and most of its many imitators proved equally profitable. In part this was because the country's increasing industrialisation was creating new audiences among the growing urban population. Unlike elsewhere, however, the Indian sound film was restricted to just one genre – the musical drama with set-piece songs and lavish dances. These musicals drew on the two thousand-year-old tradition of Sanskrit theatre, which had been enjoying a popular renaissance. But they were also successful because they transcended, if to a limited degree, the linguistic fragmentation of the sub-continent. With production centred in Bombay, these Hindi films have continued to find vast audiences across the whole of India. Nonetheless, other regional centres were and are active, shooting films in Bengali, Marathi, Tamil, Malayalam and other languages.

Domestic production expanded rapidly in the 1930s, led by companies like Prabhat, whose most prominent director was V. Shantaram, and New Theatres, who employed both Dhiren Ganguly and Debaki Bose. Prince P. C. Barua was another director associated with New Theatres, and his films like *Devdas* (1935) and *Adhikar* (1938) are striking social melodramas. The avowed commercial aspirations of these films, and of the thousands which have followed, have posed problems for critics seeking to assess them by

Raja Harischandra, *the first Indian feature film*

criteria deemed appropriate for other cinemas, and the commercial Indian cinema is frequently dismissed as escapist. But such a view refuses the rich pleasures which many of these films offer, and the multi-layered relationships established with them by the huge audiences they attract.

The Second World War stimulated further industrialisation and heightened the demands for political autonomy. The war also made fortunes for a number of unscrupulous businessmen, and the film industry was flooded with cash looking for a quick return. The relatively stable, studio-based system of the 1930s was overturned, and independent productions built round increasingly expensive stars became the norm. The colonial government, however, exercised significant control by its allocations of film stock, which was in short supply. Companies had to agree to make films to aid the war effort, even though such productions often proved unpopular at the box office. The most interesting of these films was *The Journey of Dr Kotnis* (1946), about Indian doctors serving in China during the Japanese invasion. It was shot from a script by the journalist K. A. Abbas, who was to play an important role in the post-Independence cinema.

In the years following Partition and Independence, films continued to draw audiences with ever more lavish production values. S. S. Vasan's *Chandraleka* (1948) was the most expensive Indian feature to date, and was important in consolidating the South Indian industry. Mehboob Khan's *Aan* (1952) and *Mother India* (1957) are other well-known spectaculars. But a number of other films, like Abbas' *Children of the Earth* (1949) and *Munna* (1954) and Raj Kapoor's *Awara* (1951) and *Shri 420* (1955), both co-written by Abbas, exhibited a new social concern. This was also notable in the work of the Bombay directors Bimal Roy and Guru Dutt. Sentiment, and song and dance, were now often combined with realist elements which reflected the considerable social tensions of the time.

Mehboob Khan's Mother India

A comparable and roughly contemporaneous injection of realism can be recognised in other non-Western cinemas. The influence of Italian neo-realism is often cited, although this was in no sense the only factor involved. Nonetheless, the feature which established Indian films in art cinemas abroad, *Pather Panchali* (1954), can be traced directly to this source. Its director Satyajit Ray has acknowledged the impact of seeing *Bicycle Thieves* in London, and has recalled that he was 'pleasantly surprised to discover that one could work exclusively in exterior settings, with non-professional actors, and I thought that what one could do in Italy, one could do in Bengal as well, in spite of the difficulties of sound recording.'

Ray came from a family steeped in the Bengali culture of his native Calcutta. But he also responded to Western ideas, and his film-making career has combined both traditions. The minimal budget for *Pather Panchali* – the first of the 'Apu' trilogy which traces the experiences of a man from rural childhood to marriage and life as an aspiring writer in the big city – was scraped together over two years; and a production without songs or stars met with little enthusiasm from Indian distributors. But after a success-

Shyam Benegal's Junoon, *with Shashi Kapoor*

ful screening in New York, the film was well received at the 1956 Cannes festival. Ray has continued to work on the margins of the Indian film industry, and with one or two exceptions his films – social dramas, political

Satyajit Ray's Charulata

fables, even fantasies for children – have been better appreciated abroad than in India itself. His work is impressive for the manner in which it reflects grand themes within the compass of intimate relationships, for its understatement and its sympathy, best evidenced perhaps in his masterpiece *Charulata* (1964), a delicate study of a woman caught in an emotional triangle in the stultifying atmosphere of Victorian Bengal; or in *Days and Nights in the Forest* (1969), in which a quartet of young men discover some revealing truths about themselves during a holiday in the country.

Two other Bengali directors have also worked mostly on the fringes of the commercial mainstream. Ritwik Ghatak's films, like *The Hidden Star* (1960), were inspired by his Marxist convictions, often dealing with the scars of Partition. Mrinal

Sen, also a Marxist, has combined formal experimentation with neo-realism in films like *Bhuvan Shome* (1969), *And Quiet Rolls the Dawn* (1979) and *Genesis* (1986). Sen's uncompromisingly committed films offer a trenchant analysis of power relations and the potential for change.

Shyam Benegal is another film-maker whose work reflects a concern for social and political change. His films often focus on the role of women in Indian society, as in his debut *Ankur* (*The Seedling*, 1974), about a rural servant girl; or in *The Role* (1979), which focuses on a film actress to reveal how women have traditionally been treated in the Indian cinema. Other notable film-makers of what has been loosely called the Indian 'new wave' include Mani Kaul (*In Two Minds*, 1974); M. S. Sathyu, whose *Hot Winds* (1973) is a clear-eyed view of Hindu-Muslim relations in the violent aftermath of Partition; Girish Karnad (*The Forest*, 1973), who works in the state of Karnataka; and the Keralan G. Aravindan (*The Circus Tent*, 1978). These are merely some of the new generation of film-makers who have brought to contemporary Indian cinema its rich diversity of theme and style.

Although these regional cinemas are now well established, Bombay's output of Hindi musicals is still the mainstay of the commercial industry. Films like Benegal's *Junoon* (1979), with superstar Shashi Kapoor, and Karnad's *Utsav* (1985) have attempted to integrate elements of the New Indian Cinema into productions aimed at a popular audience. But it is the traditional formulas that retain their appeal. The national market is still one of the few in the world large enough to sustain the domestic industry, particularly since television in India – although beginning to make inroads – does not yet provide serious competition.

Cinemas of South-east Asia

The historical details remain hazy, but silent film production is recorded in both Burma and Thailand. Both countries have sustained industries ever since, although few of their products have reached the West. Most of the output is for a mass audience. Among veteran figures of the Thai cinema the director Vichit Kounavudhi is particularly admired, especially for *The Mountain People* (1980) and *Son of the North-East* (1982). A younger film-maker, Cherd Songsri, has had popular and critical successes with *The Scar* (1978) and *The Gem from the Deep* (1987).

Rather better known in the West is the cinema of the Philippines, in particular the work of Lino Brocka. The history of the Philippine industry dates from the feature *A Girl from the Country*, made in 1919; and by the end of the 1930s at least five major companies were turning out comedies, musicals and melodramas. After the Japanese occupation there was a vogue for lavish spectaculars, like Manuel Conde's *Genghis Khan* (1950). Work from the 1960s and early 1970s is invariably dismissed as escapist, although like much Asian cinema it awaits further exploration.

A new wave of Philippine cinema is dated from 1976, with the release of features by Ishmael Bernal, Eddie Romero, Mike de Leon and Lino Brocka. Romero's *This is the Way We Were Then, How Are You Now?* (1982) is a historical comedy, tracing the adventures of a naive peasant through the early years of the century. Brocka's work is often urgently contemporary, made within the mainstream industry but developing a critique both of the Marcos government and of exploitation. *Manila* (1975) is a melodrama which exposes the slums of the Philippine capital. *Bayan Ko: My Own Country* (1984) is about a worker forced into crime.

Lino Brocka's Manila

Since the Second World War Hong Kong has supported a thriving film industry, which around 1960 was producing some 300 films each year. Today the figure is around half that, although cinema is still enormously popular. Both the Cathay company and the Shaw Brothers organisation, which dominated production in the 1950s and 1960s, were linked to large cinema chains throughout Singapore and Malaya. A third company, Golden Harvest, was founded in 1970 and achieved notoriety in the West for its cycle of Bruce Lee martial arts films. Such films have dominated Hong Kong cinema over the years. Many of them are mediocre, but the dazzling epics of the director King Hu stand out. Born in Peking, Hu has worked in both Hong Kong and Korea since he was stranded in the colony when the borders with China were closed. *A Touch of Zen* (1968) is a remarkable visual experience, combining choreographed acrobatics and astounding cinematography. *The Fate of Lee Khan* (1973) and *The Valiant Ones* (1974) are equally bravura action movies which also relish their striking moments of grace.

Since the mid-1970s, as the fortunes of the three large production companies in Hong Kong have declined, many smaller independents have entered the market. Working with directors who cut their teeth on innovative television dramas, these companies have sustained a lively 'new wave'.

King Hu's A Touch of Zen

Among the best known of these films are Allen Fong's *Father and Son* (1980), a sympathetically observed drama of generational conflict; and Ann Hui's controversial *Boat People* (1982), which presents a photo-journalist's view of the Communist takeover of South Vietnam.

Latin America

In the years after the First World War, Hollywood sought the same dominance of South American markets that it was achieving elsewhere. Brazil had witnessed a flowering of local production before 1911, but distributors and exhibitors throughout Latin America relied mostly on European suppliers. As the war caused increasing disruption, and as the United States government encouraged film companies to export more aggressively to the South, the influence of North American companies was rapidly extended. In 1920 one New York exporter estimated that 95 per cent of screen time in South America was occupied by American films. Mexico attempted to resist the invasion, and in 1922 the government there banned films from any foreign company that had made movies portraying Mexicans in an offensive manner.

The economic colonialism of South by North has continued to this day. Until well after the Second World War, Hollywood's influence prevented the emergence of viable domestic industries. The exceptions were in the larger countries like Mexico, Brazil and Argentina, where the home market was large enough to make possible a return on low-budget domestic productions, and where investment monies were available to cover the costs of introducing sound. Colonialism of the imagination has continued as well. Racist stereotypes of Mexicans and other Latin peoples have been the villains in countless thrillers and Westerns. Brazil and Argentina have provided the 'exotic' but often threatening backdrops for many more films. And Hollywood's musicals and comedies were endlessly imitated by Latin American producers endeavouring to compete with the popular imports. The New Latin American Cinema, which took root in the mid-1950s, was an explicit challenge to both economic and imaginative colonialism.

Mexico, Argentina and Brazil each supported a significant silent cinema industry, and sound consolidated the production base in each of these countries. But only in Mexico did government support (introduced in 1934) and a quota system (forcing each cinema to show one Mexican film each year) underpin the high level of domestic production. The melodramas of director Emilio Fernandez are particularly well regarded from this period. And from 1946 Luis Buñuel found a congenial home in the industry, for which he made twenty-one films including *Los Olvidados* (1950), *Nazarin* (1958) and *The Exterminating Angel* (1962).

Buñuel in Mexico: The Exterminating Angel

Both in Brazil, which had supported the most extensive silent cinema in Latin America, and in Argentina the post-war years offered some opportunities for film-makers to make self-consciously artistic dramas, like Leopoldo Torre Nilsson's *The House of the Angel* (1957). In Brazil too the musical

256

chanchadas found commercial success from the 1930s. But until the mid-1950s there were no signs of a cinema about and for the majority of the people. This period, however, saw the emergence of a militant nationalism throughout the continent, and since then the New Latin American Cinema has been intimately entwined with changes of political fortune. The Chilean cinema, for example, flourished under the brief democratic regime of Allende. But as repressive dictatorships took control in several countries during the 1970s, much of the most creative work came to an end. Now the political struggles in Nicaragua and El Salvador are reflected in vigorous film and video cultures. And with the cautious moves in the mid-1980s towards broader democracy in Argentina, Brazil and Uruguay, film-makers have engaged with a new and genuinely popular cinema.

In the early 1950s Fernando Birri was one of several aspirant film-makers from Latin America who studied at the Centro Sperimentale film school in Rome. In Italian neo-realism Birri and his colleagues recognised the potential of a cinema which on slender resources could represent the 'invisible' poor and oppressed. After the overthrow of Perón in 1955, Birri returned to his native Argentina to found the Documentary Film School of Sante Fe. Believing that the first step to be taken by an aspiring national film industry is to 'document national reality', he made documentaries like *Tire Dié* (1959), which showed the living conditions of shanty town dwellers, and in 1961 the remarkable neo-realist feature *Los Inundados,* a comedy about bureaucratic reactions to the flooding of a squatter settlement. But after the imposition of a military regime in 1963, Birri had to leave Argentina and since then he has worked mainly in Italy and Cuba.

Fernando Birri's Los Inundados

Birri's documentary initiatives were echoed by film-makers like Mario Handler and Ugo Ulive in Uruguay, who combined the techniques of *cinéma vérité* with an agitational impetus. In Colombia, Jorge Silva and Marta Rodriguez made a series of sociological documentaries about unskilled workers and peasants. And throughout the 1960s the Cuban director Santiago Alvarez assembled a number of polemical film documents, including *Hanoi Tuesday 13th* (1967) and *LBJ* (1968). But perhaps one of the most impressive documentary projects from Latin America is the three-part *The Battle of Chile* (1973-9), made by Patricio Guzmán and a team known as Equipo Tercer Año. In the years leading up to Allende's election in 1970, Chilean cinema had begun to produce a range of remarkable work, including *The Jackal of Nahueltoro* (1968), a powerful reconstruction of a notorious murder made by Miguel Littin. Recognising the import of the events they were living through, Guzmán and his colleagues began to document political and social events throughout what turned out to be the final year of the Allende government. The result, which was edited in Cuba over the next six years, is a unique achievement, integrating rigorous political analysis with a sweeping chronicle of social transformation.

The Battle of Chile

Documentary and neo-realism were two influences on what came to be known as 'Cinema Nôvo' in Brazil in the early 1960s. In *Vidas Secas* (1963)

Glauber Rocha's Antonio das Mortes

257

Nelson Pereira dos Santos produced a powerful realist drama, which was soon followed by remarkable features from Glauber Rocha, Carlos Diegues and Ruy Guerra. Rocha's films, like *Black God, White Devil* (1963), *Terra em Transe* (1967) and *Antonio das Mortes* (1969), assimilate many influences, including the French new wave, mysticism and popular theatre. Allegorical fables of repression and revolt, these are films of startling imagery and often operatic intensity. Ruy Guerra's films follow a similar path, from the agonised picture of oppression in *The Guns* (1964) to the florid, violent allegory of *The Gods and the Dead* (1970). Increasing censorship and political repression within Brazil, however, forced both Rocha and Guerra into exile, and the coherent force of Cinema Nôvo was dispersed.

In Bolivia meanwhile Jorge Sanjines and others were also working for a new national cinema. With the Ukamau group, Sanjines attempted to create a cinema of mass participation, directly addressed to furthering liberation struggles. In *Blood of the Condor* (1969) and *The Courage of the People* (1971) Andean peasants re-enact their experiences of exploitation, in the former case resisting the sterilisation policies of the US Peace Corps, and in the latter reconstructing a massacre of tin miners in 1967. But after 1971 Sanjines too became an exile from his own country.

In 1963 the Argentine directors Fernando Solanas and Octavio Getino wrote 'Towards a Third Cinema', a manifesto in which they called for a film-making practice which was neither that of Hollywood nor the 'authors' cinema' which had developed in Argentina and elsewhere after the Second World War, but a cinema which 'attempts to intervene' in a political situation and which invites its audience to be an active participant rather than a passive spectator. This new practice was exemplified by their film *The Hour of the Furnaces* (1966), a dynamic collage of Argentinian history which draws together newsreels, slogans, documentation and individual testimony, and which Solanas and Getino described as 'an act, before being a film: an act of liberation'. The film was widely shown, often clandestinely.

Another attempt to create such a 'third cinema' can be observed in post-Revolution Cuba, whose film industry is one of the most developed in Latin America. Prior to the overthrow of Batista in 1959, the domestic industry had produced some unremarkable commercial features, but for Castro and the new regime the cinema was of fundamental importance. The Cuban Institute of Film Art and Industry (ICAIC) was immediately established, and the task begun of building both a production base and audiences. Cuba had long been used as a kind of testing ground by entertainment companies from the United States interested in exploiting markets to the South. The sophisticated understanding of the cinema which this had fostered was to result in a remarkable programme of writing and production.

In 1955 Tomas Gutiérrez Alea and Julio García Espinosa had collaborated on the clandestinely shot, neo-realist *The Charcoal Worker*, which had been suppressed after its first showing. ICAIC's debut feature was *Historias de la revolución* (1960), directed by Alea and also strongly influenced by neo-realism. In his subsequent work Alea has explored a more varied cinematic vocabulary. In *Memories of Underdevelopment* (1968) a writer confronts the meanings of the Revolution and his ambivalent place within it. *The Last Supper* (1976) is an allegory cast in the form of a black comedy, set just after the Haitian revolution in 1795.

The films of Humberto Solás, in particular his *Lucía* (1968), also combine realist conventions with formal experiment. The three episodes of *Lucía* are set in three different historical times, corresponding to the colonial period, neocolonialism and the Revolution. The lessons for today are clear, as they are in a number of other films set in the Cuban past, like Manuel Octavio Gómez's *The First Machete Charge* (1969) or the same director's *Days of Water* (1971), a baroque account of the manipulation of religious hysteria during the 1930s. The Cuban cinema has produced fewer films which directly engage with contemporary questions. Sara Gómez's *One Way or Another* (1974) is a striking exception, not least in its confronting of the patriarchal nature of Cuban society. Another is Pastor Vega's controversial *Portrait of Teresa* (1979), which also offers a feminist perspective.

Accompanying this surge of film-making in Cuba has been a vigorous debate about the role of cinema, an influential contribution to which was a

Humberto Solás' Lucía

call by Julio García Espinosa for an 'imperfect cinema'. Espinosa, who took over as head of ICAIC in 1981, argued that emerging cinemas should not necessarily aim for technical perfection. The surface of a Hollywood-style feature was a way of prompting audiences towards passive consumption of films. A revolutionary cinema should be seen as 'a way of learning', and should engage the viewer in an active dialogue.

In recent years the film industries in both Brazil and Mexico have enjoyed a significant amount of state support, facilitating active production programmes but also imposing a degree of political orthodoxy. In Brazil, directors like Carlos Diegues and Nelson Pereira dos Santos, working with the state film agency Embrafilme, have endeavoured to work with song, dance and spectacle to create a new popular cinema. Dos Santos' *A Estrada da Vida* (1980), for example, is a comedy featuring two well-known singers which also deals with the problems faced by rural peasants entering an urban culture. Ruy Guerra has also sought an aesthetic which is very different from that of 'Cinema Nôvo'. His *Malandro* (1985) is a musical which reflects his conviction that dance and music – as strong cultural components for Latin America – should be integrated into the work of film-makers.

State support in Brazil, at least until the military dictatorship was banished in 1984, entailed significant restrictions on the subjects that could be tackled. Film-makers like Carlos Reichenbach, however, used the popular genre of *porno-chanchadas* (soft-core erotic comedies) to explore political issues in ways which would not have been permitted in more 'serious' features. Such an intriguing option has not been open to directors from other Latin American countries, and many have had to work in exile. Of the most prominent Chileans, for example, Raul Ruiz has been based in France and Miguel Littin has worked in Mexico and Spain, although he entered Chile clandestinely in 1985 to film *General Statement on Chile.* In Bolivia, even under the extreme military repression, film-makers secretly used Super 8 equipment, and the somewhat tentative restoration of civilian rule has allowed Jorge Sanjines to begin working there again. His documentary *The Banners of Dawn* (1984) chronicles events in the country during 1983.

In Nicaragua and El Salvador, film and video are making major contributions to the political struggles there. An internal production like *El Salvador – The People Will Win* (1980) is an important counter to much of the news and current affairs coverage seen outside the country. And while there was next to no tradition of production in Nicaragua the Sandanist National Liberation Front set up a national Film Institute in 1979, which has made documentaries as well as the feature *Alsino and the Condor* (1982), directed by Miguel Littin.

One other significant aspect of Latin American cinema today is the emergence of women film-makers like Maria Luisa Bemberg and Suzana Amaral. Bemberg's *Camila* (1984) and *Miss Mary* (1986), both made in her native Argentina, explore the links between sexuality and political control. Like these two features, Suzana Amaral's *Hour of the Star* (1985), made in Brazil, has been seen widely abroad. A sympathetic portrait of the fantasies of a poor young girl in the big city, the film has an innocence, yet also a political strength, removed from the histrionics of some Cinema Nôvo films.

Africa
African film-making encompasses a number of different traditions and identities. In the Arab world the most prominent industry is that of Egypt, which developed in the 1920s and which in the pre-war years reflected the growing national identity. Many of the earliest productions were colourful romances, melodramas and musicals; and a thriving commercial industry is today producing some forty features a year.

Kemal Selim's *The Will* (1939) is seen as the Egyptian cinema's first attempt to tackle social concerns, and in the 1950s it was the ideas of neo-realism that motivated the important films of Salah Abu Seif and Youssef Chahine. Chahine's *Cairo Station* (1958), centred on a crippled newspaper seller, depicts the grim world of a depressed underclass. His subsequent work reveals a broad range of approaches, and includes a dense, allegorical study of schizophrenia, *The Choice* (1970), and a critical analysis of the 1967 war with Israel, *The Sparrow* (1973). In the 1960s the Egyptian state began to support certain productions, including Abu Seif's *The 68 Trial*

(1968) and Chahine's rural epic *The Land* (1969). A first feature by Shadi Abdel-Salam, *The Night of Counting the Years* (1969), which examines the traces of the British Imperial presence, made an international impact. Few other recent productions, however, apart from Chahine's autobiographical reflections *Alexandria . . . Why?* (1978) and *An Egyptian Story* (1982) have been seen widely outside the Arab world.

Cinema in Egypt: The Night of Counting the Years

In the 1960s a number of Egyptian producers contributed to the establishment of a commercial industry in Lebanon. While this was largely curtailed by the civil war, a handful of interesting documentaries have been made in the past decade, including Georges Chamchoum's *Lebanon . . . Why?* (1979) and Heiny Srour's *Leila and the Wolves* (1984). Elsewhere Syria, Iraq and Kuwait have supported some domestic feature production, as have Tunisia and Morocco in the Arab West. Here, however, it is Algeria that has to date developed the most distinctive cinema. The years after independence saw co-production involvement in Gillo Pontecorvo's tribute to the resistance movement *The Battle of Algiers* (1966), and in Visconti's version of *The Stranger* (1968) after Albert Camus. In the 1970s Algerian film-makers investigated the problems of their country in features like Mohamed Bousamari's *The Charcoal Burner* (1972) and Mohamed Lakhdar-Hamina's *Years of the Brazier* (1975). Merzak Allouache (*Omar Gatlato*, 1977) is another talented Algerian director.

While this domestic production is clearly significant, cinema screens in the Arab world and throughout black Africa are still mostly occupied by Hollywood movies or by the commercial output of India and Hong Kong. Hollywood made a conscious expansion into Africa during the 1960s, creating the American Motion Picture Export Company (Africa) in 1961 to co-ordinate activities in seven of the 'anglophone' countries which were achieving their independence from Britain. And until recently the circuits in the 'francophone' countries were controlled by a French distribution duopoly, which denied all access to African films. So while it is important to recognise the differences within black African cinema, a powerful cultural colonialism remains a problem common to all those seeking to create distinctive national cinemas.

Souleymane Cissé's Brightness

Distribution is still a major difficulty. In 1981 CDIC was formed as a distribution agency promoting African cinema in fourteen francophone

261

countries, but it has not proved effective either in building new audiences or in generating revenue. Production resources remain scarce, and attitudes to the one scheme of extensive foreign funding were equivocal. This was set up in 1963 by the Ministry of Co-operation in France, and involved the advance purchase of non-commercial distribution rights for a sum usually significant enough to complete production. Over a hundred films were supported in this way, but the scheme was of little help in finding African audiences and protests at its implicit paternalism led to its being wound up in 1980.

In the anglophone nations, such as Kenya and Ghana, the British legacy was the documentary, and film production has to date been largely confined to educational shorts. The situation in Nigeria is similar, although here the director Ola Balogun has made features, including filmed versions of theatre works like the Yoruba drama *Ajani ogun* (1975) and *Aiye* (1980). Production and distribution remain at an early stage of development.

It is in the former French colonies that the most vigorous cinema in black Africa has been produced. A group of exiles under the supervision of Paulin Soumanou Vieyra made the first black African film, *Afrique sur Seine.* Shot in Paris in 1955, it was followed by other productions by black film-makers who had studied at the Paris film school IDHEC. Then in 1963, in Senegal, Ousmane Sembene completed his short feature *Borom sarret* (1963), a simple drama about a cart driver in Dakar, which is generally regarded as the beginning of black African cinema. Sembene had studied film-making on a scholarship in Russia, and in his subsequent work he has distanced himself from French influences. His features, beginning with *The Money Order* (1968), were made without subsidy and in the Wolof language, although he also produced French-language versions. *Emitai* (1972) looks at resistance against the French during the Second World War, and *Xala* (1974) is a satire about black politicians and businessmen working in complicity with neo-colonialism. Its comment was pointed enough to be subjected to censorship cuts before it was shown in Senegal. *Ceddo* (1977) is more complex, working with allegory, slipping through historical time and dealing with the slave trade, European oppression, Catholicism and Islam.

Another film-maker who studied in Moscow is Souleymane Cissé from Mali. His *Baara* (1979) is about a hand-cart porter in Mali's capital and his encounters with all levels of society. *Finye* (1982) introduces elements of myth into its contemporary story of students protesting against a corrupt university system. *Brightness* (1987) is a mesmeric, stunningly photographed account of the rivalry between two tribal magicians. These film-makers have gradually sought to break away from Western narrative conventions. Another African film-maker, Med Hondo from Mauretania, rejects them entirely. *Soleil 0* (1970) draws on Hondo's work in the theatre in France, but pulls together documentary, direct address, symbolism, fantasy and much else in an explosive assault on neo-colonialism. *West Indies* (1979) is equally unconventional, a chronicle of the slave trade done as a dance drama filmed on a single set.

262

The Senegalese Safi Faye is one of the very few African women directors. Her documentaries – *Letters from a Village* (1976) and *Fad Jal* (1979) – are partly ethnographical, partly personal reflections on the village in which she grew up. The Ethiopian Haile Gerima's *Harvest – 3000 Years* (1976) also relates personal experience, the memories and songs of Gerima's father, to a wider canvas, its traditional story-telling techniques encompassing a smouldering protest against three thousand years of oppression.

Gerima's film has yet to be seen in his native country because of political censorship and the practical problems of distribution. These problems are multiplied throughout black Africa. Only when they are solved will the achievements of African cinema be recognised in the continent itself as a vital cultural force.

Further reading

Roy Armes, *Third World Film Making and the West*, Berkeley and Los Angeles: University of California Press, 1987.

Erik Barnouw and S. Krishnaswamy, *Indian Film*, Oxford: Oxford University Press, 2nd ed. 1980.

David Bordwell, *Ozu and the Poetics of Cinema*, London: BFI Publishing, 1988.

Noël Burch, *To the Distant Observer: Form and Meaning in the Japanese Cinema*, London: Scolar Press, 1979.

Julianne Burton (ed), *Cinema and Social Change in Latin America: Conversations with Filmmakers*, Austin: University of Texas Press, 1986.

Michael Chanan (ed), *Twenty-five Years of the New Latin American Cinema*, London: British Film Institute/Channel 4 Television, 1983.

———*The Cuban Image: Cinema and Cultural Politics in Cuba*, London: BFI Publishing, 1985.

John D. H. Downing (ed), *Film and Politics in the Third World*, New York: Praeger, 1987.

Teshome H. Gabriel, *Third Cinema in the Third World: The Aesthetics of Liberation*, Ann Arbor: UMI Research Press, 1982.

Randal Johnson and Robert Stam (eds), *Brazilian Cinema*, East Brunswick N. J.: Associated University Presses, 1982.

Jay Leyda, *Dianying: Electric Shadows – An Account of Films and the Film Audience in China*, Cambridge, Mass: MIT Press, 1972.

Angela Martin (ed), *BFI Dossier 6: African Films: The Context of Production*, London: British Film Institute, 1982.

Tony Rayns and Scott Meek, *BFI Dossier 3: Electric Shadows – 45 years of Chinese Cinema*, London: British Film Institute, 1980.

17
Video

An electronic television signal was first successfully recorded on magnetic tape in 1956. A decade later this new technology of videotape had been adopted by broadcast television around the world, and the Japanese company Sony had introduced a relatively cheap and flexible adaptation known as a 'portapak'. Ten years on, video was firmly established both as a new art form and as the foremost medium for social and political documentary. Sony and other companies had unveiled variants of the domestic video cassette recorder (VCR). By the mid-1980s the VCR was a familiar household accessory. Hollywood was recognising the potential of a new market, and an original form of the moving image – the 'music video' or 'video clip' – was making its mark on both television and the cinema. Even directors who had worked exclusively on film were beginning to recognise the potential of video as a creative medium.

Both the portapak and the domestic video recorder were hailed as technological advances which could democratise the moving image industry. Both have been used creatively in just this way, but in the late 1980s, with a video recorder in around half of Britain's households, by far the most popular uses are the screening of rented movies and the 'time-shifting' of broadcast television programmes. As before, the structures of the moving image industry have had to adapt to a new technology and new expectations. But, again as before, the industy has proved exceptionally adept at doing so, and in making the adaptation profitable.

The breakthrough
In April 1956 the Chicago Hilton was hosting the annual convention of the National Association of Broadcasters, the trade body of the American radio and television industries. Halfway through the first morning the engineer Charles Ginsburg blanked out the live picture on the closed circuit system and played scenes recorded minutes before. 'There must have been two or three minutes of excruciating silence,' he recalled, 'and then all hell broke loose. They were hollering and screaming and jumping out of their seats. It was a bombshell.'

Filmed images of an electronic screen were the basis of the Fernseh television system in the 1930s, and this idea had been further developed during the war. American reconnaissance planes were fitted with electronic cameras, which recorded images on film for subsequent analysis. Prior to 1956, broadcast images had either been live or electronic recordings known as kinescopes, which were simply films shot off a screen. As the networks had spread across the United States, and as television services had opened up overseas, kinescopes had become increasingly significant; but they remained an unsatisfactory solution to the problem of storing television images. The dramatic demonstration by Ginsburg and his employers, the Ampex Corporation, signalled a breakthrough of enormous potential.

Ginsburg and a small team had been working towards video recording for some four years, an objective also being pursued by other research initiatives, including one at RCA. Among Ginsburg's colleagues was Ray Dolby – later to find fame for his work with stereo sound and noise reduction – and together they conceived of up-ending the technique of recording audio. The basis of audio recording, in which a narrow magnetic tape passed across a fixed head, was being used in separate explorations by both RCA and the Bing Crosby Laboratories, where as early as November 1951 engineers had demonstrated crude video recording on tape. Ginsburg and Dolby built a rapidly revolving head which scanned a slower, two inch-wide tape. In this way they could record the 4 million cycles per second necessary to create a picture which the human eye would find satisfactory.

Just months after the Chicago demonstration the system was being used for broadcast programmes, the first being the relay to the West Coast of CBS' New York-produced *Douglas Edwards with the News*, on 30 November 1956. Despite high costs the process was eagerly embraced by television stations, and early in 1958 Associated-Rediffusion took delivery of the first Ampex recorders in Europe. The BBC, which had been experimenting with their own system, also began using the Ampex recorders.

At first videotape was used solely to record programmes produced live in the studio. Editing tape was almost impossible, and it was only in 1960 that the technology became available to allow a video recording to be cut together with a live signal. By 1963, however, tape could be edited, albeit laboriously, with an accuracy of one tenth of a second. Working for Granada Television, producer Denis Mitchell and director John McGrath made *The Entertainers* (1963), the first British video-tape documentary. But the technology's disadvantages were considerable, and editing remained difficult until the introduction of electronic systems in the late 1960s. The cameras and recorders were also cumbersome, permitting none of the flexibility offered by the new lightweight film cameras used by documentary film-makers like Richard Leacock and Don Pennebaker.

The portapak

Not only was early video technology awkward to operate, it was also, because of its cost, effectively restricted to broadcasters and large corporations. Recognising a potential market for video in training and education, and eager to break into the American consumer market, the Japanese electronics firm Sony developed a far simpler camera and recorder, the 'portapak', which stored black-and-white images on half-inch tape. Compared with broadcast standard television the quality of both picture and sound was crude, but it was well-suited for closed circuit use.

Image-making was now within reach of almost anybody. Previously, of course, independent film-makers had worked extensively with both 16mm and 8mm film equipment, but the video portapak was simple to use, needed little supplementary lighting and could be operated by an individual. The cost of a unit was relatively low; and, unlike film, tapes could be re-used. Direct playback also eliminated the need for a laboratory, synchronous sound was built in, and although editing possibilities were limited this very restriction was adopted as one element in what was soon a distinctive video aesthetic. At the same time, in the United States at least, there were other moves towards television becoming more available to a wider range of interests. New Federal Communications Commission rules in 1964 specified that all television sets would in future have to be capable of receiving both VHF and UHF signals. Groups could now set up new channels on local UHF broadcast wavebands. With the gradual introduction of cable television, within a decade numerous community groups were exploiting both distribution systems to show their portapak-produced work.

The portapak and its later variants were to be widely used in education and training, but they also stimulated two distinct, occasionally overlapping new traditions. One involved social and political initiatives, usually in documentary form and often addressed to a particular local problem. The other adopted the rather unsatisfactory label of video art, as a number of visual artists took up video as a medium to use alongside the more traditional means of painting, sculpture and photography. From the early experiments of these artists has developed a culture which has offered some of the most intriguing and startling images of the last twenty years.

Video art
Just as painters were drawn to film in the 1910s, so in the early 1960s a few visual artists began to explore the possibilities of television, and then video. In Cologne in 1959, Wolf Vostell mounted an exhibition of television sets which had been broken, daubed with paint, and even shot at with a gun, and in 1963 he recreated this show in New York. As his conception might suggest, video art's relationship with television has always been uneasy. Acceptance of television's centrality in our culture, together with a certain envy of its audience impact, has often been balanced by hostility towards its politics and aesthetics. But even before Vostell's first shows, at least two major figures were exploring many of what were to become video art's concerns from, as it were, the inside.

Neither Ernie Kovacs, a popular television comedian in the United States in the 1950s, nor Jean-Christophe Averty, who worked in France in the 1950s and 1960s, would have described himself as a video artist. They were entertainers, interested in reaching a broad popular audience. But they were both fascinated by the possibilities of breaking with the codes of broadcast television. As early as 1951 Kovacs was slyly exposing the mechanics of television production, with an edition of his NBC show *It's Time for Ernie* featuring whispered instructions from the camera operator. Over the next decade his anarchic tricks grew ever more sophisticated, and in 1957 he mounted *Eugene* (NBC), a 30-minute drama with sound effects and music but no dialogue in which gravity appears to have gone haywire. The visual comedy, often achieved by simple but imaginative camera tricks, is probably the closest the small screen has come to the art of Buster Keaton.

Jean-Christophe Averty began making jazz programmes for French television in the 1950s. But it was in his 1964 series *Les Raisins verts* that he first fully exploited the creative potential of electronic images. Marrying the surrealism of playwright Alfred Jarry with the idea of the screen as a page on which all manner of graphic effects could be achieved, Averty created an entirely original style. Adaptations of Cocteau, Jules Verne, Shakespeare and Lewis Carroll followed, but Averty's vision was only grudgingly supported. Ideas at the heart of his and Kovacs' work have surfaced again in, for example, the anarchic comedy series *Monty Python's Flying Circus* (BBC), in *Saturday Night Live* (NBC), and in the frenetic visual fantasy of *Pee-Wee Herman's Playhouse* (CBS); and a concern to explore the specific qualities of the medium also informs many of the strands of avant-garde video.

Monty Python's Flying Circus

Legend dates the history of video art from 1965, when the Korean artist Nam June Paik took delivery of one of the first Sony portapaks to arrive in the United States. Paik, who had trained as a musician, had visited Cologne in 1958 to work with the composers John Cage and Karlheinz Stockhausen, and they instilled in him an interest in technology and the teachings of Zen Buddhism. 'Happenings' and other multi-disciplinary art events of the time were another important influence, as were the ideas of the Fluxus group, described as 'a fusion of Spike Jones, gags, games, vaudeville, Cage and Duchamp', of which Paik became a central member. Recognising, along with other artists associated with Pop Art, the new significance of television, Paik had mounted an exhibition of televisions in 1963 in which the image on each of the sets was electronically distorted. Two years later he used the new portable camera to shoot, from a taxi, an impression of a papal visit to New York, and showed the result the same night in a club. 'As collage technique replaced oil paint,' he said, 'the cathode tube will replace the canvas.'

Even before Paik collected his portapak, however, there was an interest in the abstract possibilities of video at WGBH, the Boston public television station. The producer Fred Barzyk had been experimenting with visuals to accompany live music, and in 1964 he made five short tapes called *Jazz Images*, which featured the patterns of a toy kaleidoscope. Jazz was one important influence, as were composer John Cage's ideas about the creative possibilities of chance and serendipity. In 1969 Barzyk put together the first broadcast programme devoted to artists using video and television, *The Medium is the Medium*. Among those featured was Nam June Paik.

By the end of the 1960s Paik was recognised as video art's guru, a position which his constant inventiveness and gnomic utterances have retained for him to this day. At WGBH, with the Japanese artist Shuya Abe, Paik built the Paik-Abe video synthesiser, which could generate and transform electronic images in a quite new way. Among its first creations was a four-hour live show for WGBH called *Video Commune*. His other works have included a *TV Bra* for cellist Charlotte Moorman; *Television Garden* (1974), an installation of televisions and greenery; and two inter-continental live satellite broadcasts.

Many artists have used video as an extension of work in another medium. Bruce Nauman's tapes in the late 1960s, for example, paralleled his sculptural interests. Subsequently, artists have built installations in which screens and tapes are themselves used as sculptural elements. Vito Acconci, in tapes like *Theme Song* (1974), developed a form of personal address to the viewer, the quirky personal narratives of which are a form of performance poetry. And choreographers like Alwin Nikolais and Merce Cunningham have both conceived dances for videotape and integrated video cameras into live performances. Another response to the medium was the attempt to understand and isolate the technical and formal qualities specific to it. Much of this work can appear sterile, but a piece like Peter Campus' *Three Transitions* (1974) creates a visual poetry out of simple uses of video mixes and 'keying' effects.

William Wegman's tape with his dog Man Ray (right)

Both humour and music are extensively exploited, often to provide points of access to an audience unfamiliar with video art. William Wegman's simple sketches made with his dog Man Ray in the 1970s are among the most immediately appealing tapes of this kind. In one, the fuzzy half-inch image shows Man Ray and a canine friend undertaking what appears to be an elaborately rehearsed routine in which their heads twist and turn in perfect synchronisation, until it is revealed they are simply watching the out-of-frame movements of a tennis ball. Another tape features Wegman teaching Man Ray to spell.

Video artists at first generally avoided narrative, believing that the forms of cinema and television were simply too dominant. But as practitioners gained in confidence, attempts were made to challenge and deconstruct conventional narratives, and to create subversive and fragmented alternatives.

Video was also recognised by artists like Juan Downey as an appropriate form for the subtle treatment of aesthetics and philosophy.

Initially video-makers had to work with the simplest and cheapest technology, but in the late 1970s corporations like Sony recognised the value of allowing artists to experiment with the latest machines and effects. John Sanborn and Dean Winkler, for example, in tapes like *Luminare* (1985), push high-tech systems to their limits, in the process discovering their capabilities and restrictions for both engineers and potential clients.

Mainstream television continues to be video art's Big Brother, and many artists have sought ways of confronting it. Martha Rosler's influential tapes *A Budding Gourmet* (1974) and *Semiotics of the Kitchen* (1975) are just two examples of the appropriation of a television format — in this case cooking programmes — in the service of quite different ends. Dara Birnbaum's tapes of the late 1970s, like *Kiss the Girls* and *Wonderwoman*, cut together rapid, repeated fragments of network shows in an attempt to break open television conventions. Other strategies include Ilene Segalove's naive comic tales of the small screen's influence; and the powerful satire of Max Almy's *Perfect Leader* (1984), in which a political candidate is created by computer and moulded for his television appearances.

Among the most impressive personal video creations are the works of Bill Viola and Gary Hill. Viola's non-narrative tapes, in which sound is as important as image, seek to create new visual and aural languages by abstracting and juxtaposing elements caught on tape. *Chott el-Djerid (A Portrait in Light and Heat)* (1979), for example, is an intense record of snow-covered and desert landscapes, which is partly concerned with specific qualities of the electronically recorded images and sounds but which is also a kind of meditation. Gary Hill's tapes explore other aspects of verbal and visual languages, playing games with words, manipulating them to reveal the ways in which they construct our sense of the world.

In the 1980s, in both the United States and Europe, television has begun to recognise the potential of video art. In Britain, broadcasters have been cautious in their engagement with the medium. The first experiment was in 1971 when the artist David Hall made ten short pieces (on film) for Scottish Television, intended as interruptions in the schedule and programmed during the Edinburgh Festival. Since then there have been only a handful of similar projects, although Channel 4 supported the video opera *Perfect Lives* (1983), made by the American artists Robert Ashley and John Sanborn, and has commissioned several anthology programmes of video.

Television has also begun to exploit video art as a mine of new ideas and styles. The compilation series *Ghosts in the Machine* (1986, Channel 4) was carefully studied by graphic artists and advertising agencies looking for an original way to sell products. And the video technique known as 'scratch', which cut together, often to a music track, elements of broadcast television so as to give them a new meaning, was rapidly assimilated into commercials. As used in *Death Valley Days* (1985), scratch could offer a sharp

From the video opera Perfect Lives

269

critique of President Reagan's foreign policy, but within months the same idea was being used in television commercials to sell Brylcreem.

Social action

Alongside those who took video into the visual arts, another group of pioneers saw the potential of marrying the new technology with documentary and especially agitational film-making. One early initiative was made at the National Film Board of Canada, which financed *VTR St Jacques* in 1969. Part of the 'Challenge for Change' series, which endeavoured to 'promote citizen participation in the solution of social problems', *VTR St Jacques* encouraged citizens from the largely poor St Jacques district of Montreal to express their problems on videotape. Cameras and recorders were operated by members of the community, and the testimonies became the basis for discussion meetings and a way of convincing local officials of the need for action. Those involved found in the medium an effective political voice.

One of those involved in this project, George Stoney, went on to set up a video resource group called the Alternate Media Centre at New York University. Stoney saw the possibilities of using portapaks to document labour, housing and health disputes, and then air them on public access cable channels. Bypassing the traditional channels of communication, this strategy was to prove extremely effective in empowering individuals and groups often denied a voice by television and the other media. Broadcasters, however, were able to reject many such initiatives by pointing to the poor technical quality of the black-and-white images. But the technology was being steadily improved. Sony brought out its first colour portapak in 1973, low-budget and better quality systems using threequarter-inch tape began to be available, and other advances facilitated better sound recording and even greater flexibility.

The movement loosely described as the counter-culture soon recognised the possibilities of video, and the early 1970s saw the formation in the United States and elsewhere of independent groups who were interested in challenging the conventional forms of broadcast news and documentaries. Guerilla Television was one such collective. Another was the Downtown Community Television Centre in New York, set up in 1972 by Jon Alpert and Keiko Tsuno, who made a tape about the problems of taxi drivers which became an effective organising tool for their union. D C T V was soon

Making video documentary

swamped by the many people who wished to use their facilities and undertake training courses. Another successful group was Top Value Television, who in 1972 produced documentary accounts of that

270

year's Democratic and Republican conventions which were purchased for showing on local television. Two years later, using better equipment, they sold both *Lord of the Universe* and *Gerald Ford's America* to public television.

Video documentaries became increasingly sophisticated through the next decade, and by the early 1980s broadcast television was using video for a wide range of news reporting, current affairs and other factual programmes. In 1983, for example, Channel 4 Television screened *The Birth of the SDP*, a four-part series documenting the founding of a new political party in Britain. Shot entirely on threequarter-inch videotape, it was British television's first video documentary series, and demonstrated the medium's flexibility in this area. Numerous comparable projects have followed.

Within this rapid growth of video documentary production important strands of work have retained the oppositional imperatives which inspired the pioneers of the early 1970s. In 1977, for example, Alpert and Tsuno made *Health Care: Your Money or Your Life*, a powerful portrait of the inadequacies of a city hospital which was an implicit attack on government spending priorities. In the same year, in *The Police Tapes*, Alan and Susan Raymond documented the working lives of policemen in the South Bronx, in tapes which presented a quite different view from that which a network television documentary would have shown.

In Britain during the 1970s a number of community video groups were established with the intention of creating similar alternatives to broadcast television's presentation of — or silence about — social and political issues. Channel 4 Television, set up in 1981 with a brief to make programmes with and for those normally denied access to television, began to fund (along with other agencies) a number of these video and film-making projects. These groups, known as Workshops, produce tapes and films for both broadcast and other forms of distribution and exhibition. They work closely with trade unions, and with ethnic groups and other minorities.

In 1984-5, during the lengthy and often bitter miners' strike, several Workshops collaborated in the production and subsequent distribution of *The Miners' Campaign Videotapes*, ten 20-minute videos which put across the miners' viewpoint and examined the operations of the police and the media in relation to the strike. The tapes were widely seen at trade union and other meetings throughout the country and were an important corrective to mainstream television coverage. Extending the tradition of agitational newsreels from the 1930s, the tapes provided powerful evidence for the democratising potential of video technology.

Video in the home

As with radio, the American pioneer David Sarnoff was among the first to recognise the domestic potential of video technology. 'Magnetic tape recording of video signals,' he suggested in 1953, 'should make possible simple means by which a TV set owner can make recordings of television pictures in the home. And they can be "performed" over and over through

271

the television receiver just as a phonograph record is played at will.' Both Sony and Panasonic introduced cassette-based applications of this idea in 1969, although their systems were incompatible with each other, and with a number of other products which followed rapidly into this market. Eventually, the half-inch tape cassette emerged as the dominant format in the late 1970s, with the market split between the (again incompatible) systems of Sony's Betamax, introduced in 1975, and the video home system (VHS) created in 1976 by the Matsushita corporation's subsidiary, Japan Victor Company (JVC). VHS had an early advantage because it could record for up to two hours, compared with the Betamax system's one hour, and could thus tape the full length of a movie. In later models, however, the capabilities are comparable. Most other companies entering the market have adopted one or other of these systems, apart from Philips-Grundig, which has persevered with its largely unsuccessful V-2000 system.

Video in the home

1979 is generally seen as the turning point for the VCR home market. Sales of machines in the United States passed one million in that year, and by 1981 more than three million were being sold each year. In Europe, too, a remarkable rise in sales began in 1979, and continued throughout the early 1980s. 1979 was also the first year in which the major Hollywood corporations began to make their products widely available on cassettes for home use. This industry grew dramatically in the early 1980s, generating profits from both sales and rentals of pre-recorded tapes.

By 1985, revenue returned to distributors in the United States from home video sales and rentals was at a level comparable to that expected from cinema releases. In Britain in 1987 the video market was worth an estimated £500 million, several times that of the total for cinemas. Companies spend large sums on marketing the video releases of movies, and certain films have made significant profits as videos, despite being unenthusiastically received in cinemas. 1987 also saw the first advertisement on a video-cassette, when the video release version of the movie *Top Gun* was preceded by a commercial for Diet-Pepsi. The traditional dependence of home video on the cinema market has ended (although critical reaction to a cinema release is highly valued), and by 1986 the Chairman of Vestron Video, Austin Furst, could suggest that releasing films to cinemas was now ancillary to video.

Producing at home

In the earliest years of cinematography there was no distinction between amateur and professional equipment, although the British pioneer Birt Acres designed the first low-cost camera and projector for the general market in 1898. But it was not until the early 1920s that both the French company Pathé and Eastman Kodak introduced systems intended to appeal to a wide amateur market. Pathé's Pathé-Baby projector showed 9.5mm films, either shot by the owner on the accompanying camera or chosen from the range of commercial releases soon available for sale and hire in the new format. Eastman meanwhile had designed another new format, which was

272

16mm wide, and the 1930s saw keen competition between the two gauges. Both colour and sound were also available to the amateur at this time.

A viable 8mm system was first marketed by Eastman Kodak in 1932, with a camera which took a 25-feet roll of film that was 16mm wide but with twice the usual number of perforations. The film was run once through the camera, exposing images one quarter the size of a normal 16mm image; it was then reloaded and run through again, exposing images on the other half of the film. The two halves were split after processing and run end to end. 8mm systems became increasingly popular after the Second World War, and then in 1965 Eastman made a further innovation with its Super 8 package. The new format made a far more efficient use of the film strip, increasing the picture area by 50 per cent, and its convenient cartridge-loading meant that it soon dominated the amateur market. In the mid-1970s Polaroid even brought out an instant film for the 8mm market, but it was expensive, produced poor quality images, and was rapidly withdrawn.

During the 1970s companies sought the videotape equivalent of Super 8. Akai were one of the first into the market with a quarter-inch monochrome system in the late 1970s. Then in 1980 Sony introduced Video 8, a tape format which corresponds in size to 8mm film; and their 'camcorders' – a camera and a recorder in one lightweight unit – have become increasingly popular. Competing in the same market are a camcorder using a standard Beta cassette and a JVC system which records on to a standard VHS cassette. Many more weddings and holidays are being recorded than ever were on film, and both artists and documentary-makers are beginning to explore the potential of these systems. In 1987, for example, the French television channel Canal + screened a documentary about Shanghai, made on Video 8 by Régis Debray. Seen on a good television screen, the image quality was all but indistinguishable from professional systems. Video 8's ease of operation renders image-making as easy – in purely technical terms at least – as it has ever been in the history of the moving image.

Video and television

While video artists and documentary-makers have either chosen – or been forced – to set up new means of distribution and exhibition, others have initiated a parallel integration of previously distinct media. For more than a decade now, the potential of video has been explored in often startlingly innovative ways within the established structures of television and the cinema. In the younger medium most prestigious drama productions, for example, are still made on film. But there is a steadily growing tradition of mainstream video creativity which indicates that the achievements of video may soon begin to match those of film.

In British television, as elsewhere, video was initially used to record a programme produced live in a studio. Drama on videotape was a captured trace of what was essentially a stage production. But as the possibilities grew for editing the video image, and then manipulating it in other ways, a few

Innovative TV drama: And Did Those Feet? *(1965)*

directors started to break with this way of working and to create dramas which were neither studio theatricals nor unachieved attempts at movies. As early as 1965, in the B B C play *And Did Those Feet?*, the writer David Mercer and the director James MacTaggart were experimenting with a bold, fragmented style which combined studio drama with film inserts. MacTaggart's subsequent work included other non-naturalistic dramas, of which one of the most remarkable is his videotape adaptation of *Candide. The Chester Mystery Plays* (1976, B B C), directed by Piers Haggard, was a comparably ambitious version of a classic text, and was among the first television dramas to exploit the recently introduced potential of the electronic manipulation of images: highly stylised paintings and tapestries are used as backdrops before which the 14th-century dramas are acted out. And as new image-processing devices became available, other writers and directors were attracted by the creative potential of this new technology.

In *The Journal of Bridget Hitler* (1981, B B C), director Philip Saville created an elaborate 'electronic investigation' of a diary by the wife of Hitler's half-brother which alleges that the young Adolf visited Liverpool in 1912. *The Adventures of Frank* (1980, B B C), written and directed by John McGrath, uses video effects to relate a picaresque comedy of a young man's experiences in contemporary Britain. At the same time other directors were using improved studio cameras, single set-ups rather than multiple-camera shooting, and carefully planned lighting, to achieve a new precision in conventional video drama produced in the studio. Richard Eyre's production of *The Cherry Orchard* (B B C, 1981), from Trevor Griffiths' version of Chekhov's play, is one immaculate demonstration of this approach; another is the presentation of Büchner's *Danton's Death* (B B C, 1978), directed by Alan Clarke.

Television in the United States has produced little comparable work, but a number of European broadcasters have collaborated with prominent directors to produce bold, distinctive work on videotape. Rainer Werner Fassbinder's *Nora Helmer* (1973), for example, made for the West German regional station S R, is a visually striking videotape version of Ibsen's *A Doll's House*, in which the action is constantly veiled and obscured so as to suggest Nora's emotional imprisonment.

Film-makers and video

Television, in this case the Italian service R A I, also provided the finance for *The Oberwald Mystery* (1981), Michelangelo Antonioni's first involvement with video, which was transferred to 35mm film and released as a feature. For Antonioni the experience was liberating, especially in the possibilities it offered for the manipulation of colour, but he has not returned to the medium since. 'The electronic system is highly stimulating,' he said at the time. 'When you approach it, it seems like a game. They sit you in front of a control panel full of levers, and by moving them you can add or remove colour, intervene in the quality and the relations between the various tonalities. You can also obtain special effects that are impossible in normal film-making. Yet you soon realise it is not a game at all, but a new way of making films. Not television, but cinematography. A new way of finally using colour as a narrative, poetic, medium.'

One notable precedent for Antonioni's explorations was *OFFON*, an avant-garde work made in 1967 by Scott Bartlett and Tom DeWitt. Images shot on film were transferred to video, manipulated with colour processes and feedback, and then put back onto film. In the commercial cinema the first feature of electronic images was *Hamlet* (1963), a black-and-white kinescoped record of a stage production with Richard Burton, which more than covered its costs on its initial theatrical release. A second video feature, the rock show *T.A.M.I. (Teen Age Music Incorporated)*, was shown in 1966. And Frank Zappa later experimented with a tape-onto-film system for his concert movie *200 Motels*, which used video effects to create psychedelic images. A number of other movies since have been made in a similar way.

OFFON

In his *One from the Heart* (1982), Francis Coppola brought together video and film technology in a different way. Many directors had begun to use a video camera as a way of instantly evaluating shots and performances which they would not otherwise see until the next day's film rushes. Coppola used video to store storyboard drawings and rehearsal dialogue, so that he could roughly sketch out the film before going near the set. Sections of this 'rough cut' were later replaced with photographs and video recordings of rehearsals. Coppola, production designer Dean Tavoularis, cinematographer Vittorio Storaro and others could assess the film as it was coming together in a unique way. Editing was also facilitated by extensive use of video. Coppola claimed that this form of 'electronic cinema' led to considerable savings in production costs. But the film performed badly at the box office, Coppola was soon forced to sell his studio, and no prominent commercial director has been interested enough to explore the system further. Only in 1987, with the shooting of the first feature in a high-definition television system (see Chapter 19), has the idea of 'electronic cinema' taken another major step forward.

The film-maker who since the late 1970s has undertaken the most rigorous investigation of video is Jean-Luc Godard. In 1972, with Anne-Marie Miéville, he set up in Grenoble a production company called Sonimage, and began to explore the possibilities of video production. In 1975 Godard and Miéville made *Numéro Deux*, a controversial analysis of class and sexuality which is played out on two studio monitors. Two series of programmes for French television followed, *Sur et sous la communication* (1976) and *France/Tour/Détour/Deux/Enfants* (1978), both of which endeavour to stand apart from the conventions of the medium in an attempt to provide a better understanding of how it functions. Just after his feature *Passion* (1982), which is itself partly about the shooting of a television film, Godard made *Scénario du film Passion* (1982), a personal meditation on film and

275

Godard and Miéville's Numéro Deux

Music and film: In Lamplight Land, *made by George Pal in 1935*

video. He has continued to explore aspects of video in his subsequent work, which includes a thriller on videotape for French television, *Grandeur et décadence d'un petit commerce de cinéma d'après un roman* (1986). Supposedly an adaptation of a novel by James Hadley Chase, it is actually an original comedy about financing and producing features.

Music videos

The music video has proved to be one of the most ubiquitous forms of the moving image in the 1980s, although the idea of synchronising music and picture is as old as the cinema. Indeed even before Edison's phonograph, first shown in 1877, music halls presented songs accompanied with appropriate projected slides, and such entertainments continued to pull in audiences as supplementary attractions in nickelodeon programmes. Films of vaudeville acts and opera, accompanied by music and singing on a record, were popular from around 1900.

Among the film pioneers who wanted to do more than simply capture a live performance on film was the German animator Oskar Fischinger, who from 1921 made abstract films to accompany both jazz and classical music. Fischinger later emigrated to the United States, where he worked first for Paramount and then for Disney, for whom he designed the opening sequence of *Fantasia* (1940). Another animator who explored similar ideas was the Hungarian George Pal, who in Holland in the 1930s created a series of musical shorts extolling the virtues of Philips' electrical products. Pal also went to Hollywood, where he continued to make animated short films with jazz musicians like Duke Ellington and Woody Herman. (And today of course many music videos, despite their name, are still made on film.)

In the later 1940s in the United States musical shorts were made not only for the cinema but for visual jukeboxes marketed as Panoram Soundies. In return for a coin, a small rear-projection screen showed black-and-white film – sometimes of the performer, sometimes of a simple story – while the appropriate record played. The idea was revived in the 1960s by the French Scopitone system, which played colour films featuring popular performers. But visual jukeboxes were essentially of novelty value, and they did not reappear until around 1983 after the music video was firmly embedded in the culture.

Throughout the 1950s and 1960s rock music enjoyed uncertain relationships with both television and the cinema. As early as 1949 *Paul Whiteman's TV Teen Club* (ABC) was presenting popular music for young people, although its musical tastes were conservative. In Britain the BBC's *6.5 Special* (1957-8) and Associated Rediffusion's *Ready, Steady — Go!* (1963-6) put pop on television with a vigour more appropriate to its audience. *Ready, Steady — Go!* was produced by Jack Good, whose high-energy presentation of groups in what was clearly a television studio with a mess of cameras and cables was to prove influential for at least twenty years.

As music buying patterns changed, the presentation of live music became

276

more complex and ever more dependent on technology. Visual impact was important for certain groups, as is reflected in a concert movie like *Pink Floyd at Pompeii* (1971). Short promotional films continued to be made in the early 1970s, but they remained a sideline until 1975 and the clip for Queen's *Bohemian Rhapsody*, a visualisation with rather crude video effects, made by television director Bruce Gowers. The BBC's *Top of the Pops* played the spot twice and the record reached the Number One slot in the charts. Other record companies were immediately interested, and the show began to feature new music videos on a regular basis. *The Kenny Everett Video Show* (BBC), directed by David Mallet, increased interest in the clips by building elaborate video tricks around them.

Music video: David Bowie's Loving the Alien *(1985)*

Music videos have continued to offer inventive images, from the dazzling sequence of sight gags in The Cars' *You Might Think* (1984, directed by Jeff Stein) to the imaginative wizardry of *Rene and Georgette* (1984) and *Boy in the Bubble* (1986) from Paul Simon, or the boundless energy of Michael Jackson's *Beat It* (1983, directed by Bob Giraldi). Most music videos, however, are hackneyed concoctions of fantasy images, concerned simply to make an immediate visual impact. Their images are often misogynist, and they endlessly pillage cinema history.

In 1981 Warner Cable's Nickelodeon service was carrying a weekly programme of music videos called *Popclips*, and both the cable and music divisions of the corporate giant (Warner Communications was now merged with the American Express company) recognised the promotional potential of a cable television service, with stereo sound, running clips twenty-four hours a day. The service was called Music Television (MTV), and record companies were persuaded to allow their music videos to be played without fee. Gradually the music industry became convinced that the right clip could sell millions of records. In 1983 Sony released the first video 45s, and numerous music video shows began to appear on the networks and on other cable services.

Almost every aspect of the moving image industry felt the influence of music videos in the early 1980s. Commercials quickly adopted the rapid cutting style of the music clips, probably the most influential example being the Levis 501 campaign in Britain in 1985 whose glossily produced mini-narratives, backed by nostalgic soul music tracks from the 1960s, sold the jeans as never before. Many rock videos are made on film, and prominent directors have been attracted to the form, among them Lindsay Anderson, Nicolas Roeg, Ken Russell, Jonathan Demme and John Landis (who shot Michael Jackson's *Thriller* in 1985). Other directors who had made their name with music videos

Flashdance, *promoted by a rock video*

277

crossed over to feature film-making. And Universal's successful television series *Miami Vice*, with its stylish visuals and pounding soundtrack, is one example of the influence of the music video on mainstream television.

Flashdance (1983), made by former commercials director Adrian Lyne, was the first movie to be sold successfully by a rock video. The film's fantasy of a young dancer making the grade was ideally suited to be cut down into a three-minute clip. Repeated, free plays on MTV and elsewhere promoted both movie and record, and the marketing technique has been used frequently since. Rock scores, together with accompanying albums and singles, have become increasingly common elements of major Hollywood movies; and the cross-promotion of film, clip and record, together with book, video game, computer programme and much else, is a profitable enterprise for the large conglomerates which now own Hollywood. The rock video has been a key element in the increasing interconnectedness of the music, movie and television industries in the 1980s.

Further reading

Roy Armes, *On Video*. London: Routledge, 1988.
John Ellis, *Visible Fictions: Cinema, Television, Video*, London: Routledge & Kegan Paul, 1982.
John Hanhardt, *Nam June Paik*, New York: Whitney Museum of American Art, 1982.
Sara Hornbacher (ed), *Video: The Reflexive Medium*, a special issue of *Art Journal*, vol. 45, no. 3, Fall 1985.
Independent Media, the only regular British magazine concerned with video art and with community-based video practices.
Journal of Communication Inquiry, vol. 10, no. 1, Winter 1986 is devoted to essays on MTV.
E. Ann Kaplan, *Rocking Around the Clock: Music Television, Postmodernism & Consumer Culture*, London: Methuen, 1987.
David Kirk (ed), *25 years of Video Tape Recording*, Bracknell: 3M United Kingdom, 1981.
Andy Lipman, *Video: The State of the Art*, London: Channel Four, 1985.
OneTwoThreeFour, no. 5, Spring 1987, is a special issue on music video.
René Payant, *Video*, Montreal: Artextes, 1986.
Michael Shore, *The Rolling Stone Book of Rock Video*, London: Sidgwick & Jackson, 1985.
Graham Wade, *Street Video*, Leicester: Blackthorn Press, 1980.
————*Film, Video and Television: Market Forces, Fragmentation and Technological Advance*, London: Comedia, 1985.
Brian Winston and J. Keydel, *Working with Video*, London: Pelham Books, 1987.

18
The Moving Image Industry Today

At the end of the 1980s a mammoth amalgam still identifiable as Hollywood retains the dominance of the moving image industry that it established in the early 1920s. This Hollywood, however, is a very different concern from that of seventy years ago. Today's Hollywood still makes movies, and the names of the 'majors', including MGM, 20th Century-Fox and Columbia, still precede these movies wherever they are shown. But the majors are no longer the autonomous groups they once were; they are elements in large corporate entities which are by no means exclusively concerned with movies. Television, records, video-cassettes and many other related items now make significant contributions to their profits.

Elsewhere in the moving image industry, the forms of television distribution and exhibition are also changing rapidly and the previously unchallenged power of the three television networks in the United States is being eroded. Video-cassettes, cable services and direct broadcasting by satellite are transforming the television landscape. Even more fundamental shifts may occur in the near future. Yet having established close links with the once rival medium, it is the restructured Hollywood of the 1980s which seems likely to consolidate its power by setting up new forms of vertical integration appropriate to the 1990s.

Corporate raids and *Easy Rider*
In the early 1970s the decline of Hollywood's major corporations (begun by the 1948 divorcement proceedings) appeared to be entering a terminal phase. Between 1969 and 1972 the seven major studios lost over $250 million. 20th Century-Fox was particularly badly hit, recording huge losses in 1969 and 1970. Cinema admissions in the United States dropped to an all-time low in 1971 of just 820 million. Blockbuster attempts to repeat the family audience success of *The Sound of Music* had failed. Production costs were rising rapidly and interest on bank debts was a large burden.

Even before these problems became apparent the companies – most of which had enjoyed an independent existence for more than four decades – were exposed as susceptible to takeovers. And towards the end of the 1960s several of the main movie corporations were absorbed into larger conglomerates, just as Universal had been bought by the Music Corporation of America in 1962. In 1967 Gulf and Western Industries completed their acquisition of Paramount, and Transamerica Corporation took over United Artists; and in 1969 Warner Communications Inc emerged from a merger of the film company with Seven Arts and Kinney National Services. These diversified conglomerates, which now owned most of Hollywood, were attracted by the studios' valuable real estate holdings, by what were seen as their undervalued share prices, and by the chance of very large returns for comparatively small outlays. Their immediate over-investment, however, financed by lavish borrowing, only compounded the problems of the studios.

In retrospect, the problems of the majors in the early 1970s can be seen as symptoms of a necessary period of readjustment. At the time, however, the changes in the film industry were perceived to be as significant and as potentially destructive as the broad social shifts which were, in the eyes of many, threatening the fabric of American life. The film which was recognised as a potent concentration of all these shifts was *Easy Rider*, released in 1969. Moreover, its startling commercial success gave notice of a new order which prompted immediate adjustments by the 'old' Hollywood, but which would soon be assimilated into a restructured and revitalised industry.

Easy Rider

The genesis of *Easy Rider*, and of many of the other key 'New Hollywood' films of the 1970s, should be located in the exploitation films turned out in the 1960s by producer Roger Corman and American-International Pictures. Their speciality was low-budget films whose central sensational idea could be expressed in a snappy title. These films were sold through fringe distributors to specialised audiences, such as the teenagers at the drive-in cinemas. To save money, non-union crews were used, often recruited from the film schools which were beginning to flourish in the 1960s. Corman undeniably exploited his protégés like directors Peter Bogdanovich and Martin Scorsese, but at the same time he offered them a chance denied by the mainstream industry.

A picaresque odyssey by hippie bikers across middle America, made by Dennis Hopper on a very low budget, *Easy Rider* took $50 million in a year at the box office. This was the sort of commercial success only glimpsed by the industry since *The Sound of Music*, and it prompted all the by now despairing majors to seek out their own 'youth' pictures. The film's unconventional production company BBS secured a deal with Universal for a package of films, including Bob Rafelson's *Five Easy Pieces* (1970) and Peter Bogdanovich's *The Last Picture Show* (1971). But the euphoria was not to last. Poor returns from over-calculated 'youth-appeal' pictures like *Strawberry Statement* (1970) convinced executives that their supposed saviour was another chimera. The future direction of Hollywood lay elsewhere, along a path taken by another graduate of Corman's 'school'.

Francis Coppola had attended film school at UCLA and then undertaken a variety of tasks for Corman. On location in Ireland in 1963, for example, with actors still contracted after a shoot, he put together a horror film for Corman for just $40,000. Subsequently he scripted and directed films for the new Warners-Seven Arts group. In 1969, just after *Easy Rider's* success, Coppola and his film school friend George Lucas set up their own production group, American Zoetrope, and secured $3.5 million backing from Warners. After their disappointment with Lucas' science-fiction film *THX 1138* (1971), however, Warners pulled out of the arrangement and Coppola contracted with Paramount to make arguably the most influential film of the decade, *The Godfather* (1972).

Movie brats

'We want one big picture a year,' Frank Yablans of Paramount was quoted as saying. 'The rest are budgeted to minimise risk, and hopefully, they will make money too.' *The Godfather* was to be the studio's big picture of 1972. Made on the comparatively modest budget of $6 million, it was backed up with blanket promotion and a special release pattern. Paramount's confidence was justified: it was a huge success and the first of the decade's blockbuster films. For the remainder of the 1970s the studios would chase with mounting desperation a hit such as this.

Coppola's subsequent career has been wayward but full of interest. He made the intriguing *The Conversation* (1974) and the conclusion to his baroque Mafia dynasty tale in *The Godfather, Part II* (1974). He mounted the grandiose but also intensely personal Vietnam epic *Apocalypse Now* (1979). He endeavoured to enter the distribution business; he set up Zoetrope again on a far more lavish scale, only to see it fall apart for a second time; and he has constantly experimented with new production technologies. At the same time, he has produced a number of proficient studio pictures like *Peggy Sue Got Married* (1986). But perhaps his most significant achievement is as mentor and catalyst to a generation of directors which includes George Lucas and John Milius, as well as (although the connections are less direct) Martin Scorsese, Brian De Palma and others.

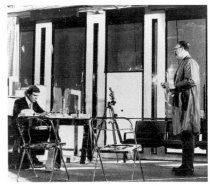

Coppola's The Conversation (*Gene Hackman*)

By the time *The Godfather* (and *The Poseidon Adventure*, 1972) began to break box-office records, the studios had recognised that the small-scale films made in the *Easy Rider* mould were not going to generate sufficient revenues, and they now looked for projects which could be major events: disaster spectaculars like *The Towering Inferno* (1974), on which a $12.5 million budget was carried jointly by 20th Century-Fox and Warner Bros. The director who was to generate several of the most successful of these 'motion picture events' started working for the small screen. After several television episodes for Universal (the first made when he was just twenty), the well-liked tele-movie *Duel* (1971) and a modest feature debut with *The Sugarland Express* (1974), Steven Spielberg made the 'monster' hit *Jaws*. Packaged by independent producers Richard Zanuck and David Brown for Universal, *Jaws* (1975) was an immaculately crafted, visceral movie which was brilliantly promoted. Two years later Spielberg proved, with the release of *Close Encounters of the Third Kind* (1977), that he could once again make the most successful movie of all time. This science-fiction spectacular, the thrill-packed adventure *Raiders of the Lost Ark* (1981) and the fantasy *E.T.* (1982) combined instant emotion and childhood movie memories with the physical sensations of video games and rollercoaster rides. Their nostalgic appeal was a brilliantly timed antidote to the disenchanted mood of these years. By the mid-1980s Spielberg was concerned, in *The Color Purple* (1985) and *Empire of the Sun* (1987), to prove himself as a more 'mature' film-maker.

Spielberg's popular success was matched only by the films of Coppola's former partner George Lucas. After the disappointment of *THX 1138*, Lucas and producer Gary Kurtz tapped into the tail-end of a programme established at Universal to back young talent. Executive Ned Tanen provided the limited budget of *American Graffiti* (1973), and against all the studio's expectations the film was an enormous hit. Just before its release, Kurtz and Lucas had made the deal for *Star Wars* (1977) with 20th Century-Fox, and it was this studio that shared in the science-fiction fantasy's vast profits. For not only did the film become the biggest box-office film ever (briefly supplanting *Jaws* before it was itself overtaken by *Close Encounters*), the attendant marketing of toys, books and other spin-offs had been carefully prepared to take full advantage of the success. An adventure fantasy became a gigantic commercial operation, which set the form for many subsequent marketing campaigns and guaranteed the success of later episodes of the *Star Wars* saga.

Coppola, Spielberg and Lucas, together with a number of their colleagues, have been identified as 'movie brats', a generation that had grown up with Hollywood movies and early television. Their films express a love for this tradition, but also an understanding of the fantasies and desires of the younger audience of the 1970s. In part influenced by the French 'new wave', they saw themselves as making personal statements, but they also enjoyed exploiting the power of Hollywood to appeal to a mass audience. Directors such as Brian De Palma, Martin Scorsese and John Milius endeavoured to reconcile these tendencies in their films. And when successful, as in Scorsese's musical *New York, New York* (1977) and his boxing drama *Raging Bull*

(1980), they created movies which must be recognised as among the most exhilarating of their time.

The conglomerates which now owned the film studios increased the pressure on their subsidiaries to make instant profits. Whereas in the early 1970s the studios had kept costs under control, the desperate search in the latter half of the decade for 'mega-buck' movies, coupled with the grand demands of some of the directors, led to spiralling costs. The budget for Michael Cimino's ambitious Western epic *Heaven's Gate* (1980) escalated to an estimated $36 million, and its spectacular failure was used by the studios as a way of reasserting rigorous overseeing of budgets and production. *Heaven's Gate* was also responsible for Transamerica's decision to sell its subsidiary United Artists – which had backed the film – to MGM.

New roles for the majors

Although the trend had begun back in the 1950s, the early 1970s brought the consolidation of a significant shift in the primary interests of the majors. A concentration on production was replaced by a concern for financing and distributing projects brought to the major companies by independent producers. The package for this would often include a best-selling book, ideally one or two of the increasingly powerful stars like Robert Redford, Warren Beatty, Dustin Hoffman, Robert De Niro or Barbra Streisand, and a 'star' director. United Artists, which owned no physical plant, had worked in this way for some time, and the other majors gradually sold off their back-lots or, like Warners and Columbia, set up their studios as separate companies. Independents proliferated, but the majors retained their dominance because of their control of distribution.

Much of the continuing strength of the majors was based on this control of distribution, but they had also been helped by new forms of financing. Columbia, for example, was saved by 'tax shelter' money, after it had accumulated debts of some $223 million by 1973. 'Tax shelters' were an ingenious way of spreading the risk of financing movies, by off-setting film investments against tax demands, and they undoubtedly contributed significantly to American production until 1976, when they were effectively outlawed by the government.

By the end of the decade overall theatrical returns were strong, both at home and internationally, and Hollywood was continuing to find ways to work with new distribution media like cable and satellite television and video-cassettes. Only escalating costs seemed to pose any threat. One indication of the film industry's profitability was the entry into the game of companies like Tri-Star and Orion. Another was the new round of corporate shifts in the early 1980s. MGM, for example, had cut back its film operations throughout the 1970s and had wound up its distribution concerns, releasing films through United Artists. Majority shareholder Kerk Kerkorian, who had gained control of the company in 1970, had concentrated resources in the hotel business. When the buoyant industry encouraged him to expand

Spielberg's Close Encounters of the Third Kind

Scorsese's New York, New York

'Mega-buck movies': Heaven's Gate

film production, he acquired United Artists from Transamerica in May 1981. A month later the oilman Marvin Davis purchased 20th Century-Fox. And later in 1981 Coca-Cola bought Columbia Pictures.

It is the importance of ancillary markets like cable and satellite, however, that is indicated by the next entrants to the round of buying and selling the majors. Towards the end of 1983 the press magnate Rupert Murdoch made an unsuccessful attempt to buy Warners, which was weak after the collapse of the videogame market in which it had invested heavily. Two years later Murdoch did take control of 20th Century-Fox. And in 1986 Ted Turner, who had made his money with a cable television operation, purchased MGM, leaving the United Artists subsidiary with Kerkorian. Both Murdoch and Turner had substantial interests in television operations, and saw a Hollywood major as an essential element in the creation of new forms of vertically integrated media empires.

Towards the end of the 1980s one further trend was becoming clear, which also suggested the re-establishment of the forms of vertical integration outlawed by the 1948 anti-trust decrees. Throughout the decade the majors gradually re-entered the exhibition area, from which they had been barred by these decrees. In 1986 the Justice Department formally recognised that 'the 1948 consent decrees are outdated'. Much of the history of post-war Hollywood was directly shaped by those decrees, and with the official acknowledgment of their demise a new chapter opened in the history of the moving image industry.

The television networks

Much as the majors still dominate the cinema industry, so the three networks — NBC, CBS and ABC — remain the most significant forces in American television. Like the majors also, the networks have been subjected to far-reaching changes in the past two decades. Both the corporate companies which controlled ABC and NBC, for example, have been taken over by even larger conglomerates, and CBS has been massively restructured. In contrast to the flourishing film majors, however, the networks' grip on the television industry is being eroded, and this process is likely to continue.

The position of the networks throughout the 1960s was grounded in the Nielsen ratings. The prices each network could demand from advertisers depended, in essence, on its overall audience share. In 1970, however, a subtly different notion entered these calculations, as networks and advertisers alike recognised the importance of 'demographics'. Research revealed that urban women in their twenties and thirties were the prime consumers of the kinds of goods mostly offered on television. And certain shows, although they attracted large audiences, were found to have little appeal among this target group of consumers.

External factors also contributed to what was seen as a major realignment of network television. Student protest and general social unrest suggested that television's relentlessly upbeat tone was not the most appropriate response to the nation's troubles. 'Relevant' series like *Storefront Lawyers* (CBS) were enthusiastically embraced, although many were welcomed more by network executives than by audiences. Nonetheless, the success of Norman Lear's comedy series *All in the Family* (CBS) appeared to justify the new attitude, as did the strong ratings for another original series, *The Mary Tyler Moore Show* (CBS), which featured a young independent woman and attracted an audience with a high proportion of her own kind.

All in the Family

Both Norman Lear and the team behind *The Mary Tyler Moore Show*, who set up MTM Enterprises, were able to capitalise on these hits (not least by 'spinning-off' characters into shows of their own) and to build strong independent production groups which have made significant contributions to television ever since. By 1977 independent companies, led by Lear's TAT Communications and MTM, were making more network shows than the majors.

The networks' monopoly was also under attack from the White House. Speeches by Vice President Agnew in 1969 and 1970 suggested that President Nixon and his close staff were angered at what they saw as the networks' bias against them, and Agnew's invective did contribute to a muting of critical analysis. Nixon, however, exploited television to great effect in the election year of 1972 when he made the first visits by an American President to Communist China and to Moscow. The landing in Peking was precisely scheduled for American primetime television; and, although it meant waiting several hours in Anchorage airport, so was his return home. The medium was also to contribute to Nixon's undoing. In 1973 an impoverished Public Broadcasting Service elected to air lengthy coverage of the Congressional Watergate hearings, and when exceptional ratings were achieved the networks followed suit. The White House 'dirty tricks' were exposed to the nation, and the process began which led to Nixon's at times almost incoherent resignation on television in August 1974.

In the early 1970s CBS and its programming chief Fred Silverman promoted respected shows like *M*A*S*H* and *Kojak*. But in 1975 Silverman left the network for the ailing ABC, where the only hits were shows like *The Billion Dollar Man*, aimed at children. Advertisers were increasingly demanding demographic profiles with high proportions of young viewers, and the Nielsen ratings could now supply this kind of breakdown on the day after a show had appeared. Drawing heavily on audience research, Silverman constructed an output that was, in the words of one critic, 'a deliberate formula of puerile comedy, fantasy and sophomoric sex'. At the end of the 1976-7 season ABC was leading the ratings.

Dubbed a 'living schedule', Silverman's new strategy depended also on the relentless exploitation of high-profile movies made for television, and on spectaculars like the coverage in 1976 of the winter Olympics and celebrations of the Bicentennial. The schedule was also complemented by television 'events' such as the mini-series *Rich Man, Poor Man* (1976) and *Roots* (1977). The mini-series became a new vogue, and in 1978 NBC screened the controversial series *Holocaust*.

Silverman moved again, to NBC, but similar success eluded him and in May 1981 he was replaced by Grant Tinker, the man who had guided MTM's spectacular growth and had overseen the highly respected series *Lou Grant* (CBS) and the innovative *Hill Street Blues*. Tinker's commitment to 'quality' shows such as this (others included *St Elsewhere, Cheers* and *The Cosby Show*) ensured that by the mid-1980s NBC was again dominating the ratings. Series like this appealed to the all-important younger, urban viewers, who were thought the most likely to be attracted by pay-cable. For by the early 1980s the networks were recognising the very real challenge from other forms of television distribution. Between the late 1970s and 1987 the networks' combined share of the total audience had dropped from 90 per cent to 76 per cent. Uncertainty about future advertising revenues was also increased by the controversial introduction in 1987 of a new method of ratings assessment. Early results from the 'People Meters' (which require a sample viewer simply to press a button when he or she starts watching television) indicated that people watched less network television than was thought, and that it was indeed the younger, more affluent audiences who were defecting to cable.

MTM's Hill Street Blues

The effect of this was radical cost-cutting. In 1985 ABC was taken over by the giant conglomerate Capital Cities Communication, and NBC's parent company RCA was purchased by General Electric. The new head of CBS was Laurence Tisch (whose company had previously bought Loew's Inc, the former owners of MGM), who instituted drastic economies, concentrated in the once sacrosanct news division. CBS and the other networks also cut back on blockbuster mini-series and specials. The takeovers were in part motivated by the still extraordinarily high level of profitability sustained by the networks during the early 1980s. But they also reflected the deregulatory philosophy of the Federal Communications Commission under the Reagan administration. The FCC was now committed to a policy of allowing the market to dictate the structure of the television industry.

Along with pay-cable, another aspect of the challenge to the networks is the growth of independent or non-affiliated television stations. At the end of 1987 the three networks counted 637 affiliates between them, but the number of independents had grown to 275, with the capacity to reach 85 per cent of all homes. The Australian press baron Rupert Murdoch began his attempt to put together a fourth network among these independents in March 1985 when he bought a half-control in 20th Century-Fox. By the end of 1985 Murdoch had picked up the remaining share of the film company as well as the Metromedia group of seven independent television stations. The exceptionally high cost of these acquisitions forced him to sell one of the stations immediately, and in early 1988 he was still fighting anti-trust rulings that, as part of the deal, he would also have to sell his newspapers in the United States.

In April 1987 the newly inaugurated Fox Broadcasting Company went on

286

the air, offering a schedule – initially on just one night a week – to 105 affiliates. These stations included the six former Metromedia stations, which guaranteed Fox access to the major broadcasting markets. The schedule was calculatedly pitched at young urban viewers, but the response from both advertisers and audiences was mixed. Fox product, both movies and series, can be profitably exploited not only on the fourth network but also on Murdoch's Sky Channel satellite service across Europe. The venture is the most intimate linking yet of Hollywood and television; and with simultaneous access to production, distribution and exhibition, it creates a vertically integrated operation of unparalleled scope.

Cable television

Another component of the challenge to the three networks' dominance emerged in November 1972, with the introduction of modern pay-cable services in the United States when Home Box Office (HBO) made its first transmissions to 365 subscribers in Pennsylvania. The history of cable broadcasting dates back to the 1920s, when poor radio reception – and the possibility of picking up foreign stations – prompted the spread of cable retransmissions in Holland. Similar 'rediffusion' in Britain after 1925 compensated for interference in coastal towns by shipping signals. In the United States, AT&T had developed by 1936 a wideband coaxial cable which could carry television pictures, and after the war this was used to bring television signals to places denied broadcasts either by obstacles like mountains and skyscrapers, or by the FCC's licensing freeze from 1948 to 1952.

Cable's spread throughout the 1950s, in the United States as elsewhere, was restricted to improving or extending broadcast signals. In Britain, for example, the first cable television service was started in Gloucester in 1951, but like all the other systems it carried only the channels available in the airwaves. This retransmission was at first unrestrained, and in the United States it was only when the FCC assumed in the mid-1960s the right to regulate the growing cable industry that any restrictions were imposed. Local rebroadcasting remained cable's main function, although early in the 1970s the FCC instructed operators to make time available for 'public access' services. Meanwhile operators had recognised that new services could be created solely for the cable audience. The most elaborate early attempt was Subscription TV's plan to offer programmes on cable alone in San Francisco and Los Angeles, but a referendum late in 1964 showed that voters believed pay-TV to be against the public welfare and the operation had to be wound up.

The idea was reintroduced a decade later by Time Inc and cable operator Charles Dolan, who had wired lower Manhattan. The response to their HBO service was initially disappointing. The turnaround came by combining cable with satellite technology, so that a service could be provided simultaneously to the scattered cities and towns with systems which carried HBO. This was first achieved with the transmission of the Ali-Frazier boxing match from Manila in September 1975, and the response provided the foundation for HBO's subsequent success. The fragmented cable audience could now be brought together to provide sufficient revenue to fund productions which that audience demanded, but which it could not receive from broadcast channels. Two rival services were started, offering much the same mix of movies and sport; but Viacom's Showtime (from 1978) and Warners' The Movie Channel (1979) found that the market could not support them both, and they amalgamated in 1983.

By the early 1980s HBO was three times larger than any pay-cable rival, and was fully or part-financing a production programme of movies and television specials. HBO subsequently formed a partnership with CBS and Columbia Pictures to found Tri-Star, which was intended to develop as a new Hollywood major. On anti-trust grounds, the Department of Justice stopped the majors themselves (who were all too aware of the growing power of HBO) from entering the distribution and presentation ends of the pay-cable business. But in December 1983 Paramount signed a deal with the new Showtime/The Movie Channel partnership for exclusive rights to the studio's films over the next five years.

The television networks also tried to start up their own pay-cable services. But both CBS Cable, intended as a cultural service financed by advertising, and RCA's The Entertainment Channel closed down after heavy losses. Only ABC's joint venture with the Hearst Corporation, now known as Arts and Entertainment, has found any real success. Such ventures are not, however, the only potential use of the technology. Community cable services were experimented with in Britain in the early 1970s; and because of 'public access' regulations in the United States comparable operations have become familiar although infrequently watched elements of American broadcasting. But the fanciful dreams of democratic access to the media and of a community's images being controlled by that community appear to have vanished.

The grand hopes of a fully cabled Britain with a plenitude of services, as envisioned by the 1982 Hunt Report on the future of cable television, have also yet to be translated into reality. Certainly variants of the technology offer the possibility of a fully interactive system capable of providing home shopping, banking services, security alarms, games and much more. But the physical structure of the system is expensive to install, and development has been slow. Moreover, many observers believe that hardware which is quite inappropriate to future needs is being put in place.

Electromagnetic wires, similar to telephone cables, are being laid in the vast majority of new cable networks. Yet their limited capacity will soon prove to be an enormous restriction on the development of cable's potential. It is argued that only fibre optic networks, in which information is transmitted as light, can offer the versatility that this potential will soon demand. A fibre optic system was installed in 1984 in Birmingham, Alabama, and the following year Denmark was the first country to commit to reconstructing the full telephone system with fibres. But as the story of the moving image has indicated many times, it is not technology alone which determines the development of our culture, and until political, economic and social factors begin to bear on the issue the possibilities of fibre optic cable are likely to remain undeveloped.

Satellites

In July 1962 the United States space agency NASA launched the AT&T-built Telstar I, the first satellite capable of relaying all forms of communication, including television signals. The idea of using a space satellite as a communications vehicle had been formulated by the writer Arthur C. Clarke in the October 1945 edition of the British magazine *Wireless World*. His conception was of a 'high-orbit' system, with a satellite set some 42,000 kilometres above the equator. In this position the satellite would remain in a stationary position relative to a point on the Earth's surface, and so just three satellites could be used to send signals right round the world. In 1954 the American scientist J. R. Pierce, Director of Research at AT&T's Bell Laboratories, determined that a 'low-orbit' system was also feasible.

Pictures by satellite

In the 1950s scientists had bounced signals off the moon as a way of communicating around the curvature of the Earth. In August 1960 a metallised balloon dubbed Echo I was launched for a similar purpose, and two years later it was used to transmit a degraded television image between California and Massachusetts, but this technology needed an inordinately complex receiving station. Intensive research at Bell Laboratories, however, developed the possibility of satellite communications, and in the rush to compete with the Russians in the early days of the Kennedy administration Congress approved a marriage between AT&T's privately financed plans and the public monies behind NASA. Telstar then initiated live television transmissions between France, Britain and the United States on 23 July 1962.

AT&T's interest in the technology was motivated by their concern to control both telephone communication by satellite and the relay of television signals, on the station-to-station cable transmission of which they still held a monopoly in the United States. Just after Telstar's pioneering transmissions the Communications Satellite Act of 1962 acknowledged that the development of international satellite communication should be solely the concern of the private sector, and the Comsat conglomerate was formed, with the active participation of AT&T, RCA, Western Union International and ITT. One year later a synchronous satellite, as envisaged by Clarke, had been built by the Hughes Aircraft Corporation; and by August 1964 one of this series, Syncom III, was successfully placed in its geostationary orbit over the equator. Among the first live pictures which it relayed back to the United States was coverage of the Tokyo Olympics.

The potential of a cable-satellite combination was demonstrated in 1975 by HBO's boxing match transmission from Manila. Two years later Ted

Turner, owner of an independent station in Atlanta, started to distribute his schedule by satellite to four cable affiliates. The programme of older movies, sports and re-runs was unremarkable, but this 'superstation' WTBS was soon being picked up by cable operators across the country, and Turner could generate significant revenues by selling advertising at national rates. By 1987 WTBS could be received in over 40 million homes, and two other 'superstations', beamed from New York and Chicago, had begun operations. Turner also set up both the 24-hour news service Cable News Network (CNN) – now expanding in Europe and elsewhere – and an abortive rival to Warners' MTV.

The distribution of cable services by low-power communications satellite is by the late 1980s also well established in Britain and throughout Europe. Rupert Murdoch's Sky Channel, which offers an entertainment service to some 10 million subscribers in 19 countries, was the first to be established, but even after five years in the sky it has still to make a profit. Super Channel, launched in January 1987 by the ITV companies (excluding Thames) and Virgin, also found revenues elusive. A European variant of MTV, with finance from press magnate Robert Maxwell, British Telecom and Viacom, has been available since August 1987. Other British-based services include the Children's Channel, Maxwell's Premiere, Screen Sport and Lifestyle. Several of these British services had started up after the 1983 Cable and Broadcasting Act which promoted the private development of cable systems. But delays in installing the physical structure of the cable network led the owners to look to satellite transmissions.

All these operations have subsequently combined low-power satellite transmissions with local receiving stations, equipped with large dish aerials, which have then relayed the signals to homes on a cable system. But individuals, in the United States as elsewhere, have also installed comparatively large dishes for private reception. Although the necessary arrangements to ensure good reception are quite complex, by 1984 some 500,000 dishes had been sold in the United States and it was clear that they were beginning to dent cable revenue. Initially there was no effective method by which a channel like HBO could exact payment for their service if it was picked up in this way, but more recently those who produce the channels have started to encode their signals, necessitating their unscrambling with a special device.

A home-built dish aerial in California

In the past decade the technology has been developed which permits the direct broadcasting by satellite (DBS) to small domestic dish aerials, which can be placed unobtrusively in a garden or on a roof. Yet DBS has so far largely failed to fulfil its potential. In the United States in 1984 United Satellite Communications set up a service in the Northeast and Midwest, but it failed to attract enough subscribers and quickly folded. Industry opinion is that the market there is now sufficiently well served by the penetration of VCRs, cable and the non-DBS satellite services, and that a DBS service for the United States is not at present a viable option.

290

In Europe, the available DBS frequencies were shared out more than a decade ago. Each country received five, and after much delay the franchise for three of the British channels was awarded in December 1986 to British Satellite Broadcasting. BSB intends to begin transmissions by December 1989, with its signals directed at a 'footprint' on the ground which is largely restricted to Britain. But BSB may be pre-empted by the Luxembourg-based SES group, which is backed by a range of European banks and intends to sell channels on its medium-power, RCA-built Astra satellite. The Astra channels will be capable of being received across Europe, but they will require a larger dish and may not give comparably sharp reception.

One element in the irresolution about European DBS is the concern felt by many broadcasters that DBS services will undermine the revenue bases of the national networks, and that public service operations will be threatened by entertainment-oriented channels over which the regulatory authorities in each country will have no control. Yet the experience of cable in Belgium, where some 75 per cent of all homes are passed by cable and around 60 per cent subscribe, and where foreign stations are consequently freely available, suggests that an audience's loyalty remains with national networks.

The fears about DBS are prompted by the probable form that it will take in Europe, but it is also possible to conceive of a far more radical use of the technology. In India, for example, the Satellite Instructional Television experiment (SITE) has since 1975 been sending educational broadcasts to dishes and communal television sets in more than 2,000 villages.

Further reading

Erik Barnouw, *The Sponsor: Notes on a Modern Potentate*, Oxford: Oxford University Press, 1978.

Jane Feuer, Paul Kerr and Tise Vahimagi (eds), *MTM 'Quality Television'*, London: BFI Publishing, 1984.

Todd Gitlin, *Inside Prime Time*, New York: Pantheon, 1983.

Diane Jacobs, *Hollywood Renaissance*, New York: A.S. Barnes, 1977.

Robert Phillip Kolker, *A Cinema of Loneliness: Penn, Kubrick, Coppola, Scorsese, Altman*, New York: Oxford University Press, 1980.

David McClintock, *Indecent Exposure: A True Story of Hollywood and Wall Street*, New York: William Morrow, 1982.

James Monaco, *American Film Now*, New York: Oxford University Press, 1979.

David Pirie (ed), *Anatomy of the Movies*, London: Windward, 1981.

Michael Pye and Lynda Myles, *The Movie Brats: How the Film Generation Took Over Hollywood*, London: Faber and Faber, 1979.

Paul Sylbert, *Final Cut: The Making and Breaking of a Film*. New York: Seabury Press, 1974.

John Taylor, *Storming the Magic Kingdom: Wall Street, the Raiders and the Battle for Disney*, New York: Ballantine, 1987.

Robin Wood, *Hollywood from Vietnam to Reagan*, New York: Columbia University Press, 1986.

19
Looking at the Future

Most visions of tomorrow's moving image culture share the conviction that major changes are imminent. New technologies, it is claimed, are already bringing about a 'revolution'; cable systems and satellites will replace today's forms of distribution, both to the home and to social environments like the traditional cinema. New forms of exhibition are also promised, including enhanced film projection systems like Showscan and flat, wall-sized television screens suitable for high definition pictures. In many ways, however, the most significant forseeable changes in our conceptions of the moving image are those prompted by the possibilities of computer-generated digital images.

One of the convictions informing this book is that new technologies alone do not initiate fundamental changes. Economic, political and social influences combine in complex ways with technology to bring about the major shifts in our engagements with moving images. Most of the systems discussed in this final chapter have yet to make a pronounced impact on our culture. Some, such as Imax and Omnimax, may remain as diverting but marginal variants of familiar forms. Others, like laser video discs, may change moving images in ways undreamt of by their original creators. But it would seem that the achieved applications and the potential of computer-generated images are provoking as fundamental a reassessment of the ways we visualise our world as was heralded by the first photographs.

Television technologies tomorrow

Within a decade, in many homes, the currently familiar domestic configuration of television aerial, monitor and video-cassette recorder will have been transformed. As we have seen, the aerial for the reception of terrestrial broadcast signals is likely to be supplemented by other receivers, including cable inputs and a small DBS dish. Screens in the late 1990s will be larger, with high definition capability, and the monitor will be flatter and probably wall-mounted. Sound reproduction will be greatly enhanced, and for many consumers the integration of both compact disc and digital audio tape systems will be essential. The VCR may also store images in digital form, and

292

could be complemented by both a laser video disc system and by a personal computer installation, offering the possibility, along with certain of the cable services, of limited interactivity.

Research into High Definition Television (HDTV) was begun by the Japanese Broadcasting Corporation (NHK) in 1970. The inadequacies of the picture produced by the three international standards (the NTSC system with 525 lines in the United States, PAL 625 in Europe, and SECAM) had been apparent well before that, as had the problem of their mutual incompatibility. A new system, in which the picture was built up from a greater number of lines, could offer enhanced image quality and perhaps a single international standard. Eventually the engineers in Japan settled on an optimum of 1125 lines, which delivered a picture perceived as comparable to that of 35mm film, and a screen aspect ratio (width compared to height) of 5:3 rather than the current 4:3. The increased resolution and a reduction in screen 'flicker' meant that viewers no long perceived the lines which composed any image, and the screen size could consequently be considerably increased. With this new clarity viewers acknowledged a heightened realism, a greater illusion of depth and a more pronounced sense of inclusion within the image. As Anthony Smith has observed, HDTV 'provides an experience as different from colour television as colour television is from black and white and, at the same time, as different from traditional cinema as television is. It combines the instantaneity of television with the full illusion of well projected film.'

Sony and other Japanese manufacturers began to manufacture the necessary hardware, and over the past decade they have mounted an effective campaign for HDTV. CBS in the United States has thrown its weight behind the worldwide introduction of HDTV, and a range of advertisements and music promos have been completed, together with one full-length feature film. But HDTV signals are not compatible with any existing television hardware, so both broadcasters and consumers would have to be completely re-equipped if the system were widely adopted. Nor has Sony or another manufacturer yet demonstrated a large-screen domestic monitor which could be manufactured relatively inexpensively. Moreover, the bandwidth needed to transmit HDTV signals would occupy three to four contiguous broadcast channels, which are already exceptionally scarce.

A recognition of these problems stimulated consideration of alternative schemes, and especially 'enhanced' television. One proposal from Germany called Imagevision posits a 655-line standard, combined with other improvements but with a standard picture ratio, which produces an image close to that of 35mm film. In Britain the Independent Broadcasting Authority's engineers favour an enhanced system known as C-MAC. Another was unveiled in 1987 by NBC's conglomerate parent General Electric, which took over RCA two years earlier. Advanced Compatible Television (ACTV), it is claimed, offers a widescreen, enhanced-resolution picture of 1050 lines which – in essence because this is double the number of lines in the NTSC standard – would be compatible with present television sets. In addition, and unlike several other enhanced systems, its signal could be transmitted on a normal broadcast bandwidth.

ACTV has become one further element in the enquiries and tests being undertaken in the late 1980s, by the Federal Communications Commission and other bodies, to determine the course to which television in the next decade should be directed. By this stage, however, it is clear that HDTV, or at least High Definition Video (HDV), with the same technical specifications but not necessarily designed for broadcast, is well ahead of its competitors. At the end of 1987 two 'films' shot in HDV had been completed, RAI-TV's *Julia & Julia*, and *Do It Up* from the HDV facility owned by producer Barry Rebo. HDV commercials and promos have also been shot, again primarily for theatrical exhibition, and the medium is exercising the talents of innovative image-makers like Zbigniew Rybczynski and John Sanborn.

Increased speed and flexibility in post-production means that origination in HDV is cheaper than 35mm film, and the possibilities of video image-processing make available an extensive range of special effects which would be either impossible or exorbitantly expensive on film. During 1987 CBC in Canada, for example, produced an HDV drama series for which elaborate exterior shots were created by limited sets being matched with electronic images laid into the shot in post-production. These advantages are of course also offered by other enhanced television systems, but given its limited acceptance already HDV's future for theatrical presentation appears bright. Yet because of its incompatibility with both NTSC and PAL receivers, as High Definition Television it undoubtedly faces strong resistance to its establishment as the international broadcast standard of the future.

Whatever system, or systems, are adopted, distribution to and exhibition in both cinemas and the home will undoubtedly undergo major changes. (One likely possibility, of course, is that 1125-line HDV establishes itself for a theatrical market, but that broadcasters take on one or more variants of enhanced television.) Initially, HDV productions will be transferred to film for public screenings, but by the early 1990s circuits of HDV 'cinemas' may develop, equipped with specialised video projection equipment. Distribution to these could eventually be undertaken by DBS or via cable, although HDV pictures would take up a significant portion of the available space on electromagnetic wires. DBS transmission, however, or fibre optic cables would not only contribute enormously to print and transport economies but would also permit the relay of live events, with exceptional picture quality, into these theatres or, eventually, into the home. The 1940s dream of 'theatre television' (see Chapter 12) will finally become a feasible and attractive alternative. The savings, however, would be in distribution costs, and the considerable conversion costs would not necessarily be covered by any increased exhibition profits.

At home, HDTV images will in any case probably be seen on wall-hung, large-format screens which will use not cathode ray tubes, but liquid crystal display (LCD) technology, a crude version of which is currently employed in digital watches and calculators. The difference between public and private screenings will simply be a matter of how the spectator pays; although at home that spectator will probably also be able to call on a whole range of alternatives, including some form of laser disc-based interactive system.

Discs and digital technology

In September 1927 John Logie Baird demonstrated an early form of image storage on discs. His Phonovision system, which was briefly and unsuccessfully marketed in 1935, inscribed information from 30-line television pictures as well as sound onto wax discs. 78rpm gramophone records made from these could then provide up to six minutes of playing time. Later research in the United States endeavoured to impress the waveform of a video signal onto film, but it was not until the 1960s, after the widespread professional adoption of videotape, that the potential of domestic video stimulated further research into other storage systems. At the end of the decade CBS brought out Electronic Video Recording, which utilised 8mm film; and RCA launched HoloTape SelectaVision, in which a laser read holographic images implanted in transparent film.

Image storage on disc: Baird's Phonovision

Both CBS and RCA were concerned to develop domestic playback hardware for which the images could be strictly controlled, as they were not in cassette systems capable of off-air recording. Consumers, of course, saw personal recording as a great advantage, and neither initiative sold well. Almost a decade later RCA launched a new variant of Selectavision, in which images were stored on a disc; but the discs were fragile and again no significant advantage over cassettes was offered to the consumer.

Philips meanwhile developed a quite separate technology, which used a laser to read images from a disc. The key difference from the other systems was that the images were inscribed on the disc in digital form. That is, the images were converted into many discrete and individual elements of information, rather than into a continuous – or analogue – form like a line, the bumps and grooves of a long-playing record, a conventional film image or a magnetic signal. (One example often cited to define the difference is that a traditional wristwatch is an analogue device, since it registers the time continuously on its dial. A 'digital' watch presents the time discontinuously, as a series of discrete numbers.) The distinction is fundamental, not least because information in a digital form can be fed into a computer, manipulated and then offered in an altered form.

A Philips video disc system

The laser disc system offers enhanced picture quality (although this is limited by the line standard of the monitor) and the possibility of immediate access to any frame. Moreover, largely because there is no physical contact between laser and disc, it is the most durable form of visual information storage yet conceived, with a guaranteed life of 600 years. A domestic version, prepared with MCA which supplied the programming, was launched as DiscoVision in the United States in 1978. But neither this, nor a similar venture by Pioneer, was successful in appealing to the individual consumer. The technology of laser discs, however, remains exceptionally important, not least for their potential as the storage and retrieval components for interactive systems.

The laser disc also spawned the audio-only compact disc for the digital reproduction of recorded sound. Philips teamed up with Sony in 1979, and their joint product, launched two years later, has found a major and rapidly expanding market. In 1987 CD Video was announced by Philips, which had created 8-inch discs, from which both picture and sound could be read by a single laser. The discs could carry some five minutes of video and sound (ideal for a music promo) together with an additional twenty minutes of sound. If these discs win market approval, Philips is looking to reintroduce longer laser discs for the release of movies, concerts and other attractions.

Cinema technologies tomorrow

Despite prognostications about its demise since at least the early 1950s, the cinema in its familiar form continues to thrive. As earlier chapters have demonstrated, this cinema has successfully adapted both its exhibition strategies (adopting widescreen technology in the 1950s, for example) and its forms of production and distribution. The major producers in Hollywood accommodated broadcast television, and more recently cable, video-cassettes and other carriers of the moving image. Shifts in the market have shaped – and been shaped by – these adaptations, but the conventional cinema, and the American corporations at its heart, have retained a dominance which currently demonstrates few signs of decline.

As we have seen, both HDTV and satellite distribution may stimulate changes in accepted exhibition patterns. Theatrical exhibition, however, faces a different challenge as the possibilities of watching the moving image at home more closely approximate to the experience of cinematic projection. For it seems likely that audiences, to be tempted from their homes, will increasingly expect new forms of the moving image. In the 1970s many exhibitors predicted that the only future for theatrical presentation of films was the convenient provision of greater choice, and many large cinemas were converted into multi-screen venues where three, four or more films played in small auditoria. More recently, a number of purpose-built 'multiplex' cinemas have opened, offering twelve, eighteen or even more different shows under one roof. At the same time there is a recognition of the audience demand for at least a scattering of 'ultra-luxury' cinemas to showcase major 70mm films.

Parallel to these changes within mainstream cinema, the past fifteen years have seen the commercial development of the large-screen Imax system, together with experimental presentations of other large-screen processes. In an Imax theatre the image, often shown on a slightly curved screen, is so large that the spectator's field of vision is almost completely occupied. Any awareness of the frame is effectively banished, and there is a quite unique sense of being *within* the picture. With Omnimax, which is a modified version of Imax, this sense is heightened as the image is filmed with a fisheye lens and projected, through a similar lens, onto a dome. The spectator is engulfed by the picture as the eyes, aided by audio cues from an elaborate arrangement of speakers set in the dome, have to search the visual field for the centre of interest.

Imax was first seen at Expo 70 in Osaka. But there were numerous precedents for such large-screen moving image experiences, which were also often shown for the first time (and frequently the last) at World's Fairs. At the 1900 Universal Exposition in Paris, for example, visitors could 'travel' in a balloon over Paris and Brussels, courtesy of an elaborate projection system using ten 70mm projectors. These projectors threw hand-coloured aerial views onto a circular screen – much like that of the 19th-century Panoramas – which was 30 feet high and more than 300 feet in circumference. At the same Exposition, the Lumière brothers projected images onto both sides of a screen 70 feet by 53 feet. Such elaborate film presentations were often featured attractions at later Fairs; and at Walt Disney's Disneyland a multiple-projector 35mm system called Circarama (or later Circle Vision 360) has since 1955 impressed visitors with the encompassing images of *America the Beautiful*.

Imax, however, was developed for more than occasional specialised screenings, although few existing cinemas have proved large enough to accommodate it. Shot on film 65mm wide, but printed on and projected from 70mm film (like the widescreen process known as Super-Panavision), Imax runs this film horizontally through both the camera and projector. As in the original VistaVision developed in the late 1950s, this re-orientation of the image means that a far greater area of film (more than ten times that on 35mm stock) is exposed for each frame. Consequently, the image can be shown on a screen as large as 120 feet by 85 feet high without appearing unacceptably grainy.

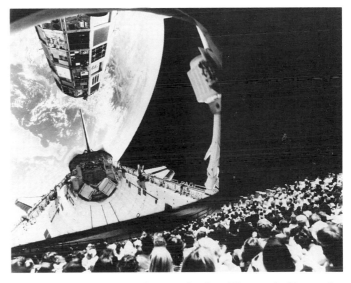

Imax and Omnimax projectors are elaborate engineering projects, with large horizontal steel plates to carry the enormous reels and a parallel system for rewinding. The film also travels exceptionally fast through the projector gate, moved by air-jets rather than an inertia-inducing mechanical process. Rewinding one print while another is playing has until recently restricted the running time of any one film to under one hour. Another problem is the production cost, which in 1984 was calculated at about $1 million for a 20-minute film, largely because of the film stock and the rental charges for a camera, which can only be hired from the Imax Corporation. Moreover, these cameras are

Interior of an Imax Theatre: the film was shot in space by members of the US space shuttle Challenger mission in April 1984

only able to house magazines holding 1,000-foot rolls, restricting each shot to a maximum length of three minutes. And the systems usually need specially built theatres for only a few existing buildings are tall enough. Nonetheless, Imax and Omnimax have proved to be exceptionally popular, and lucrative.

The films initially produced for exhibition in these formats were short travelogues or popular science items. In 1981 George Englund produced *My Strange Uncle*, a 30-minute comedy and the first narrative film for the system. Other dramas have followed, including *Flyers* (1982), about a Second World War flying ace who becomes a stuntman; and *Behold Hawaii* (1983). One of the most elaborate Imax documentaries, *The Dream is Alive*, about the American space shuttle programme, opened in 1986. March 1988 saw the premiere of the first Imax feature, *Alamo . . . The Cost of Freedom,* made at a cost of $7 million primarily for the Imax theatre near the site of the Battle of the Alamo.

The projection system known as Dynavision was also developed in the early 1980s for large-screen presentations. With a film image about half the size of an Imax frame, it is significantly cheaper and can be run through an adapted 70mm projector. Equipped with an exceptional sound system, it can be employed to produce a large-screen image, blown up from 35mm, on a portable 60 feet by 80 feet screen. The feature-length concert film *We Will Rock You* with the rock group Queen, marketed in this form on a roadshow basis, suggested a possible future alternative to live tours.

The Showscan system, conceived by Douglas Trumbull (renowned for his special effects on *2001: A Space Odyssey* and *Close Encounters of the Third Kind*), also offers enhanced image quality and a more intense theatrical experience. Showscan uses widescreen 70mm film, photographed and projected at 60 frames per second. This increases the resolution of the image, but as with Imax necessitates the construction of new theatres with special screens. Having failed to interest his former employers Paramount in the process, Trumbull has been developing it himself since 1975. His first hour-long production, *New Magic,* was released in a few venues in 1985, and Trumbull is convinced that his process holds enormous potential as one of the moving image experiences of the future.

Douglas Trumbull's New Magic, *which uses the Showscan system*

Holography

Alongside the creation of new exhibition processes, recent years have also witnessed research into new methods of creating moving images, including moving holograms. A hologram is a visual record of a whole object which produces a true stereoscopic image of that object. Unlike the 3-D processes exploited by the cinema in the early 1950s, a holographic image will reveal different facets as a viewer's eyes are moved in relation to it. The viewer can look round the sides of such an image, just as if he or she were looking at the object itself.

Holography was conceived in 1947 by the British researcher Dennis

Gabor, who wanted to improve an electron microscope so as to reveal atomic structures. He used a coherent light source, generating light in which – in contrast to that from the sun or from a lamp – the photons are strictly regimented. When coherent light is reflected this regimentation breaks down, and the pattern of interference, together with another 'reference' beam of coherent light, can be recorded on film. Passing the same reference beam through the developed film recreates the 'wavefront' made by the original object, and produces a true three-dimensional image. Gabor worked with a high-pressure mercury lamp as his coherent light source, but the bulk of work with holograms since the early 1960s has been undertaken with lasers.

A laser provides exactly the kind of strong coherent source required for holography, and with a simple arrangement to split the beam both the disturbance caused by an object and an undisturbed 'reference' can be recorded on film. The first holograms made in this way were shown in 1963 by Emmett Leith and Juris Upatnieks, and the first real-time holographic moving images were created some six years later, using pulsed lasers which emitted exceptionally rapid bursts of light. In 1969, at the Hughes Research Laboratories in California, Alex Jacobson and Victor Evtuhov produced a very grainy, monochromatic moving image of an aquarium, which could only be viewed by one person at a time. But despite the availability of the technology, progress in the subsequent two decades towards the realisation of holographic cinema has been negligible.

Holography's advantages over normal photographic processes include the potential for a much greater brightness range and depth of field. Real-time holographic moving images, however, require very powerful and potentially dangerous lasers. Nor, without a special optical screen, can the images be viewed by more than a small number of people from one vantage point. And although full colour holograms were achieved in the 1970s, at present they require an exceptionally complex coordination of three separate pulsed lasers.

Computer images

After a comparably lengthy development over some forty years, computer images are far more advanced than holographic ones. Holography remains an intriguing curiosity, whereas computer images are now integral to our culture. Computer images represent a quite new form of picture-making, and their introduction will be seen by future historians as comparably significant to the appearance of moving pictures in the 1890s, or the invention of photography some seventy years earlier.

The phrases computer images and computer graphics are applied to a variety of creations and techniques, and a number of distinctions should be recognised. The central notion, however, is that computer images are the product of numbers in digital form. The images may have been created by feeding into the computer pre-existing pictures, which have been changed and manipulated; or they may be the result of a complex algorithm for which no previous visualisation has been made. And they may be realised on a monitor, or as animated film, or as printed 'hard' copy, or in other ways. But in essence they are digital numbers, and their uniqueness is derived from this simple radical notion.

Once the source of computer images in digital numbers is recognised, fundamental differences have to be acknowledged between two-dimensional and three-dimensional work, and between still and moving, or animated, images. Computer animation is another term which confusingly subsumes a range of techniques, although it is true that there is a common pre-history for all computer imaging, dating from work in the early 1950s at the Massachusetts Institute of Technology (MIT). The Whirlwind computer, built there in 1949, was one of the first computers capable of carrying out calculations in digital form and then converting and displaying the results on a cathode-ray screen (CRT), much like that used in domestic televisions. In 1951 Ed Murrow's CBS series *See It Now* even showed some of the earliest MIT experiments, including the simulation on screen of a bouncing ball.

The idea of using a CRT in this way was a fundamental breakthrough in the development of computer images. Comparably important was the inter-active quality of an American air defence system known as SAGE, which was operational by the mid-1950s. To use this, an operator indicated potentially unfriendly aircraft with a light pen on a display screen, and so alerted a computer to their position. A third breakthrough was the picture-processing technique produced at the National Bureau of Standards. Although crude, this was the first method which permitted a computer to 'see', and later to manipulate, existing images.

Genuine interactive graphics were first achieved by Ivan Sutherland's 'Sketchpad' software, written at MIT in 1962. Data could be entered into a computer, displayed on a CRT almost immediately, and then manipulated in a number of ways. In particular, points on a line could be indicated with a light pen, and the computer could then be instructed to 'draw' the line between them. Programmed instructions enabled points to be moved, thus also shifting the lines and producing the now familiar 'wire-frame' moving graphics. The next important step, and the shift from two to three dimensions, was to input instructions which included the conventions of perspective and the automatic erasure of lines which would be 'behind' closer objects. Software which entered these instructions permitted the wire-frame models to be moved in what appeared to be three-dimensional space.

This technology soon became increasingly flexible and cheaper, and its potential was recognised both because it could draw more accurately than any human hand and because the representations could be moved and manipulated. The three-dimensional capability, for example, meant that car manufacturers could simulate and test a new model. Architects could produce the outlines of a proposed building, and use the screen to view the project from different angles. By the early 1970s computer-aided design was making an important contribution to many industries.

Designers also benefited from computer images with the introduction in the late 1970s of a number of 'paint' systems which facilitated the creation of two-dimensional images by an operator using a light pen as if it were a brush. The results of movements across an electronic tablet, combined with a choice of colours, thicknesses of stroke and so on, are displayed directly onto a video monitor. The Quantel Digital Paintbox is probably the best-known of these systems, offering the 'artist' an electronic palette on screen before each mark is made. Paintbox is now extensively used in commercial design and television graphics, but its creative capacities have also been explored by artists like David Hockney who are intrigued by the possibilities of 'painting' directly onto a video screen. Comparatively cheap paint systems are also now available for running on relatively humble personal computers.

Such interactive imaging should be seen as distinct from image processing, in which a video picture is digitised and then manipulated in some way. Quantel and its founder Richard Taylor also played an important part in these developments, marketing the first full-scale digital-effects device, the DPE-5000, in 1977. The key was a way of 'quantising' television signals; that is, converting them into digital information which could then be stored and manipulated within a computer system. Taylor's first achievement, around 1975, was the compression of a television image and its positioning – in its own frame – anywhere on a screen. Other possibilities – soon realised by Taylor, and by researchers at the American company Grass Valley Inc – were movement around the screen, rolling, flipping and the other visual tricks which are now accepted (and often overused) elements in television news and entertainment programmes.

Subsequent innovations in this field have included both colourising techniques and image-mapping, which was introduced to the television industry in 1985. With a system like Quantel's Mirage, an image could be digitised and the information, and consequently the image, 'wrapped round' an apparently three-dimensional model – of a sphere for example, or a wine-glass shape — the configuration of which was stored in the computer. This model, with the image mapped onto it, could then be moved in the three dimensions of the world represented on the screen. A further generation of digital effects, first widely available in 1987, is the range known by names such as Harry and Abekas 64, which facilitate the complex matting of images, allowing the user to cut and collage both still and moving images.

Computer images and image-processing are now widely used in television production. Simple computer-generated graphics are essential elements in news broadcasts, and image-processing is employed extensively in programme production and in commercials, music promos and title sequences. Such short items, which enjoy comparatively generous budgets, need to make an immediate impact and they also use extensively the forms of three-dimensional animation discussed below. Designers and production

Computer graphics in television: the opening title of ABC's Wide World of Sports

301

houses compete to exploit the latest technologies in the most attention-catching ways, and it is these television fragments which offer some of the most surprising and pleasing of all small-screen images. Another stimulus for computer image creation and manipulation, in both the United States and elsewhere, is the transmission of major television events. The ABC network revolutionised the look of television sports in the early 1980s with their committed use of computer images at the Lake Placid Winter Olympics of 1980. From that date the familiar see-it-now relays of mainstream sports coverage began to be transformed into highly choreographed, graphics-intensive visual extravaganzas.

Three-dimensional imaging and animation

Both paint systems and image processing essentially involve either the creation or the manipulation of two-dimensional images. Parallel with such developments there was a great deal of research into the possibilities – suggested by the wire-frame models of the late 1960s – of image creation in three dimensions. Surfaces to give body and volume to these wire-frame outlines were first developed around 1970 by Ivan Sutherland and his partner David Evans. Their funding, like that of many other computer image pioneers, came from the military, specifically the US Department of Defense which was concerned to build a realistic flight simulator. Throughout the 1970s other computer graphics experts worked at representing light and shade on these surfaces, achieved with a process known as 'ray-tracing'; and at developing 'texture mapping' which could define the 'feel' of the surfaces, whether they were smooth or rough, shiny or dull. Pre-eminent in this work was James Blinn, based at NASA's Jet Propulsion Laboratory, who by 1979 was creating astonishing animated simulations of the Voyager 1 spacecraft's approach to Jupiter.

One further important technique involved the introduction of fractal geometry. Conceived by Benoit Mandelbrot in 1975, this system is non-Euclidean and defines a class of shapes that, as it were, exists between the dimensions of lines, planes and solids. As computer graphics artist Loren Carpenter among others discovered, fractals could be used to model mountains and natural terrains which had previously eluded the most complex of programmes. And the resulting images could be progressively magnified to reveal increasingly perceptible detail.

A number of different techniques are subsumed by the term computer animation. Computers, for example, are used to speed-up conventional cartoon animation, with software to colour areas of hand-drawn frames and to create the 'in-between' frames once the start and end of a movement have been defined by a human artist. But computer animation most frequently designates the more high-profile work, now usually undertaken in three dimensions. Although a direct video interface can be used, most computer animation is carried out with frame-by-frame filming of a monitor screen. The computer creates an image on the screen, this is recorded on a single

302

frame of film; then the computer presents the next image in the sequence, which is recorded on the next frame of film, and so on. Real-time animation in three dimensions is also feasible, but even comparatively simple modelled imagery manipulated in this way requires a vast computer memory.

The first computer-generated film is generally recognised to be Edward E. Zajac's animation made at Bell Laboratories in 1963, created with a recently introduced electric microfilm recorder to represent a satellite path around the earth. The following year, also at Bell, Ken Knowlton and Stan VanDerBeek started to work on computer-generated patterned films, which have been seen as the first such work produced primarily with an aesthetic intent. Comparable, and spectacular, geometric abstracts were also produced from the late 1960s by computer pioneer and experimental film-maker John Whitney Sr, with the active support of IBM.

In 1978 Whitney's son, John Whitney Jr, produced one of the first computer graphics animations incorporated into a television commercial. And during the 1980s the techniques have become increasingly common in advertisements, in programme title sequences and in presentation breaks. One of the first computer animations to make an impact in Britain is the logo for Channel 4 Television.

The computer-video interface has also been increasingly explored in recent years, an important early creation being artist Ed Emshwiller's collaboration with computer graphics expert Alvy Ray Smith. In *Sunstone* (1979) they scanned a face into a computer and then manipulated it in real time through changes in which it became, among other images, a sun and a mandala, and also appeared on the sides of an animated cube which broke apart and began to replicate itself. More recent examples include John Sanborn and Dean Winkler's collaboration with composer Philip Glass on *Act III* (1983), and Winkler's work with singer Laurie Anderson and art director Perry Hoberman for the video clip *Sharkey's Day* (1984).

Since the early 1980s, 3-D computer animation has been increasingly exploited to create special effects for movies. The first example is probably *Futureworld* (1974), in which a computer-mapped image of Peter Fonda's head was featured on a video screen. The company responsible for this effect, Triple-I, later undertook the 3-D work for *Looker* (1981, directed by Michael Crichton) in which a character was supposedly digitised and the data base used to create simulations. In 1982 the Walt Disney company released *Tron*, which contained some fifteen minutes of computer-generated imagery. The film was widely recognised as a breakthrough, but audiences were unconvinced by the thin narrative and Hollywood's initial enthusiasm for the new technique waned.

Nonetheless, computer-generated imagery has been integrated into many recent science-fiction films. Its most extensive use to date is for the special effects in *The Last Starfighter* (1985), for which John Whitney Jr and Gary Demos, co-founders of Digital Productions, created a claimed twenty-five minutes of animation. In contrast to the abstract fantasies of *Tron*, these images were designed to appear as 'real' as possible, or at least to simulate closely an audience's expectations of outer space. The film was a modest success, but the cost of the imagery – generated with a Cray supercomputer – has deterred further production on such a scale. Further important work has been undertaken at Lucasfilm, where the Pixar system was developed to marry digitally created backgrounds with live foreground action.

Interactive images

The digital generation of images is now one essential component of the form of the moving image. Another is a fully interactive system: that is, one in which images are engaged by and actively respond to the commands and directions of a human operator. Such interactive imagery was made possible by the laser disc technology developed by Philips. The optical laser disc stores the information which comprises each image in digital form. On the standard disc, some 54,000 individual frames can be accommodated, which if recorded or played consecutively give a total playing time of about thirty minutes on each side. But the disc can also produce still frames, slow-motion, high-speed scanning and, most importantly, random access to each image. The disc player can, with only a brief delay, locate the position of a particular frame and move the laser to it.

This random access facility makes laser discs particularly suitable for training purposes and for point-of-sale advertising and promotion. Video jukeboxes are another application. If this facility is combined with a simple computer, one image from the disc can 'ask' a question to the user and then access particular images depending on the responses. Such responses might be given on a keyboard, or by making contact with a touch-sensitive screen on which the image is being shown. Or it might be relayed through a joystick, or in other ways. One experimental application of this potential was a visual 'map' of Aspen, Colorado, produced at MIT in the late 1970s. Images from the disc showed the view through a car windscreen; at each crossroads the display requested the user to indicate left, right or straight ahead, and then produced the appropriate sequence. Another applica-

Computer generated imagery: Tron

tion was for arcade video games, which began in 1972 with Atari's *Pong*. Despite the crude computer-generated animation, and the limited interactivity, games such as this and the later *Space Invaders* (1978) and *Pac-Man* (1981), proved exceptionally popular and for a while hugely profitable.

Throughout the 1980s both digital generation and disc technology have continued to be refined for arcade games. And by 1987 there was a new twist. From the laser disc Philips had developed compact disc technology for digital sound reproduction. CD video was the next step, and interactive CD (or CD-I) followed. CD-I will require a simple computer to be added to a CD video player, and these are already being manufactured, as is appropriate software.

CD-I is obviously restricted by the storage capacity of the disc. A screen and personal computer, however, could be linked by a fibre optic cable network to an interactive system which, backed by a supercomputer, could accommodate many 'players' or participants simultaneously. Gary Demos is certain that such home simulations will be created: 'The real-time simulation would be a direct feed from a supercomputer . . . and available on a subscription basis. So you just tune in and . . . you become part of the movie . . . You control things, create a custom movie that will never be seen by anyone else. The entertainment value of interactive characters . . . all customed to your command, would be incredible . . .' Yet even a system such as this would be constricted by a flat screen. Imagine instead the possibilities of a fully interactive environment.

The Hale's Tours railway carriage, 1904

Environments and alternative realities
Moving image environments date from at least the Hale's Tours attraction at the turn of the century. In this the audience was seated inside a mock stationary railway carriage, and a film of the view from the engine was projected onto the front wall. The 'passengers' were enthralled, and Hale's Tours, first seen at the 1904 St Louis Exposition, was a striking commercial success. Sound, rushing air and a swaying carriage were later added as refinements. But even prior to this the 1900 Universal Exposition in Paris had featured the 'Mareorama', which placed viewers on a mock-up of a ship's bridge and 'sailed' them, via film, across the Mediterranean.

At the 1939 New York World's Fair 'passengers' entered a 'rocket' which, with a similar use of projected images, flew them to London; and at Disneyland after 1955, another rocket, equipped with flashing dials, shaking seats and synchronised animation of travel through outer space, proved to be one of the most popular attractions. An updated version of Hale's Tours was mounted at the Brussels Exposition in 1958. And today, in the base of the CN tower in Toronto, a rocket flight featuring digitally generated images continues to thrill intrepid voyagers.

The Brussels Fair also included an attraction called 'Polyecran', a Czech process combining live stage action with images projected onto variously sized and shaped screens. In 1967 at Montreal a new version of this, 'Laterna Magika', also incorporated a facility which the audience, in choosing to press different buttons, could determine which form of the plot would be followed. 'Laterna Magika' should thus be counted as one of the first truly interactive moving image systems. Meanwhile non-interactive environmental simulations entered amusement arcades with 'Sensorama', in which the participant sat on a motorcycle seat and held on to mock handlebars. A film was projected as if the bike was hurtling down a city street, sound and air flow were synchronised, as was even the smell of a pizza stand which the bike supposedly passed.

More elaborate simulations were developed for the military to train pilots, and in the early 1980s research workers at MIT created a digital holographic simulation of a small section of forest, which would respond to the head movements of the participant. The most exciting digital simulation to date, however, is that conceived at the NASA research laboratories. Developed to control robots working on the outside of space stations, it is based round a lightweight helmet, inside which are two LCD displays linked either to a remote camera or to a computer generating images. The displays offer a convincing stereoscopic image of the relayed or simulated environment, and the digital generation will respond as the viewer turns his or her head or moves forwards or backwards. At present, a data base has been created which simulates in wire-frame form two rooms linked by an escalator, on which the viewer can appear to ride up or down.

With a linked glove, equipped with sensors to indicate the position of each joint of the hand, the participant can 'pick up' objects in the simulated environment, or by using a set code make objects expand or contract, float or fall, simply by making hand movements. Although this is restricted at present to wire-frame representations, there is no reason why, with greater comput-ing power, the simulated environment should not be modelled and shaded, and eventually be made to simulate sufficiently precisely either a pre-existing reality or a fantasy world in which entirely 'unrealistic' events could be made to happen. Several helmets could be linked to the same image simulation, and the participants would be able to take part in a fully inter-active moving image environment. The viewer would enter an alternative reality or 'virtual world' with a comparable sense of surprise and excitement to that experienced by those who saw the first photographs, or went to the Panoramas of the 1840s, or were present at the earliest Lumière shows.

Not yet a century old, the moving image holds many wonders yet.

The wonder of the image: a Chinese gaming counter, c. 1800

Further reading

Joseph Deken, *Computer Images*, New York: Stewart, Tabori and Chang, 1983.
James D. Foley, 'Interfaces for Advanced Computing', in *Scientific American*, Octo-ber 1987 (about the NASA project).
Cynthia Goodman, *Digital Visions: Computers and Art*, New York: Harry N. Abrams, 1987.
Ben Keen, 'Play It Again, Sony: The Double Life of Home Video Technology', in *Science as Culture*, no. 1, London: Free Association Books, 1987.
Myron Krueger, *Artificial Reality*, Reading, Mass.: Addison-Wesley, 1983.
Mark Mancini, 'Pictures at an Exhibition', in *Film Comment*, New York: McGraw-Hill, 1984.
Robert Rivlin, *The Algorithmic Image*, Redmond, Washington: Microsoft Press, 1986.
Anthony Smith, 'High-Definition Television: The Politics of Perfection', in *Sight & Sound*, Spring 1983.

Index